Embr...
En...

Embracing Philanthropic Environmentalism

The Grand Responsibility of Stewardship

WILL SARVIS

McFarland & Company, Inc., Publishers
Jefferson, North Carolina

ISBN (print) 978-1-4766-7736-1
ISBN (ebook) 978-1-4766-3574-3

LIBRARY OF CONGRESS CATALOGUING DATA ARE AVAILABLE

BRITISH LIBRARY CATALOGUING DATA ARE AVAILABLE

Front cover image © 2019 Sarunyu_foto/Shutterstock

Printed in the United States of America

*McFarland & Company, Inc., Publishers
Box 611, Jefferson, North Carolina 28640
www.mcfarlandpub.com*

Acknowledgments

First, I would like to thank Layla Milholen and all the good people at McFarland, who saw this project through from beginning to end. Obscure independent writers like me have no connections with powerful people, and thus no leverage in the world of publishing politics. So we appreciate the rare occasions when complete strangers take the time to examine our work, then find merit in it. My hope is that their every minute has been well spent. Like the rare insightful editor she is, Layla said the most by saying the least. Her penetrating yet succinct comments became an important guide during the final draft.

I thank *Counterpunch Magazine* for publishing a preliminary essay in 2012 that broadly and briefly explored some of the themes developed here.

Large and small environmental stewards everywhere are out there trying to do the right thing, and I've had the privilege to meet a few of them. Back in the 1990s, the late Leo A. Drey and his admirable chief forester Clint Trammel generously granted me interviews and touring time, showing me firsthand one of the most magnificent examples of forest stewardship I've ever seen. No doubt, Drey's German ancestors would be very proud. On the urban side of things, arborist James Cummings and his crew continue to demonstrate remarkably conscientious tree and community care. I hope to gather more stories from them in the future. It's always enjoyable meeting working people who also ponder their endeavors philosophically. In some small way, I hope this book serves as a tribute to them and the efforts and vision of environmental stewards everywhere. Arborists and tree planters do sacred work.

On a more personal note, I thank my niece Emily for our discussions regarding science and the politics of science. Like the best of environmental stewards, she possesses a wonderful combination of practicality and high ideals. I hope to watch a stellar career unfold for her.

Last, but far from least, many thanks to my oldest and dearest friend, Teresa Chen. She always offers moral support, and for the third time she has generously contributed her photographs to one of my books.

Table of Contents

Preface

This book has been kicking around in idea and note form for more than a decade. During that period the focus of the study has taken some major divergences. There were times when I felt very reluctant to pursue the project at all, mainly due to the "religious" nature that environmentalism has taken on since the more "innocent" days of the 1970s. Undoubtedly back then I was largely unaware of problematic precursors that now heavily color contemporary environmental philosophy and policy (the Endangered Species Acts come to mind). But in the 1970s there were also some comparatively straightforward matters that preoccupied many people and that the majority of reasonable people would find uncontroversial. Ending widespread point-source pollution, cleaning up Lake Erie and the Cuyahoga River, removing lead from gasoline, and other such practical measures did much to improve the environmental quality of life in the United States. But environmentalism quickly moved on to other matters that have proven far more problematic. I deal with some of those issues in this book.

The final iteration of this work is also related and partially inspired by the "Misanthropic Eden" chapter in my previous book, *Sacred and Ephemeral*.[1] In fact, for a while I even wondered if I should extract that chapter and make it the basis for a new book. But in the end I decided *Sacred and Ephemeral* should remain intact as originally conceived, and that any overlap in themes would not be all that significant, especially where further research and contemplation has opened new ground or invited substantial elaboration upon preliminary ideas. This particularly became the case regarding climate science, which receives far more treatment here.

Speaking of which, I'm sorry to report how emotional reactions apparently blind otherwise intelligent people when it comes to the topic of (anthropogenic) climate change. Many people put climate science debates into a false dichotomy. You are either an "alarmist-liberal" or a "denier-conservative." Among other offenses, the false dichotomy shuns an informed, logical debate. No one can refute the basic fact that science is incapable of predicting the

1

future. That's because we've never had any means by which we can predict the future—scientific, religious, or otherwise. Apologies to all psychics who might offer personal prognostications. If we did have future prediction tools, the stock market alone would explode in hyperspace trading within hours if not minutes. And yet people fear climate predictions as if they were somehow more tangible. People I know to be rational and intelligent, who would agree about the impossibility of future prediction in general, nevertheless have balked when I raised this simple truth regarding climate change. Such is the emotional baggage that accompanies this topic. By contrast, in the following pages I have tried to offer a sober assessment heavily based in logic and philosophy of science.

For a moment let's say that philosophy majors study philosophy with a large "P." This involves reading the giants, beginning with the pre–Socratics (in western culture) and continuing from there. It also means learning about systematic subtopics such as existentialism, phenomenology, and pantheism. In contrast, I think of this volume as philosophy with a small "p." Though touching upon grand subjects such as empiricism and epistemology in a general way, I think of this book as much more in the vein of common sense.

Anyway, almost accidentally I've ended up with a book of "philosophy" embracing guarded environmental optimism and a celebration of humanity. This was not a preconceived agenda. I drifted away from the field of environmental history after losing my Forest Service job in 1993. I did some brief environmental history research in the Missouri Ozarks a few years later, but that focus was more on property law and eminent domain, which captivated me for many years. By then I had given up on an earlier Forest Service history manuscript as unpublishable, but was in for a happy surprise about a decade later (the University of Tennessee Press published it). In a way that brought me back into the field of environmental history. Still, I was reluctant to continue working with contemporary environmentalism due to the prevalence of ideology.

So instead, the book vaguely began on peripheral topics, mostly centering on trees and urban forestry, now incorporated in the following "Rural Stewardship, Old and New" and "Modified Habitats" chapters. By then I had met an arborist (James Cummings) who, like so many people in Eugene, Oregon, defied occupational stereotypes. James had almost gone to law school, but instead decided to become (basically) a steward of the urban environment. He had some very thoughtful and philosophical observations that inspired me to think about a book regarding urban forestry. That, and a large pile of earlier notes, slowly continued to develop.

As the work progressed, I also began to see this volume as (ironically) an unplanned and much-belated response to the first environmental dooms-dayist I met in person, in 1984 (of all years!). He was a geology professor whose specialty was the Jurassic, hence his preoccupation with dinosaur extinction. He was convinced that we ourselves would be extinct soon. Of course, I had been hearing one thing or another since my childhood during the 1960s: the population bomb, the next ice age, the threat of nuclear winter, silent spring, and all the rest. I'm embarrassed to think of how vulnerable I was in the face of that geology professor's gossip-like glee over being a messenger of bad news. At the time I descended into one of the blackest depressions of my life. But eventually I got over it, and then without knowing it, I began to build up an immunity to prophets of doom.

Writing this book has been quite an education for me personally, for good and ill. Like many people, I had a general idea about the sensationalist, superficial aspects of our news media. Some of this cannot be helped; it is part of the journalism business model working with short deadlines, catering to a public thirsty for bombshell stories, and the general unprofitability of investigative reporting that makes deep news the exception rather than the norm. Having said all that, I was stunned to discover just how inaccurate our media has been in perpetuating environmental myths, particularly of a doomsdayist nature. For example, ABC, CBS, NBC, NPR, PBS, and other media outlets ~~both~~ all seem to accept anthropogenic climate change as an irrefutable scientific fact rather than a working hypothesis. So if anything, this study reflects a cautionary tale regarding common-sensical empiricism and epistemology involving data that circulates in popular culture. Internet data (too often not elevated enough to be called "information") has merely exacerbated problems long inherent in human communication.

On the other hand, I was heartened to encounter scholars like Alston Chase, Bjørn Lomborg, Alan Freeze, and Frances Drake who, many years ago, published substantial works that serve as antidotes to popular misunderstanding, especially the alarmism and sensationalism in the media. While writing, sometimes I would ask myself, have I slowly overreacted after having been too vulnerable to the doomsdayists of my youth? But I think not. Skepticism seems to come more naturally when your detractors are not really proving their case through evidence, logic, common sense, or anything else.

One of the surprises in writing this book was to discover some stark socioeconomic class dimensions of environmental topics that seem obvious to me now. I should have seen them coming. As the Greek historian Thucydides wrote, "the strong do what they can and the weak suffer what they must."[2] He was talking about warfare, but the same applies to the wealth and poverty that remain inextricably related to environmental matters. Many years ago I became generally aware of environmental racism, clearly related to poverty, but only later did the full contours of the environmental elite and their green rhetoric come into marked relief. SUVs with green bumper stickers were always too obvious and too predictable. But, on the other hand, I had always thought of veganism as more or less a reflection of a lifestyle choice, usually (but not always) ideological in nature. What I learned was, the elaborate workarounds vegans must undergo to avoid malnutrition are only possible in a wealthy nation with an ample and varied food supply. Of course. Why hadn't I thought that through before? As Michelle Obama helped publicize, the food deserts in the United States reveal (all by themselves) how poor people struggle just to find basic good nutrition.

I chose the term "philanthropic environmentalism" for two reasons. First, as a counter stance to misanthropic environmentalism, or what I sometimes call Green Calvinism. Misanthropic environmentalism shows up quite commonly in American culture. In my view, it mistakenly separates humanity from nature and perpetuates an impossible Edenic ideal regarding the environment. It also fosters some odd and sometimes untenable environmental policy choices.

Second, I agree with a great number of people who have decided the central issue is human poverty. Even if you were an misanthrope, the irrefutable logic holds that environmental improvements follow alleviation of human poverty. No one volunteers to live in a toxic habitat, but only the wealthier societies can address such contamination. Yet it would be nice if we cared about people for their own sake, in their environment. Misanthropes hate humanity, and hating our species is one of the easiest traps to fall into during our brief passage through this life. Humans have done and will continue to be capable of doing terrible things. But besides misanthropy becoming a cancer for its bearer, it quickly degenerates into a broader negative force in the world, taking much and contributing little.

Introduction

"Did God file a Draft Environmental Impact Statement before Mount St. Helens erupted?"

This was one of the sarcastic comments I heard in 1992 during my brief employment with the U.S. Forest Service. An old forester said this—a man who remembered the agency before it became so much more bureaucratized—before Draft Environmental Impact Statements, litigation, public protest, revised Environmental Impact Statements, and the months and years of processing such policy procedure had made demoralized paper pushers out of foresters who once spent more time in the woods. He was a little bitter over the bureaucratization of the agency, but also the development of environmental philosophy that had come to seem untenable.

The old forester could be forgiven his irony. The 1980 eruption of Mount St. Helens leveled or buried well over 200 square miles of forest, an area obviously vastly larger than any clear-cut timber sale, and of course with far more devastating effects on flora, fauna, water and air quality. Who knows, maybe Mother Nature has an "ecocidal" aspect to her. Joking aside, even the most dogmatic environmentalist would hardly "protest" an inescapable natural disaster. Contemporary environmental thinking views human-caused changes in a different category, and that to a significant degree is what this book is about.

By the way, the Mount St. Helens environment recovered itself quite rapidly.[1] Nature has a remarkable tendency to do exactly that, despite humans panicking all around. Many Americans expect Eden, which is a perfect, static habitat not reflecting human influence. But nature is just nature, regardless of human expectations. And yet environmental stewardship is inevitable, even if the current American cultural milieu fails to embrace this fact when not denying it outright. The fallacy of an "unspoiled natural paradise" surrounds us in the United States, replete with (ironic) human attempts to stop or slow "natural" changes. With mixed results (good, ill, and often ambiguous), humans are influencing practically all flora and fauna species on the

5

planet, one way or another. We rescue wild animals, kill others, encroach upon habitat, set habitat aside, and take innumerable other actions large and small. Humans preying upon lion fish or Asian carp, humans pulling up English ivy or Himalayan blackberry—this is stewardship whether or not these people are embracing or accepting stewardship as a philosophy. Ironically, even the Eden preservers (such as the National Park Service) are acting as stewards of a sort, whether or not they are cognizant of the philosophical basis.

As the age-old observation goes, we are self-conscious creatures who cannot escape our own animal nature, which puts us in the middle of the classic paradox of the overseer role while still being subject to the same natural laws that govern all creatures. We consume life to perpetuate our own, and yet one day we too shall be consumed—by other life, if we allow it, or by fire. Even saturation in formaldehyde merely delays our bodies' elements from transforming to other elements. And yet we have no other choice when it comes to our overseer role. Our self-consciousness alone prevents us from doing anything except stewardship.

*   *   *

The rise of the three major monotheisms—Judaism, Christianity, and Islam—all followed much more ancient religious worldviews that combined polytheism within an "Cosmos versus Chaos" dynamic. By contrast, the monotheisms came to embrace a "Good versus Evil" dynamic. The latter is familiar to all who understand western civilization, with its additional dichotomy of heaven and hell (and, for the Christians, Satan and Jesus). The Cosmos versus Chaos worldview is quite different—sometimes more ambiguous, never truly dichotomous, and containing an understanding of human struggle without inserting the artifice of "sin," a theological invention of later centuries. Primeval Chaos is just the nature of the world and the universe before Cosmos came out of it. There are huge mythological traditions associated with this, but it can also be understood as an individual's daily self-discipline to get up, go to work or study, clean house, or what have you—and generally not succumb to decadence. Decadence would be a reflection of allowing Chaos to win the day, for it is in the eternal nature of Chaos to keep reasserting its original dominance.

In the ancient world people were in awe of what humans could create, and if their understanding was appropriate, these accomplishments were in tribute to the larger creation that was everything around them on planet Earth. To this very day structures like the Parthenon, the Egyptian pyramids, Machu Picchu, or Stonehenge still awe us and often confound us in trying to understand how people once created these monumental tributes. In the ancient world this awe, properly understood, was not in opposition to natural phenomenon. Neither should it be now, even though we view "wild" lands differently than they did.

On the other hand, Edenic thinking shows up everywhere in American environmental philosophy, policy, and day-to-day thinking. It is how we see common usage of buzzwords like "sustainability" (as if any civilization avoided sustaining itself). It is how "biodiversity" acquired philosophical value in the name of scientific proof. It is how we came to "preserve" nature in national parks and wilderness areas, as if nature stood still. As National Park Service Director Jon Jarvis said in 2016, the focus of their agency was the impossible task of preventing change in the national parks.[2] This is classic Edenic thinking. What would serve well in its stead would be a reconfiguration of our environmental philosophy, in which Mother Nature is an indifferent, mysterious, non-anthropomorphic force for us to respect and adore. In the meantime we could do what we can for the life forms we like, including our fellow humans. In contrast, Edenic thinking is also where a strain of misanthropy enters, where people want to have the illusion of nature without humans, themselves excepted.[3] It also greatly explains the species preservation movement that offers an untenable philosophical worldview that flies in the face of common sense and observable scientific fact of dynamic nature.

These differing lenses offer some insights into seeing contemporary environmentalism. A Cosmos versus Chaos worldview readily accommodates humans as part of nature and celebrates human achievements as our mundane version of rendering Cosmos out of Chaos. Cultivating a garden or a forest, caring for a suburban landscape, building houses and cities—and, yes, even setting wilderness aside—can all be appreciated as humans exercising their stewardship roles. The Good versus Evil tradition, on the other hand, carries some unfortunate baggage, especially in the United States.

In the monotheistic traditions, especially those of Judeo-Christianity, the Garden of Eden is a mythological paradise. Humans are there, but they spoil it, and thus they have defiled nature. This worldview has lent itself to some Americans viewing humans as apart from nature, with human actions distinct from the influences of nonhuman species. Developed further, especially through Calvinist theology, an environmental misanthropy creeps in, with humans representing evil in contrast to good nature. Human actions have an obvious and undeniable level of influence and magnitude—but we wield it self-consciously, or at least we should. Thus, Eden becomes ultimately untenable when posited alongside the distinctly different approach of philanthropic environmental stewardship.

Largely ignoring prehistoric native impacts on land in North America, it was no surprise that Americans would nurture wilderness worship and eventually Green Calvinism, a sort of misanthropic strain of environmentalism that separates humanity from nature and blames people for marring an imaginary environmental Eden. I derive the term from John Calvin's theology, which I regard as fundamentally misanthropic. To hazard a vast oversimplification, the gist of Calvinism implies that you're probably going to hell and you deserve it. This is and has been found widely in the various Protestant churches influenced by Calvinist theology—not just fundamentalist or evangelical sects, but past and present forms of congregational puritanism, Methodism, Presbyterianism, Wesleyanism, Baptist churches, and so forth. Translated into environmental terms: you will experience environmental apocalypse and it's your fault.

If we reject Green Calvinism, and particularly the separation of humanity from nature, we begin to better understand things like the co-evolution of species. Co-evolution presents an array of additional problems, but at least it is a scientific fact. But even in the Calvinistic worship of wilderness there is a refreshing alternative, which includes the celebration of landscape gardens. Wonderful traditions of gardening are found in both Asia and Europe, tellingly where the long historic presence of humanity has probably diminished fantasies of "untouched" nature.

Save the Planet: Kill Yourself.

So runs the humorous bumper sticker. But this joke also reveals a fundamental hypocrisy in most if not all of Calvinism, Green or otherwise. The wide and deep streak of misanthropy in Calvinism is unmistakable, and perhaps represents the Original Sin guilt trip taken to its furthest (and most absurd) extreme. Even poor John Muir epitomized (to some degree) the old adage about becoming what you hate. He abandoned his admittedly horrific Calvinist upbringing (far worse than my father's or Ed Abbey's) but merely became the obverse Green version, worshipping (as he described it) nature as his church. But at least he wasn't a hypocrite in that regard, as so many of the rebellious Calvinists become.

Ironically, many of the would-be children of nature from the Counterculture (and their contemporary, very latter day imitators along the West Coast) inadvertently perpetuated the dualism that separates humanity from nature. Otherwise, there would never have been a need to "return" to nature, as they did during the "back to nature" sub-movement of hippie communes celebrating the *Foxfire* books, the *Whole Earth Catalogue*, the re-discovered *Five Acres and Independence*, and all that romanticizing of rural life. Like children in a fit of pique, they insisted on running away when they only ran in a circle, ever toward the source they thought they were escaping. And that is regardless of returning to the suburbs once those trust funds kicked in.

Communing with nature often has an artificiality to it. Sometimes it is downright affectation. Those who actually live in nature or close to it generally have a different perspective compared to urbanites who almost invariably romanticize the wilds. Muir, who talked to rocks and plants, was really only talking to himself and reporting it back to his enamored audience safely removed from nature. There is, in fact, a deep tradition of armchair naturalism in American culture, in which various people (Thoreau, Muir, Ed Abbey, Aldo Leopold, Annie Dillard) record their journal entries in the wild for vicarious enjoyment among those sitting in comfortable climate-controlled living rooms. Together they form a cult, of sorts, and there is prestige and pecking order within this movement, as in all movements.

And so many movements end up focusing on the same thing: the people in the movement, not the supposed cause. This is a perennial feature of humanity, a social species. This is how some of the Sixties rebelliousness became about hell raisers having fun rather than stopping the Vietnam War or changing the world. This is the "art scene" in New York City, which has little to do with art. Most real artists work in obscurity, far away from Big Apple schmoozing. And likewise, genuine children of nature rarely send their accounts to press. They are reluctant to relate their stories, and with good reason. In fact, to do so would seem downright sacrilegious.

*   *   *

Even before the Neolithic, when humans began adopting a more sedentary lifestyle, there have been complex interchanges and co-evolutions among humans and various flora and fauna that we're just beginning to understand. Fifteen-thousand-year-old mice skeletons in the Levant reveal changes in teeth formation because of cohabitation with people, and these were still the wandering hunters and gatherers of the Paleolithic.[4] More dramatic changes commenced with farming. It is fairly easy for us to find or invent reasons why certain wild animals (cows, pigs, horses, et cetera) became domestic livestock. Possessing fellow mammalian intelligence, they somehow sensed that humans were now offering them regular food, shelter, and protection from predators. And so they abandoned their wild ways, and further selective breeding (a sort of anthropogenically enhanced evolution) encouraged domesticity as well as greater milk production, wool growth, or what have you.

More challenging for us to consider is how plants changed. The best explanation we have so far, for all flora behavior, tends to center on chemistry. Somehow plants communicate chemically with each other in their competition and cooperation to consume nutrients and propagate. They also communicate with other creatures, like pollinating insects. And so somehow they "sensed" that humans were now cultivating them—coddling them with irrigation and fertilizer, and removing competition (what we now call "weeds"), and protecting them from consumers, such as birds. Thus, the reasoning goes, they stopped using their energy for survival, and produced "food" consumable by humans rather than expending energy on camouflage, thorns, or poison.

The Galapagos finches are famous in Darwin lore for helping him develop his theory of evolution. But so were domestic animals. In a sense, human domestication speeds up the evolutionary process, wherein we manipulate the gene pool for the traits we want. This is how we have dairy cows and beef cows, guard dogs and sheep dogs, and various breeds of sheep growing wool with distinct characteristics. It is also how we get sweet corn and corn fodder, all derived from maize (still called Indian corn in the American Southwest). It is also how you get orange tomatoes if you plant your red and yellow varieties too close together. So, in this sense, plants and animals have been "genetically modified" for thousands of years. But all interacting flora and fauna (including us) experience genetic modification, given enough time, through the very process of our interaction. Genetically modified organism proponents would argue that today we are just utilizing ultra-sophisticated tools. Detractors, critics, and those concerned that the scientific ramifications remain dangerously unknown, would disagree.

*   *   *

If internal distortions in contemporary science were not enough, the news media sometimes fosters—inadvertently or otherwise—additional layers of misunderstanding. This is particularly true with today's hot button issues of (anthropogenic) climate change and species extinction. One of the most astonishing experiences of writing this book was to discover what a gulf separates popular understanding of these issues and the wide array of ambiguity in the scholarly literature. Popular understanding, in a nation that cherishes free speech and press, is intertwined with an entire subfield of journalism involving the communication of science. The most honorable people working in this field function, to a significant degree, as translators of esoteric knowledge, but we all appreciate how nuances and complex details are easily lost in this process. That, all by itself, might not be so bad—except that we have dedicated billions of dollars to science that feeds into poorly-reasoned policy and vice versa. Perhaps that is an unavoidable aspect of policy. But it is all the more a shame when we have an array to real environmental problems that no reasonable person could deny.

Many things are done in the name of science now, much as they were done in the name of institutionalized religion in the past. And yet, like the abuses in religion, it is the *authority* of science that the propagandists and sensationalists so often claim, not the true scientific method. An easy illustration of common abuse concerns prognostication, something science has never been able to do, save the guarded anticipation of replicable results in controlled, limited, and comparatively focused experiments—and even that is not future prediction proper, but rather verification of past experiments and progress within a given scientific paradigm which (as Thomas S. Kuhn famously described)[5] itself will eventually shift. The scientific method can no more predict the environmental future than stock market analysts can predict future booms and busts. In both there are too many variables, too many combinations of variables, and too many unforeseen forces that instantly destroy all models, including the pet computer models of climate change alarmists.

Anthropogenic climate change has become an information war far more than it has become scientific inquiry, partly because the subject does not lend itself to scientific inquiry as simply as some of the grant recipients blithely claim. Most fundamentally, science cannot predict the future. Claiming otherwise is just a crystal ball with a bow tie. Also important, regarding the anthropogenic aspect, we have no "test group" and "control group" in this field, further compromising measurements of human influences. But none of this has diminished the information war that sometimes readily degenerates into propaganda.

Probably more than any other environmental subject of late, climate change has fed into false dichotomous thinking that has greatly hindered rational discussion. The false dichotomies are basically liberal alarmist versus conservative denier. Undoubtedly many accept self-identification in these simplistic categories, which carry much additional baggage regarding free markets, government regulation or deregulation, immigration policy, health care problems, and all the other topics that have been dividing Democrats, Republicans, populists, and socialists of late. This is very unfortunate. The reality regarding climate change for some of us is far more interesting partly because it is far more complex. Nuance plays a prominent role. The scientific method takes center stage. Distinguishing prediction from scientific observation of empirical evidence is utterly crucial.

Instead, emotional responses have hopelessly obscured what should be the most rational of debates. Disbelieving bogus science does not indicate lack of concern for the environment. In fact, the current political contentiousness regarding climate possibly hinders practical solutions. For example, if atmospheric carbon turns out to be the main culprit in global warming (a debated topic among atmospheric scientists), we could already be removing significant amounts through carbon capture and sequestration instead of spending those billions on the impossibility of predicting future climate. But welcome to politics.

Far less uncertain than climate science, we're living in the aftermath of a chemical revolution that requires caution at every turn. Edenic thinking has led to hysteria of any "contamination," which has turned out to be mis-founded or overplayed in some sensational cases, such as those associated with Love Canal or Times Beach. But that is not to deny unambiguously toxic substances that we have refined and spread, especially lead and mercury, now readily found in our plumbing and in the oceans (the latter delivered to the sea by rain falling through coal smoke). If we followed European Union stan-dards, we would put chemicals like the herbicide atrazine or the chemical BPA (used in plastics) closer to the categories of lead and mercury. So far, we have not. And then there are a huge array of chemicals we would rather not ingest, if possible, though many medical questions come into play here, including chronic or acute dosage, genetic predispositions, and issues of pre-existing health conditions. The jury is still out on much of this, but substances involved are especially that wide category of endocrine disruptors. We don't live in a perfect world, and the human body is generally far more resilient than some of the purists think … at least if you are properly nourished in the first place.

This brings us to the environmental justice issue. Far less covered in the press than species preservation or climate fears is the fact that the greatest environmental burdens have always fallen and continue to fall upon poor people. That remains true in developing countries, but very prominently in the United States as well, particularly the American South, and particularly in African American neighborhoods. This pattern is no accident, and is one of a great many legacies of slavery. When the "Black Lives Matter" movement began, I preferred a different slogan that, admittedly, requires study of history. That slogan was, "The Legacy of Slavery Is Everywhere." It is particularly bothersome to contemplate the billions we have spent chasing chimeric envi-ronmental issues when this one persists. Depressing as that is, the only solu-tions will arise from improved social justice combined with green science and technology.

I am no Pollyanna, but if you consider the unambiguous environmental messes we have made—such as hexavalent chromium contamination of Cali-fornia groundwater, or dioxin contamination of Vietnam—the only way out or through is with the same tools that got us into trouble in the first place, science and technology. We made the messes; only we can clean them up. Of course, they will generally clean themselves up, eventually, even if the worst of nuclear waste has a depressingly long half-life. In the meantime people and the greater ecology suffer disease, premature death, and reproduction problems, not to mention terrible aesthetics and grim physical surroundings.

An astonishing array of green technology awaits further development and distribution, depending upon how things unfold. Bioremediation and phytoremediation are helping with nonpoint source pollution. Similarly, bacteria is one way to address oil spills and even plastic garbage. And then there are alternatives to plastics, just as there are to fossil fuels (though the latter sure seems to be dragging its feet). But even regarding fossil fuels, carbon capture and sequestration is a contemporary technology more than half a century old. Geothermal energy is making a small comeback; desalination technology is advancing, modern nuclear power plants make the old water-cooled models of the Cold War era seem almost like Model Ts. The list of innovations and ideas goes on and on.

My enjoyment of what scientists and engineers do is purely vicarious, but philosophically I see it as our only option. Some years ago, where I live (Eugene, Oregon), a small and loud group of "primitivists" romanticized the Paleolithic and pretended that going backward in time was a viable alternative to imminent environmental doomsday. Very few people would even try that. Entire societies are not going to do it.

Perhaps it is easier to get discouraged with "civilization" when living in a city, which is where most of the world's population resides now. After all, Rousseau himself invented the romantic "noble savage" child of nature in contradistinction to his depressing urban environment. But lest we forget, rural Americans have a long tradition of stewarding the land. There really is no other choice, unless you seek (literally) to stop sustaining yourself. Farmland cannot be exhausted, trees must be cut in rotation. And we have learned greatly from mistakes like the Dust Bowl, cut-out-and-get-out stripping of entire forests (which makes clear cutting appear moderate by comparison), and boom and bust mining towns with their piles of slag and tailings still leaching heavy metals into waterways. Contemporary rural stewardship is alive and well, employing more sophisticated tools and a better understanding of ecology. A love of the land has never ceased; country people are regularly astounded at why urban folk seem to miss that most salient of points. Ironically, not everyone appreciates that urban folk also live in interesting natural habitats.

If I had to choose one adjective to describe nature, I might choose "persistent." This seems like a good way to understand urban nature as well. If nature were not so persistent we wouldn't spend so much time and energy maintaining our city parks, urban trees, and millions of yards. In the Pacific Northwest the annual moss accumulation alone will make short work of asphalt roofs, initiating a top-down structural deterioration that picks up speed and momentum if unchecked. Nature is here. Nature is everywhere, and not merely in the common urban flora and fauna species.

Some will have objected to the association of "natural habitats" with cities. But this is an inevitable end point of non–Edenic thinking. In philanthropic environmentalism, city buildings and bird nests merely occupy different points on a continuum. Remember, humans and their creations have to be a part of nature, according to this philosophy. Separating people from nature not only creates an untenable standard against which to measure human influence, but it does not focus enough attention upon realizing our full potential as environmental stewards.

Nature is so much easier to enjoy, cherish, worship … if we stop Edenizing it. It is everywhere. It is the volunteer plants that populate your yard if you do not kill them. It is Old Growth forest, but also a young forest returning from logging. It is wilderness and city parks. It is most definitely the wonderfully cultivated grounds of campuses and landscape gardens. It is hummingbird nests and timber frame houses. Weeds growing out of sidewalk cracks. Saplings. Thus, some of the best "naturalists" are the unpaid ones. They explore nature out of interest and love; there is no need for a funding agenda involving pseudo-theories or even intensive case studies.

We should take joy in things like gardening or building better cities or developing green technology. Not only is this a celebration of human ingenuity, but it is really the only option to environmental problems. No human society has volunteered to return to earlier cultural configurations, and even partial returns (perhaps the European tribes after the fall of the western Roman Empire) do so with irrevocable knowledge of what they have seen regarding new culture. No culture lives in a vacuum, despite romantic wishful thinking. Groups like the strict Amish operate within a mutually influential modern context. For example, Amish buggies travel on modern technology roads, not the rough turnpikes of the 19th century. Also, ironically, Amish organic animal dung compromises trout habitats by absorbing oxygen from rivers like the Susquehanna.

Wilderness is a myth in any ultimate sense, partly because a massive glass dome does not separate it from the rest of the world. Instead, there is the earth with all places effected variously by the human presence. And this isn't *the* garden in an Edenic sense, but it is our garden, and there is sacredness in our stewardship role.

The trajectory of American wilderness worship stems from the Romantic period, which was partly a reaction against early industrialism. It was partly predicated upon the myth of the United States as a land "unspoiled" by people; wilderness dialogue and concepts regularly ignored indigenous peoples, and did not yet appreciate the extent of aboriginal environmental alteration. Wilderness worship gained new momentum during the prosperous economy following World War II. It was culturally contingent upon these historical and geographical factors, and makes it easy to forget that worship of the pastoral has been a powerful force in the human experience as well. The pastoral setting is one modified by humans for practical purposes, but inspired no end of poets and painters who found spiritual bliss in the countryside. The pastoral represents rural order in contrast to urban order—but both in contrast to wilderness.

Humans like order, for we like to plan ahead to be prepared for calamities we know are coming. An orderly food supply is protection against famine. Orderly structures protect us from homelessness and (worse) loss of shelter.[6] Such planning gained massive momentum beginning with the Neolithic. And, despite the romantic picture that primitivists paint of the Paleolithic, our species was probably doing its best to plan ahead even then. The hunt is notoriously uncertain; prehistoric nomadic people would not have survived had they not thought ahead to future seasons. As the philosopher Susanne Langer wrote, "[Man] can adapt himself somehow to anything his imagination can cope with; but he cannot deal with Chaos."[7] This quest for order manifests itself in both the mundane world of daily life as well as the ancient metaphysical concepts of Cosmos and Chaos.

Unless you are hopelessly naïve, or unless you have lived a sheltered life, or unless you were fortunate enough to have an unusual personality—you might agree that insecurity is a fundamental aspect of human nature. There's nothing wrong with this. We fear for our loved ones' safety in a dangerous world in the face of an uncertain future. But if we recognize this as a natural disposition, we can also see how it has fed into a certain environmental hysteria based far more in sensationalism and emotion than in scientific knowledge. Worse, fear-mongering is a potential distraction from real environmental problems, often leading to misbegotten policies addressing chimeric crises and neglecting pragmatic approaches to genuine issues. And sadly, unfounded worry subtracts from the joy and privilege of environmental stewardship. We're probably a lot better at it than we credit ourselves. A sober, logical assessment of where we stand may free the mind for the emotional embracement of loving the natural world as much as we can.

One way to view order with a small "o" is as an extension of the more metaphysical Order or Cosmos from ancient thinking. What we would call civilization in general is what the ancients would call rendering Cosmos out of primeval Chaos. This is a grand way to view our current responsibilities of environmental stewardship, which flies in the face of an untenable concept of Edenic order. The Edenic order exists only in our imaginations; it may or may not make for a fine fantasy, but it does not lend itself to realistic environmental policy or philosophy.

Human "disturbance" is everywhere, and yet we have not really come to accept that yet, at least not in the elite environmentalist circles of western society. We have created enormous habitats quite inadvertently, even if we have destroyed other habitats quite deliberately. We stumble semi-coherently toward embracing a comprehensive stewardship role when we should accept stewardship as our very premise. Historic rapacious resource exploitation was a mistake, at least according to today's values—but our current milieu favors an overreaction manifested in impossibilities like preserving every species, stopping invasive species, controlling the climate, freeing the world of toxic chemicals, et cetera. The Edenic premise has been untenable from the outset.

Chapter 1

Cosmos and Chaos

Much dualism in western civilization derives from monotheism. This began with Zoroastrianism's concept of a spirit of light (Ahura Mazda) versus a spirit of darkness (Angra Mainyu).[1] Judaism, Christianity, and Islam continued this trajectory to create familiar (and often falsely dichotomous) struggles between good and evil, sin and virtue, with rewards in heaven or punishment in hell.[2] "Us v. them" is practically a universal aspect of humanity involving the territorial imperative (famously described by Robert Ardrey)[3] and other matters, but western culture's dualism certainly enhances this with a mentality of the True Believer versus heretic or infidel. And yet, there have always been other ways of looking at the world.

As Elaine Pagels demonstrated in her 1995 book, *The Origin of Satan*, Jewish sectarianism preceding and coinciding with the Jesus era and involved much demonization of the opposition. Good v. evil, already well established in Judaism, received new fuel as the early Jesus Movement sought to distinguish itself from apocalyptic Jews pitted politically against the Roman Empire. The four canonical gospels thus depicted a spiritual teacher harmless to Roman hegemony ("Render unto Caesar the things which are Caesar's," etc.), unlike the Essenes and various zealots who anticipated holy war in which the theocratic state of Israel would triumph.[4]

The Bishop of Lyon, Irenaeus (died circa 202 CE), whom scholars recognize as the architect of the Four Gospel Canon, continued the well-established concepts of good v. evil, especially denounced mystical interpretations of Jesus, and heavily emphasized "original sin."[5] The latter became fundamental in all subsequent western Christian understandings of heaven and hell. Believing that humans are originally good or bad should be seen as a purely subjective philosophical point of view, not an objective reality handed down from on high. But claims of original sin offer clear manipulative possibilities which institutionalized Christianity, taking the torch of politics from the declining Roman Empire in western Europe, has carried ever since. Here is one example where Protestants are not so nearly rebellious as they claim to be, for they merely took the Catholics' original sin in new directions without ever coming close to rejecting it altogether. One much more radical departure from this entire legacy is a rethinking of paganism.

Preceding the development of monotheism by many centuries, and certainly coinciding and following it, have been ancient concepts of primeval Chaos out of which came Order or Cosmos. In the most metaphysical version of this worldview, primeval Chaos is not equivalent to "disorder" in a mundane sense. Rather, it is the primal nothingness out of which came all creation.[6] A secondary, but equally engaging concept follows this more metaphysical depiction. It lands more in the world of mythology, and involves trickster figures who often represent true disorder, but also present qualifications upon conventional truth in order to keep the latter honest and humble. In this mythological world of Order v. Chaos, a regular (sometimes daily) struggle is necessary to maintain Order and keep Chaos limited to minimal damage. In both the metaphysical and mythological concepts, Chaos and Order do not represent a dichotomy. In fact, they seem vaguely evocative of the Chinese concept of yin and yang, in which each principle contains the seed of the other principle.

Before Hesiod rendered his version of the story, the Greeks saw Cronus (Time) as the first principle. Time created Chaos (the Infinite) and Ether (the Finite). Chaos and Ether together produced Phanes (Light), which in turn produced Gaia (Earth), heaven, and Zeus. All other creativity and life commenced from there. Hesiod modified this cosmology to make Chaos the first principle, from which all life and creativity arose.[7] Hesiod's version is more typical among archaic cosmologies in general. But what they all have in common, including the Greek original, is a morally-neutral concept of Chaos. Whether the primary principle or a latter stage of primary principle creativity, Chaos is not anarchy or disorder in the mundane sense, or negativity in the ethical sense, but rather approximating metaphysical nothingness. It followed that archaic societies reconnected with this nothingness in numerous rituals, in order to recreate the world. This leads us to the trickster concept.

The trickster shows up in innumerable prehistoric and early historic societies. Among American Indians, the trickster is Coyote in the Desert Southwest, Raven in the Pacific Northwest, entities called Napi (among the Blackfeet), Inklonmi (among Assiniboine), Nihancan (for the Arapaho), and many other names among other tribes. In Norse mythology, this is the famous Loki. Like all tricksters, Loki is complex and ambiguous. He or she (for gender ambiguity is a trickster trait) is mischievous and destructive, but also self-sacrificing, repentant for her or his previous vandalism, and sometimes plays a role of vital creativity as, for example, a Promethean-like bringer of the fire. In other words, Loki is a classic representation of the mythological Chaos.[8]

This is not to romanticize archaic models of Cosmos and Chaos. After all, from a modern point of view, we have great difficulty accepting the idea of human sacrifice as a reenactment of primeval Chaos, out of which we recreate the world. Some societies still practice human sacrifice and, of course, nations like China, Iran, and the United States continue to do so (in a way) through the convoluted guise of capital punishment. But beyond that, the virtues of ancient worldviews may be adopted and adapted to contemporary life, just as other aspects may be abandoned.

The highest metaphysical questions involving primeval Chaos came full circle in the 20th century with the development of "chaos theory" in mathematics and physics. Chaos theory has raised possibilities of a role for seemingly random forces in what is, overall, an ordered system. This gets back to other very old ideas involving teleology. Maybe there is a purpose to what seems like purposelessness. The layer of possible primary causes recede back, a step further before every scientific discovery and explanation.

A worldview that sees struggle to maintain order, by keeping Chaos at bay, has much to offer us today. It avoids the simpleminded false dichotomy of good v. evil, and thus acknowledges unavoidable ambiguities that might better be addressed with endless Socratic questions rather than reactionary answers. It avoids the manipulative tools of heaven, hell, and the entire premise of sin; the latter being a questionable premise at best. In fact, you can take the opposite premise, such as Mencius (or Mengtzu, 孟子, ca. 372 BCE–289 BCE)[9] did, of humans being originally good and potentially corrupted by the world (ironically, this "veil of tears"). At that point, humanity's task is quite practically one of improving ethical behavior. The inability to eradicate all crime and bad behavior is the Chaos ever-knocking at the door. By taking the Original Sin premise, we get political manipulation, perpetual infantilization of humanity bowing to a heavenly anthropomorphic deity and "his" self-appointed representatives on Earth. Or, in the version of Han Feizi (韓 非), we get Legalism and totalitarianism. I'll take the Mencius perspective, if I have to choose.

The Greek view of dignified human nature, its revival among Renaissance humanists,[10] or the philosophy of Mencius—all offer worldviews that embrace human environmental stewardship without apologies for the place of humanity within the rest of the natural world. They form something of a general foundation for the premise of human involvement with nonhuman life that informs this book.

All creativity brings Cosmos out of Chaos. This is not limited simply to "art" per se, but to all creativity—in business, science, technology, law, child-rearing, vegetable gardening, or what have you. Our small acts of creativity can thus be seen as tributes to the larger creation that is our world and all its life. The heaven/hell worldview makes no sense from this perspective. Us v. Them also seems largely irrelevant. Good and evil are unavoidable actors in the scenario (as in all scenarios), but they are not the main point, nor are they dichotomously opposed. The main point is to be creative, to bring your portion of the Cosmos out of the Chaos.

The Zen master Shunryu Suzuki (鈴木 俊隆, 1904–1971) said many wise things; among them, to practice Zen anywhere, anytime. He wanted people to know that quitting work or school to go (literally) to a mountaintop was to miss the point. Sitting in meditation and bowing were important formally, but cooking without wandering thoughts was also Zen, as was limiting one's grief or joy, and being aware that (for example) ideal perfection in parenting was impossible.[11] So the self-conscious (often fake) rapture in the wilderness is obvious; rapture is readily available amid urban ecology, if you care to recognize it. This fits nicely with the Cosmos/Chaos worldview, but not at all with the heaven/hell worldview.

Nassim Nicholas Taleb is an example of a contemporary person interacting with the Cosmos/Chaos worldview. Taleb uses terms like "antifragility" and "robustification" to describe facing Chaos and deriving Cosmos from it. Among other remarkable accomplishments, he has made a fortune in the financial world by applying these ideas. In 2009, British journalists Bryan Appleyard included Taleb's 2007 book, *The Black Swan*, in his list of books that have changed the world since World War II. The title of Taleb's 2012 book, *Antifragile: Things That Gain from Disorder*, practically speaks for itself.[12]

Here is a further story, this one of two wealthy men as understood through the Cosmos/Chaos worldview. One man, Leo Drey, was heir to the Drey Mason Jar fortune. He could have invested his vast wealth and increased it many fold, but he chose instead to be a steward of land. Through decades of discipline and work, he created the Pioneer Forest, about 154,000 acres in the state of Missouri. This was and is a working forest that utilizes old German silvicultural techniques of individual tree selection, and avoidance of clear-cutting. Besides being a closet idealist (often the best kind), Drey and his Pioneer Forest provide a small staff with good jobs. They give forestry and biology students a free laboratory for their field work. And finally, Drey gave the world an example of conscientious yet utilitarian environmental stewardship. This was one man's way of creating Cosmos out of Chaos.

I was once acquainted with another man of great independent wealth. I'll call him Nelson. If Nelson had followed a Cosmos out of Chaos worldview, his challenge would have been to work creatively with his money and hopefully do things for the less fortunate. This would have been his Cosmos. The

Chaos, ever looming on the horizon, would have been keeping opportunists at bay and trying to avoid the many unintended consequences and mistakes of charity. Instead, Nelson gave in to a different aspect of Chaos and did little with his life, wasting some of it in drunken self-pity. He accomplished little creatively, and helped very few, himself among the least.

Viewing these men through the heaven/hell worldview makes little sense to me. Leo Drey did not live in heaven, but he disciplined himself and created Cosmos. Nelson experienced a sort of living hell, partly as a consequence of the vicious circle of fate, depression, laziness, and self-pity—but most importantly, he did not create Cosmos; in fact, there is very little evidence that he even tried. As for their destiny in the after life, my favorite response to that question comes from Confucius (孔子), who said we have enough to rectify in this life without concerning ourselves with the hereafter. In other words, Confucius was interested in our ability to achieve or approach Cosmos.

If we can agree that struggle explains some of our main ontological questions, then a cosmology explaining struggle becomes centrally important. Creative struggle itself comes to answer teleological questions. Here, one's worldview need not be taken so seriously, as so many of the monotheists are indoctrinated to believe. Rather, it can be more like art—a matter of taste.

For many reasons the primeval Cosmos out of Chaos conception is greatly appealing. It is non-dogmatic, flexible and tolerant, appeals to the aesthetic and philosophical imagination, and (quite importantly) transposes itself in daily life. You need not consider philosophy to appreciate the inescapability of struggle, whether for sheer existence for the poor or for the wealthy to keep decadence at bay. We would not want Chaos to disappear. It gives us purpose in life. It's fringe benefit is that of the court jester, reminding us not to take ourselves too seriously, reminding us that the emperor has no clothes, and constantly dispelling narcissistic self-mythology. It is not Satan. It is not evil. It is not hell. It is or should be inspiration to continue.

Cosmos and Chaos have ancient roots for what we would today call environmental stewardship. Until the post-industrial world, human creations constituted sacred landscape, almost precisely the opposite of contemporary wilderness worship. Wilderness represented Chaos in the ancient world; cities, houses, groves, gardens, and other human creations were among the efforts that represented Cosmos. Americans in particular—with all their Edenic cultural baggage, purity preoccupations, and wilderness worship— would do well to consider cultivated gardens as an important expression of sacred landscape.

* * *

Meanwhile, nature is indifferent to us. Lao Tzu, the founder of the school we call Philosophical Daoism, wrote such an observation over 2,500 years ago.[13] This is readily evident to anyone who has ventured into the wilderness. I remember a Canadian tour bus driver whose route was the Banff National Park. He was also a part-time voluntary park ranger who made regular stops to chastise the tourists for violating explicit park rules against getting out of their vehicles to photograph the grizzlies.

"They're urban folk," he said. "They think this is a zoo. Then they get too close to an irate sow who turns around and swats them one, and then we have to airlift the bear to another location because it's deemed a human hazard. It was the human who was the hazard all along."

It takes very little imagination to appreciate how wild land threatened ancient humans, and even contemporary humans. When I worked as a commercial fisherman in southeastern Alaska during the early 1980s, a friend of mine up there used to say, "Your chances of dying here are about as good as the inner city. The difference is, instead of someone killing you, you are likely to make a mistake."

Or, as Emerson wrote in 1849, nature "pardons no mistakes."[14]

We used to see it all the time; the chainsaw dealer who flipped his skiff and drowned within a stone's throw of land due to the frigid water draining the strength from his limbs, rendering him unable to swim. The unlucky fishing crew who hit a "deadhead" (a semi-submerged, partially-waterlogged tree trunk) that punched a basketball-sized hole in their wooden hull. The careless hiker who fell off a rock cliff on Mount Verstovia, apparently while sunbathing in the nude. His father flew up to Sitka to retrieve his son's body; a grim mission for him that we all heard about in the small town.

Nature in southeastern Alaska was exquisitely and electrically beautiful, but there was no ignoring its potential deadliness. Anyone who has fished the northern seas and watched the icy ocean water wash over the deck, through the gunwales, must come to some appreciation of this.

In any case, it puts wilderness worship into an entire different framework, and one comes to appreciate armchair environmentalists taking comfort in the oft-mentioned "knowing wilderness is there" concept, even though they never visit it. Those who do venture in rely completely upon modern technology of lightweight backpacking gear, dehydrated foods, excellent footwear and most of all, the knowledge and design of the wilderness trek as a strictly temporary sojourn based firmly in civilization. It is a recent luxury. On the other hand, human-altered landscapes are one of the components marking the beginning of civilization.

Despite numerous cultural variations upon the theme, gardens throughout history and across continents have certain commonalities. Chinese literati gardens (first arising during the Tang Dynasty, 618–907 CE) were urban sanctuaries where creative people might contemplate and seek their muse,[15] something artistic people the world over appreciate. Chinese literati gardens could also mark social status and prestige,[16] not unlike the political intent of Versailles or its European imitators large and small. The religious significance of gardens appears the world over. The Aztecs built elaborate gardens replete with spiritual references.[17] In Israel, some sacred landscapes precede monotheism and thus Judaism as the world came to know it, and yet incorporate the collective Jewish religious experience.[18] The same can be said of Sufi gardens in modern day Iran, which have traditional roots that precede the Muslim faith by many centuries.[19]

Ironically, human-created gardens (such as Chinese Daoist gardens) became places to commune with nature and mystical forces[20]; things wilderness worshippers associate with the illusion of remote lands with (the wishful thinking of) missing human influence. Chinese gardens were places of aesthetic beauty, deliberate religious symbolism, and where individuals could discover their personal self, as well as how and where that self fit into the larger world.[21]

"Civilization" in the most generic definition (attempting a neutral description of culture) begins with the Neolithic. The Neolithic lasted between 6,000 and 8,000 years (beginning around 10,000 BCE) before giving way to metal technology cultures (the Bronze and Iron ages). The Neolithic was when humans began domesticating plants and animals, farming on a more sedentary basis, inventing writing and systematic religion, developing social stratification, and other features quite distinct from the earlier nomadic traditions of hunting and gathering. The Neolithic is also when we find our earliest gardens.[22] More appear in the earliest civilizations of the western tradition, in Sumer (a subset of Mesopotamia) and in Egypt.

The Sumerian hymn "Lugale" captures a classic example of humanity rendering Cosmos out of Chaos by building a garden out of the wilderness. Here wilderness begins as a "wild and inimical space," but humans are able to make it a safe and nurturing place.[23] This appeals to our common sense if we try to imagine the fragility of ancient societies in particular, but even today if we consider trying to survive in the wilderness without benefit of (or even *with* benefit of) contemporary technology. Rendering Cosmos out of Chaos in gardens also made them instantaneous places where humans felt they interacted with divine forces and sources of creation. This was readily evident in Egyptian gardens, as it is in ancient gardens in general.[24] Yet Egyptian gardens retained elements of "wild" nature, especially compared to intensely constructed gardens of later eras.[25]

Greek sacred groves resembled Egyptian gardens in their religious associations as semi-wild places. Greeks planted sacred groves of trees, both in rural and urban settings, dedicated to various deities.[26] Sometimes they associated specific species of trees with particular deities, such as the oak with Demeter or the ash with Apollo. Greeks appreciated what the Chinese would conceptualize as the *feng shui* (風水) of a grove's natural features, such as caves or fresh water springs.[27] Like gardens, parks, and groves in other cultures, ancient Greek groves ultimately featured a combination of human and nonhuman attributes. Natural landforms and pre-existing flora species coexisted with religious sculpture and planted tree species.[28]

By Plato's era, Greek gardens had acquired additional attributes as places for learning and meditation. Scholars and students held discussions in gardens, exercised physically, and learned to cultivate good manners. In this sense they had added a secular side featuring human intellect and social behavior. Greek philosophers created a precedent in western civilization (followed for over two millennia now) that associated gardens with intellectual thought.[29] Alexander the Great and his conquests were the first phenomena to spread Greek gardening traditions, yet this was also the era when monumental gardens of the Persian Empire influenced Greek ideas of gardening. This hybrid began to show up in the new cosmopolitan cities of the Hellenistic kingdoms, particularly Alexandria, Egypt.[30]

In general, the Hellenistic period was when the urban garden came to the fore in western culture. The Epicurean school of philosophy in particular sought to create oases of rural nature within cities.[31] This human impulse to retain aspects of rural nature in the city has been a constant theme throughout urban history. Marked highlights include the Versailles garden complex initiated under Louis XIV and all the European imitators that followed. Frederick Law Olmstead might be the most famous garden designer in American history, perhaps most noted for helping to produce New York City's Central Park.

We have often thought of urban quality of life in relation to its absence or presence of green space. A sad feature of slums is their absence of redeeming parks. Practically all urban design today, and certainly the "green city" concept, includes liberal accommodations for trees, ponds, fountains, berms, parks, and other sanctuaries of nature among and even enhanced by buildings surrounding them.

As they did with so much Greek tradition, the Romans absorbed and transformed Greek gardening practices.[32] From that tradition came a wide variety of European gardens containing many reiterations of earlier themes. Medieval "pleasure gardens" represented both primitive leftovers of Cosmos

College campuses often offer garden-like sanctuaries sequestered from vehicular traffic and urban noise. This view of Burruss Hall is taken from the quad behind Williams Hall on the Virginia Tech campus in Blacksburg. Except for the occasional maintenance vehicle, the Williams Hall quad accommodates only pedestrian traffic. As much as houses, farms, gardens, and ziggurats, Archaic people would consider such human architectural and landscape creation as a tribute to the larger creation that is the entire world and all life within it (photograph by Teresa Chen).

rendered out of Chaos, as well as religious associations that had grown more complex since ancient times; i.e., some garden aficionados associated "pleasure" with earthly delights, others with Christian notions of divine love, or admixtures thereof.[33] As with the new genre of fine art portraiture, Renaissance gardens came to reflect social standing and status of the rising merchant class. Albeit royal status, Versailles became the penultimate expression of this trend, widely imitated at the royal level outside of France, but also all over Europe in much more modest suburban gardens reflecting the growing *nouveau riche* status.[34]

Speaking of Versailles, many people have noted how western gardens supposedly follow rigid geometric forms "imposed" on nature, in contrast to East Asian gardens that supposedly "harmonize" with nature. There is no doubt that East Asian gardens generally do indeed blend into the nonhuman environment in ways starkly contrasting a garden like Versailles.[35] But the east-west contrast is ultimately an overly-simplified false dichotomy for a number of reasons. First, it raises the perennial philosophical issue of whether or not humans are *a part of* nature, and therefore whether or not any human creation is "artificial" or natural. But the east-west contrast only works specifically with certain western gardens. The earliest Mesopotamian and Egyptian gardens employed geometric design simply for practical reasons, being that the straightest and shortest irrigation route made sense in a desert or semi-arid environment.[36] As for the Versailles-type of geometric garden, it was a specific product of the Scientific Revolution and its preoccupation with mathematics.[37] As we have already seen, the Greek sacred groves were quite different from this and had more in common with East Asian gardens than geometric gardens. Perhaps the most striking thing about Eurasian gardens in general was their reflection of various peoples and cultures all embracing humanity and its role in nature. It is the United States with its odd notion of Eden where some people view human influence, ingenuity, and stewardship as somehow "unnatural" and thus somehow opposing nonhuman nature.

If it were not obvious already, one premise of this book is that humans are indeed a part of nature. It is hardly an original idea, stemming back to Greco-Roman culture.[38] In fact, it might seem absurd to have to mention it at all (like all mammals we live, breed, kill, and die) were it not for the "misanthropic Eden" strain in American environmental thinking. It has given rise to what I call Green Calvinism, given the puritanical strains of it all. Ironically, such misanthropy reflects a rebellion against a false premise: i.e., the cherry-picked biblical notion that humans are above and domineering over nature.[39] In 1967 Lynn White wrote a regrettable essay with this very thesis, debunked at length and in detail afterward by a great many scholars, writers, and thinkers.[40] A false premise leads to a false argument as well as a false rebellion. As I described at length in "Misanthropic Eden," there is a stronger counterargument that uses Judeo-Christian sources (if that is what appeals to you) to support conscientious environmental stewardship.

In any case, misanthropic Edenist ideology shows up all the time in standard environmental dogma, such as "invasive species" ecological purity concepts, the carbon footprint cliché, concepts of wilderness as well as official American wilderness policy to "leave no [human] trace." It is the idea that habitats are better left "untouched" by humans, as if humans were not part of nature, and no matter that all habitats are nonetheless influenced by humans one way or another anyway.

Way back in 1961 amid the national trend toward wilderness worship, Jane Jacobs objected to the idea that human structures were any less "natural" than bird nests or bear lairs.[41] This was the sort of idea that became blasphemous to many of the Sixties children, but actually just ahead of the curve from what we face today. We are self-conscious members of nature who wield enormously significant powers to alter the nonhuman environment, but we are every bit as "natural" as any other living being.

More about this later.

The individual experience in gardens began during the Romantic period and continues today.[42] Gardens function as private sanctuaries featuring individuals' aesthetic expressions. Urban gardens can help foster community.[43] They can be places of weddings or wakes. As in times past, they are places of meditation. Some even see gardens as expressions of peace. And, in direct continuity from the most ancient gardens, contemporary gardens remain sacred space,[44] at least for those who appreciate them as such. In this sense they reflect universal aspects of humanity and the environment. Despite comparatively recent wilderness worship, we still understand the human-created sanctuary that the ancients understood.

As Catherine Howett wrote, quoting the centuries-old Haggadah of Judaism, "Our new gardens … must be modest gardens, expressing our wonder and reverence for the world as we discover it, our humanity a part of the whole mystery." She also recognized gardens as expressions of tribute to the renewed earth and its people.[45] As Jennifer Cousineau described it, "even" an urban environment like Manhattan can be consecrated into sacred space that fosters a sense of home and community, embraces material culture, but sanctifies it according to ancient Jewish law.[46] This would be consistent with the theme of this chapter; rendering sacred Cosmos out of primeval Chaos.

The point would be to act as a Grand Steward, a Zen gardener raking the gravel or "pointlessly" carrying stones from one corner to another.[47] The *gardening* is as important as is the garden, just as playing a musical instrument is as important (or more important, for the musician) than the resultant music.

Gardens are a celebration of civilization and human ingenuity, for pre-garden society was a nomadic existence passing through wild lands. What a comparative luxury to be able to cease constant relocation, enjoy more stable sources of food, and demarcate sacred space out of the wild space, as people from Neolithic times to the present have done. We create *feng shui* by working with nature, and this is the best of all worlds for humans. The instinct to make a statement from nature and in nature during our transience is very important. We create a little temporary place to enjoy, whether it endures for later generations or not. We are not "harming" nature by doing such things, as the misanthropist environmentalists would have us believe. In fact, ulti-

The Japanese Garden in Portland, Oregon. This is a classic example of human stewardship expressed in a beautiful landscape design. Ancient peoples all over the world considered such creations as religious expressions of rendering cosmic Order out of primeval Chaos. Joseph Campbell once said, "in some of those [Japanese] gardens you don't know where nature begins and art ends" (Joseph Campbell, *Power of Myth*, episode two, "Message of the Myth") (photograph by Teresa Chen).

mately everything we do is like a traditional Navajo sand painting or a Tibetan mandala (or "Dust in the Wind," the tune by the rock band Kansas): a temporary creation that should be in tribute to the vast creation that is our world, ourselves in that world, and our appreciation of the unique role allotted human beings regarding an unescapably self-conscious care for the environment.

That is, in a nutshell, what philanthropic environmental stewardship is all about.

A final note about order and chaos. Order, in a much more mundane sense, deeply appeals to human nature. We organize our thoughts and seek order and patterns in nature, whether they exist or not. Obviously you could go down the rabbit hole of metaphysics regarding this topic, and perhaps the most plausible immediate argument would indicate the more mythological concepts of Cosmos and Chaos naturally arising in conjunction with or because of our more mundane organizational penchants. But to stay within the realms of science and common sense—this penchant for organization creates potential problems.

Imposing scientific order upon a messy phenomenon such as species definition, for example, creates endless policy headaches (not to mention litigation) when it comes to habitat protection. As R.C. Lewontin points out, we create "scientific facts" out of an "undifferentiated nature." If the results fail to pan out as we wished, we can always change the organizational scheme.[48] This becomes a way to "bring order out of confusion."[49] But obviously such a constructed order, as we shall see, runs the risk of prejudicial or at least subjective agendas. Perhaps the strangest prejudicial agenda is premised upon strange notions of Eden, in which Americans try to freeze the environment in time, banning undesirable species, and pretending that humanity has not "sullied" the garden. The latter is most easily dispensed with if we simply consider people *part of* the garden.

Mythologically, Eden is a commonly misunderstood archetype. Ecologically, the garden that is Earth is our habitat, and we are its self-conscious stewards. We cannot escape this stewardship role, nor should we try. Instead, we should accept it with gratitude and humility. I've met a number of gardeners, landscape architects, arborists, and others who love a particular land—who tend to know all this intuitively. It is a tremendous privilege to care for a small portion of home. That hasn't stopped us from doing a very bad job of it sometimes, but we also have the opportunity to learn from past mistakes and to employ better tools and better understanding as we follow our inevitable stewardship path.

Earth as our mundane garden is okay. Technology is here to stay. Fear and insecurity are natural; this is why courage is a virtue. We need to reunite with the mythos. Very few of us have the ability to unite with the Immortal Principle itself. The mythos will have to do. When misunderstood, both science and religion (usually of the institutionalized variety) can become deviations from the mythos, and certainly from the Immortal Principle. This is unnecessary and potentially very wrongheaded indeed. Science, religion, and the mythos can all be embraced; in fact, science and religion (together or separately) can and should lead to mythos. And we can do it all during our short time on post–Pandora Earth. We have no other choice, really. We cannot go back, so we might as well go forward as enlightened as possible in all realms.

Chapter 2

Untenable Eden

Just before I turned eleven my family moved to Blacksburg, Virginia. Near there, to the west, were remnants of the old 460 Highway that had been bypassed by the new and improved (and straighter) version of that same numerical roadway. The abandoned curvy sections were kind of fun to explore; they featured old guardrails in an advanced state of rust. Faded remnants of painted lines remained barely visible if at all. The edges were crumbling, sending pieces of deteriorating asphalt into the ditches beside the old road. There was a palpable sense of history there, ludicrous as that might sound; but I could not help but think of the old vehicles that had once rolled over that highway when it represented a major improvement over the dirt and gravel roads that had preceded it.

Influenced by some of my father's ideas and comments, I had a fantasy about digging holes in the middle of those abandoned highway sections and planting trees, which roots would help hasten the disintegration of the remaining asphalt, thus quickening a process that would take place anyway. There was something satisfying about nature "taking something back" from humanity's imprint. But perhaps just as important is accepting the inevitable reality of this happening. Eden and "untouched" wilderness are cultural constructs; the striving of all life forms to survive and perpetuate themselves is observable scientific fact. This is how Yucatan jungles overtook Mayan ruins. This is how flora and weather erase abandoned highways. It even shows up repeatedly in human drama, wherein the hero sacrifices her or himself, with the parting admonition to "carry on without me." Carrying on is what nature does, and that includes practically all life, from bacteria to blue whales, from eucalyptus to egg plants. Humans are no exception.

Sometimes we forget how much energy we invest in maintaining civilization. Just imagine how quickly your house would begin to crumble without maintenance. A human life can easily outlast a structure's life, unless humans maintain that structure. Roofs begin to leak, which in turn cause foundation timbers to rot. If you've ever examined a crumbling house, you can see that it begins from the roof or the foundation, but quickly becomes both in a vicious circle. As an old house renovator once told me, regarding the fixer-uppers that he rescued: "Stabilize the foundation and the roof first. The rest can wait." By contrast, the life force of "nature" requires no maintenance at all, for it will perpetuate itself in one form or another until the sun dies and the planet becomes uninhabitable for all life. As Alston Chase observed many years ago, fragility characterizes civilization, not wilderness.[1]

"Wilderness" has a way of returning and inherently continuing regardless of its natural details and how we define or value them. So in a sense we cannot escape our self-preservation as a species, nor would any arguments to the contrary be very persuasive. Along with our fundamental attempts to thrive, we carry selective valuation for other life. We value life that feeds us and non-utilitarian life as much as possible (or at least we should). On the other hand, we're glad to kill infectious bacteria and viruses that are attempting to survive (like all life forms), but at our expense. We also do not hesitate to kill predatory mammals and reptiles that threaten us.

According to Bjørn Lomborg, despite environmentalist propaganda, humans with rifles are the number one cause of polar bear death, not melting ice habitat.[2] Lomborg's critics rejected his assessments here, of course, but eight years after he made it the Norwegian Polar Institute actually reported an increased population in the Svalbard region.[3] In fact, in recent years, the Arctic ice in general has remained constant or actually grown.[4] But in classic circular reasoning and an untenable conflation of policy and science, Howard Friel triumphantly declared that the Republican President George Bush's Department of the Interior listing the polar bear as endangered from global warming proved Lomborg wrong.[5] Perhaps we may safely conclude that polar bears, like the World Wildlife Fund's panda poster child, is more emotionally evocative than scientifically indicative.

The "untouched wilderness" of the western Amazon was actually once home to various civilizations.[6] We've also recently learned that the Mayan civilization was much more extensive than archaeologists previously thought.[7] In both cases, it was only the rapid re-growth of the rain forest that created the illusion of past absence or diminished presence of humans. Other non-jungle places on the globe simply take longer to achieve the same results.

Land left alone can be just as wondrous as "wilderness." This makes sense if we accept Eden as a false premise. Eden concepts potentially make wilderness disappointing. Trekking into the wilderness can be an amazing, enriching experience, but it is predicated upon an assured return to civilization. The only other option is death. Native people knew this, and did not venture into the lands that we now call wilderness: high elevation places fea-

turing sparse food supplies and harsh weather. No wonder they derived omi-
nous religious associations with the high elevation mountains. No wonder
they lived in the valleys. A person with the right sensitivity can easily appreciate this today. Conversely, as Michael Crichton wrote (regarding "ecopsy-
chology"), "the movement projects the dissatisfactions of contemporary
society onto a natural world that is so seldom experienced that it serves as
the perfect projection screen."[8] In other words—nature as Eden, including
wilderness—is more of a sociocultural construct that often has little connection to actual nature and most certainly ignores what science can tell us about
our environment.

*　*　*

I used to go hiking with a retired schoolteacher in the northern Washington Cascades. I'll call him Joey. He was a kind and gentle man who, like
so many sensitive people, had experienced bouts of severe depression in his
life. In his youth he had wanted to roam the world, but his bride wanted to
nest in the same county of their birth. He relinquished his wanderlust for the
sake of the marriage and paid a price for his sacrifice, which choice still
seemed ambiguous four decades after the fact. Time had brought him some
peace, but only some.

In any case, Joey was my only benevolent acquaintance during a ten-
month temporary job in a small town that was too small for me. Every weekend
I ventured to Seattle or Bellingham, or to one of the many surrounding Indian
reservations to do research on a canoe culture project then occupying me. But
on some weekends Joey would take me high into the Cascades on hikes he had
been walking over and over his entire life. It was a real privilege to see that
country, and I could not have done it without him or his guidance.

One day in August we were well above the tree line and ventured into
a glacial field. Quite strangely, Joey found an ice ax lying there in the com-
pacted snow and gave it to me. He already owned several and I owned none.
He even briefly described a life-saving technique.

"If you start to slide down the mountain, do not sit up or resist. Cling to
your ice ax like dear life and begin slamming it into the ground to slow your
dissent. With any luck that will end your slide and you can recover from there."

Less than an hour later we were in precisely the landscape that could
precipitate such an emergency.

The trail at this point was along the narrowest of ridge spines, revealing
bare ground and rock in the late summer. But the flanks on either side were
still many inches thick in snow-ice that melted a little during the day only to
re-freeze at night, creating extremely slippery conditions.

We found a small exposed rock outcrop to eat our lunch. In ceasing our hiking, the silence began to move in. And in looking out over that eerie, high elevation landscape, I said, "It's like we don't really belong up here."

"I know," Joey said solemnly, instantly recognizing a kindred intuitive appreciation.

There was no need to say anything else. We both sensed the foreboding nature of the land we were in. We were not macho men (nor young men) out "conquering" mountains. We were visiting a sacred place that included no little dark mystery. And I was thinking, no wonder the pre-contact aborigines rarely if ever ventured into this country. Why would they? There was no practical point. Even their solitary vision quests took place in the lower elevation forests in this particular part of the country. The forests, after all, were and are replete with life and (if you wish) no end of spiritual forces.

So what we call wilderness certainly has a special place in our philosophical spectrum, but so does (or should) nearly every other place. I admit, places like the western Utah alkali flats stretch that concept for someone like me, but that is also a subjective opinion. Desert people say similar things about feeling alienated in the northern rainforest that I prefer. But all of this is important because every non-wilderness place tends to reveal human influence rather clearly. There is no problem with this in general as long as we abandon misanthropy and embrace the idea that humans are both part of nature and stewards of habitats in general, whether we like the latter role or not. Where things get interesting is acceptance of a very realistic premise involving the striving struggle of all life. This is how landscapes formerly reflecting marked human influence can hold wondrous prospects.

Speaking of Utah—I once saw photographs of soil exhaustion in 1920s North Carolina, where land had been overplanted in tobacco. Portions of it vaguely resembled parts of the Claron Formation in Utah. The top soil and much of the subsoil had all washed away in rainstorms, leaving wide and deep swaths of erosion. Practically everyone would condemn this landscape as a product of poor agricultural stewardship. Yet, we admire Bryce Canyon National Park, which features such erosive geography on a massive scale. In fact, we tend to enjoy it especially when we are assured of passing through this uninhabitable land (unless food and water are imported). In ancient societies, transforming desert lands into habitable space would have been a sacred act, a rendering of Cosmos out of Chaos. So it is important to remember value judgments.

Comparing eroded North Carolina tobacco fields and the Desert Southwest may seem absurd, but consider the remnants of a rock quarry cliff compared to one made by nature. What if you saw a photograph of one and were not sure whether it was the product of human behavior or not? Why would we see them so differently, even if the resultant geography is similar? It is worth remembering how misanthropy sneaks into these considerations, and how we usually do not separate our aesthetic sensibilities from our philosophical values.

We reflect our philosophical values in "restoring" various landscapes as well. There is an entire subdivision of ecology called "restoration ecology." The Society for Ecological Restoration publishes a journal by that name. The immediate question that comes to mind is, restore to what configuration and why? After much mulling over the definition of restoration ecology, in 1995 the Society for Ecological Restoration's described it as "the process of repairing damage caused by humans to the diversity and dynamics of indigenous ecosystems."[9] The return to paradise theme is evident; the misanthropic streak is reflected in the choice of the word "damage" instead of the more neutral "alteration." This was partly in response to Pickett and Parker's earlier observation that restoration ecology could not recreate some imagined standard of pre-human perfection.[10] Picket was one of the pioneers of disturbance ecology some years earlier,[11] so his point of view was no surprise.

Restoration ecologists publish many helpful technical details about their work, but in their early years their official goal was restoring an imagined nature that existed before human influence. As Jacques Swart and team wrote in 2001, "The wilderness approach may be considered the dominant valuation approach in nature development and often in restoration."[12] Swart, et al., continued that "pristine, indigenous ecosystems" served as restoration goals. Thus, an imagined Eden is the standard against which all else is measured, "situations prior to human settlement" serving as the supposed guide,[13] as if we even know what the pre-aborigine landscape looked like, as if we could even reconstruct the impossible with all the missing species, minus the air pollution, reversing all the evolutionary changes since human settlement, et cetera. And never mind that, in a final oxymoronic twist, it is humans implementing this "nature development."

In that same June 2001 issue of *Restoration Ecology*, R. van Diggelen, et al., complained about the 1998 Groningen Conference on Restoration Ecology held in the Netherlands. "Due to its geographic position in Europe, the conference was clearly biased toward cultural and semi-natural ecosystems," they wrote,[14] making their Edenic frame of reference quite clear. This included the old familiar American misanthropic streak found in such thinking, objecting to the conference's location amid western Europe's densest human population that "unfairly" gave high priority to society rather than nonhuman life.[15]

Yet, in the same collection of articles, Jörg Pfadenhauer offered a very different perspective pertaining to the realities of a crowded Europe where misanthropic Edenism is not only impossible, but impractical. He recommended that restoration ecologists view their projects on a site-by-site basis, working with the local societies they encountered. He saw interaction with political leaders and policymakers as inevitable and unavoidable.[16] "Ecological restoration is not only the recovery of the former state of a disturbed or destroyed ecosystem," he wrote. "It also includes the construction of new ecosystems" with multiple aspects, making things like artificial wetlands do double duty treating wastewater.[17] This is a much more realistic approach to restoration ecology, partly because it recognizes and even embraces the human agency. It recognizes the impossibility of returning to some pre-anthropogenic landscape, and at least tacitly appreciates the philosophical valuation invested in such restoration efforts, changing course from earlier valuations.

By 2004, Mark Davis and Lawrence Slobodkin were adopting a stewardship idea of restoration ecology that apparently contradicted many of the Society of Ecological Restoration's philosophy.[18] Davis and Slobodkin advocated that restoration ecologists be sure to distinguish between their science and their philosophical values, and to see their work for its place square within policymaking.[19] "That restoration ecologists must involve themselves with values, public policy, and science is, no doubt, one of the reasons so many students are attracted to the field as a career option," they wrote. They saw the acknowledgment of philosophical values as an asset, not a liability or deterrent. The science could remain focused on the task at hand.[20] Keith Winterhalder, et al., found much of this upsetting and proceeded to respond with an essay that seemed to miss Davis and Slobodkin's most salient points quite completely. They argued that the Society for Ecological Restoration made it clear that the endeavor was value-driven within a social context.[21] So how, then, were Davis and Slobodkin contradicting the SER?

In any case, this sort of controversy seemed to reflect growing pains in the young discipline of restoration ecology. Sometime after the early and mid–2000s, the Society for Ecological Restoration appears to have become far less Edenic. The "definitions" section cited above no longer exists on their website. Instead, their mission statement now reflects a far more philanthropic environmentalism. They seek to engage society in ecology, including aboriginal people whose actions and influences many Edenists (like the early Yellowstone National Park managers) have ignored in the past. Now they seek to "re-establish an ecologically healthy relationship between nature and culture."[22] That's a far more reasonable approach.

Outside of the confines of the Society for Ecological Restoration, any number of semi-coherent philosophical valuations might be found. For example, federal and state governments, the Nature Conservancy, and other groups have spent hundreds of millions of dollars restoring rivers. These efforts include removing old dams, planting trees, reestablishing old flood channels and floodplains. In western Oregon, the Willamette Focused Investment Partnership has utilized many millions of said dollars doing such work on the McKenzie and Willamette rivers. Their general aim is to undo past agricultural modifications of the watershed and restore the riverine environment to pre–European settlement configurations. But they've also "reclaimed" leftover gravel pits, which function well as artificial fish habitats—so apparently there are limits to recapturing Eden when alterations suit contemporary values.[23]

Many eastern rivers in New England and the Mid-Atlantic states are so altered that it took a couple of geologists to point out that millions of dollars' worth of "restoration" was not restoring the landscape to pre-colonial configurations at all. These landscapes had been altered so much that, without test bores and other geological investigation, the naked eye could not appreciate the extent of change. Some places featured megatons of accumulated silt filling in old wetlands and terraces created by tens of thousands of early, small dams. Only scientific investigation could reveal pre-colonial river and stream channels and former wetlands, and it is questionable whether these landscapes could be "restored" at all, or if we would even want to go that far.[24]

Obviously farmers everywhere have altered landscapes with levees, irrigation ditches, dams, and channels excavated to drain swamps. The practical aims were agricultural productivity and protection from flooding. Now we no longer need certain areas for farming, and thus seek to return it to an earlier habitat configuration featuring the usual *cause du jour* of native species. This is generally Edenic and quite expensive, but impossible in any ideal sense. It does reflect the values of our time, as part of the reaction to an earlier era's widespread and somewhat indiscriminate utilitarian alteration of the land. These days we have the luxury of not needing so much utility, at least in certain landscapes.

Attempting to undo past environmental changes is one component of contemporary thinking. Another is predicting (or fearing) possible future scenarios. Since recorded history we have tried to peer into the future. It is part of the human condition; our inherent insecurity and seeking of reassurance, our desire to plan ahead and create order out of chaos, sometimes as a basis for hope, and sometimes just out of mere curiosity. So we have cast yarrow sticks, read Tarot cards, consulted oracles, read horoscopes, read palms, gazed into crystal balls, and assembled a mind-numbing array of portents and omens.

As mentioned, that Jurassic specialist was my introduction to doomsdayism. I have so much respect for geologists, and some of the professors at Virginia Tech (Gerald V. Gibbs of Jerrygibbsite fame comes to mind) were world class. So naturally I listened when this Jurassic era specialist preached environmental apocalypse. I did not know he was merely a doomsdayist.

But this was an instructive episode for several reasons. First of all, the Jurassic specialist is long dead, and we're all still alive. Knowledgeable as he was about the geological past, he was no better than a kook on the street corner when it came to prophecy, and his scientific training should have made him know better than to confuse the scientific method with futureology. Finally—and here was an irony apparently lost upon the geology professor himself—the dinosaurs went extinct because of a massive asteroid hitting Earth. Short of nuking such a future asteroid in outer space before it hits the planet, we're just as vulnerable to such an astrophysics event, which would render null and void all our fears and concerns, merited and not, regarding anthropogenic environmental change.

When will the misanthropists ever learn?

But doomsday is coming! Now! I mean *right* now! No? Okay, then sometime soon!! *Real* soon! Watch out! Be afraid! Or be *outraged*. At least *be concerned*. At least *raise awareness*.

The environmental apocalypse has been just over the next horizon since I was a child during the 1960s. Rachel Carson's 1963 book, *Silent Spring*, sounded an early warning regarding injudicious use of pesticides, particularly DDT.[25] The spring would be silent because, beginning with the insect end of the food chain, all other animals would be dead. A few years later Paul and Anne Ehrlich predicted massive human death through famine caused by overpopulation in their 1968 book, *Population Bomb*.[26] There was also Lynn White's 1967 essay laying environmental damage at the feet of the Christian cultural tradition, as well as Garrett Hardin's 1968 essay "Tragedy of the Commons."[27] DDT remains controversial to this day, for proponents indicate the human lives saved by eradicating mosquitos bearing deadly diseases. The Ehrlich's prediction flopped, and both White's and Hardin's points have been thoroughly qualified if not outright debunked.[28]

But earlier prophecies proven false in no way diminishes the minor industry in predicting doom. Environmental doom is but a variation upon a much larger theme.

Ironically, by the time eco-apocalypse had gained currency, the early Baby Boomers (around a decade older than me) were already making fun of the doomsday fear of their childhood, that of nuclear holocaust. "Duck and cover" had fallen out of fashion. This must be one of the more bizarre stories involving the age-old theme of apocalypse in the human imagination. Innumerable doomsdayists have come and gone throughout the millennia without their predictions coming true, and yet nuclear annihilation is now—and possibly forever—a genuine scientific, political, and military possibility. Still, in my lifetime, it has gone from existential threat to forgotten afterthought. Not only do the surplus of nuclear weapons still exist (that is, more than enough to kill all humans many times over), but nuclear technology is a genie that will never reenter the proverbial bottle. So why are we no longer afraid? Perhaps this illustrates the faddish nature of doomsdayism.

In any case, a succession of hysterical predictions of ecological collapse has been cycling through popular culture ever since, paralleling the nuclear fear during the 1960s, then overshadowing it as a more popular apocalypse variation. The Amazon rain forest was going to disappear. A fifth of Earth's species were going to be extinct by the 1990s. A hole in the ozone layer was going to grow and kill us. The sun was losing its power and we were facing solar dimming and a new ice age. No, the planet was warming because of human activity—or, to hedge all bets and win the propaganda wars, humans were causing the climate to change, thus safely interweaving partially-understood natural changes with whatever influences we are having.

Doomsday has been around since recorded history, long before contemporary environmentalism.[29] Lately it is epitomized by the ludicrous "Doomsday Clock," which began seriously enough during the height (or nadir) of nuclear holocaust fears. Serious physicists from the Manhattan Project (in requisite white coats) stood before a cheap theater prop of a huge clock with the large hand set ten minutes before doom. As one wag recently asked, "What happens when we have to set our clocks an hour forward?"[30]

Much of this is childish, quite literally. "Scientists" posing as seers try to frighten us with their predictions, the way parents try to frighten children into behaving with tales of monsters, bogeymen, and Santa punishing those who are naughty and not nice. But no one can predict the future and "authorities" who claim otherwise discredit themselves through the "cry wolf" dynamic.

Related to future doomsday is the lost Golden Age. Since the environmental movement began, this Golden Age is vaguely associated with pre-nuclear, pre-industrial society. But this variation upon paradise lost is but one manifestation in a much larger theme. A lost utopia shows up in many if not all cultures. These include the Garden of Eden, Shangri-La, the Peach Blossom Source, and a great many others.[31] In America of recent generations, this lost utopianism has manifested itself in environmental philosophy, policy, and politics regarding most especially national parks and wilderness areas. It has taken on "religious" attributes, as many scholars and writers have observed.[32] Where religion bleeds over into philosophy, we begin to find all sorts of value-laden ideas masquerading as "science," including the science of ecology.[33] This would have enormous potential for distorting any hope for "objective" understanding of nature as it is, but add to that "politicized science" and ecological studies teeter dangerously close to propaganda. Some would argue they cross the line altogether.

Especially since the industrial revolution, doomsday has become part two of a fictional way of viewing the world, the dark future linked to a bright past, both almost wholly imagined. The dark future is usually (at best) an uninformed guess over what cannot be predicted. The bright past is a lost paradise that advocates, activists, and various other preachers admonish us to return to.[34] With environmental preaching it takes on a highly romanticized nostalgia for the pre-industrial past. We saw this as soon as industrialism began. For example, the English Victorians were prone to romanticize the pastoral cottage life they had just lost.[35] American worship of wilderness followed the same dynamic.[36]

But the lost golden age story combined with future apocalypse uses, in a way, the same manipulative device as the child's version of the Adam and Eve story (not to be confused with the mythological archetypes that the story actually represents). We live in a troubled world and always have. It's easy to be seduced into believing that it was somehow better, once upon a time.

Some of the professional environmental advocates seem as far removed from everyday life and common sense as the most eccentric Ivory Tower denizen. If you just walk around and ask people about climate change or species extinction or plastic recycling, they usually only have general or even vague ideas that there is supposed to be a problem according to what "they" say. But most people are naturally too preoccupied with their own lives to be all that concerned. Except for the wealthy, most of us have to focus on surviving. We worry about crime in the neighborhood, or how our children are doing in school. We worry about our aging parents and maintaining their quality of life and independence. We worry about job insecurity and having enough money during our old age, if we live that long. We *really* worry about getting sick and losing everything through predatory medical expenses.

You begin to realize that doomsday is a preoccupation for a small group of people trying to stir up trouble or gain attention or funding for their cause. Sometimes they just seem to have too much time on their hands. There are both humorous and commercial aspects to environmental doomsdayism.

One of my local doomsday preachers, John Zerzan, got upset when Guy McPherson, one of the professional doomsdayists, came to town a'preachin' and hawking his book. According to Zerzan, McPherson was just another doomsayer who missed "the cardinal realities of the impending eco-catastrophe."[37] Oh my gosh, did the pot just call the kettle black? Was the pot unaware he had just done that? How? Goodness forbid a veteran attention seeker like Zerzan get out-doomsday-ed. But, you can't expect much from someone parading as an anarchist (communism having lost its shock value and attention-getting potential back in the 1970s) while living off the fat of the land. It seems infinitely more unfortunate to have entire societies buy into the doomsday dogma. From my point of view, a good place to begin buying out would be an abandonment of the Edenic premise.

In an odd way, and in an effort to be charitable, I sympathize with the young environmental protestors. I was once just as impressionistic, just as uninformed, and just as fearful for the future of the planet's ability to sustain life as we know it. I also had my entire life ahead of me and harbored a certain terror (perhaps particular to the young) that the world would end before I had a chance to live my life and fulfill my destiny. Fortunately, I never became a crusader for a cause I did not understand. Last year I encountered such a person, or rather had her encounter me—demanding I donate some of my substandard wages (I'm a part-time teacher) to his environmental cause. I pointed out that the directors of his charity (one of the famous global environmental organizations) pulled in six-figure salaries, that he probably had a trust fund waiting in the wings, and how I had once planted tens of thousands of trees and had thereby actually *contributed* something. It stopped him in his tracks.

What a shame to have to mention such a thing, if only as an effective defense against a gauche, self-righteous zealot invading your privacy. Besides, the facts in my defense were apparently devastating and, in any case, effectively reclaimed my peaceful walk through campus.

I have planted somewhere between thirty and forty thousand trees. I have an estimate of the number because I was paid by the white pine and scotch pine seedling when I planted in Virginia (nickel a tree). In Oregon I received the princely sum of $7 an hour, an unprecedented wage for me in 1982. At the time I did not think to count the unpaid commute to the logging site, sometimes two hours one-way. And it was many years later that I realized this was migrant labor, and boy did you earn every penny of those $7. You got fired from the Oregon crew if you planted less than a thousand trees a day, and I would be surprised if I exceeded that bare minimum by more than a few dozen trees any given day. It was easily the most exhausting work I have ever done in my life. I've never eaten so much food just to avoid *losing* weight (at 120 pounds, I had none to spare back then).

To put it all in perspective, my *entire* contribution was merely a single long season's worth of trees compared to professional tree planters who, quite literally, plant millions of trees before their bodies simply cannot take the punishment any longer. Yet in those few thousands of trees I planted, I contributed more carbon sequestration (if that's what concerns you) than most of the Eugene tree-hugging protestors combined. Still, for the gregarious, protesting is good social fun; labor always carries a sense of solitude, even when performed with a group.

In this age of tree farms and forest crop rotation it makes absolutely no sense to cut what little Old Growth forest remains. Still, the pseudo-silvicentric dogma and ideology surrounding Old Growth remains lost upon tree religion's acolytes—all of whom hypocritically use forest products. I'm still waiting to meet one who has planted any significant numbers of trees, or any trees at all. The privileged urban tree sitters would rather leave that sort of work to the migrant workers. There is much more of a socioeconomic class aspect in radical environmentalism than the protestors want to admit. But righteousness tends to be a blinding force like that.

Protesting against logging often becomes classic Edenism. There is a Calvinistic aspect to this, for Calvinism is sometimes preoccupied with purity concepts. Still, there must be many reasons why a strain of purity runs through American culture. Some would automatically jump to the Puritans themselves and their hyper-misanthropy regarding all things "sinful" and dirty, particularly as they pertained to "fallen" humanity. But others have concluded that the land itself, free of Old World cultural baggage, fed into American purity concepts. One theory does not exclude the other, of course, as Winthrop's famous 1630 "city on the hill" sermon illustrated, in which Winthrop anticipated the new land becoming the place where the Puritan strain of Protestantism would be an example to the world.[38] This might be the most noted example of combining religious purity concepts with the "pure" North American landscape. But it continued and continues to show up these centuries later.

In 1949, famous conservationist Aldo Leopold wrote that wilderness was an non-renewable resource that could "shrink but not grow."[39] This was a classic Edenic point of view. Once you "fall" from the Garden you can never go back. Ten years later Richard Neuberger echoed Leopold when he wrote, "Once wilderness is mined or grazed or logged, it can never be true wilderness again."[40] The 1964 Wilderness Act institutionalized this perspective, out of fear of losing lands in "their natural condition" uncorrupted by humanity.[41] Obviously native peoples had entirely different perspectives upon the topic. At the time, before the 1970s, white mainstream society (including scholars and policymakers) regularly ignored native people and their influences upon the environment; to have done otherwise would have complicated the Edenic premise, to say the least.

In any case, we can find the purity premise in a great many places today. As John Mortimer has his character Rumpole say, "be careful of … living in America…. The purity! The terrible determination not to adulterate anything!"[42]

Purity concepts have made a fortune for the house cleaning products industry, particularly when appealing to germaphobia, which probably has some connection to John Wesley's "cleanliness is next to godliness" mentality. It shows up in the marketing genius of "organic" foods despite the contentiousness that surrounds definitions of "organic,"[43] and never mind that there is no shortage of deadly organic plants, including poison sumac and a wide array of poison mushrooms. We are right to be concerned with artificial chemical contamination, but we should remember many toxins (lead, asbestos, etc.) appear in nature.[44] So much for paradise. Objection to genetically modified organisms (GMOs) sometimes plays into misanthropic purity concepts, glossing over the fact that plants and humans have been modifying each other since at least Neolithic times.[45] Aside from this Edenic aspect, the science surrounding GMOs is indeed unsettled, complex, and controversial. More about that later.

The ideologues love the quote from Thoreau, "In wilderness is the preservation of the world." But like most bumper sticker thinking, this phrase is full of holes. In wilderness is the preservation of … well, wilderness. Or at least an environment with a minimum of human influence, with the misanthropic aspect quite obvious. In human ingenuity is the preservation of the world as a friendly habitat for life as we now know it; that is, plants, us, and other animals.

Unsurprisingly, there are strains of Edenic thinking in many political movements and crusades, including anarchism, socialism, libertarianism, and even the Classic Liberalism of the 18th century (think Adam Smith). This is because many of these movements or at least sub-movements within them operated from various legal fictions of a state of nature that approximated a lost Golden Age. John Locke and Jean Jacques Rousseau were but two Enlightenment era thinkers in this vein, both seeing their contemporary societies as having fallen from an earlier mode of life, even though their political philosophies went in very different directions. Locke fed heavily into American ideas of property ownership; Rousseau found friendlier reception in subsequent strains of socialism. So, the present time in any given age is always a mess—thus an intellectual and emotional escapism can arise in a paradise lost.

Aside from Green Calvinism strains, misanthropic Eden thinking is a worldview based upon a premise of nature being an entity of order, stability, and harmony. The idea of a balanced or orderly nature has ancient precedents, but also dominates much of contemporary, popular environmental thinking.[46] As early as 1930, biologist Charles Elton dismissed the existence of "nature in balance."[47] By the 1960s, other ecologists had begun to doubt the balance myth as well.[48] And yet, as recently as 2009, biologist John C. Kricher still felt compelled (with good reason) to write an entire book debunking the balance-in-nature idea as unsupported by scientific evidence.[49]

Harmony in nature was wishful-thinking philosophy; not scientific fact. It also feeds into extinction hysteria, as if extinction were not the overwhelming story of life on the planet. All species eventually go extinct. How humans are now contributing to this is an important topic, but one not to be framed in terms of humans disrupting Eden. How wonderful it would be if we could reduce the human population and cease encroachment upon nonhuman habitat—that, in a nutshell, is the real story of accelerated or human-influenced extinction. No wonder it would end up being a problem so difficult to solve, interwoven with entire societal levels of education and income, yet largely out of fashion since the "population bomb" apocalypse came and went as the *doomsday fad du jour*.

*   *   *

Imagine being steeped in the biblical scholarship of Elaine Pagels, Karen Armstrong, Paul Winter, and other greats—and then trying to have a conversation with a biblical literalist. It is unlikely you would have a very worthwhile theological discussion. This would not be all that different from having a knowledge of environmental history, an appreciation of the limitations of the human condition, some thoughtful approach to environmental philosophy and science, and then trying to converse with environmental True Believers.

True Believers of any stripe have already assembled their worldview. They are suspicious of questions; even open questions. Instead, they find comfort in answers, and sometimes the simpler the answer the better. In the case of the natural environment, they seem incapable of appreciating the problematic characteristics of evidence, the scientific method, the limitations of science, or where philosophy and science intersect. Their conclusions fuel their crusade, which is often as simple-minded as it is self-righteous. Bikes not bombs, man.[50]

As mentioned, I live in one of the buckles of the Green Belt. There is a similarity in not being able to speak rationally, backed by evidence, against the emotionalism of religious feeling or belief. So naturally, fake Eden shows up here in many places here. I love my home, and have lived here more than four times longer than any other place (after dozens of lifelong relocations). But there is a "bubble" aspect, one that shows up in many college towns. Unfortunately, here it fosters no shortage of self-righteous environmental elitism and its close cousin of token environmentalism, all in lieu of even appreciating greater levels of complexity, much less actually doing anything substantial about it.

American token environmentalism is akin to children enjoying a good horror story. Kids like to be frightened as if to find reassurance in secretly knowing all was well all along. Many Americans confirm climate change propaganda and impending environmental doomsday in their own beliefs, and yet they keep living their materialistic lives of high energy use and conspicuous consumption.

Many a cynical atheist has commented upon religious hypocrites going through the motions of their creed, listening and repeating mere words without living the life. But the same is true of so many Green Belt denizens. They repeat the dogma of climate change, species extinction, carbon footprint, sustainability, and all the rest ... but continue driving four-wheel drive vehicles with tire studs that disproportionately destroy the streets, just so they can get over the mountain passes on their weekend ski trips. They "buy organic" and some practice vegan speciesism, and many shop or advocate shopping locally except for all the electronic gadgets made in Asia that they buy through the Internet.

I had a former colleague who epitomized this lifestyle. She taught a course concerning the environment that featured only the radical fringe perspectives, inaccurately depicted in the college catalogue as covering the topic broadly. There wasn't even any mention of the Endangered Species Act, much less a sampling of other major litigation (such as the National Environment Policy Act, Clean Air Act, or Clean Water Act). Instead, it was all radical data of the Deep Ecology sort; Earth First!, tree sitters, timber cutting moratoriums, neo-Pantheism, climate change hysteria, and the usual menu items of ideology and dogma. You have to suspect classes like this as platforms for preaching personal beliefs more than teaching complex subjects. Meanwhile, she and her spouse pulled in a handsome six-figure income, enjoyed lives of conspicuous consumption and a "high carbon footprint," then bought a four bedroom house for the two of them in the swanky part of town. Outside her office, she put that recently-popular satellite photograph compilation capturing the entire Earth at night. This montage showed the prevalence of electricity-powered lights in the developed world compared to the unlit developing world. And yet, she couldn't even be bothered to take the stairs. And this is supposed to make us feel guilty about our admittedly high energy consumptions?

But then, hypocrisy is one of the more common aspects of human nature; it is hardly limited to one group or another. Hypocrisy stopped surprising me a very long time ago, but I remain wondrous at the apparent inability of its bearers to see it for what it is. Or maybe some of them just cannot bring themselves to admit it. The easiest remedy would simply be to stop preaching in the first place.

Much of the green consciousness in Eugene and elsewhere reflects token environmentalism, anti-garden aesthetics, an untenable pretense that humans are separate from nature (for good or ill), and a willful ignorance of environmental concerns that merit serious attention. Notions of Eden also make for bizarre ecological notions that defy common sense. Trivial gestures abound, such as Catherine E. Southward righteously announcing her intention to save all her plastic container lids, since the recycling company cannot process them.[51] The fact that China has finally grown weary of sorting through our contaminated recycled materials, which will now send megatons to the landfill every month, is a real issue. Southward's issue is the sort that arises from those who apparently have too much time on their hands.

Or take a recent edition of the BBC World News Service's show, *The Real Story*, about the proliferation of plastics as an environmental topic. The host, Carrie Gracie, asked her contributors to confess their personal behavior regarding environmentally-correct credentials. Graham Thompson (Greenpeace) said he was very careful about what he bought, foregoing plastic water bottles. Adina Renee Adler (Institute of Scrap Recycling Industries) said she separated plastics and recycled them. Jennifer Turner (China Environment Forum at the Woodrow Wilson Center) said she was a "fanatical" recycler who "even" composted her biodegradable garbage. Roger Baynham (British Plastics Federation) heroically declared that he avoided using tea bags to preclude their end product as garbage.[52] Never mind that tea bags compost very nicely, thank you very much.

The comedian Lewis Black did a hilarious skit on the Jon Stewart show back in 2007, pointing out this combination of environmental elitism and tokenism.[53] Black showed Oprah Winfrey giving away florescent light bulbs and advocating cloth grocery bags, but also giving away cars. The ABC show *20/20* flew reporters to six continents to file live reports on supposed environmental emergencies that came and went from public consciousness. The television show *Pimp My Ride* advocated using biodiesel (an ultimate example of buzzword), as if this could offset one of the more frivolous expressions of car-culture America. And then there were various television personalities and Hollywood celebrities advocating using less gasoline, reducing paper usage, and using tissues from recycled paper.[54]

I used to check out materials at the Eugene City Library before its nasty-tempered, pseudo-public servants made the place intolerable (to sympathize, the place is as much a homeless shelter as it is a library). At the self-check terminal, a screen would appear with a picture of planet Earth and a moral message about whether or not to print a receipt of items checked out. So, save the planet by avoiding printing 3×4 inch slips of paper. On the way home I would bike past a school with SUVs and mini-vans lined up around the block to pick up kids; the more efficient school bus of yore is not what it used to be. So much for reducing the much-touted "carbon footprint." But, environmentalism in the age of helicopter parenting doth have its hazards.

Among the more flagrant examples of fake Eden around Eugene include the Cheshire Prairie, Delta Ponds and the "natural landscape" feature at Lane Community College. The latter features irregular tree spacing and native flora species, without irrigation, mowing, or fertilizer. As a result, more trees than those in the forest just simply die. This is classic token environmentalism. Ignored is the ambient heat from abutting masonry buildings and the heat island effect of the campus in general. The soil configuration beneath the "natural landscape" was long ago disrupted when the area was logged, possibly farmed, and then radically altered (bulldozed, refilled, and graded, then seeded in grass) decades earlier to create the campus itself. Then there is the completely "unnatural" precipitation run-off from surrounding concrete and asphalt, air quality infected with tailpipe emissions, et cetera. And what natural state does the landscape pretend to represent? The pre-aborigine landscape? The pre–Columbus landscape? What about the pre-glaciation landscape of tens of thousands of years ago? Instead, this landscape is obviously contrived; neither "natural" nor cultivated by stewards, and thus the worst of all worlds. It is a fraud.

There are many other examples of fake-natural landscapes in Eugene, including Hendricks Park, an artificial creation admonishing against invasive species seeds. The west Eugene "wetlands" is actually a drained swamp, a result of the Army Corps of Engineering digging a massive trench to channel the Amazon Slough. The Cheshire Prairie features a patch of invasive thistles and native plants that accommodate homeless campers during the summer before late summer's fire hazards apparently necessitate the city's annual autumn mowing (with organic, solar-powered electric lawnmowers, as nature intended it before the white man arrived).

But one of the more egregious examples of token environmentalism and a lost opportunity lies with the Delta Ponds. These are leftover human-made gravel pits adjoining the Willamette River that (ironically) came to function as valuable aquatic habitat. The river water feeds into the old pits through

The sign in the foreground reads, "Habitat improvement area. This storm-damaged tree is being left to enhance the environment for wildlife." The is a classic example of Edenic thinking, wherein a clearly cultivated environment (a college campus) pretends to accommodate "wildlife"—in this case, life forms like insects, bacteria, moss, and lichen; clearly not poisonous snakes, over-browsing deer or elk, and any large predator. These sorts of good intentions nevertheless leave us with the worst aspects of all worlds: the missing aesthetics of a well maintained human-created environment, and the missing ecology and aesthetics of an environment with minimal human impact. Such token "natural" areas oddly use human agency to pretend humans are separated from nature (author's photograph).

small, slow-current channels. This is one of the most obviously human-altered environments you can find around here, and yet now we are supposed to leave it "untouched," as if it were a wilderness, as if it were Eden. Again, what we get is the worst of all worlds. It would be better to embrace the Delta Ponds as a human-created environment and proceed to make it into a park with features such as an arboretum, footbridges to islands, pagodas and tea houses situated along the existing foot trails, and any number of cultivated landscape features. It could become a jewel of the West Coast if only we would render Cosmos out of Chaos and stop pretending that a bastardized landscape constitutes some approximation of nature uncorrupted by human beings. Here, Eugene might take a cue from eastern Germany, where people are flooding former lignite mining pits in an effort to transform the place into a "lake district" for recreation.[55]

But Eugene is hardly alone when it comes to this weird variation of Edenism that is really just token cessation of change amid a landscape altered so radically that even earlier generations of transplanted people do not recognize it. For example, this is how University of Cambridge zoologist Jonas Geldmann perpetuates the pre–Columbian Exchange Edenic idea when he objects to imported European honeybees (supposedly) competing for pollen with native bees. He concludes that the honey bees are not natural.[56] This is

Here is an ironic Forest Service sign. Apparently they do not mind if human waste gets buried in the wilderness, but not dog waste. Why does one violate Eden and the other does not? Obviously the Forest Service must be thinking in practical terms here. But this merely illustrates the odd choices and policies that arise when we pretend some environments are "pristine" and others are not. In fact, all environments reflect the influences of a great many species, including humanity. Yet philosophically, "wilderness" continues to serve as the core proxy for Eden (author's photograph).

absurd on many levels. First, the European imports are largely dealing with introduced crop pollen fostered by massive human agriculture that did not exist before the bees were imported. The entire ecology is unrecognizable compared to the pre–Columbian Exchange era. And imported honey bees also pollinate pre–Columbian plants, to their benefit. Are we to pick and choose individual species that we object to, but not others? How could we possibly separate the interactions among pre– and post–Columbian exchange species? All of this stinks of untenable Edenism.

We'll discuss this much further when we get to notions of invasive species, biodiversity, extinction hysteria and other philosophical values masquerading as scientific fact. Philosophical values tend to carry less clout when influencing policy, hence the resort to claims of science. In a way this is just power politics as usual. But the integrity of true science suffers in the process.

So, to reiterate, puritanical premises often show up in environmental thinking, which assign all sorts of poorly considered philosophical values that shape policy and compromise (or even contradict) science. Philosophical values are *ipso facto* debatable, but it is important to recognize them for what they are, accept alternatives with an open mind, and especially to avoid confusing philosophical values with science. The latter is no small feat, especially when applied to something so contentious as environmental policy. As we shall see, too often we mistake the purported "authority" of science for science-proper, even though framing the topic as such raises many further questions and problems.

Chapter 3

Some Problems
with Science

Science has no utility in its pure form. Pure science is strictly a quest for knowledge and understanding. It is more like fine art in that regard. Applied science is another matter entirely. Applied science that requires funding enters an obvious economic realm. Science out in our world now, most definitely including the environmental sciences, usually have controversial political and policy implications, which almost always creates gaps (sometimes enormous) between applied and pure science.

Since 2017 I have read about or seen on television a number of protests in which scientists (sometimes wearing lab coats) decry the government's position "against science." But obviously what they're most worried about is the possible loss in *funding* for science. I'm still waiting for a journalist to mention this salient point. After all, it was almost sixty years ago that Eisenhower gave probably the most famous presidential farewell address of all time. It was 1961. Not only did he mention the notorious "military-industrial complex" that so many anti–Vietnam War protestors later repeated (many not knowing the irony of the source), but also of the "danger that public policy could itself become the captive of a scientific-technological elite."[1] Both prophecies had a significant amount of truth in them even in 1961, and since then the magnitude has only grown.

My niece Emily recently finished earning her biology degree. She has a natural scientific mind, but she also has her feet on the ground when it comes to academic politics. She recently declared, "There is no more pure science." It is regrettable to conclude that this is probably only barely an overstatement. Perhaps safely tenured professors not seeking grants are still able to approximate pure science, but academic departments in general have gone the route that Eisenhower foretold in 1961. Emily is interested in studying an obscure parasitic worm called *Dendritobilharzia pulverulenta*. Her advisors wisely told her she would need to "connect" this worm to humanity, somehow, were

50

she to seek funding for her research. Pure science, of course, would be studying the worm for its own sake whether or not it had a direct bearing on humanity's interests.

Science is not the only endeavor to succumb to the politics and potential corruption involved with grant-seeking. I've seen colleagues in the humanities and social sciences attempt to put the right "spin" on their grant applications. Advisors coaching students applying for scholarships have similar techniques. All inevitable subjectivity aside, it seems unfortunately naïve to expect the world to appreciate merit for merit's sake. Instead, we in the United States especially are in a context of hyper salespersonship, in which everyone must "sell" their idea or credentials to the government funder, endowment board, college admissions board—or, for that matter, literary or talent agent.

* * *

As recently as my parents' generation people lived in fear of polio. My mother remembers one summer that may have changed her life. There was a polio outbreak in the San Francisco Bay Area, and her parents would not let her socialize with other children out of fear she might catch the dreaded disease. She learned how to play by herself that entire summer and later appreciated that, unlike the compulsively gregarious, she was perfectly capable of keeping her own company.

By my generation (late Baby Boomer) polio was among the horror stories our elders told, but we had all been inoculated. We rightly took for granted that any number of earlier killer maladies (small pox, measles, cholera) would not touch us. Such medical advances alone have helped lead us to worship at that altar of science, as well we should in many ways, all aspects of our current highly faulty healthcare system aside. A major problem of late, however, is the *authority* of science substituting for actual science. To see how this happened, we should briefly retrace the steps of the so-called Scientific Revolution.

Major advances in astronomy during the 16th through the 18th centuries helped initiate the modern scientific era. William Whewell coined the term "scientist" only in the 1830s; before that people working in the fields we call science generally called themselves "natural philosophers."

Many historians of science no longer accept the "Scientific Revolution" of textbook lore, on the grounds that the traditional depiction was entirely too linear, too simplistic in conceiving of events in a Whiggish fashion of "progress," and not nearly so "revolutionary" as earlier scholars had claimed.[2] Fewer would disagree with the idea of a revolution in astronomy, which took us from geocentrism to heliocentrism. Having said all that, we can still appreciate the astonishing advancement of knowledge in all the fields we now call science. The advances in astronomy based in mathematics generally contributed to something of an infatuation with the mathematical approach in other fields of endeavor,[3] with consequences quite evident today. Those who see this reliance on science as misapplied, overly applied, or too narrowly applied use the disparaging term "scientism."[4] More about that later.

Between 1543 and 1687, in western civilization, the sun-centered universe we know today replaced the medieval concept of an Earth-centered universe. European scientists benefited immensely from astronomical data going back to the Greeks and Romans, subsequently enhanced by Muslim intellectuals. Muslims also crucially advanced higher mathematics (algebra comes from the Arabic *al jabr*) that would make later astrophysical calculations possible. Imagine Newton trying to do calculus with Roman numerals.

The geo-to-helio revolution began with Copernicus's 1543 work *De revolutionibus orbium coelestium* ("On the Revolutions of the Heavenly Spheres") and culminated with Isaac Newton's 1687 work *Philosophiæ Naturalis Principia Mathematica* ("Mathematical Principles of Natural Philosophy"). In between those two publications was much additional work, particularly by Johannes Kepler and Galileo Galilei. Without getting into the modifications that Einstein made to the Newtonian worldview, there was a great beauty and elegance to the astronomical revolution, especially during its own historic context. This was largely because of mathematics.

By the way, contrary to popular belief, there has never been a simple conflict between science and religion. Early modern science was actually most properly appreciated as a *servant* to religion.[5] Even Galileo's much-repeated clash with the Catholic Church (often the only early example people cite) was not a "science v. religion" argument in simple terms, involving Galileo's lack of diplomacy and ridiculing of the pope as his fictional character, "Simplicio." Contemporary debates between creationists and Darwinists tend to obscure Darwin's religiosity and Darwin's endorsement by people like the Reverend Charles Kingsley. Decades ago official endorsement for Darwinian evolution came from the Vatican, the United Presbyterian Church, Lutherans, Jews, Episcopalians, and Unitarians, among others.[6]

The truth and the details involving science and religion are much more interesting than the oil/water depiction of a loud few. Copernicus and Newton alone considered themselves very religious men. Copernicus reasoned that the geocentric model of his milieu must be wrong because the math did not work. Math is perfect, Copernicus thought, and so is God. God would not get the math wrong, so humans must have.

By the 18th century, intellectuals were fond of Deism, an approach that

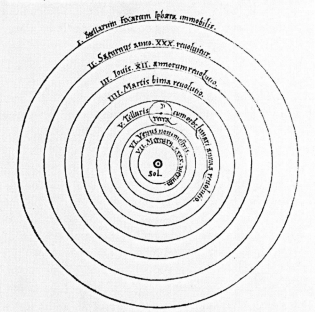

NICOLAI COPERNICI

net,in quo terram cum orbe lunari tanquam epicyclo contineri
diximus . Quinto loco Venus nono menſe reducitur.,Sextum
deniq̃ locum Mercurius tenet,octuaginta dierum ſpacio circũ
currens,In medio uero omnium reſidet Sol. Quis enim in hoc

pulcherimo templo lampadem hanc in alio uel meliori loco po
neret,quàm unde totum ſimul poſsit illuminareꝛSiquidem non
inepte quidam lucernam mundi,alrj mentem, alij rectorem uo‹
cant. Trimegiſtus uiſibilem Deum,Sophoclis Electra intuentē
omnia.Ita profecto tanquam in folio re gali Sol reſidens circum
agentem gubernat Aſtrorum familiam. Tellus quoq̃ minime
fraudatur lunari miniſterio , ſed ut Ariſtoteles de animalibus
ait,maximā Luna cũ terra cognationē habet.Concipit interea à
Sole terra , & impregnatur annuo partu. Inuenimus igitur ſub
hac

What people often refer to as the "scientific revolution" of the 16th and 17th centuries
actually arose from a revolution in astronomy, in which the heliocentric model of
the solar system replaced the previous geocentric model. Copernicus conceived of
the sun at the center of the universe, then the mathematics of Johannes Kepler proved
the orbits were elliptical rather than round. Finally, after Galileo overturned Aris-
totle's physics, Newton's calculus tied heliocentrism together with gravitational theory. The revolution in astronomy was elegant and seductive, for mathematics
precisely explained cosmic phenomenon. Applying such mathematical approaches
to other fields we now call science—including all the environmental sciences—has
proven problematic, at best (illustration by Nicolas Copernicus, ca. 1543).

reconciled religion and science by viewing God as a Divine Watchmaker or Divine Clockmaker. It was a seductive concept that married important concepts; old notions of the all-creator deity, an eternal human desire for order, and the precise mechanics of then-recent astronomical discoveries. Sadly, as we shall see, mathematical application of science ran into immediate problems once outside the realm of physics, but all these centuries later we have yet to accept the imprecision of so much study done under the guise of science. Over-confident, misapplied reliance on science to reveal the "truth" has ironically contributed to environmental alarmism and beliefs more akin to superstition than fact. This is deeply ironic.

As mentioned, the success of the astronomy revolution inspired intellectuals to apply a math-oriented scientific approach to terrestrial topics, such as medicine. Medical science pioneers like Lister, Harvey, Vesalius, and many others made enormous strides in surgery, the circulatory system, and anatomy. And yet all these generations later, medicine remains far less scientific compared to mathematics or astronomy. Ingenious philosopher and surgeon Sherwin Nuland appreciated this profoundly, calling medicine the "uncertain art."[7] Nuland embraced often mysterious phenomena involving the doctor-patient relationship, a patient's outlook on life beyond having any maladies, how western science is an inadequate method for understanding Chinese medicine, and other sometimes murky aspects of healing.[8]

Obviously medicine includes much "hard" science, particularly when it involves such things like immunology or blood tests and chemistry. But as Nuland, Ted Kaptchuk, and others have understood, there can be much "unscientific" mystery as well. Furthermore, there is plenty of sloppy science, wherein scientists are unable to reproduce experimental results—replicable results being a hallmark of the empirical scientific process.[9] And today, of course, massive greed in the American healthcare industries compromises medical science on a regular basis, wherein hospital corporations, Big Pharma, and (saddest of all) highly paid doctors themselves often give priority to the bottom line with healing an afterthought at best.[10] But that's another story highly documented elsewhere.[11]

To return to our historical summary, by the 19th century the enthusiasm for science reached new heights (some would say delusional depths) with the invention of all the so-called "social sciences," like sociology, psychology, and anthropology. Economics gets somewhat more respect among "hard" scientists, especially when there is heavy involvement of mathematics. History existed for thousands of years as a humanity, and is still classified as such in some academic departments, but gained new techniques and new foci influenced by the social science movement.

Critics have found much fault in the social sciences and especially psychology, but this criticism is really nothing new. Back in 1973 a Stanford psychologist conducted the notorious Rosenhan Experiment[12] that amply illustrated the problematic nature of psychological diagnosis. Since then an array of psychological pseudo-science has come to light.[13] And yet much of this can be appreciated through "mere" common sense.

There is a semi-serious joke among mathematicians that ranks math as the only "pure" science. I'm sure mathematicians have a great deal of respect for physicists and chemists. Geology also employs physics and chemistry, but stands out for its particular difficulty in reconstructing past earthscapes.[14] Hats off to the geologists. Things tend to get messier thereafter—even in the life sciences (biology, medicine, and their branches), which employ plenty of physics and chemistry. By the time we get to "social science" (an unfortunate term) we are dealing with a great many factors that do not lend themselves to the scientific method whatsoever. In fact, mathematicians, physicists, chemists, geologists, et al., sometimes disparage the "social sciences" as the "soft sciences." Nassim Nicholas Taleb goes further (Taleb often goes further!) and distinguishes science-proper as "smart science" in contrast to social science.[15]

There are obvious perennial frauds involving psychology: the impossibility of measuring things like "happiness," the eternal hazards of subjects' self-reporting, the impossibility of reading subjects' minds, skewed samples (think of who volunteers for psychological studies), troubled people drawn to the profession of psychology for reasons of self-therapy, understandable researchers' subjective distortions that sometimes arise from constantly dealing with aberrations, et cetera. But aside from the obvious problems involving psychology and other social sciences, and to be as charitable as possible, perhaps we could simply use a different term for the better work just to avoid confusion with science-proper. I propose SEASF (Semi-Evidentiary Attempts at Systematic Findings).

I'm absolutely certain no one will ever use SEASF.

It is important to remember this when dealing with environmental sciences. They can offer much weaker conclusions than we might expect or hope for, though for different reasons compared to the flaws of the social sciences. Because we care about our planet, our only home, it is easy to let emotion cloud logic when it comes to distinguishing real problems from manufactured or ambiguous ones.

I remember when the Environmental Movement was still comparatively pure. I'm sure that back then I was also far less exposed to propagandists and not yet aware of the distinctive environmental elite. But we were dealing with tangible negatives like smog and point-source water pollution that so obviously needed rectification. Tangible negatives have never disappeared since the 1970s, but during the intervening decades the Environmental Movement has certainly gained many more characteristics of a crusade that (ironically) now obscure and overshadow some of these ongoing non-negotiable problems. Worse, it fostered a weird sort of negativity that merged guilt, false science, and the government as a false panacea for curing invented environmental ills. "Despondency became the measure of moral seriousness," Alston Chase wrote. "If people believed that nature was threatened, they could not feel good about their society or the environment."[16] The guilt and bad feelings were predicated upon supposedly imminent doomsday, human greed and freedom supposedly run amok, ecosystems that did not exist (much less "balance" within them). Like children looking for parental guidance, the federal government was supposed to make things better. "Only coercive powers of the state could protect us from ourselves," Chase wrote.[17]

To a significant degree, that is still where we stand today. It is a classic expression of Green Calvinism: feel bad about yourself and your species, but don't abandon your SUV or high energy use. Like other hypocrites, Green Calvinists have continued to enjoy the fat of the land while babbling environmentally-correct rhetoric. The antidote proposed here is basically philanthropic environmental stewardship that embraces humanity as a part of nature, calls upon us to abandon doomsday rhetoric, figure out what informs our philosophical values and why, and utilize our tools of green science and technology to address unambiguous environmental problems.

*   *   *

Darwin struck upon the sort of scientific theory that scientists dream of: successive generations of biologists have constantly reaffirmed biological evolution and elaborated upon it with additions that Darwin could only puzzle over, particularly the driving mechanism of that we now appreciate as part of the field of genetics.

Occasionally I'll get a Creationist student in class who says something like, "Darwin could be wrong. After all, evolution is only a theory." Gently I respond with an explanation that "scientific theory" is something much more than the more general use of the term. I usually end with the local joke about there being a theory that "Eugene is where old hippies come to die."

Scientific theory is supposed to be an advanced stage in the scientific method that begins with a question, idea, or a working hypothesis. A hypothesis-proper is apparently where much science ends. To reach the theory stage is a monumental advancement indeed. There was an old idea that the rarest, highest stage in the scientific endeavor was scientific law, as in the law of gravity, the law of conservation of mass, or the law of conservation of energy. I imagine that theoretical physics wreaks havoc with all of the above. But it gets messier when you consider science from a philosophical point of view.

The mathematician and philosopher of science Henri Poincaré pointed out that things like geometric axioms are reflections of our selective penchant for order, not reality *per se*.[18] In other words, we could and can choose different axioms or classifications or patterns as tools for defining our world. This fascinated Robert Pirsig, who appreciated the infinite number of potential hypotheses at the beginning of a scientific inquiry. Pirsig regarded hypothesis-forming as the most mysterious act in the entire scientific process. Only un-ordered data comes out of nature.[19] It is we who try to "make sense" of this data, and in so doing reflect our cultural values and biases as well as our personal subjectivity.

So there is no single "scientific method," of course. Researchers employ both inductive and deductive reasoning. There is dumb luck and also propitious timing. Newton appreciated the latter, humbly acknowledging the research that preceded his era and how it gave him the foundation for doing what he did, which was basically completing the astronomy revolution with gravitational theory. Hence his famous quote, "if I have seen further, it is by standing on the shoulders of giants."[20]

Characteristics of the scientific endeavor are supposed to include empirical observation. This is why they made you dissect the frog in biology class, not because they expected any different results from the millions of previously dissected frogs, but to give students a taste of hands-on biology. Another hallmark of science is supposed to be replicable results. This is how the grand dream of cold fusion keeps getting debunked; no one has been able to replicate claimed results. This is also how the vaccination-autism link got debunked, after a 1998 study slipped past the peer reviewers and into *The Lancet*.[21]

So the actual work of science in the contemporary world is far from ideal. Just think of how pre–Clovis archaeologists kept quiet for years lest they risk their academic careers by questioning the Clovis-first paradigm. Apparently many an older generation geologist also resisted the advent of plate tectonics, which is now standard theory for all of geology.

Aside from purely academic politics (destructive enough), there are many terms that describe compromised science both in academia but especially out in the wider world: politicized science, mission-oriented science, agenda-oriented science, policy-driven science, and (worst of all) "post-normal" science. The latter relies upon a presumptuous premise of emergency and impending doom, thus feeding off of our current frenzied environmental thinking as well as exacerbating it.[22] Even the best science cannot escape its subjective context and the limitations of its given era,[23] but the terms just listed often represent various levels of outright propaganda. No surprise that sciences involved with the environment would regularly feature subjective philosophical values and received worldview—neither of which are surprising, though the claim to the *authority* of science remains untenable in too many cases. As we shall see, for a number of reasons exterior to the intellectual core of science (funding sources, insecurity over the future, cultural biases), a great deal of purported science turns out to be not all that scientific. But to return to problems involved with the intellectual core of the scientific endeavor, we're still dealing with the legacy of the inapplicability of mathematics to the life sciences.

Reflecting the then-ongoing infatuation with math, physics inspired the "ecosystem" concept and concurrent schools of biological thought derived from physics. For example, the ecologists George Evelyn Hutchinson, Eugene Odum and Howard Odum all believed ecosystems to be closed energy loops facilitating the equivalent of perpetual motion machines.[24] This concept (popular during the 1950s) was part of a tradition established by A.G. Tansley, who coined the term "ecosystem" in 1935.[25] These early concepts of ecosystems turned out to be quite a naïve, and vastly over-simplified habitats into systems that were not closed energy loops at all.[26]

Hutchinson was an early proponent of creating ecological models in the face of the impossible task of cataloguing everything and all interrelations in a given habitat. He also advocated detailed fieldwork. Combining the modeling abstractions with representational fieldwork would reveal preexisting patterns in nature.[27] But the patterns only preexisted in Hutchinson's scientific imagination, and these two approaches (basically deductive and inductive) were married for practical reasons in a quest for the impossible. Pattern-seeking, as Taleb reminds us, is a human desire. Metaphysics aside, we are ever in danger of imposing them where they do not exist in nature.[28]

Botanist Frederic Edward Clements advocated a wishful-thinking "holism" in ecology, which again conceived of habitats as a fairly neat series of orderly successions culminating in a "climax" habitat. Ecologist Henry Allen Gleason disagreed with Clements, and offered his "continuum ecology" idea of complex habitats featuring more individualistic competition among flora and fauna, not necessarily configured in successional stages at all. Gleason interpreted ecological succession categories as simplistic human constructs imposed upon an infinitely complex nature.[29] Gleason was on to something.

Even to this day environmental habitats are typically too complex to understand in the way (for example) that Newton, et al., came to understand heliocentrism. The comparatively neat and clean energy exchange models of physics turned out to be so misapplied to highly complex habitats in nature as to render the entire premise nearly worthless.[30] As the biologist John Kricher observed, it is biological evolution that is the driving force in nature, not the ecosystem construct.[31] By stating it as such, Kricher makes an important juxtaposition between a true scientific theory (evolution) and a notion (ecosystem) that does not really survive as a scientific hypothesis. Ecological case studies continue to be of great value,[32] but only when we interpret them for what they are: inherently circumscribed case studies, not small parts indicating a (fictitious) ecosystem whole.

As Taleb wrote, the imitation of physics by other sciences is like trying to "make a whale fly like an eagle."[33] R.C. Lewontin described biology in the context of general scientific laws as "nothing but a small set of informing and organizing metaphors."[34] And finally, as Paul Griffiths observed, regarding the laws of nature, biological study only reveals specific examples of chemical and physical laws.[35] Beyond those physical and chemical laws, biology and ecology run into all sorts of difficulties. This may not amount to much inside the world of science itself, but immediately runs into troubling implications when we get into policy supposedly informed by science.

As K.S. Shrader-Frechette and Earl D. McCoy argued, weak and subjective ecological theory—such as balance in nature, ecosystems, and ecological stability—does not help policymakers. Instead, policymakers would benefit from specific case studies and what narrow conclusions we may reasonably draw from them.[36]

Ecology falling short of anything approaching a precise science did not stop the Environmental Movement of the 1960s and the 1970s from seizing upon the ecosystem idea, apparently not even realizing it was far more philosophical (no matter how untenable) rather than scientific. This period also witnessed ecology receiving its first substantial infusion of governmental funding,[37] and thus there was major incentive to crank out tons of "ecological science" that was not necessarily all that scientific.[38] Ecologists fatefully turned to mathematical modeling in lieu of empirical observation of systematic evidence and experiments therefrom,[39] as per standard science procedure. Concepts such as impending species extinction became a premise for funding.[40] This is a classic example of how science gets politicized. Even my modest local university has lately been getting about $100 million annually to finance scientific research, including the standard environmentally-correct topics of rising sea levels, carbon acidification of ocean water, and climate change.[41]

Again, ironically, ecosystem thinking and especially ecological computer models reflected and reflect a philosophical desire for logical and orderly results that science could not and cannot verify. As R.G. Collingwood observed in 1960, "An event in the world of nature becomes important for the natural scientist only on condition that it is observed."[42] Collingwood lived and wrote before the days of widespread computer modeling, when ecologists and climate scientists began offering their best *guesses* at the evidence that might be out there, instead of the classical empirical approach that Collingwood described.

The merging currents of funding, ideology, and fear created much claim to the *authority* of science to bolster a subjective worldview of misanthropic Eden. But there were many precedents. This was how the nature "preservationists" (think John Muir) set themselves above "conservationists" (think Gifford Pinchot). This is how the National Park Service tried to create an Edenic myth out of Yellowstone, although it turned out to resemble a Disneyland type of landscape missing major environmental actors, like Indians and wolves.[43] The latter, ironically, were wiped out by an earlier generation of park rangers who reflected then-contemporary values of large predator eradication. My, how values change.

Many people in and outside the fields of ecology and biology still think ecosystems exist, and thus it easily lends itself to the worldview of environmental activists and policy-makers. But as Alston Chase wrote many years ago, where does one ecosystem stop and another begin?[44] All one has to do is consider that old high school biology concept of "edge ecology." As many have observed (and as deer hunters and crocodiles appreciate) a great deal of fauna activity takes place where one general habitat meets another: forest abutting field, meadow merging into scrubland, Old Growth forest adjacent to a grove of younger trees, and especially anywhere land meets water. Also, as many suburbanites have come to appreciate, their yards and neighborhoods are often rich habitat that we now call part of the "wildland-urban interface." Considering this, where does one "ecosystem" begin and other end? Ultimately one could argue that the entire planet is an ecosystem, which led to fanciful ideas such as James Lovelock's "Gaia Hypothesis," in which Earth is a living organism.[45]

In reality—and as the wiser biologists and ecologists appreciate—the reality of natural habitat is one of constant change. In ecological terms, this is dubbed unpredictable and irregular disturbance.[46] Not only does current ecology confirm this, but it also appeals to common sense. So too do qualifications of "invasive species," which term is classic Edenesque thinking. This concept gained momentum after 1958, when Charles Elton published his book, *Ecology of Invasions by Animals and Plants.* This volume contained many concepts that ecologists later rejected or qualified, including the idea of natural balance and "dislocations in nature" resulting from migrating flora and fauna.[47] Elton also separated humans from nature, seeing wilderness free of people as containing "rich natural communities," whereas the human-modified Earth reflected being "knocked about."[48] And yet Elton also celebrated human-modified landscapes that featured a mixture of sheep pastures, forests, and the legendary hedgerows of England's countryside.[49] Perhaps England was too far removed from a western hemisphere style of "wilderness" to ignore so many ancient and accumulated landscape modifications. But Elton, anticipating so many contemporary environmentalists, feared ecological change amid an age of accelerating globalization. In this context he celebrated "variety,"[50] a precursor to biodiversity, and feared homogenization—something unlikely to happen in reality, given the struggle of all species to prevail, including adaptation to changes.

In reality, millions of years of habitat changes have moved all sorts of species around, driving some extinct, forcing others into monumental migrations, even if such movements took place over a great many generations.[51] Considering this undeniable natural history reality, the entire concept of "invasive" becomes a clear cultural construct, and ironically so since Euroamericans and other "invasive" immigrants to the United States have largely invented and perpetuated it as a part of popular culture. As biologist John Kricher observed, "Ecosystems [that is, habitats] are anything but closed to immigrant species."[52] So all the familiar terms—alien, exotic, invasive, non-native, introduced—reflect philosophical values as much or more than they reflect science.

In a way this brings us full circle to the non-loop of ecosystems. As K.S. Shrader-Frechette and Earl D. McCoy pointed out, case studies of specific species and their habitats (not ecosystems) provides sound scientific evidence for specific policymaking decisions.[53] And yet the 1973 Endangered Species Act (ESA)—one of the most influential and consequential pieces of environmental legislation of all time[54]—is premised upon the Edenic concept of stability in nature and the absence of extinction on a systematic scale.[55] Thus, as the Congressional Information Services itself freely admitted, the ESA "can become a surrogate battleground in debates" that mask other agendas.[56] One of the more noted examples of this took place during the 1980s and 1990s in the Pacific Northwest involving Old Growth forests and the northern spotted owl controversy. The spotted owl as a purported endangered species became the surrogate for the real issue of cutting down or preserving trees.[57] You can agree or disagree with whatever timber policy is being debated, but the Old Growth preservation advocates immediately hijacked the very preliminary "science" behind the spotted owl.

First, a single graduate student (Eric Forsman)[58] had only examined fourteen owls and radio-collared six. I doubt he had any idea how his innocent graduate work was about to be used. Forsman only examined Old Growth forests and never made the claims that Old Growth preservation advocates later attributed to this extremely preliminary work. To this day, more than forty years later, no one has ever taken a true population census of northern spotted owls, partly because such wildlife population counts end up being little more than guesswork dressed up as science.[59]

Contrary to earlier claims, northern spotted owls did not depend exclusively on Old Growth forests. In fact, as far back as the mid–1980s scientists observed that mixed growth and the old "edge environments" produced higher reproductive rates and greater overall health in northern spotted owls. Edge environments have proven important to northern spotted owl survival from northern California to Washington state.[60]

In any case, in 1994 President Clinton signed the Northwest Forest Plan that reduced timber harvesting on Pacific Northwest federal lands, thus supposedly protecting the owl's habitat. And then, guess what—the aggressive eastern barred owl had the temerity to fly into the Pacific Northwest and "invade" the spotted owl's territory. The Edenic gamekeepers quickly devised a plan to kill the barred owl.[61] Anything for Eden.

It gets more absurd from there. Typical sensational media stories (often based on mere anecdotal information) decry all things "invasive"; plants, mammals, birds, amphibians, and even earthworms. The tsunami off the coast of Japan, a "natural" geological event if ever there was one, nonetheless became a focus of hysteria regarding Japanese species rafting their way across the Pacific. Misanthropic environmentalists might argue that these life forms were rafting on the wreckage of human-created phenomenon (the remains of boats and piers), but what about the "natural" logs that carried them? But such details become a whirlwind in a piss pot considering that humans cannot stop the "invasion" of such species regardless of their vehicle. What we're really seeing so often in fears regarding "ecosystems" and species is really a fear of change—and we should know that change is the single constant on planet Earth for us and everything else.

I remember when I first learned about the northern spotted owl controversy, and people were throwing around vague population numbers. At the time I thought, "There's no way an army of biologists are combing through thousands of acres counting owls, and even if they were, how would they know if they were counting the same birds multiple times or not?" They were not counting them physically, of course, but I was disappointed to realize that "computer modeling" was their highly imprecise method for guessing the population.

Philosopher of science Jay Odenbaugh described environmental science models in general as very idealized, utilizing very imprecise information.[62] This makes sense, for gathering precise data is impossible in any practical sense. Environmental scientists also tend to hold certain subjective, philosophical values that we should regard with caution when their work crosses from science into advocacy.[63] We also have to remember that this sort of science requires a great deal of funding and, humans being humans, grant-writers will kowtow to established paradigms.[64] Studying an invasive species rendering detrimental effects (according to commonly held values) may win you and your team several years worth of salaries and expenses. Proposing to study domestic livestock as invasive species would likely raise more eyebrows than funds. Never mind that all domestic livestock (even the re-introduced horse) are foreign species who rely upon artificial habitats.[65]

If it were not obvious at this point, clearly there are many forces compromising the objectivity of environmental sciences. From a physics point of view, and certainly from a mathematical point of view, a great deal of this endeavor at least borders upon outright pseudo-science. This is, unfortunately, abundantly clear in what has probably become the most contentious environmental science of all time, that of anthropogenic climate change. That merits an entire chapter (coming up).

One last note, lest we forget.

There have been plenty of mistaken scientific ideas in the past, along with outright pseudo-sciences: craniometry, Aristotelian physics, geocentric astronomy, alchemy, eugenics, physiognomy—and indeed—the "scientific claims" that bolstered the social construct of race and racism ... and the latter, long before imperialists used the pseudo-science of Social Darwinism to justify or rationalize their mistreatment of colonial peoples. The very fact that Social Darwinism (vis-à-vis Herbert Spencer) was a bastardization of Darwinian evolutionary theory should sound an extra cautionary note, for here the *claim to authority* linked with a genuine science made for an extra-harmful pseudo-science.

By the way, many would include Galen's medical theories of the four humors in the list of mistaken scientific ideas, but along with alchemy, we have not undergone a comparatively simple and straightforward revolution in chemistry or medicine as we did in astronomy. Alchemy, after all, helped *propel us* toward the field we now call chemistry, albeit in somewhat convoluted fashion. More recently, open-minded doctors like the late Sherwin Nuland were appreciative of medicine's continuing mysterious aspects. So if theoretical *qi* energy and acupunctural meridians help heal patients, maybe we should not care too much whether or not western medical concepts can

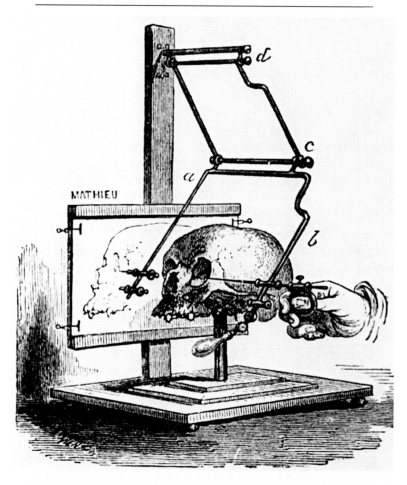

Paul Broca was one of those unfortunate anthropologists who equated science with measuring or attempting to measure things mathematically. In this case, Broca was one of many who believed in "craniometry" and "physiognomy," or the belief that the contours of individual human skulls reflected differing degrees of intelligence. We now appreciate that human intelligence is far more mysterious and does not lend itself to such simple calculations, mathematical or otherwise. This should serve as a cautionary tale regarding our contemporary beliefs in scientific measurement or assessment (*above* from Paul Topinard, "Anthropology" [1878], *following page* from George Combe, "Elements of Phrenology" [1835]).

incorporate them. If western medicine needs to understand acupuncture as releasing endorphins, then so be it.[66]

But the point should be obvious. Many a person in earlier eras thought they knew the scientific "truth." They should have been more humble then, and we should be more humble now. Scientific inquiry, by its very nature,

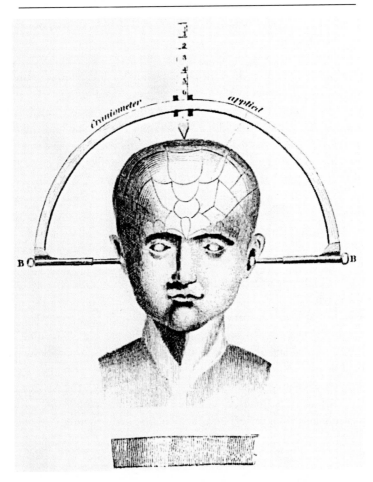

has no end, no arrival point. The more we explore the more we realize just how vast the terrain is, and thus how little we actually know. Rarely do we even appreciate the contours of our ignorance. This should be a source of excitement! But it should also be a cautionary note regarding epistemology and authority.

One of those humble silviculturists I worked with during my brief employment with the Forest Service gave the following account: "When we were in college in the late 1950s, the scientists pretty much thought that we knew practically everything we needed to know about forest ecology. During my career we increasingly discovered that we knew less and less."

It was a remarkable statement from someone in 1992, nearing the end of his career. It was more or less the opposite disposition of politicized ecology, where advocates present scientific understanding as authoritative rather than tentative or (goodness forbid) unknown. This is a shame, but it is also the way of the world.

Our desire for order is related to our teleological inclinations. Most people want order and purpose in the world, and if they can't find it or are unsure of its existence, they'll invent it. We do not really understand most of the details involved with the science of ecology, and we may never know. This is because there are too many variables, which are constantly evolving and influencing one another. Revealing historic ecological patterns will always be impossible, providing far fewer details than the ecology that confronts us now. Still, we pretend to understand ecology, ranging from fantasies of "balance" in nature and mythical Garden of Eden wilderness worship, to the bastardized concept of "ecosystem management," conditional wildfire suppression or generation policies, highly irregular ideas of what constitutes "invasive" species, and so on. If all of this were not bad enough, we have highly politicized policies that make pursuing ecological science in a pure sense even more difficult. Ecological study is highly worthwhile, but often it does not approximate any true scientific method.

"We should keep our mind a blank tablet which nature fills for us, and then reason disinterestedly from the facts we observe," Pirsig wrote.[67] It was a reminder of ideal science which, sadly, seems almost quaint in the day-to-day world of contemporary scientific activity. Nowhere is that more evident than in the endeavor of climate science, but it is true of all the environmental sciences. Troubling as this is, an added dimension of communication challenges arise when such uncertain information passes through science journalism.

Chapter 4

Environmental Science and Journalism

In the 1997 movie *Wag the Dog*, a president manufactures a fake war and manipulates the media into believing he has heroically ended the conflict and saved the day, thereby salvaging his career. An enjoyable farce, it nonetheless illustrates the power of the media to shape public perception, and the power of various entities (in this case, the president and his circle) to influence the media. Even a cursory glance at our society indicates the "power of the press," often referred to as the Fourth Estate or informal branch of government. It is amusing to find journalists who deny their power, when even a modicum of common sense indicates otherwise.[1] But the process works in many directions, including how-to manuals for activists publicizing their cause.[2] These factors also play out in many other matters, including any number of environmental issues, particularly as they appeal to notions involving the environmental sciences and all the authority such fields are supposed to merit. Despite our reverence for the myth, there is no true free press.[3]

I'm not here to trash journalists; in fact, I have seen many good reporters laboring nobly in a compromised profession (all professions being compromised). So I could say the same of teachers and nurses. This always reminds me of that passage in Max Ehrmann's wonderful prose-poem, *Desiderata*: "Exercise caution in your business affairs, for the world is full of trickery. But let this not blind you to what virtue there is; many persons strive for high ideals, and everywhere life is full of heroism."[4] Thus, we should probably consider professionals within the context of their particular profession, not some detached ideal, partly because that illustrates the situation so many of us find ourselves in; limited free will within greater institutional or sociocultural constraints. The constraints of journalism are many.

The oft-observed resort to media sensationalism is part of the old "if it bleeds it leads" credo of the print journalism of yore. This makes journalism and the gawking public a bit of a chicken/egg phenomenon, as any impatient police officer will tell you while trying to wave the rubber-neckers past a gory car accident. So an airplane landing safely is not a news story. The absence of impending environmental catastrophe is not a news story. Add to this the competition among journalists to "get the scoop" and the excitement of "getting the story" inherent to the profession, and no wonder journalists often end up sacrificing facts and accuracy. The short lead time may be the most damning factor of the profession, as that leaves little or no room for explanation and analysis, much less critical thinking or reflection.[5] And then there is the "news cycle" which affects the timing and spacing of stories.[6] Jack Stapleton, Jr., described one such scenario in 1997.

Stapleton was the former owner and editor of the *Daily Dunklin Democrat* in far southeastern Missouri, a rural area called the Bootheel that received periodic sensational attention from the St. Louis press. "The [St. Louis] *Post-Dispatch* is always being accused of sending a reporter down once a year to rediscover poverty in the Bootheel." He laughed while relating this story. "And it's a good, standard story for the *Post-Dispatch*," he said, "to send out some reporter who discovers, to his horror, that there are as many poor people in the Bootheel as there are in the city of St. Louis. Actually, they have many more today than we do."[7] Timing such stories was choreographed by the *Post-Dispatch*, just as global warming stories have been timed more frequently in summertime.[8]

Few journalists have graduate degrees, and thus little or no preemployment experience in scholarly research. Sometimes they fail to grasp the esoteric science they are reporting.[9] An undergraduate degree and work experience constitutes the usual career path. Work experience can be wonderful way to learn investigative skills, at least for the few media employers who have the finances and interest in supporting such endeavors. But investigative journalism is expensive and time-consuming, and thus (sadly) the exception in reporting. No wonder so many media stories substitute anecdotal information instead of any attempt at systematic overviews or conclusions.

Since the 1980s, and especially after the Internet became media competition, so-called mainstream journalism probably took a sharp turn toward what used to be tabloid journalism. On the other hand, it was the 19th century that brought us Yellow Journalism and all its sensational inaccuracies, including the explosion of the U.S.S. *Maine* which helped launch the Spanish-American War. So maybe today's news media (after a hiatus of comparatively sober news) is only different in its volume, itself exacerbating its inherent propensity toward sensationalism.

In any case, what we get from the bulk of media is not so much a "mirror of the world" as a homogenized information package tailored for middle

America.[10] This plays right into the desires, concerns, and expectations of the environmental elite. So, for example, except for conservative exceptions, much of the American media generally seems to take anthropogenic climate change as a settled scientific fact. As mentioned, it is more than a curiosity that more media stories of global warming showed up during hot summer months compared to other seasons.[11] It is also important to remember that such reporting is based on little if any critical investigation. Few even mention the hazards of prediction and climate modeling. Anthropogenic climate change may end up being one of the most mis-reported topics in the history of journalism. Some of the climate alarmists, with elite credentials and institutional affiliation, have undoubtedly promoted the view of scientific certainty, scientific consensus, and other non-facts (all detailed in the following chapter). So how and why the media have bought into this seems suspicious, other than it being the *doomsday du jour* of our times, which raises the issue of "socially robust knowledge."

In the previous chapter I mentioned how forces like politics and policy, agenda and funding can compromise "pure" science. Socially robust scientific knowledge operates in this arena as well, but can be somewhat more nuanced, for it involves society speaking back to scientists and influencing their work, whether or not society is fully informed, and whether or not those doing the speaking are demographically representative of society as a whole. Some call this the "contextualization" of science,[12] when "reliable science is not enough."[13] It also must meet social expectations and address social concerns. This particularly influences the environmental sciences in contrast to the types of sciences employing controlled lab experiments.[14] Science journalism is in the middle of this socially robust knowledge involving environmental sciences.

Hans Peter Peters and Sharon Dunwoody described aspects of socially robust knowledge in science communication. The media covers scientific disputes and scientists air their differences publicly (including their take on policy implications). Scientific fraud and hoaxes also make the news, as well as possible influence or corruption of science by vested industry interests.[15] The media itself is obviously a major player, but so are scientists. Scientists may want to influence government oversight of their endeavor. Groups of scientists may agree upon a policy agenda, such as mitigating second-hand smoke or influencing climate policy. Then, of course, there is the ubiquitous association of publicity and fundraising.[16] Media often becomes the central agent of communicating such interests (overt or veiled) to the interested or general public.

Where an earlier era of journalism reported "just the facts" (ma'am), science journalism has plunged into analysis and even science itself, with mixed results.[17] The chemicals alar and BPA (Bisphenol A) offer contrasting examples. On one hand, CBS's *60 Minutes* failed to investigate an advocacy report by the Natural Resources Defense Council suggesting alar (a chemical some apple growers used to retard rotting) was possibly carcinogenic. Naturally this caused a collapse in the apple market. But panic turned out to be unfounded, a product of shoddy science and media sensationalism.[18] Danielle Haas described the process that can fuel such reporting, when "too often scientific reports received insufficient skeptical scrutiny." Reporters got the scoop and advocates received attention and/or funding for their cause.[19] But Haas described a very different process when it came to the *Milwaukee Sentinel-Journal* and BPA.

One of the more interesting examples involving journalism and science pertains to the American Association for the Advancement of Science, which offers media fellowships to upper division science students.[20] One such recipient was Susanne Rust, who left a doctoral program in biological anthropology to pursue science journalism, with an eventual particular focus on BPA. Along with Cary Spivak and Meg Kissinger, they published the "Chemical Fallout" series for the *Milwaukee Journal Sentinel* that ended up winning many journalism prizes.[21] Rust revealed a pattern in over 200 "scientific studies" that indicated industry-funded work pronouncing BPA harmless and more or less opposite results from nonaffiliated sources.[22]

Reporters like Rust expected and experienced the difficulties of contending with wealthy and powerful corporations who have an obvious economic interest in silencing critics. Such topics get murkier when cross-accusations begin to fly, as happened with biologist Tyrone Hayes and manufacturers of the herbicide atrazine.[23] It would appear that the legal world ended up agreeing with Hayes, at least to some degree. In 2012 the city of Greenville, Illinois, won a $105 million settlement against Syngenta corporation (a manufacturer of atrazine) for drinking water contamination.[24] But it is practically inevitable in such cases that it will be extra difficult to sort out the scientific "truth" when a lot of money, prestige, power, and corporate and individual reputations are at stake. Additionally, journalists get into rivalries with other journalists, foster jealousies that affect the news, incestuously feature each other in "celebrity lite" guest appearances on each other's television shows, succumb to peer pressure regarding interpretation of evidence, and other very human behaviors.[25]

So to give the good journalists their due, they are working in real time. By contrast, historians enjoy the luxuries of reflection when sifting through contradictory data after the dust has settled, and sometimes in light of knowledge that has advanced since the events took place. This post-real time does not mean that historians always solve the puzzle, or solve it adequately, but solving the puzzle is enormously more difficult when powerful entities are potentially withholding information, actively propagandizing against you, threatening lawsuits, or what have you. If that were not enough, the complex world of socially robust scientific knowledge has yet other aspects.

Scientists regularly complain about the difficulty in translating complex, contradictory, and inconclusive results to journalists.[26] Translation is the right word, and the interaction between popular media and esoteric science risks vital information being lost in translation. Yet the sword cuts other ways. Undoubtedly some scientists use media hype to gain attention and thus funding for their pet projects.[27]

Biologist Stephen H. Schneider described trying to straddle adherence to the scientific method while pandering to media sensationalism. He called it a "double ethical bind" requiring a proper balance "between being effective and being honest."[28] But this is the very problem that comes from mixing policy advocacy (effectiveness) with the intellectual endeavor of science (being honest). Who would *not* be honest about the latter, at least in its pure form? In fact, some scientists and philosophers would argue that policy advocacy inevitably compromises anything approaching "objective" truth. Of course, no thoughtful observer of journalism (or knowledge in general) thinks ideal objectivity is possible, and science journalism is particularly beset with reporting uncertainty.[29] And yet too often uncertainty gets reported as fact or gets cloaked in doomsday prediction from "experts."

Science communication, including science journalism, is a massive field containing hundreds of books and articles analyzing all sorts of aspects in the field. Entire journals dedicate themselves to this topic, including *Public Understanding of Science* and *Science Communication*. But we can take a look at a few environmental topics to see some things for ourselves.

Every year billions of dollars in cargo travel up and down the Mississippi River. This economic reality necessitates the dredging that is, unfortunately and undeniably, compromising if not destroying some of the old habitats of the silt-enriched delta. A compromised delta supposedly also exacerbated the damage of Hurricane Katrina. But it is difficult to know what is happening in any detail from news reports.

Between 1971 and 1986 the *New York Times* reported that the Louisiana coast was annually losing between 16.5 and 40 square miles of land to coastal erosion.[30] In 2015 Jesse Hardman reported that "a football field of coastal wetland disappearing every half-hour."[31] In January 2018 NBC News took the baton and reported 13.5 square miles of wetlands lost annually.[32] In May 2018 Travis Lux reported that more than 2,000 square miles had been lost since 1918.[33]

But this lost coastal Louisiana remains only vaguely accounted for. The annual dredging of the Mississippi River is undoubtedly removing silt, and thus common sense would dictate that we have markedly compromised the coastal land. And yet, Google Earth Engine's time-lapse satellite photographs from the past quarter century[34] reveal a Louisiana coastline that does not reflect the radical loss of earlier and ongoing predictions. The Google Earth imagery shows inevitable coastline fluctuations, with innumerable additions and subtractions, but that is typical of all silt-laden coastlines. One would think that hundreds of square miles of missing land would be rather obvious. Thus we are left to wonder if the media has exaggerated or otherwise misreported the story.

Still, in a wise countermove, today's artificial barriers may well begin to offset the negative effects of dredging.[35] If so, this could end up as a positive stewardship story.

Somewhat similar to the alar topic, the "hole in the ozone" story turned out to be an unfortunate example of scientist-advocates planting a story and manipulating the media.[36] Apparently it is a scientific fact that chlorofluorocarbons (CFCs) destroy ozone.[37] But when the "hole in the ozone" became a media sensation, scientists studying the atmosphere were not actually measuring ozone globally. Nor were they knowledgeable of fluctuating ozone levels over past millennia, or even any precise data of contemporary natural variability. For the media, CFCs became the culprit for ozone without any consideration given to natural influences such as volcanic eruptions. The "science" was—you guessed it—based on computer modeling.[38]

At this point it is difficult to give the computer modeling approach even the credit of an educated guess. When we function with this level of ignorance, incomplete information, unknown variables and even lesser known interactions among variables, it is practically mere guessing. Throw in the grant-seeking scientist-advocate ingredient and all other bets are compromised.

The Amazon deforestation (or rather, "destruction") story was a much more protracted one that unfolded in the media over many decades. The end results have been quite surprising, similar to the coastal erosion phenomenon with its false prophecies of doom.

According to the *New York Times*, between 1982 and 2007, various environmental advocates and supposed "experts" made widely varying estimates of annual Amazon rainforest loss, from 22,000 square kilometers to ten times that much.[39] In 1980 the *New York Times* reported estimates of world rainforest deforestation between 40K to 95K square miles annually,[40] a suspiciously broad range.

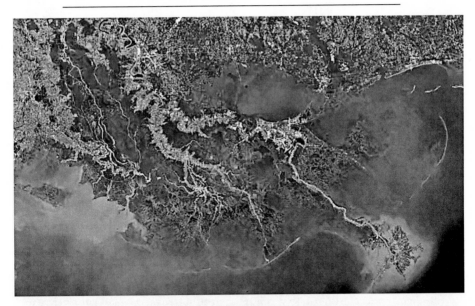

Satellite photographs of the Louisiana coast in 1984 (top) and 2016. Mississippi River dredging unquestionably compromises silt enhancement of the delta, but these photographs do not support decades of media reports claiming annual loss of hundreds of square miles of land. Such dire reports run the danger of following the progression of the Boy Who Cried Wolf. The public remains generally uninformed regarding details of the changing delta environment (enhanced from Google Earth Engine images).

For a moment let's suspend the fact that the future is unpredictable, scientifically or otherwise. In all of this the great *New York Times* (and I mean that sincerely) nevertheless succumbed to a common problem in science reporting; many of the estimates relied upon interviews with "experts" rather than examining the scientific data itself.[41] This is understandable. Deadlines are tight and data is a long haul study. But when the "experts" are giving subjective opinions based in fear or fear-mongering instead of sober, detached assessments, this sort of inaccuracy is bound to be the result.[42]

Even more sensational were predictions of when the forest would disappear completely. Between 1971 and 2003, the *New York Times* reported wild estimates of no forest remaining by 1999, 2006, 2019, 2081, or 2083.[43] Related to these predictions was more false science involving the supposed "high loess" soils that would turn to desert following deforestation. According to this line of reasoning, which I remember well at the time, was that rainforest nutrients were stored in plants, not soil. Desertification was supposed to follow deforestation.[44] Instead, as also reported in the *New York Times* (to their credit) standard crop rotation rendered productive farmland, year after year, and particularly successful were the cattle grazing pastures sown in grasses.[45]

Obviously there is bound to be an enormous variety in soil quality over such a huge area, but the reality has still turned out to be much less dire than earlier predictions. In 2002 José Luís Campana Camargo and others demonstrated that bare soil in Central Amazonia actually generated more directly-sown seeds than did partial forests or pastures, likely because of the absence of certain fauna eating seeds or sprouts, or absent flora-related soil pathogens compromising seed germination and survival.[46]

Ironically, as a rural-to-urban migration began, people abandoned farms that the rain forest began to regenerate. We knew rain forest regeneration was possible over a hundred years ago, but in 2009 it made breaking news at the *New York Times*.[47] In fact, since the late 19th century the Costa Rican rainforest reclaimed abandoned sugar plantations.[48] Similar regenerations occurred throughout the 20th century in Puerto Rico, after farmers abandoned coffee plantations. In fact, second growth rainforest is actually more common than first growth throughout Central America and among the Caribbean islands. But rainforests also began regenerating in India, Bangladesh, and North Vietnam during the 1980s, and in Papua New Guinea and the Dominican Republic by the late 20th century.[49] Compared to any part of North America, the Amazon rainforest grows back *much faster*, with hundred-foot-plus trees in only fifteen years.[50]

And this does not take into account much earlier indigenous ruins in South and Central America that were swallowed up by a long-recovered forest that many, apparently, had mistaken for "virgin" forest.[51] As for more recent regeneration, some of the stalwart pessimists, very belatedly accepting the second-growth reality, and have been reluctant to acknowledge such good news.[52] The fact was, the doomsdayists' dichotomy of forest/non-forest was always false. As on North American cattle farms and ranches, Amazon pastures featured and feature many trees to provide shade for cattle. Decades after predicting climate change from Amazon deforestation, no one has yet bothered to measure the carbon sequestration of such habitats.[53] That would be another variable in climate prediction ignored (more about that, next chapter).

The Amazon rainforest's death, world rainforest death, and Mark Twain's death, all turn out to have been greatly exaggerated. And I'm writing this in 2018, when over three-fourths of the *original* pre–1970s Amazon rainforest remains intact.[54] According to the Mongabay environmental news site, about 81 percent of the Brazilian rainforest remains intact as of 2017.[55] This was the forest that was supposed to be disappearing. It is Brazil's *Atlantic* rainforest that has suffered far more timbering, with perhaps as little as 11 percent still intact in small, disconnected fragments.[56] But even 11 percent is far more than the massive forests Anglo-American colonists encountered all along their eastern seaboard of what became the United States.[57] Those forests are practically all gone now, replaced by cities, farms, highways, industrial parks, and neighborhoods. The disconnected remnants are much smaller than in Brazil, and practically non-existent in New England. Thus, despite being colonized generations earlier by the Portuguese, Brazil's Atlantic rainforest has survived in greater magnitude than its eastern seaboard counterpart in the United States. In one last ironic note, the world's largest urban forest exists in Rio de Janeiro, mostly a remnant of the Atlantic rainforest.[58] No such urban forest exists anywhere in the United States, eastern seaboard or anywhere else.

Granted, Brazil has a very different (tropical) geography compared to the temperate one of the United States. But it is worth noting that the remaining Amazon rainforest amounts to over a billion acres of Old Growth forest in a total area of 1.3 billion acres. "Virgin" is a misleading term, considering that some of this jungle grew back after ancient people lived there. But if only we had such enormous swaths of Old Growth timber left in the United States. Instead, our ten largest Old Growth forest areas combined constitute less than eleven million acres, and Alaska's Tongass National Forest accounts for half of those.[59]

When I did research for the Jefferson National Forest in Virginia, then-octogenarian Martin Hassinger showed me some photographs his father had taken of the old highland forest around Konnarock in southwestern Virginia.

Until that moment, I had no idea trees had grown so large in the east. One black oak measured eight feet in diameter; a tulip popular measured eleven feet in diameter. And this was among the higher elevations in the Virginia Appalachians, around 3,000 feet, where tree growth is slow and (compared to the lowlands) somewhat stunted. A century later, the forest in and around Konnarock is unrecognizable compared to the pre-logging era. A century of growth in the logged portions of the Amazon will be a different story. If you love big trees, it will be a better story. That's one of the obvious differences between a tropical rainforest and an eastern North America high country temperate forest.

During the late 20th century, the Amazon became a classic Edenic symbol for the American environmental elite.[60] It also became a very convenient location for species extinction hysteria and the fostering of biodiversity as a philosophical value cloaked in (supposed) scientific fact.[61] Brazilians in particular became sensitive to the hypocrisy of Americans from a wealthy country that previously stripped most of its forest acreage, now dictating that their impoverished neighbors to the south avoid doing the same thing. In fact, maybe they could eat cake if they ran out of bread. Of course, the elitists will never admit that is what they are, in effect, advocating (they'll say vaguely sympathetic things about the poor). But this is why the general run of policy ideas from people like Bjørn Lomborg or Wilfred Beckerman is more appealing than those of the Edenists and certainly those of the doomsdayists. Improved standard of living fosters inherent environmental concern, just as we witnessed in the United States during the Progressive Era of the late 19th and early 20th centuries, when agencies such as the Forest Service and National Park Service came into being. Undoubtedly the majority of Brazilians, like the majority of Americans, would like to enjoy enough wealth to be selective when it comes to natural resource use, including rainforest resources.

*   *   *

We have quite a mixture here: socially robust scientific knowledge, the power and influence of the media cutting several ways, some scientists who have difficulty communicating their complex uncertainties, and others who use or try to use the media to generate publicity and possible future funding for their projects. One of the results is the so-called "garbage can model" of policy-making, which particularly describes the environmental sciences during and after the 1970s. In the garbage can, both science and policy are thrown in together, but not necessarily in a coordinated fashion, sometimes resulting in discordant results. Unanticipated political developments, sometimes originally remote, come to influence the garbage can mixture. The environmental movement itself becomes an obvious player (often even a heavy hitter), and thus this all favors environmental elites.[62]

Among those elites I would include the comfortable middle classes. In fact, I would include almost everyone outside the demographic of environmental injustice victims, groups of people who never seem to make the news as much as stories about ozone depletion, Amazon deforestation, or climate change. More about environmental justice later.

Katherine E. Rowan described a wonderful ideal of science journalism. "The trick," she wrote, "is to indicate broad support for claims that have survived rigorous testing but still help audiences see that currently accepted perspectives are [only] the best working hypotheses."[63] The scientific paradigm may be only forming or nonexistent, and claims to scientific consensus may be slight or even missing. Science journalists are supposed to report their topics as such.[64] But, as with all endeavors, the ideal often gets lost in the endeavor. No wonder when that endeavor is science journalism, because most of the results of current and ongoing science are uncertain, not conclusive.[65] Many journalists probably sense that their audiences are hungry for clear and (overly) simplified answers. After all, humanity in general prefers answers to questions. As veteran *New York Times* science journalist Cornelius Dean said, "people tend to read over the caveats"[66] even if the science journalists put them in the story. As in the cases of ozone depletion, Amazon deforestation, or Louisiana coastal erosion, scientific uncertainty and surprise results often leaked out over time (sometimes requiring decades). But by then few were comparing today's headlines with yesteryear's, and socially robust scientific knowledge contemporary to any era may reflect the latest story, an echo from the past, or some hodgepodge of both.

Chapter 5

An Ever-Changing Climate

To a significant degree, anthropogenic climate change is a debate about competing predictions. It is tempting to dismiss the debate entirely because of that basic fact, for we are not able to predict much of anything, and never something as complex as climate. Probability and statistics do well regarding simpler problems with clearly defined limits when employing ultra-accurate data. Inaccurate data destroys probability, even with comparatively simple problems, like locating someone lost at sea.[1] Inaccurate data ruins even short-term weather prediction of a few days or less. And yet thousands of climate scientists receive billions of dollars[2] to undertake the opposite: long-term predictions with uncertain data, uncertain variables, and the impossibility of knowing how all these variable might interact. In other words, they seek to do the impossible. And yet few are willing to say the emperor has no clothes.

Climate change prognostication is a form of "futureology," not to be confused with attempts at scientific prediction in controlled experiments.[3] I already mentioned SEASF (Semi-Evidentiary Attempts at Systematic Findings) as a tongue-in-cheek substitute for the so-called social sciences. In some ways, futureology does not even rise to SEASF's level. Sometimes climate prediction has more in common with astrology than astronomy. More thoughtful scientists and philosophers of science even reject *controlled experiment prediction*. They have reason for doing so.

None other than the eminent physicist Richard Feynman wrote that the process of physics experiments entailed trying new things and observing the results, and how "we cannot say ahead of time successfully what it [the result] is going to look like."[4] And remember—Feynman was referring to the uber-science of *physics*. Even the best biological experiments seem endlessly open-ended and sloppy by comparison. As the mathematician Henri Poincaré demonstrated, predicting the future would require ever greater precision in calculations when, in fact, even small initial errors in data exacerbate inaccuracies that end up compounding inaccurate calculations.[5] As if to prove Poincaré's point, the much-noted "butterfly effect" arose when mathematician and meteorologist Edward Norton Lorenz discovered that slightly different data made profound differences in weather forecasting results.[6]

Back in the 1950s, long before climate prediction became the cause *du jour*, Albert Einstein wrote, "when the number of factors coming into play in a phenomenological complex is too large, scientific method in most cases fails us. One need only think of the weather, in which case prediction even for a few days ahead is impossible."[7] This remains true, despite the development of Doppler radar, satellite data, and other advances in meteorology since Einstein's era. Even today, billions of hourly data from numerous geographical locations instantaneously fed into computers only give us (in the best conditions) probability tools for about three days of weather prediction, a general improvement from one day, circa 2008.[8]

So if the science of weather prediction remains eternally problematic and inconclusive, it would only stand to reason that climate prediction would be thousands of times or even infinitely more difficult to predict—and thus far, far beyond the abilities of even probability science. In other words, we are lucky to predict the weather a few days in advance. How could any rational person have confidence in climate predictions set for years, decades, or even centuries from now?

Again regarding the uber-science of physics, Feynman illustrated how we can never know when we are definitely correct about scientific conclusions, but how we can always prove existing theories or suppositions wrong. Finding flaws with earlier ideas, in fact, is the only way science progresses.[9] If Feynman were alive today he would undoubtedly find the claims of climate prediction amusing, at best.

And yet it is astonishing how widespread, and how deeply believed, is the foregone conclusion of anthropogenic climate change and its inevitably dire consequences. This is bad science, but as already indicated, it also testifies to an absence of common sense.

This isn't Jimmy Stewart in *It's a Wonderful Life*, wherein a simplistic alternative world is revealed by removing one variable (Jimmy Stewart himself). In environmental science, and especially in climate science, there are simply too many variables for such a simple story; i.e., emission of natural and anthropogenic greenhouse gases, solar variations, unpredictable future volcanic activity, future human ingenuity involving green technology, human population trends, future asteroid impacts, global pandemics, cloud formation patterns, et cetera, et cetera. Furthermore, these variables interact with each other in infinite possible combinations depending upon their relative magnitude, timing, and duration.

So what do climate modelers do in the face of such overwhelming complexity? They simply artificially limit the variables they insert into their pro-jections. Thus, to no surprise, even the Intergovernmental Panel on Climate Change (IPCC) admitted that different models render different results.[10] Far more than resembling science, this seems much more like elaborate guess-work.

For example, the importance of atmospheric carbon in climate change continues to elicit varying opinions among scientists. While sharing the IPCC's assumption that increased atmospheric carbon will indeed warm the planet, Peter Cox and his team offer less drastic warming projections based upon atmospheric carbon calculations compared to the IPCC's. Naturally they are employing an alternative climate model, the only major tool available to climate futureology. Cox and team assume that observable warming data is not in dispute,[11] which it actually is[12] (more on that, below). But aside from that, Cox and the IPCC offer another case of dueling predictions. To name just one other variable, Ben Houlton and others have discovered that previous climate modelers failed to calculate anything near an accurate measurement of terrestrial nitrogen. Said nitrogen, Houlton argues, could have a hitherto unappreciated effect on flora growth and thus carbon sequestration.[13] This science is obviously preliminary, but already it indicates the fatally flawed basis of climate modeling as a worthwhile forecaster.

Houlton raises the nitrogen variable—and who knows which variables await further appreciation. Even if we knew all the variables, they could be assembled in literally infinite combinations of how they might work out (including time and magnitude variables of each causal factor), thus render-ing infinite possible results. In other words, the variables all play out differ-ently over time depending upon how they are added in the first place and when or if they are added along the sequence, and what level of impact they might or might not have, thus effecting other variables, *et cetera, ad infini-tum.*

More recently, Nicholas Lewis and Judith Curry's study claims the IPCC's warming predictions are vastly exaggerated in general.[14] We could keep listing competing models and studies. As the back issues of the *Journal of Climate* and *International Journal of Climatology* amply demonstrate, there are literally hundreds if not thousands of articles all predicated upon modeling; simula-tions, predictions, projections, and past trends that cannot predict the future—in other words, futureology. At least some admit uncertainty and seek to correct past modeling mistakes,[15] but such modeling and modeling correction could go on and on—and, if nothing interferes and funding con-tinues—will go on indefinitely, without illuminating us regarding future cli-mate.

Climate change prognostications often seduce the naïve by their reliance on computer modeling. As science ethicists Adam Briggle and Carl Mitcham wrote, climate change has become a "secular religion" replete with exaggeration and fear-mongering. Furthermore, we have developed an "assumption that defining and responding to climate change are scientific and technological in nature."[16] But computer models are really the only tools available for such futureology. They are not the equivalent of telescopes showing us astronomical details or microscopes showing us bacterial details. Models predicting future climate are like maps made of terra incognito. We have not seen the territory, so how can we draw a map? But even good maps should not be confused with actual territory.[17]

Worse, much of the climate change gospel depends upon a violation of a Logic 101 lesson, which is to avoid conflating correlation with causation. We are releasing carbon and other gases from burning fossil fuels, and at least some people think the overall global temperature is rising. It is tempting to jump to the conclusion that one is causing the other, but we know better. Atmospheric science is too complicated to reach such simple cause-and-effect conclusions.

So even if we can agree that the climate is warming (a determination more problematic than the crusaders will admit), the cause of the warming is even more difficult to determine. Is it partly a continuation of the warming trend since the last ice age? If so, how much is this long term geological trend contributing to the current climate change? Are humans contributing to enhanced warming through their activities? If so, how much? In the current and recent socio-political climate, such "simple" questions generate highly contentious responses. Trying to predict the future when we're not even sure about present causal factors becomes downright ludicrous.

For a moment, simply consider the prognostication problem of wholly unforeseen factors, like the aforementioned eastern barred owl showing up to compete with the northern spotted owl. Regarding the future climate, what would happen if we finally had our technological revolution that ended fossil fuel consumption and combined that with technology (already readily available) that removes carbon from the atmosphere? If, indeed, carbon is the culprit—another bit of gospel relying more upon guesswork than science.[18] Predictions of technology alone are worthless for a number of reasons— partly because we do not yet have future tools (not yet imagined) that will enable future technology, and if we did we would build the technology instead of predicting it. Technological forecasting is just as spurious as scientific forecasting.[19] Given any number of unforeseen variable insertions, interactions, and behaviors, climate modeling predictions could actually run in a direction closer to *the opposite* of what some of them are predicting now. It all depends upon what data we feed into the models, and that data is inevitably faulty and incomplete, and inevitable errors (as Poincaré warned) will result in fatally flawed conclusions.

It only stands to reason, not to mention common sense.

Taleb believes "the future will be increasingly less predictable,"[20] which makes sense if you consider growing complexity, which adds new variables and new interactions among variables.

Another problem lies in the myth of the "scientific consensus" regarding anthropogenic climate change. Science without dissent is like democracy without dissent; they exist in name only, not reality. Maybe it was pure coincidence, but a few years ago the first four books I pulled off the shelf at random in the University of Oregon science library all qualified or contradicted this so-called "scientific consensus" regarding human-created climate change.[21] It appears that the "consensus" is propaganda picked up (like climate change in general) by the media uncritically.[22]

Instead of a scientific consensus, the more we dig through the scientific literature, the more we discover exactly what we would expect of most sciences: far, far more questions than answers. A main corollary problem with the scientific consensus myth lies in what we now call confirmation bias. As Francis Bacon warned us centuries ago, confirmation bias of preconceived agendas is detrimental to the scientific endeavor.[23] And as Thomas Kuhn wrote decades ago, "there is no such thing as research without counterinstances."[24] Thus, even one scientist's work contradicts or at least qualifies a given scientific paradigm, much more so hundreds of scientists' work. But it is the nature of those accepting a paradigm to dismiss anything that deviates from their accepted worldview.[25] This natural and common human desire for order often compromises the scientific method. Sometimes we cannot help but impose our artificial notions of order upon phenomenon independent of it. Metaphysicians and philosophers of science have explored this juxtaposition, which makes a fascinating philosophical topic, but potentially compromises scientific endeavor.

And so we probably *do* have a scientific paradigm that generally embraces anthropogenic climate change, but that should indicate to us a future shift of said paradigm. Yet we hate to admit the impossibility of predicting that shift— when, and in what direction. Again that eternal human trait of seeking an orderly world, deviations be damned.

So obviously the paradigm holders are not necessarily accurate in any detail, or even basically correct. Ptolemy was wrong in his conception of geocentrism, as was Paul Broca in his notions of craniometry. And, as already illustrated, any number of recent environmental doomsdayists have also made wrong predictions involving species extinction, human famine, peak oil, global cooling, solar dimming, et cetera.

In any case, I was stunned at the ready availability of materials contradicting popular culture conceptions. Even at that early stage in my exploration, I suddenly had a strong suspicion that there must be a huge difference between what climate scientists as a group think they might know, and how the news media has come to depict the anthropogenic aspect of climate change as a foregone conclusion. Now I've developed a Pavlovian cringe every time I hear a journalist on the radio or television say "climate change," for it is invariably stated in the institutionalized dogmatic terms that dominate our times. Of course (ironically) I avoid the news outlets that supposedly support climate skepticism. Anyway, apparently few journalists walk into science libraries and poke around. Or maybe their editors would shoot down their stories if they tried. After all, in our cultural milieu, the True Believers quickly dismiss any dissenters as "deniers" or "naysayers," even if the latter suggest modifying the gospel only a little bit.[26] As with other tribalistic bigotries, we are living amid a false dichotomy of environmental True Believers and heretics. In the case of climate change, many have observed that partisan politics has helped foster and solidify this false dichotomy.[27]

*   *   *

Back in 2000, climate scientist Frances Drake recognized the then-current milieu of global warming (later changed to climate change in a bet-hedging move) as a paradigm vis-à-vis Thomas Kuhn's appreciation of science as a reflection of its social context.[28] Drake concluded that "scientific certainty is no longer about some objective truth but that which is accepted by a majority of scientists."[29] The minority of scientists outside the paradigm (itself a contradiction of the "consensus" myth) function as skeptics that may feed into an eventual "paradigm shift." But the majority still define the paradigm, which also colors the responses against it.[30] This is actually a more sober way to understand the issue than the media-fueled false dichotomy of alarmists v. deniers. Drake, in a rare voice outside of advocacy on both sides, offers (probably) the best single non-specialist volume about the subject I have encountered.

Drake debunked many of the myths surrounding climate change, comfortable with questions in lieu of simplistic and factually-unsupported answers. For example, we do not yet know how much or how fast oceans and flora absorb carbon. We are also ignorant of how long carbon remains in the atmosphere. And finally, we cannot measure how much atmospheric carbon comes from natural sources (such as deteriorating vegetation) or human sources.[31] The list of other rational observations and excellent questions in Drake's book goes on and on. Rational observations and eternal questions are, by the way, supposed to be core to the scientific endeavor.

Drake appreciated the aforementioned causation/correlation problem that regularly obscures the climate science topic.[32] She recognized solar variations[33] as another wild card (yet crucially important) variable virtually invisible in climate change debates. Drake concluded that global surface temperature statistics are simply unreliable[34] (blasphemy! blasphemy!) and dared to ask an honest question: "How do you set a baseline, an average climate, from a constantly changing climate?"[35] This question appeals to our common sense as well as our appreciation of science.

Even if we *could* determine a baseline climate, what would it be? Presumably one that was not too hot or cold, not too wet or dry. How nice it would be to have fewer catastrophic events, like prolonged droughts. Goodness forbid we experience another ice age, like the one experienced in medieval Europe.[36] Obviously our ideal climate would be one that supports us and our agricultural endeavors. There's nothing wrong with this. But pretending that there is an ordained ideal we are somehow deviating against defies science and merely reflects common human insecurity. There's that craving for order again.

Think of how many times a meteorologist has called a certain temperature above or below "normal." The correct word would be "average," and as the years pass the averages slowly change one way or another. There is no "normal," just the wishful thinking for stability. Even "average" offers an artificial status, being merely added statistics divided by the number of days they were recorded. There are no real "deviations," for cold snaps, droughts, heat waves, and other extreme phenomenon are unusual only in our short frames of reference, not in the broader scheme of things. This is obvious in the way nature carries on. Severe enough heat waves cause trees to drop their leaves in the Midwest, but generally those trees live on. Animals die in blizzards, but the species tends to endure. The very durability of so many life forms testifies to millennia of exposure to wild fluctuations in weather.

These subjects, all by themselves, would do much to defuse the hysteria surrounding climate apocalypse, if only mainstream dialogue acknowledged them as unsolved scientific mysteries. Instead, such dialogue often goes the other direction toward alarmism and anti-science.

But, as we well know, a great many people are uncomfortable with questions, and thus quickly resort to "answers," often the simpler the better. But here is where science and philosophy have something wonderful in common:

the greatest thinkers who have studied either or both are perfectly comfortable with questions, knowing absolutely that many of their questions are unanswerable, at least in any definitive sense.

As the physicist Robert L. Park noted, climate is "the most complicated system scientists have ever dared to tackle."[37] No wonder there is so much (unreported) disagreement. Park distinguishes two main camps in the climate science debates, "Malthusian pessimists" and technophile optimists.[38] Thomas Malthus (1766–1834) is an excellent example of a futureologists who got it entirely wrong.

Malthus predicted periodic and unavoidable famines because (he reasoned) agricultural yields could only increase arithmetically (1, 2, 3, 4, etc.) while human populations would increase exponentially (1, 2, 4, 8, etc.).[39] It was a reasonable calculation for his times, but failed to anticipate a veritable revolution in agriculture (associated with the industrial revolution) that would increase farm yields beyond what Malthus could apparently imagine. The massive innovations in industrial technology alone have rendered agriculture in Malthus's day unrecognizable. As Steinbeck illustrated in *Grapes of Wrath*, "One man on a tractor can take the place of twelve or fourteen families."[40] And that was a primitive tractor. Now we have rotating shifts of one guy in a GPS-guided combine (complete with stereo, air conditioner, massive headlights, and a six-figure price tag) harvesting twenty-four hours a day, if necessary, when the crops are ready. Add to that monumental advances in soil science, horticultural techniques, fertilizers, et cetera, and Malthus's prediction seems quaint at best. Yet it is amusing to see someone still citing Malthus uncritically, as if the decades had not thoroughly disproven his population forecasts.[41] And Malthus's utter failure did not prevent Paul and Anne Ehrlich from forecasting their updated population doomsday scenario in 1968, complete with predicted famines in the 1980s that (like Malthus's) did not materialize.[42]

All of this should serve as cautionary tales regarding climate prediction. But ultimately we should reject climate forecasts upon the simple basis that we cannot know. As Taleb wrote, "The problem with experts is that they do not know what they do not know."[43] Or, as Park put it, "the further we try to project ourselves into the future, the more certain it becomes that some unforeseen, perhaps unforeseeable, advance in science or technology will shuffle the deck before we get there."[44] Climate science cannot predict the future because *science* cannot predict the future. Prediction is not what science does.

If only we had a second planet Earth following the same orbit around the sun, except without people. Then we would have a "control group" planet and the one we live on (the "test group"), and then we could most definitely measure at least some of the ecological changes humans have influenced, including climate. Of course, that would involve traveling to the human-free Earth and thus (in the old scientific paradox) possibly influencing the results simply by observing. This human-free Earth might provide a strange and ironic utopia for misanthropic environmentalists, for it would feature the Earth we know and love in its fostering of human existence, yet without the humans. But back to the science: without a control group there can be no true measurement of how much humans are influencing the climate.

Too often "climate change" appears without the "anthropogenic" precursor that should always be added. That's to remind people that climate has been changing since climate began, literally hundreds of millions of years before primates evolved. Strictly from an intuitive, non-scientific point of view, it is difficult to believe that we are *not* altering the climate in some fashion or another when you consider the megatons of carbon we put into the atmosphere daily.[45] On the other hand, even the IPCC admitted that wildly fluctuating pre-historic carbon levels (long before humans burned fossil fuels) remain an unsolved mystery.[46] At the very least, this would seem to indicate that we should not jump to conclusions about atmospheric carbon.

An inability to measure against a "control group" planet this impact of carbon—or methane, or ozone, or sulfur oxide or what have you—is a serious setback for any precise scientific conclusions. We cannot even predict long term cloud formations, which can significantly affect climate.[47] Understanding feedbacks among numerous climate variables (water vapor, incoming and outgoing solar radiation, cloud formations, atmospheric particles, greenhouse gases, etc.) continue to challenge scientists, who (as they should) hold strong disagreements with each other.[48]

Rarely does any of this complexity appear in the media. In fact, too often "climate change" becomes just another environmental buzzword. Now, every time there is a catastrophic flood, hurricane, or even the large California wildfires of 2017, a great many people (especially journalists) automatically resort to the simpleminded cause and effect catch-all of "climate change." The anthropogenic part is always implied if less often stated. Even other obvious factors such as more real estate existing in disaster-prone areas (thus giving rise to more measureable economic destruction) does not enter their calculations. The annual dredging of the Mississippi River is what is really causing coastal erosion in Louisiana, not the fictitious bogeyman of rising sea levels.[49] Drake thinks that the global scale evidentiary record does not support the conclusion that climate-related extreme weather events have increased. In fact, it's possible that hurricanes may have even recently *decreased* in activity.[50]

Marco Island housing development, southwest Florida, 1973. Many new neighborhoods in hurricane-prone damage areas naturally raise economic damage tallies in the wake of storms. Such tallies are practically irrelevant indicators of storm severity changes, themselves debated among scientists (photograph by Flip Schulke).

Let us pause to consider the "rising sea level" bogeyman associated with climate change.

We know sea level has risen hundreds of feet since the last ice age. There is no end of geological, paleontological, and archaeological evidence for this. For example, the Black Sea shows all the signs of having been a fresh water lake until the Mediterranean Sea rose too high and breached the small land bridge that is now the Dardanelles and Bosporus Strait.[51] The Cosquer cave paintings along the southern coast of France now require extremely skilled scuba divers to swim down and find the entrance, then carefully proceed into the cave itself—a clear impossibility until very recent times. And then, of course, even random undersea archaeology reveals old fire pits along prehistoric beaches. It remains problematic whether or not the oceans are still rising and, if they are, what is causing this. If they are rising it could be a continuation of the multi-thousand year trend, a result of anthropogenic global warming, or some of both. Post-industrial human activity then would be a possible catalyst or enhancer, but to what degree no one really knows. And yet, absurdly, doomsdayists rely on natural erosion of low-lying islands (ignoring creations of other islands),[52] eternally shifting ocean currents that sometimes erode beaches, Mississippi River dredging, and more development near shores. The predictions of future catastrophe from rising sea levels roll in accordingly. But rising sea level is only one of several bogeymen.

We already know that fuel accumulation in western forests has contributed massively to some of the mega-fires of recent years. And true, we've been on the dry side out here in the western United States, but we should not automatically attribute that to anthropogenic global warming. After all, a prehistoric draught of massive and prolonged proportions apparently dispersed the Anasazi peoples who once occupied places like the Wupatki ruins in northern Arizona.

But there are broader, more encompassing factors than that. Charcoal in the geological record reveals that wide areas of the planet regularly burned hundreds of millions of years ago, depending upon fluctuating levels of atmospheric oxygen. Obviously this was long before the age of primates.[53] How ironic that we blame ourselves now. But, as André Gide wrote, "man's responsibility increases as that of the gods decreases,"[54] and the trend toward secularization has only continued since the Renaissance.

So, for example, we now know that purely geological factors have caused enormous climate change in the pre-primate past, perhaps none more dramatic than the warming associated with the Paleocene Eocene Thermal Maximum tens of millions of years ago. Geologists hypothesize about the possible causes; perhaps natural release of methane, massive volcanic activity, or (like the cause of the Jurassic dinosaur extinction), a major asteroid event.[55] This, alone, should inform us about how little we are ultimately in control of the planet. It is *not*, however, a rationalization for bad stewardship. Still, climate alarmists fixating on carbon emissions—rather than asteroids, volcanoes, solar radiation variations, et cetera—reflects the misanthropic environmental mentality. We are emitting much carbon, and it might even help the economy to make a subsidized industry out of capturing it and sequestering it. But to simplify climate change to purely anthropogenic sources or causes is a fool's errand.

*　*　*

It is interesting to note how different countries depict climate change, which would indicate some cultural constructs along the way. If anything, it would appear that the media of western Europe was and is far more in sync with IPCC findings regarding anthropogenic climate change compared to United States media. Recently Michael Brüggemann and Sven Engesser wrote that "climate change is regarded as a distant problem rather than as a policy priority for the European Union"[56] And yet, ironically, American media in general is apparently much more polarized between "embracers" and "deniers" in anthropogenic climate change,[57] as well as more likely to report climate change effects without linking proactive action, such as reducing carbon emissions.[58] Perhaps the fervency of the doomsday promotion in America has engendered an equally passionate backlash. But, of course, so many things have become polarized in American sociopolitical dialogue of late. As far as partisan media sources preaching to the choir, this sounds consistent with the "echo chamber" phenomenon of the 2016 presidential election and aftermath, in which polarized audiences listened only to the news they wanted to hear. It gets more nuanced upon slightly more investigation.

Brüggemann and Engesser recently studied a broad spectrum of journalists in the United States, Germany, India, Switzerland, and Britain. They found a "consensus about the consensus" based upon the IPCC's four main points: the Earth is warming, humans are the main cause, reducing carbon dioxide emissions is the solution, otherwise the "global ecosystem" will suffer serious damage. Brüggemann and Engesser concluded that these five-nation journalists nonetheless formed an informal "interpretive community" based in their use and belief in common sources, especially the IPCC.[59]

Germany would appear to have a very different relationship between climate change science and media coverage, which very fact would probably only fuel the American "deniers." In 2013, Ana Ivanova, et al., surveyed over eleven hundred German climate scientists and found a significant level of "medialization." Medialization involves journalists interviewing scientists about their work, but also scientists tailoring their information for popular dissemination. Over 80 percent of the German climate scientists confessed that future media interactions influenced their work, such as choice in research topics.[60] This, for good or ill, is no surprise considering the previous chapter's description of "socially robust scientific knowledge." Some day historians will try to sort out who was influencing whom, and thereafter argue about the details forever. But it is also interesting to note that, more recently, German climate scientists engaging with the news media were prone to downplaying scientific uncertainties and confirming anthropogenic climate change as "historically unique, dangerous and calculable."[61] And, for whatever it's worth, many scholars studying the communication of science simply assume that anthropogenic climate change is a settled scientific fact, ignoring or downplaying any contradicting or qualifying evidence or reasoning.[62] This is not altogether surprising. The topic seems to divide people engaged in any number of endeavors; scientists themselves, journalists, sociologists, policymakers, and commentators in general. But this does not bode well for science communication.

For example, many people are shocked to discover that water vapor is the most important greenhouse gas, not carbon dioxide.[63] They'll call you a liar if you state a simple scientific fact, such as current carbon dioxide in the atmosphere accounting for less than one half of one percentile (just under 0.04 percent). They're even more shocked to discover that carbon may well warm the troposphere, but cools the stratosphere by reflecting solar radiation back into space.[64] Wise scientists conclude that we're probably influencing the climate, but ever so important details remain unknown.[65]

Confirming Frances Drake's earlier observation, the statistician Bjørn Lomborg amply demonstrated that even determining past temperature is far more difficult than neat graphs and authoritative assertions would lead us to believe. First, scientists only have "proxy indications" through things like tree ring growth. There are no ocean proxies; pretty important, considering most of the planet is covered in seawater. Even land proxy data are highly incomplete, almost only from North America, and nowhere near global. Only past summer temperatures are guessed, not nighttime nor winter temperatures.[66]

Additionally, Lomborg noted no recorded rise in troposphere warming despite careful measurement between 1979 and 2000; a warming troposphere is supposedly correlative for global surface warming. Lomborg also noted that clouds are the wild card factor in climate determination, notoriously non-conducive to modeling.[67] Finally, apparently there is a direct connection between sun spot fluctuations and Earth temperatures,[68] but there is nothing we can do to control the sun!

Climate alarmists regularly misuse shrinking glaciers when promoting their urgent doomsday message. Dramatic (and selective) photographs showing historic glaciers compared to their undeniably smaller contemporary remnants makes for effective propaganda, but lousy science. "We get a lot of information visually," glacier photographer Dan Fagre said, "and we tend to trust that even more than what we hear."[69] But glacial science, as you might expect, is much more complicated and far less conclusive. As should be the case, it raises more questions than answers. This would not be an issue, were these topics not entangled in politicized science.

For example, in 2004 Georg Kaser, et al., hypothesized (with much supporting fieldwork evidence) that increased air temperature is not the culprit responsible for shrinking the Kilimanjaro glaciers in East Africa. Instead, it appears to be an altered climate of drier air; in other words, the atmosphere itself is failing to replenish the glaciers rather than warmer temperatures melting them. This flies in the face of the simplistic dogma of global warming causing glacier melt.[70] There are more examples.

The polar ice caps regularly show up in climate change media attention and deeper scholarship. Many reports announce the shrinking of Arctic ice, but others contradict them in shorter or longer time frames.[71] The time frames themselves are problematic. A year or a decade is probably not enough time to establish a historic trend, and certainly not a predictive one.

Antarctica is one of the more problematic geographies regarding ice caps—in no small part because it is so remote with notoriously difficult conditions for mere human existence, not to mention scientific study. Back in 2002, some scientific studies concluded that Antarctica was cooler that average, and thus conducive to ice growing rather than shrinking.[72] Many media stories conveyed the idea that Antarctic was growing, not shrinking[73]; which other journalists then contradicted.[74] Then—if this were not enough of a whipsaw, newly discovered volcanic and geothermal heat beneath Antarctica was supposedly responsible for ice melting.[75] What may we conclude from all this? That we cannot conclude too much at all, except that so far we really do not understand what is happening in Antarctica.

I pity the scientists trying to do their jobs with the microscope of climate alarmists and deniers watching them. Speaking of which, in 2002, Roger Braithwaite analyzed an enormous amount of glacial data, measurements that people have only been accumulating for about a century now. Braithwaite acknowledged the difficulty of gathering accurate measurements in the field, the context of global warming fears, and the incomplete geographical history of the planet's glaciers.[76] But then Braithwaite stunningly concluded, "There is no obvious common or global trend of increasing glacier melt in recent years, and the data mainly reflect variations on intra- and inter-regional scales, which need more study in future."[77]

The foregoing studies are the types that climate alarmists often angrily dismiss as "highly selective." But whether we embrace alarmists, deniers, or neither—mere common sense should tell us that glacier studies are not what the propagandists would have us believe. It is a very new field, as far as the sciences go in general, and it has raised many more questions than it has answered. Why is it so difficult to acknowledge a topic that is majority-mystery rather than jumping to doomsdayist conclusions?

So to re-cap: science cannot predict the future climate or the future anything. We lack a "control planet" to measure the probable anthropogenic effects on planet Earth. Climate science is incredibly complex and not fully understood, as are subfields like glaciology and atmospheric chemistry. Like ecological habitats, these fields may *never* be fully understood.

Having said all that—and to repeat—it would be difficult to surmise that we are not affecting the climate *in some way or another*, locally and globally, particularly through activities such as burning fossil fuels, altering geography

A deer with "wasting disease" from malnutrition. Human elimination of predators has fostered an over-population of deer and other herbivores that now struggle to find enough food. Shortages of their preferred diet lead them to consume un-nutritious tree sprouts and other flora. They also regularly venture into the suburbs in search of sustenance. Clearly, one way or another, the human agency has altered the entire habitats and ecology of such species, raising many questions about human stewardship responsibilities (photograph by Terry Kreeger).

(forest to farm, but also farm to forest), raising massive numbers of livestock (which release methane), releasing particulates into the atmosphere, creating urban heat islands, et cetera.[78] But we simply do not know how much or in what ways.

By the way, for making the observations mentioned above, Bjørn Lomborg became a favorite target for climate change alarmists. The exchange merits some attention in an of itself, for it has broader implications for the topics of environmental philosophy, science, funding, and policymaking. If nothing else, it illustrates how prevalent emotional and illogical reactions are even among highly educated people.

*   *   *

At the beginning of this chapter I mentioned that arguments about anthropogenic climate change were often about competing predictions. And to repeat,

I regard climate predictions as unscientific because of all the reasons I mentioned; too many variables, many of which are themselves unpredictable, especially in magnitude, timing, and the infinite combination of unique interactions with other variables. Obviously there is an unending historical track record of failed predictions, and no successful predictions of any detail. That should also give us pause, to say the least, even if we hear Hegel echoing that perceptive observation about humanity never learning anything from history.

A related (mis)use of history is to study recent patterns and project them into the future, near or far. The problem is, the past is not necessarily prologue at all. It is simply past, and we just do not know when the next "consequential rare event"[79] is coming. As Taleb illustrated in a wonderful little mind exercise, the Thanksgiving turkey has every reason to believe that life is getting better and better (or is at least consistently good) as the humans fatten it up over the months and years. And then the fateful day arrives.[80]

For a scary real world example, immunologists fear we are "overdue" for a global pandemic comparable to the 1918 Spanish flu that killed more people (over fifty million) than died in World War I. If such a catastrophe were to arrive, it would alter the world's economy, various societies, global travel, and who knows what else. We do what we can to guard against it; killing poultry in fear of an avian flu crossing over to humans. But we do what we can not knowing if the pandemic is coming, and if it is, we do not know when or of what magnitude. You can argue about prediction endlessly and never really prove or disprove anything, at least not scientifically. This fact has not stopped people from doing so, of course, especially when they are afraid or wish to inspire fear in others.

So this brings us to the Danish statistician Bjørn Lomborg and the unusually concerted detraction effort his books generated. These books were *The Skeptical Environmentalist* published in 2001, followed by *Cool It: The Skeptical Environmentalist's Guide to Global Warming* published in 2007. The chronology of publications was as follows:

1. Bjørn Lomborg, *The Skeptical Environmentalist: Measuring the Real State of the World* (Cambridge: Cambridge University Press, 2001).

2. John Rennie, et al., "Misleading Math about the Earth," *Scientific American* 286:1 (Jan. 2002), 61–71.

3. Bjørn Lomborg, "Bjørn Lomborg's comments to the 11-page critique in January 2002 Scientific American," available via https://www.scientificamerican.com/media/pdf/lomborgrebuttal.pdf.

4. Bjørn Lomborg, *Cool It: The Skeptical Environmentalist's Guide to Global Warming* (New York: Knopf, 2007).

5. Howard Friel, *The Lomborg Deception: Setting the Record Straight About Global Warming* (New Haven: Yale University Press, 2010).

6. Bjørn Lomborg, "A Response by Bjorn Lomborg to Howard Friel's 'The Lomborg Deception,'" available via http://www.lomborg.com/sites/lomborg.com/files/bl_reply_to_howard_friel_0.pdf.

7. (also of interest) Gordon Moran, "The Lomborg Deception: Setting the Record Straight About Global Warming" (book review), *Journal of Information Ethics* (Spring 2013), 121–23.

Lomborg was well familiar with the famous quote about statistics, popularized by Mark Twain: "There are three kinds of lies: lies, damn lies, and statistics."[81] But this is one of the beauties of Lomborg's *The Skeptical Environmentalist*, for he claimed to use the very same International Panel on Climate Change database of statistics that informs climate change hysteria. Obviously his critics claim misinterpretation of this and other data, but Lomborg made a compelling case for exposing propaganda, in which the Worldwatch Institute, World Wide Fund for Nature, and Greenpeace (an organization he once advocated for) cherry-picked data and deliberately misinterpreted information to support a doomsday agenda.[82]

This is doubly interesting, because Lomborg believes that anthropogenic climate change is a fact; he just dares to conclude that climate change will not be catastrophic.[83] To counter the doomsday prophecy, Lomborg does resort to predictions of his own; generally of a much more moderate (and certainly far more optimistic) than those of the alarmists.[84]

There's an old saying about the most adamant preacher being the reformed sinner. This is why those of us who quit smoking cigarettes often become more adamant against smoking than those who never smoked in the first place. There may be something of that dynamic in Lomborg's work (or maybe not). Lomborg began his environmental research thinking he would confirm some of the beliefs he had formed as an activist. The evidence he uncovered began leading him to near-opposite conclusions. Of course, in a debate like this, we might do well to keep in mind Park's observation, "Both sides strive to produce better data and better analysis in the conviction that the truth will favor their prejudice."[85]

In any case, the early result of Lomborg's environmental research was *The Skeptical Environmentalist: Measuring the Real State of the World*. Of course, any book declaring to offer the "real state of the world" is bound to invite trouble, even in non-political circumstances. But rather than refuting Lomborg's findings or winning the prediction contest, Lomborg's critics did much more to reveal their own weak arguments.

The first absurdity occurred when *Scientific American* editor John Rennie declared the book a failure.[86] There's no such thing as a perfect book, but a (complete) failure? That rash over-statement set the tone for much of the pseudo-intellectualism that followed, employing the ad hominem attack, claiming misinterpretation of evidence and biased selection of evidentiary sources, and resorting to groupthink authoritarianism.[87] As Adam Briggle and Carl Mitcham wrote, the "vested interests of scientists themselves in preserving their own authoritative image should not be discounted."[88] This, unfortunately, was an example of just that.

Of course, resorting to the ad hominem is par for the course. The most notorious example I've seen was when Al Gore denounced Michael Crichton as "just some novelist," thus attempting to discredit Crichton's views on science. Never mind that Crichton was a rare genius completely regardless of his Harvard M.D. credential. Never mind (more importantly) that Crichton understood science and the scientific method, while Gore made the standard pseudo-science citations[89] to support his carbon-reduction policy agenda: the Arctic is melting (it grew recently), warming oceans are causing increased hurricane activity (unproven, and possibly the opposite), and climate-caused massive American West wildfires (we already know the major reason is fuel accumulation exacerbated by drought, the latter still unproven as connected to anthropogenic climate change).

Perhaps the problem began with the doomsday premise of Lomborg's critics, a premise that underlay their open policymaking ambitions.[90] Thomas Lovejoy (of impending Amazon rainforest destruction notoriety)[91] particularly revealed his hand when he wrote, "Lomborg seems quite ignorant of how environmental science proceeds: researchers identify a potential problem, scientific examination tests the various hypotheses, understanding of the problem often becomes more complex, researchers suggest remedial policies—and then the situation improves."[92]

Science is supposed to begin with an idea or a question—and an open, honest question at that—but for Lovejoy it begins with a problem. Maybe this was merely a poor choice in words, but *problem* is a presumption that presupposes a solution (or vice versa) and thus indicates the sort of agenda-driven quasi-science illustrated earlier. A problem begs for a solution. But what if the problem is manufactured to create a (false) need for a solution?

Lovejoy later criticized Lomborg for hindering their policy agenda regarding "urgent environmental problems."[93] But we have been talking about these "urgent problems" for over half a century now; it is the emergency that never goes away, never culminates in catastrophe, and never gets resolved. It reminds me a little of Chairman Mao's "perpetual revolution" substituting for any traditional or stable sociopolitical order. Lovejoy went on to claim that our environmental problems (arctic ice, seal level rise, etc.) had grown "exponentially"[94] when obviously that is not the case. This is just the same old doomsday premise, year in and year out. People with honest disagreements become "naysayers," according to Lovejoy's ad hominem argument.[95]

But, as Park warned, to insist that we "make policy before we understand the problem, if indeed a problem exists, is to invite failure."[96] If anything should be clear in this book and especially this chapter, it is that we do not yet understand many of our environmental problems.

Lomborg's critics developed certain pat arguments that do not stand to reason. One was to claim that the "social science" division of Cambridge University Press was not qualified to publish a work on statistics.[97] (If anything, Yale University Press should be ashamed for publishing their unscholarly diatribe *The Lomborg Deception*). This was irrelevant and a variation upon the ad hominem approach. The social science division was perfectly appropriate for a data-centric study like Lomborg's. This reminds me of other partisans who try to discredit a message based upon the messenger, rather than engaging with the evidence and its interpretation. Lomborg's critics followed up by related claims of superior authority[98] (the obverse ad hominem), not superior science. This is a form of what Alston Chase called the "Delphi approach," in which the opinion of would-be sages substitutes for scientific proof.[99] The Delphi Approach constitutes baloney, of course. For these critics, "being concerned" (preferably "alarmed") appears to be a credential in itself. Not being alarmed is heretical. They keep pretending that their competing predictions are evidence instead of, well, just predictions.[100]

Perhaps most bizarrely (or not), Lomborg's critics cited long discredited prophets of doom Norman Myers, Paul Ehrlich, and Anne Ehrlich as part of the coterie of authority discrediting Lomborg.[101] Apparently there is no expiration date in the prophesy-of-doom business, no matter how rotten the old debunked myths grow.

"Perhaps one of the most cynical critiques concerning science and the scientific method emanates primarily from politicians, interest groups, and public policy advocates who are politically conservative," Brent Steel, et al., wrote.[102] This is classic ad hominem; criticize the messenger rather than address the message, the evidence and its limitations, or the logical questions surrounding an issue.

Cynicism is the belief that all human action is explained by self-interest. But denying self-interest or failing to appreciate it is the epitome of naiveté. Recognizing the glaring facts of politicized science (masquerading as the "scientific method") for what they are hardly constitutes cynicism, nor can those millions of dollars in funding be ignored as motivating factors. The ad hominem criticism, creation of false dichotomies, and demonizing anyone outside the self-constructed consensus (itself an expression of power or an aspiration for power) is par for the course in these sorts of disagreements.

So in classic partisan name-calling, the Ehrlichs labeled Lomborg a political "conservative."[103] Climate debate in the United States, as we saw earlier, is undoubtedly polarized around general Left/Right political affiliations. But this false dichotomy is highly misleading when applied to Lomborg or any other intellectual, whose greatest "sin" was or is to have rejected the over-hyped doomsday premise. Refusing a doomsday premise is neither conservative nor liberal; it is an intellectual choice—and a very reasonable one given the long track record of fear mongering, doomsday that never arrives, and guesses dressed up as science that later turned out to be pseudo-science exaggerations. Often it is a rejection of futureology. Most importantly, it is a philosophical orientation which, as we know, cannot be proven nor disproven scientifically. Philosophy is the argument that never ends, as well it should be. So in fact, not to appreciate "science" in its highly compromised state would indeed be truly naïve.

I like Lomborg's choice for book title: the *Skeptical Environmentalist*. In graduate school we used to talk a great deal about the importance of "healthy skepticism." Healthy skepticism meant, "I'm not necessarily disagreeing with you, but I am awaiting your evidence and the logical argument you are making from it." It was not a crippling hyper-skepticism, which immediately degenerates into a metaphysical dead-end. Healthy skepticism was an antidote to gullibility or believing a source simply because you wanted it to be true, a human propensity related to Bacon's confirmation bias. I think Lomborg wrote his book in this spirit.

Finally, Lomborg conspicuously continues to focus on alleviating poverty in developing nations as one of the viable routes toward improved environmental conditions. Improve people's wealth and environmental improvement will follow. It is a compelling argument with a proven track record in western Europe, North America, and Japan. It is ongoing in India and everywhere people are struggling to get beyond mere survival. Ever since the Chinese gained an ongoing dynamic economy they have worked and are working very hard to improve their environment. No doubt this general pattern will continue in other places.

Uplifting the poor is hardly a passion associated with the "politically conservative." From my point of view, compassionate action always outweighs politically-correct rhetoric. So we could give Lomborg's action a label like "compassionate" or "humanitarian"; but is there even a point in labeling?

Lomborg is absolutely guilty of optimism. This is one reason I find his work so refreshing. He is also "guilty" of identifying the far more tangible problems of global poverty in contrast to extinction hysteria, climate dooms-day, and the all around Edenic worldview of much contemporary environ-mentalism. In other words, Lomborg focuses on global environmental justice, a far more pressing concern than the issues that preoccupy the environmental elite. Ironically, this is the more appealing environmental policy. Raise people out of survival mode poverty, and their first luxury is to clean up their imme-diate environment.

I'm not a statistician, nor am I going to re-crunch Lomborg's numbers. There are mistakes in every book, and undoubtedly he has made some. But his critics deny anything that contradicts their emergency premise and doomsday predictions. They ignore glaring facts, such as forests growing back, including rainforests. Different climate models *do* produce different results. How could they not, with humans feeding different data into them? Meyers, the Ehrlichs, E.O. Wilson, et al., *have* guessed wildly about species extinction, confusing temporary habitat disruption driving some population shifts with a conflated species-and-habitat destruction, as if creatures were immobile in a static environment.

So when Lomborg says he uses IPCC data, I am more prone to trust him than his detractors. In other words, I do not trust the Boy who keeps Crying Wolf. Why should I? Why should any of us? They have defeated themselves through past untrustworthiness alone.

It is worth mentioning that people like Lomborg are possibly more likely than alarmists in persuading skeptics that we are indeed altering the climate and warming the earth. Certainly it is the moderate voices who have reminded me not to overreact to the doomsdayists, sick of them and their well-funded lives as I am. So instead, I conclude—tentatively and vaguely—that anthropogenic climate change is likely a phenomenological fact. Drake, Crichton, Freeze, Barbara J. Finlayson-Pitts and James N. Pitts and others cited in this book have offered guarded and sober environmental assessments, avoided the ad hominem attack, and otherwise behaved far more logically (not to mention civilly). Thus, they should give us pause to consider deeply how we might be damaging the environment.

Ironically, these people trained in science would likely be disappointed even if they got their way policy-wise. Policy has a devilish way of perpetu-ating ambiguity like that. Just look at homeless policy, which resembles a half-broken wack-a-mole machine wherein one mole goes down, others come up halfway, some go sideways, others fall to the bottom of the machine—and yet the homelessness problem persists, decade after decade. There has been no policy silver bullet despite billions spent on various approaches.[104]

But aside from quasi-science supporting power agendas, some like the bogeyman. Often it is another group of people that we define as different or as an enemy. Sometimes it is a superstitious phenomenon, such as witchery or devilry. Sometimes we mix those two. Beginning especially during the 20th century, it became entire ideologies. The communism bogeyman generated untold billions during the Cold War for various military contractors (DOW Chemical, Lockheed Martin, Boeing, etc.). This was the "military industrial complex" that Eisenhower warned of during his 1961 presidential farewell address. Now the environmental bogeyman (a multi-head hydra) generates those same billions. Lomborg probably did threaten that Government-Quasi-Science Complex, but I doubt the funding will diminish significantly.

As mentioned, the western European public seem to accept anthropogenic climate change as a fact, but not necessarily an emergency nor an event with inevitably catastrophic results. That would certainly characterize Lomborg to an important degree. Why, then, the prevalence of high profile alarmists in the United States? Maybe they respond to the opposition and vice versa? Or maybe, like other topics, it has become part of a greater culture war. The climate debate in the United States seems to be as much or more about power and policy than it is science. The crusaders have made this repeatedly clear, whether or not they see themselves as doing so.

By the way, if climate change were so bad, why do so many New Yorkers retire in Florida? Just kidding. But more seriously, we are altering (micro) climates all the time already, and have been for thousands of years. This is how deserts and swamps become agricultural lands. Basically we alter the geography, but that includes climate and especially precipitation and its results. Greenhouses are microclimates constructed to enable plant propagation where it would otherwise be impossible. This is how people grow tomatoes in the Sangre de Cristo Mountains or Mexican peppers in Oregon. On larger acreage, numerous vineyards, fruit and nut orchards employ heaters and water sprayers to stave off damage from early or late frosts.

Granted, micro-climates are very different from the global climate. But given the benefits of micro-climate enhancement (plus a dose of common sense) should lead you to conclude that global climate change would have some good, some bad, and many mixed or ambiguous results ... but all only according to our subjective needs, desires, and values. Why on earth would you jump to the simplistic and indefensible conclusion that climate change could only bring catastrophe?

As many have pointed out, even if the planet is warming, all the news cannot be bad. Just examine the flora and fauna that now thrive on open land that was covered by the last ice sheet (the Wisconsin Glaciation, which covered most of Canada and parts of the northern United States in what is now the Great Lakes region). Since the mid–1980s, trees and grasses have been returning to Burkina Faso, West Africa, southern Sahara desert region. Farmers there are now growing cereal crops. Similar to the "irreversible" loss of rainforest, the old idea of desertification points-of-no-return seem to have been based more in fear than in reality.[105]

Ironically, climate trends in the Arctic and Alaska (with possible implications for Siberia and Canada) might be creating a "carbon sink" from thriving new flora, precisely where some scientists had once feared or forecasted massive carbon release from thawing permafrost.[106] As Frances Drake observed nearly twenty years ago, C4 species of flora (such as corn, sorghum, sugarcane, and many grass species) do not benefit from increased carbon dioxide, but C3 flora do (including potatoes, oats, soybeans, rice, wheat). Both groups include what we call crops and weeds.[107]

Overall the safest conclusion is that a changing climate will bring mixed results. Isn't this typical of life in general? In marriage we lose (or should lose) some of our personal freedom, and yet we hope the benefits will outweigh the losses. Or when kids grow up and move out; they anticipate all that freedom, but soon they appreciate all the new responsibility. You don't have to be a scientist to see the mistake in automatically jumping to negative or catastrophic conclusions. Talk of tipping points, runaway greenhouse effects, emergencies and urgencies, consistently end up reflecting power plays more than science. Who knows, maybe some of those privileged doomsdayists living in posh Palo Alto (and other luxurious places) actually believe their own prophecies. But even if they do, I do not anticipate such recreational fear compromising their splendid standard of living.

*   *   *

In 2009, after decades of upping the ante in their Cry Wolf alarmism, some of the doomsdayists played what would seem to be their final hand in many another scenario: they declared we had passed the point of no return for the next thousand years of climate warming.[108] Carbon capture and sequestration be damned, and any number of other future changes we cannot predict. This is the ultimate backfire, for now what would stop the response of, "Okay then, we're doomed, so let's eat drink and be merry, for tomorrow we shall die." But we haven't died, nor has the catastrophe hit. Yet the doomsdayists hang around, as they always have, and the super-funded ones will probably never stop. The 2009 study was based on one of many computer climate models, and the article carried a conspicuous section on policymaking; so much for the "detached science" of yore.

You would think the climate alarmists would eventually paint themselves into a corner, but they always seem to weasel themselves out later. Tipping points come and go and nothing happens. Maybe they have delusions of power, in which they will really be able to get their way by trying to frighten people. Not only is this prediction at its silliest, but it ends up defeating the very purpose the alarmists began with. In terms of policy effectiveness, if you're playing that game, someone like Lomborg has a much more sensible and sober approach. But just in terms of warming, the idea of a small and gradual change with mixed results appeals not only to our common sense, but what we actually know scientifically, not what we pretend to know through predictive models.

Back in the aftermath of the 1960s Counterculture it was popular to say, "If you're not part of the solution, you're part of the problem." The logic is questionable in general, and clearly false in certain instances. But to some degree you could probably apply it to the elitists' doomsday message. They are using scare tactics and living wonderfully comfortable lives with well-funded science projects and programs. Beyond that, who knows; maybe some of them actually believe their own mythology. But they are taking a great deal and giving so little in return.

We used to relegate futureology to divination, respecting omens and auspices. Now some claim to have a science of futureology, sometimes respecting prophecies of doom. It is interesting all by itself how prophecies of doom outnumber prophecies of bliss—but that's another story. Disbelieving bogus science does not indicate lack of concern for the environment. If atmospheric carbon indeed turned out to be the main culprit in global warming, we could already be removing significant amounts through carbon capture and sequestration instead of spending those billions on climate futureology.

Politics and policy move at lightning speed compared to scientific discovery,[109] and climate science very much reflects that. If, for some geological reason (such as massive planetary volcanic activity), we enter a new ice age, all the climate change alarmists will run for cover and pretend they never once predicted global warming doom. There, that's my prediction, undoubtedly completely unoriginal, and worth about two cents if you're feeling generous.

Chapter 6

Species Hysteria

The false premise of Eden extends to all timeframes. There was no past paradise, no literal lost Golden Age. Certainly we are not now living in an Eden, no matter how much environmentalists act as if we must preserve it. But what about the future? "Prohibiting extinction implies that existing species should be protected against future species that will not have the opportunity to emerge," wrote Julian Simon and Aaron Wildavsky.[1] This simple observation, an inevitable reflection of evolutionary biology, is rarely if ever mentioned among species preservation alarmists.

It is a conundrum. When I was growing up, people sometimes said, "Let nature take its course," meaning we should not interfere in certain processes, such as predators killing prey. But what does the phrase mean? Obviously we are interfering in "nature" all the time, and even when we chose to stand aside we are having an influence. Our awareness of all this creates the philosophical debates that will never end.

Like all things in our world, species and change cannot be separated, in contrast to the static world of the imagined Eden so prevalent in American environmental thought. Fluctuation of species—going extinct, emerging, and evolving—has always been a feature of natural history. Unfortunately, claims of species extinction because of human activity is more characteristic of post-war environmental doomsdayism than it is of scientific fact. Some nonhuman species would benefit if we did not interfere with or influence their habitat, but other species benefit *precisely* because we influence their habitat or because they enjoy adapting to our altered habitats of farms, parks, yards, and cities. Edenic thinking does little to inform us about the true dynamics of nonhuman species in the contemporary world. But Edenic thinking is also, to a remarkable degree, an understandable (over) reaction to past American environmental behavior.

The United States has a remarkable history of rapacious behavior toward natural resources. But let us not forget, it is also a main reason why the United States became such a wealthy nation. It is an ironic turn that we use the luxury of that wealth to look back and denounce the means by which it was accumulated. Anyway, the highly exploitative context informed George Perkins Marsh's famous 1864 book, *Man and Nature*,[2] one of the earliest and most influential studies decrying aggressive exploitation of natural resources. Miners ripped the earth apart searching for valuable metals and ores and left the tailings to pollute waterways. Hydro-mining in the California goldfields actively eroded megatons of earth in search for ore. And whether or not miners struck it rich, they left their messes behind them, of course. The marks are upon the earth to this day. And people think today's clear-cut timber sales are ugly? Marsh was living in a time when "timber stripping" and the "cut out and get out" mentality prevailed. Timber firms did not stop this destructive behavior until they cut the forests of the east and northern Midwest, then reached the Pacific Northwest and had no more massive swaths of big timber left to harvest. Replanting became a necessity.

Marsh also witnessed the beginning of the near-extinction of bison, which once numbered in the tens of millions in the tall grass prairie habitats. Hunters were killing or trying to kill any number of other species as well; eastern elk, white-tailed deer, eagles, any and all birds that ate crops, and all large predators and scavengers that preyed upon domestic livestock. In the Pacific Northwest, industrial fishers employed fish traps that helped decimate massive salmon populations. I've seen pictures in the Anacortes Museum of beaches several feet thick in rotting salmon; apparently only Chinook interested them at times, and they regarded some of the other salmon species as "trash" fish. Nineteenth-century Americans could be pretty rough on the environment.

It's wonderful that Americans now want to protect their environment and not repeat the rapacious past that rendered such environmental damage—often the sort that profited private industries, with taxpayers left with a latter day, expensive response. But it is ludicrous to pretend that our current environment resembles the pre-contact environment of just a few centuries ago, much less primeval Eden.[3] The American Chestnut trees that dominated many parts of the eastern forests are now more than a century gone, only surviving as sprouts for a few years until succumbing to the imported blight that decimated this species. Oaks and hickories have taken their place. Most of the grass species we know in yards, fields, and meadows are all European imports. Domestic livestock alone has rendered a landscape that would have been entirely unrecognizable to aborigines. Honey bees came from Europe and now pollinate plants both imported and pre–Contact. The list goes on. Parts of this picture various people might decry, others they might embrace. But there is no going back in time, and even if we could, the environment would still continue to change according to its components' volition, as it always has. Accepting change, as a matter of basic fact, might be a good place to begin debunking the premise for Edenic thinking.

Species preservation in current American habitats is, all by itself, deeply ironic considering how radically we have altered the environment since the 16th century. Some of the alteration was deliberate (nearly wiping out the bison and actually extinguishing the Carolina parakeet and passenger pigeon) and some of it was inadvertent with unforeseen consequences (accidentally importing the diseases that harmed elm trees and destroyed the American chestnut forest), and some of it was wrongheaded (according to today's values) if well-intentioned, such as transplanting kudzu to arrest erosion or English ivy as an ornamental. In any case, even if you believe that trying to arrest species extinction now is a noble idea, it still more or less epitomizes that folk saying of "closing the barn doors after all the livestock has already escaped." Appreciating and acknowledging just how much we have already altered the environment might also temper the false premise of environmental Edenism.

Instead, we're out to re-create a false Eden, whether through wilderness preservation or idealization of the Amazon rainforest. For example, regarding the depleted and fragmented Atlantic rainforest (on Brazil's coast, not the inland massive one), Milton Ribeiro, et al., wrote, "This present-day fragmentation has led to a large proportion of the forest's vast biodiversity being threatened to extinction; for example more than 70% of the 199 endemic bird species are threatened or endangered."[4] This sounds rather ridiculous from a writer in 2009, considering the Portuguese began cutting this forest over four hundred years ago, and that as little as 11 percent remains today.[5] But this statement captures the false emergency premise and extinction hysteria all in one.

Avoiding wide scale species slaughter of the past is an excellent idea, but substituting a static species preservation today is merely an obverse wrongheadedness. For example, in a television ad that aired on January 8, 2017 (and many times since), the San Diego Zoo boasted that they had reintroduced thirty endangered species back into the wild, and justified this practice "so the world works in harmony."[6] The latter is a false premise, since "harmony" (like nature in "balance") is a subjective philosophical value imposed by humanity, not a scientific fact of nature. This is Edenic Stewardship rather than realistic stewardship. Whether or not it is wise is debatable, not absolute. Current cultural aversion to the human presence does not banish said presence, and pretending to do so too often results in unrealistic and even irresponsible concepts of the inescapable role of humanity in the rest of the natural world.

So, even though few Americans are students of environmental history, one way to view our current Edenic impulses is to see them in this broader context as a reaction of regret for that earlier rapaciousness. But you can imagine the irony from the point of view of (say) the African Maasai tribe who hear Americans lecture them about killing lions that prey upon their cattle. "You mean the way you guys waged a systematic campaign against grizzly bears, mountain lions, wolves, and coyotes?" Or consider Americans upset with the Tanzanian villagers who poison elephants that eat their crops. "You mean the way you Americans wiped out tens of millions of bison? Or the ravenous Passenger Pigeon?"

Hence our overreaction extended to the rest of the world, manifested nowhere more clearly than in the final manifestation (following two earlier versions) of the Endangered Species Act (ESA) passed by Congress and signed into law by President Nixon in 1973. In a literal interpretation, the ESA mandates the impossible protection of all species.

In a primer for the ESA, M. Lynne Corn and Alexandra M. Wyatt wrote, "The gradual homogenization of the world's flora and fauna has led to a demise of many species."[7] This is a statement of fearful philosophy, not science. "Homogenization" all by itself is a wild overstatement, as anyone who has traveled even a little bit can testify. Corn and Wyatt repeat the reliable litany of common buzzwords; climate change, invasive species, and diversity loss as threats to various species.[8] They also write that "many scientists are concerned that the current rate of extinction exceeds background extinction rates over time."[9] The last phrase is not only Edenic, but Edenic with the added exclusion of humans. In other words, "background extinction rates" indicates the fantasy of how nonhuman species would be fairing were humans not on the planet. In other words, it becomes a philosophically constructed standard—at turns artificial, implying misanthropy, unrealistically removing humanity from nature or at least utilizing the questionable philosophical premise of humanity as separate from nature. The same is true in Reed Noss's use of "wilderness as baseline,"[10] making the theoretical nonhuman world the standard from which to measure our fall from ecological grace.

The same logic is employed with the "baseline" of biodiversity concept,[11] as if Eden in its current complexity is the standard against which all else is measured. Past configurations of nature and species complexities are permanently mysterious in any detail, just as contemporary configurations are. And, consistent with the prophecy of decline, the biodiversity proponents equate a loss in variety as equivalent with environmental degradation in general. Again, that is a philosophical concept, but not a scientific fact.[12] There is no teleology of maximum or minimum diversity supported by science. In fact,

Photograph by E.C. Stebinger, courtesy of Glacier NP Archives

The Blackfoot and Jackson glacier, Montana. Climate change alarmists regularly use such obvious and undeniable changes in selected glacial loss, jumping to the conclusion that anthropogenic warming is the cause. More nuanced questions arise regarding the state of glaciers worldwide, regional changes in precipitation that feed glaciers, and continuation of the earth's most recent warming trend that began thousands of years before the Industrial Revolution. We should remember that glacial science is comparatively young, and that politicized influences often obscure the highly complex questions pertaining to all environmental sciences (photograph by B. Reardon).

science could never really support any teleology. Concepts of goal-orientation (or lack thereof) involve philosophy.

The fact is, we are on the planet, and like all species, we have effects upon others. White-tailed deer in Pennsylvania have altered the forests by overpopulating and eating tree sprouts they would not otherwise consume.[13] Deer, elk, and moose in northern hemisphere forests in general have behaved similarly, also from decline of their natural predators, wolves, mountain lions, bears.[14] Of course, to a major extent, humans have replaced their natural predators with automobiles; for many years now, the most common source of deer death in the United States. Yet all these cars have not quelled the overpopulation. Lyme disease has exploded in the northeast of late, due to proliferation of mice. Various outbreaks of the Black Death (*Yersinia pestis*) were the results of an "invasive species" of *coccobacillus* that sent millions of humans to their graves. The fact that humans have been facilitators of these phenomenon is irrelevant for all practical purposes. Some humans obviously transplanted northern pike in various mountain lakes in the Cascades and Sierras, far from their pre-human contact habitat. But the eastern barred owl flew in to the Pacific Northwest—albeit across a "human-altered" continent— to compete with the northern spotted owl on its own. Other species (like the zebra mussels, Asian carp, brown tree snakes, or chestnut blight) have hitch-hiked on boats, ocean barges, airplanes, and other means of transport.

The point is, there is no environment on earth *not* influenced by human-ity one way or another. So species like the panda live on due to *our* nurturing in the wake of *us* destroying much of their habitat. Species like sparrows need no nurturing (though we feed them anyway) in urban settings that replaced earlier habitats of farm, field, and forest. This is the human stewardship rub, in many ways. We're in this mix whether we like it or not. Obviously we're already dealing with it daily, cutting back kudzu and Himalayan blackberry and English ivy, ripping out scotch broom, cutting down eucalyptus trees, and asking boat owners to check for zebra mussels before "putting in" at mountain lakes and other waters. It's just our philosophy that hasn't caught up yet, nor has our acceptance that we are not living in Eden and our stew-ardship roles carry with them philosophical value as well as some scientific knowledge (not to mention economic interests).

* * *

As many have noted, all species go extinct. But the more misanthropic doomsdayists get their glee defused if they stop and consider that "extinction" does not necessary imply the fate of specific species like the dodo bird or the Carolina parakeet. Another option is morphing into new species (hence one of the problematic aspects of our artificial category, "species"). Our primate ancestry goes back over eighty million years and even the genus *Homo* (closer to eighteen million years ago) has left many earlier species in the dust—such as *Homo habilis* (morphing from the earlier genus *Australopithecus*), *Homo erectus*, or *Homo neanderthalensis*. The latter is instructive, for the Nean-derthal genes live on in small percentages among all of the world's populations except for those originating in Sub-Saharan Africa. So, as opposed to com-plete termination, morphing and evolving is an obvious fate of species, and we humans with our penchant for categorization should not take our cate-gories too seriously. Life is evolutionary change, so of course species as we classify them disappear. Yet even dinosaur remnants live on in birds.

All species compete to survive, and competition is a driving force in both extinction and evolution. Humans have been competing to survive for a long time. Some prehistorians are convinced that early humans contributed (along with other factors, like a changing climate) to the extinction of megafauna such as mastodon or giant sloth.[15] This is not to be confused with contemporary species extinction alarmism.

One of the fundamental problems with the Endangered Species Act is an inability of scientists, philosophers, or anyone else to offer a precise scientific definition of what constitutes a species.[16] After all, Carl Linnaeus's 18th-century taxonomy was hardly handed down "from on high," and other cultures have classified life forms in radically different ways. Even Darwin himself was never able to offer a clear definition and had doubts that "species" represented a true scientific category.[17] That's no problem, in and of itself. Science is filled with far more speculation and subjective categorization than the ideal might suggest. But for a statute as powerful as the ESA to be based upon such indefinite scientific categorization is also not an ideal place to begin.[18] It gets worse when you consider the slipshod philosophy of freezing current life in Eden that is built upon such a murky scientific premise.

Even if you accept the category of "species," no one knows how many there are worldwide. The widest range of guesswork stretches from a low of 3.5 million to a maximum of 100 million. Apparently most interested parties agree on a narrower spectrum of ten-to-thirty million,[19] but even that range is so vague as to defy what precision in science is supposed to mean. Just use your common sense and it is easy to appreciate how difficult it is to count particular flora and fauna, much more so to catalogue even most flora and fauna. And since it is difficult or impossible to count—and regardless of the false premise of freezing evolution in space and time for a handy inventory—it follows that we have little idea of how much or of what magnitude is the issue of human-caused or human-influenced extinction.[20] In the face of this doomsday prediction predicament, the prominent biologist Jared Diamond regrettably resorted to a call for us to assume that a species is extinct unless proven otherwise.[21] This sounds like the aforementioned "post-normal" science premised upon unproven emergency conditions. As Julian Simon and Aaron Wildavsky put it, "This intellectual strategy suggests that the biologists now despair of making their case with the usual tools of scientific inquiry and ask instead for support on the basis of non-evidential faith."[22]

Ah ha, so there is reconciliation between science and religion after all! Just kidding.

It is sad to report that the decline or demise of nonhuman species have been greatly exaggerated. This began in earnest when Norman Myers published *The Sinking Ark* in 1979, claiming we were losing over a hundred species every day.[23] This was the doomsday cadence for the time; an acre of Amazon rain forest lost every fifteen minutes, a square mile of Louisiana coastline lost every month, or what have you. As illustrated earlier, there were many exaggerations and dire predictions. Unfortunately, species extinction has joined the Boy Who Cried Wolf chorus.

In 1980 Thomas E. Lovejoy predicted 15 to 20 percent of all species extinct by the year 2000.[24] The following year, professional doomsdayists Paul and Anne Ehrlich (of earlier false population bomb prophecy) got in on the act. The Ehrlichs invented an extinction rate more than six times that of Myers.[25] By the early 1990s, the famous ant specialist E.O. Wilson weighed in with his guesswork, claiming that 27,000 species were being lost annually in woodland habitats alone due to forest "reductions."[26] All theses numbers and similar predictions were inventions. The actual extinction rate is impossible to know or predict, and Lomborg notes accurately that they could increase, decline, or remain stable depending upon obvious factors such as habitat loss or recovery, and human population dynamics and concentrations.[27] Going out on a predictive limb, Lomborg projected a mere 1 percent extinction rate between 2001 and 2051.[28] Again, Lomborg's prediction is only a guess, but in this case he probably deserves the credit of an educated guess[29]—which stands in stark contrast to the sensationalist propaganda he his countering.

In their particular extinction book, the Ehrlichs really revealed their doomsday true colors in a breezy, breathless, anecdotal book replete with the "fallacy of the lonely fact"[30]—and that's if their actual "facts" are correct in the first place. With no cause-and-effect argument whatsoever, they argued the following in a few lines: killing Amazon species would cause climate change, which in turn would trigger an agricultural production crisis and famine, which would then cause thermonuclear war![31] It was like they were hitting all the doomsday buttons in one tour.

The funding for politically-correct biology and ecology is evident in the massive number of books since the 1970s on species extinction and invasive species alone. Most of them are barely one step removed from sensational journalism.[32] Thus this and so many other environmental prophecies also illustrate publishing politics. Confusing status (Stanford or Harvard letterhead in the case of the Ehrlichs and Wilson) with substance has always been as common as dirt. But more common are books published predicated on sales rather than substance. Goodness forbid a peasant with no status try to publish an intellectually honest book.

The passenger pigeon functions as something of a poster child for past anthropogenic extinction. Humans even named what they thought was the last known bird, Martha, that died in 1914 in a Cincinnati zoo.[33] Since the passenger pigeon's demise, ornithologists have told its story as a tragedy, and the tragedy took on especially mournful tones during and after the environmental movement of the 1970s.[34] For example, Jerome and Bette Jackson wrote, "The Passenger Pigeon is gone, a victim of the growth of our nation, excesses, bottom lines, human ignorance of the interconnections in nature, and the bird's own social behavior and accessibility to human exploitation."[35] By "bottom lines" we have to assume they mean hungry people finding a ready meal or farmers desperate to preserve their crops, for the massive flocks could and did strip entire fields free of corn.

The Jacksons echoed Simon Reeve when he described how the passenger pigeon survived for "one million" pre-human contact years, but also another ten thousand years with aborigines. (We can see the villain coming down the pike now.) "But after just 100 years of concerted attack by settlers in the New World, the graceful birds had been pushed to extinction, testimony to the

Hunters killing a flock of passenger pigeons in Louisiana, ca. 1875. The passenger pigeon, now a poster child for species extinction, often ate entire fields of crops. It remains important to appreciate past human behavior within a particular historical context. In addition to historical empathy, such an appreciation can sometimes help us understand our own contemporary context and its contingent philosophical values (from Smith Bennet, *Illustrated Sporting and Dramatic News* [July 3, 1875]).

violent supremacy of humans."[36] Farmers at the time might have argued self-defense rather than attack.

Indeed, it is sad to think of an entire species wiped out … unless you were one of those hungry farmers trying to keep your family from getting wiped out. As Robert Whaples observed, "For good or for ill, the displacement of the passenger pigeon reflects the broader agricultural history of humankind—taking control of nature, driving out wild species, and replacing them with domesticated animals that are more cooperative at growing fat and being eaten."[37] Not just cooperative, in the case of livestock, but not crop-consuming as in the case of the passenger pigeon.

It's a little too easy to sympathize with the passenger pigeon from the comfortable vantage point of the well-fed beneficiary of … well, all that successful agriculture, among other things. So to some degree this is a classic meeting of emotion and logic, romanticism and rational thought. Our mourning of the lost passenger pigeon reflects our current values, in stark contrast to our past values. As far as science is concerned, our species outcompeted the passenger pigeon species. But since we are a self-conscious species capable of and responsible for environmental stewardship, we can debate topics like this and find ourselves confounded by the usual factors of economic and environmental costs and benefits.[38]

Bird sympathy in general comes out of an unfortunate latter day development of elitism. As so many have observed, bird-watchers often tend to be a self-appointed aristocratic lot.[39] I used to see them frequently in Skagit County, Washington; a gathering of upper-end vehicles parked along the roadside, a group of the monopod-wielding leisurely nearby. The British even have a word for the avid birder affixing pride on rare bird spotting: twitcher.[40] Twitchers themselves do not care for the term. In any case, this aristocratic affectation gives bird extinction writing an insufferable air of the moral high ground. "The unwashed masses slaughtered OUR fine feathered friends"; that sort of thing. Never mind that some of those masses were feeding the rich. And never mind that aristocrats of yore hastened some species' extinction, back when bird feathers and hats were high fashion. Of course, back then, naturalists (including the famous John James Audubon) regularly and gratuitously killed birds themselves. But then the elites changed their minds. It is all rather tiresome and predictable.

So many of us have become pro-life when it comes to nonhuman species, which is easier to do in the city or the suburb where killing our competition is out of sight and consciousness. It is nice that we gained the luxury of this vantage point, which helped foster the reaction against anthropocentrism. So many of us may wish our culture to stop dominating other species, but we cannot escape our unique and self-conscious role of enormous influence on other life forms. We've driven species into extinction. Now we rescue them from the same fate and "reintroduce" them into the wild. What other animal has such stewardship power?

*   *   *

Biodiversity is a philosophical value along with related concepts like "ecosystem health," "keystone species," and especially the claim of an "extinction crisis." None of these terms stand up to scientific scrutiny. As Sahotra Sarkar wrote, those enamored of the ecosystem notion "follow a long holistic tradition in natural history that tends to deify complexity."[41] "Deify" is the right term, and it clearly indicates philosophical value, not science. And this is not to advocate for simplicity or complexity, but rather to expose biodiversity as an inherently Edenic concept.

Forest habitats are generally more complex (and thus diverse) than desert habitats but—like the anthropological concept of cultural relativism—each habitat is best understood within its own context, and not necessarily in comparison with other habitats. Desert habitats are not as "diverse" as forest habitats, but they are invaluable habitats for the species that populate them. Like so many buzzwords and buzz phrases of contemporary environmental dialogue, "biodiversity" is really just a term with scientific pretensions cloaking other matters, often of a static preservationist nature. In this case, it is overwhelming concerned with human interference with and destruction of nonhuman habitats. We *should* be concerned! And we should avoid wanton killing, especially of the historical sort involving wanton resource exploitation. But celebrating diversity and complexity in its own right is of questionable philosophical worth and most definitely obscures science.

By the way, such earlier, rapacious exploitation was literally unsustainable, like the frontier boom-and-bust mentality in general. When an economy regularly enters a bust period, following over-exploitation, it is *ipso facto* unsustainable. That, by the way, is one of the few proper uses of the term in non-buzzword terminology.

All of human endeavor since before recorded time has focused on future survival. People struggled to ensure food and water supplies. They planned ahead each spring for the next winter, gathering heating fuel and repairing clothing and shelter. They prayed to deities for herd animals to return, or for rainfall and a good harvest. They did everything they could to *sustain* their lives and, as much as possible, provide for the sustainability of future generations. It was no big deal. It was just life.

Today's buzzword use of "sustainability" is predicated upon insecurity, a universal aspect of the human condition. Anyone who has never experienced insecurity has led a sheltered life or is so arrogant as to be unimaginative and blind to the possibilities of threats to their survival. But people in wealthy societies often take the basics for granted, and even come to feel entitled to them. Compared to most societies in world history, Americans have tremendous security regarding the traditional triad of food, shelter, and clothing.

Another aspect of "sustainability" regards the aforementioned reaction to past irresponsible behavior. Examples included many 19th-century practices, such as the "cut out and get out" timbering model, massive slaughter of bison, and mining practices that caused indiscriminate erosion and water pollution. Twentieth-century chemical dumping that polluted groundwater sources was also "unsustainable" even in narrow economic terms, considering the cleanup was far more expensive than preventative measures would have been—not to mention human and ecological costs. But now there are an array of laws reflecting a broad and deep societal response against such practices and behaviors.

Today's buzzword usage of "sustainability" feeds into the doomsday predictions so commonly found in contemporary environmental dialogue; in this case, fear of running out of resources in the future. Hence we had such sensational forecasts as "peak oil," which did not anticipate fracking alone. Not to ignore the problems that have accompanied fracking, but this is one of endless examples of our inability to predict the future.

So those using the "sustainability" cliché have turned it into a token of environmentally-correct superficiality. It sells properly-labeled products in places like Eugene and Portland, but does nothing to alleviate the woes of real problems, such as those in the "Cancer Alley" between Baton Rouge and New Orleans, a sad epicenter of environmental racism. Juxtaposing a buzzword with such a deep problem reveals it for its faddish qualities.

Biodiversity became a fad during the late 1980s and early 1990s, after ecologists found that field evidence began to debunk or at least qualify earlier concepts and practices. Balance in nature and climax plant and animal communities were discredited, as was any precise definition of an ecosystem. A faddish "ecology of chaos" was popular for a while, partly out of frustration with earlier failures to impose or even find order in nature. The better scientists already saw the wishful thinking represented by the computer modeling endeavor. So the next crusade began, to stop human-caused extinction of nonhuman life.[42] It has proven rather enduring, but of course so has the pop science concept of the long-discredited "ecosystem." As Donald Worster wrote a quarter century ago, "As one set of environmental perceptions and values faded away, another began to take its place."[43]

Biodiversity's scientific pretensions break down when you consider that, ultimately, it merely becomes a synonym for biology-proper.[44] Biologists disagree about how to protect biodiversity, with some advocating a hierarchy of preferential species protection, while others argue that we should preserve all species.[45] The latter sounds hopelessly Edenic; the former is probably an inevitable aspect of human stewardship. Even the Edenic preservation of all species would require our stewardship, but that sort of all-encompassing caretaking smacks of hopeless impracticalities. Perpetuation of one species (such as ourselves) is bound to cost other species, and very few humans are willing to sacrifice themselves for the sake of other life forms. Could we mitigate our impact by reducing our own population? Absolutely. Is human population reduction desirable for the sake of non-human species and ourselves? Almost definitely. But let us wish ourselves and future generations good luck with such an endeavor.

As mentioned, biodiversity gained momentum during the early alarmism predicting the end of the Amazon rainforest.[46] E.O. Wilson, celebrity biologist extraordinaire, became a proponent of biodiversity salvation and the funding needed to accomplish that end.[47] At one level this is classic Edenism; save the planet's flora and fauna in their current configuration, or at least until we can catalogue it all. The latter is impractical, the former impossible given that constant evolutionary change is inescapable.

The cautionary environmentalist would probably see biodiversity as related to biological complexities that we do not yet understand, and thus should protect before we deliberately or inadvertently destroy something that will be lost forever. That sure seems reasonable enough, and does not really clash with old environmental conservation ethics.[48] But conservation and stewardship face daunting choices compared to the non-solution of ideal preservation. If preservation implies simply setting aside certain acreages for minimum human impact, that presents few philosophical problems, though it is bound to raise controversial policy issues. Beyond that, environmental conservation and stewardship generally consume the concerns and activities of everyday life. Preservation remains a luxury we often cannot afford, much as we might want to.

In its most regrettable usages, biodiversity is also a buzzword that means little or nothing upon closer examination. For example, John Coykendall is a Tennessee gardener on a quest to save heirloom crop seeds originally imported to America. That is all fine and well, and joins a greater movement to avoid the increased pesticide use associated with monocultures (in order to prevent reoccurrences of disasters like the 19th-century Irish potato famine). But Coykendall said his efforts took on new importance as "industrial farming practices threaten the old farming ways, and the bio-diversity of crops."[49] So now heirloom farming is part of biodiversity, but invasive species is not, or at least certain particular invasive species. Used so superficially, such a buzzword means nothing practically or philosophically, much less scientifically.

* * *

Related closely with biodiversity notions is fear of "invasive" species. In a sense, "invasive" just means aggressively successful, sort of like Euroamericans versus Indians. Many biodiversity proponents object to invasive species on ecological grounds, because one aggressive species can cost the lives of other, non-competitive species—thus diminishing biodiversity (since the addition of the invasive biology does not count, in Eden).

In any case, invasive species ideology is perpetuated by one of the most widespread invasive species of all time, that of *homo sapiens* originating in Africa and now present on every continent, including Antarctica. There could be no greater hypocrisy regarding other species, nor could there be a more simpleminded failure to grasp a central issue at play: the inescapable role of humanity in the environment. Planet earth has a long natural history of flora and fauna migrating all over the place. One of the implications of "invasive species" is the naughty human agency involved (there we go again with the misanthropic streak of Green Calvinism).

Anyone valuing "nature" would have a difficult time objecting to non-human stimuli moving flora and fauna around the globe (except for those eastern barred owls), but those who do not accept humans as part of nature see some crime in the human agency of species movement. And yet aside from our accidental or mistaken (according to us) transplantation of species, we also have a long history of fostering some life forms while eradicating or quelling "pests." For most of human history, and still yet among impoverished people, human values most often reflect survival. Aside from practical concerns that compromise our economy, it is generally a great luxury that our human values are now intertwined with notions of invasiveness.

The human agency remains ambiguous. Naturally we regret how we have introduced species like lion fish, Burmese pythons, Asian carp—and, except for a certain breed of wine makers and eclectic salad aficionados—the dandelion. But we accept uncritically our introduced agricultural species, for we depend upon them for our very survival. In this context, "non-native" versus "non-invasive" becomes a bit of a bet-hedging terminology designed to avoid obvious ecological hypocrisies.

This is not to downplay the hazards that transplanted plants and animals have wrought. But one way to approach this topic is by looking at it through three lenses: economic, philosophical, and scientific. Human valuation especially pertain to the first two. The economic devastation of introduced algae, zebra mussels, northern pike (or what have you) should never be underplayed. But we fight back, of course, and will continue to do so. All species act in their own self-interest, at least to a degree. The invasive species interferes with our self-interest, and we interfere with theirs.

Things get much murkier when we turn to philosophical perspectives of migrating species. As already mentioned, there is a fundamental irony and hypocrisy for a land-of-immigrants nation like the United States to become the headquarters of a manufactured Eden that (I assume) is supposed to be free of "invasive" species. And, believe it or not, there is a long tradition analogously associating human immigrants and immigrant fauna, and especially flora, with a concomitant "native" versus "alien" contest. Whether or not you accept this analogy, you can find it in debates of the national mood in pre–Nazi Germany (and of course the Nazi era itself) as well as in arguments over Australian eucalyptus trees transplanted in California, along with cosmopolitanism vying against xenophobia. In any case, we'll return to philosophical considerations below.

Finally, scientifically, "invasive" species—whether deliberately or inadvertently introduced by humans—is but a variation upon the theme of evolutionary biology. The biologist John Kricher is probably right; evolution is the best explanatory theme we have for understanding biology,[50] and evolution involves the life force of *everything* trying to survive and reproduce. Parasites and disease do it even at the expense of their host and thus ultimately themselves. That is what a relentless, driving, "mindless" power the life force is. And if there is one biological teleology in the world, it has always been this: to survive and reproduce.

In any case, so-called invasive species does nothing outside of this ordinary understanding of biology. It is only we, in our inescapable and self-conscious stewardship role, who assign various values to what we want and reject as flora and fauna neighbors. Despite the protests of some biologists and ecologists, when we are speaking scientifically, nature is never out of place,[51] but philosophically we definitely believe that portions of it are.

So to reiterate, what "invasive" reflects is a human valuation against various flora and fauna that tend to spread and dominate aggressively at the expense of other flora and fauna, especially the *faux* sacred "native" species. At one level this is farcical, at another it is common sense. First, the common sense.

When I was a boy we lived in western North Carolina for a few years. I remember my father coming home from work at the end of a summer day and driving over kudzu vine that had literally moved into the driveway during his absence. It grows that fast. If you don't cut back kudzu, it will literally smother centuries-old oak trees. We like oak trees, so we try to save them from the kudzu. Where I live now, the introduced Himalayan blackberry would also overtake entire yards and even houses if we did not cut it back. I've seen vehicles barely discernable underneath several summers' worth of growth. It is not nearly as aggressive as kudzu, but it requires trimming many times a year, and weekly vigilance is not uncalled for during late summer growth spurts.

The human valuation part is what gets subsumed in the Edenic worldview. For example, the Audubon Society sees various plants and animals as "introduced" in the Pacific Northwest without acknowledging that humans are also an introduced species.[52] People dislike introduced slugs and rats, but endorse introduced oysters, clams, and pheasants.[53] There is nothing wrong with this, except that such ubiquitous human valuation sneaks in everywhere, contradicting the untenable Edenic premise. Why not simply abandon the Eden premise and focus on other things, such as details of why we value what we value? Then we could attempt to distinguish between our philosophical beliefs and scientific facts (or, more commonly, scientific lacunae). Then we could decide if and when scientific understanding informs our philosophical beliefs, discuss the practical aspects of what we do, and possible compromises we want to make involving utilitarianism, pragmatism, aesthetics, and consideration for the well being of other life forms.

*   *   *

The short documentary film *Butterfly Town, USA*[54] illustrated several deeply ironic aspects of involving invasiveness and Edenic stewardship. First of all, Pacific Grove (median real estate price over $600K in the cheapest part of town; more than twice that in the ritzy sections) is one of the headquarters of the "environmentally worried elite"[55]; a place where it becomes apparent what happens, when people enjoy great comfort and have time and money on their hands. Second, the conflict involving migrating monarch butterflies centered around the presence or absence of what (in other circumstances) is an invasive species: the Australian eucalyptus tree. What did the monarchs do before Americans transplanted these trees by the tens of thousands during the 19th century?

Other ironies include a California landscape altered in radically different ways that make the presence or absence of eucalyptus trees trivial. What about the millions of acres transformed into agriculture, eliminating or vastly reducing the milkweed plant, a favorite of migrating monarchs? What about

During the nineteenth century, Californians enthusiastically planted eucalyptus trees imported from Australia. Only in recent decades have they become controversial as an "invasive species" and (more importantly) as a potential fire hazard. Yet Monarch butterflies, universally adored by environmentalists, now heavily rely upon eucalyptus groves during their annual migrations through a California massively altered in innumerable other ways since Euroamericans arrived (unknown photographer).

all the highways and reservoirs? Pacific Grove would not exist without all these landscape modifications, nor would its residents eat much food. But all these considerations are lost in the righteous outrage over whether or not to have a certain configuration of eucalyptus trees. The filmmaker fibbed and claimed that the number of monarchs had doubled after the trees were kept, as if preservation had caused a population explosion, as if they had any true census of the butterflies at any time, much less before and after Bob Pacelli planted a few immature trees.

A confession: I am a fan of the eucalyptus. Somewhere deep in my little primate brain, it is the first profound aroma of my life, in the atmosphere of the Alta Bates Hospital where I was born in Berkeley, California, and most definitely in the Oakland Hills cottage (surrounded by a eucalyptus forest) where my parents brought me home from the hospital. Aroma, as we well know, is the most powerful, profound, and even mystical among all our senses. Aroma summons memories and associations we did not even know we had, and interestingly, they bring back the past in ways that we could not consciously summon even if we tried, even if we knew what we were trying to smell.[56]

So the eucalyptus aroma signifies something I can never really ever describe; it is my lost home, the place where I could never return (too expensive), a false promise that used to wait for me in the distance before I finally accepted my permanent exile. Not that it matters worth a damn, but if there were one place on earth where I would want my ashes spread, it would be in that eucalyptus grove on the west side of University of California–Berkeley campus; an appropriate tribute to that once-grand institution that never has any association with pariahs like me.

But back to the eucalyptus debate. A great many Californians are fond of the imported tree, along with who knows how many purists or Edenists who would like to see the species eradicated (I recommend the latter stop by any California Indian reservation and ask them which species variety they would like to see eradicated from California). Anyway, Achva Benzinberg Stein and Jacqueline Claire Moxley wrote a thoughtful article in defense of the California eucalyptus that (among other things) supersedes the false dichotomy of native/non-native species.[57] After a century of popularity, Edenists only began targeting the eucalyptus during the 1960s as an "invasive."[58] This sudden change in fashion alone should alert us to the trendiness of philosophy-lite that often permeates American environmental thinking.

Stein and Moxley recognized the contributions the eucalyptus makes to California, such as their hardiness in drought, service as windbreaks, and habitat for the monarch butterfly indicated above.[59] Stein and Moxley recognized the subjective philosophical values held by those opposing the eucalyptus. The scientific considerations are far more complex, such as how transplanted species affect the soil, interact with pre-existing life forms, and tolerate pollution (also "imported," by the way). And then there are the cultural values, such as those held by yours truly.[60] The fact is, eucalyptus groves create a different habitat than the ones that existed before humans transplanted them; just as California featured different habitats before Euroamericans built cites. Eucalyptus groves are apparently not conducive to hummingbirds or fostering salmon habitat, but are favored by other species like egrets, cormorants, owls, hawks, and blue herons—and, of course, monarch butterflies.[61] As Stein and Moxley wisely concluded (decades ago), the "world is a complex system of natural and human-made environments with layers of conflicting needs and is subject to major catastrophes. We cannot approach programs dealing with natural resources in purist or finite ways."[62]

This, in brief, offers an antidote to untenable Edenic thinking. But the eucalyptus debate continues despite such sound scientific and philosophical observations. The fire danger is quite real, and eucalyptus being an oily tree makes it a special target for those fearing fires in neighborhoods like the Oakland Hills where we used to live.[63] In 2013 a pro-eucalyptus group called Save Our Big Trees fought a legal battle against the city of Santa Cruz, which had amended its Heritage Tree ordinance to allow removal of eucalyptus and acacia trees on the usual grounds of fire hazard and invasive species. The California Court of Appeal ruled in favor of the eucalyptus proponents, but did not address the scientific aspects in any detail.[64]

The fight against invasive species is really an effort to manage change, and to create or maintain habitats whose components reflect the value judgments of humans. Again, the irony of the obvious human agency flies in the face of environmental misanthropes who routinely ignore the inescapable role of people "playing God" whether they like it or not. Our self-consciousness alone creates this paradox.

Now humans, somewhat futilely, want to declare illegal immigration status on certain biota. There is something quintessentially American about this; once someone has found paradise, she wants to slam the door and keep all others out. Former Oregon Governor Tom McCall once famously told tourists to visit Oregon, spend money, but for God's sake never to move there.[65] McCall was born in Massachusetts.

The opponents of "invasive species" remind me of the hysteria recently popular around Eugene, about the variously-imagined evils of "globalism" and the global economy. So far I have responded with the following: "The United States began doing business with China during the 1790s. Arguably the so-called global economy began with the age of European exploration, if not earlier with fourteenth and fifteenth century Ming Dynasty expeditions to Africa (led by the famous Zheng He 鄭和). In other words, globalism is nothing new; it is merely a matter of degree and details."

But, as Anna Bramwell wrote, primitivism became part of 20th-century ecology.[66] Somewhat related is a social egalitarian ethic mixed in with the environmental movement.[67] By the 1970s and 1980s, when early baby boomers were reaching their thirties, the socialist chic of the anti–Vietnam War era became passé. Then some of the leftover, would-be, or retarded imitators of radicalism adopted anarchism. The early 21st-century primitivists of Eugene, it turned out, were but a belated expression of that old impulse, which ran its course elsewhere decades earlier, even if part of its legacy went mainstream in things like wilderness and species preservation, invasive species xenophobia, unfounded fear of disappearing resources (the "sustainable development" myth), and no end of misanthropic rhetoric banning humans from the Garden. In all cases, the untenable premise remains, in the romantic notion of closing Pandora's Box, abandoning technology and science, and returning to a Golden Age that never was.[68]

*   *   *

"Speciesism" is an animal liberation term that is supposed to be somewhat equivalent to racism or sexism; i.e., humans discriminating against nonhuman species. This is, unfortunately, a classic example of philosophy lite, for it masks subjective values and the imposition of human perception upon nonhuman life. Human valuation of nonhuman entities is inescapable, and this alone reveals the fallacy of Deep Ecology's so-called "biocentrism." I suspect the Deep Ecologists' ironic anthropogenic valuation here is inadvertent, but that renders it no less anthropogenic. As far as we know, no non-human species could possibly realize whether or not we are assigning them values (and what specific values) as they strive to survive and reproduce. People assigning rights to rocks, trees, rivers, forests—it is still people doing the assigning of human values to non-human entities.[69] Ironically it is an anthropomorphic response arising from anti-anthropocentrism.

David Ehrenfeld wrote that the "long-standing existence in Nature is deemed to carry with it the unimpeachable right to continued existence."[70] The passive voice grammatical construction betrays his real meaning: *We* deem the unimpeachable right, at least if you agree with Ehrenfeld. There's just no escaping human valuation, and there is nothing wrong with that—but it is misleading to pretend the human valuation is somehow absent and that we're receiving these instructions from On High. Ehrenfeld went on to advocate preservation of the small pox virus as an endangered species, claiming "the non-humanistic 'existence value' argument is the one that matters more."[71] Not too many people would agree with this philosophically (or commonsensically), though Bernard Dixon and others advocated saving the last remnants of small pox for scientific purposes.[72]

People for the Ethical Treatment of Animals filed suit against British photographer David Slater, after the "selfie" photograph of a macaque monkey became famous. The monkey had grabbed his camera and accidentally took the photograph, but PETA was upset that Slater was getting the credit. PETA

lost the case and the appeal, and a judge reasoned that the monkey was inel-
igible to receive copyright for the photograph. Nevertheless, Jeff Kerr, the
attorney for PETA, said their "groundbreaking case sparked a massive international discussion about the need to extend fundamental rights to animals
for their own sake, not in relation to how they can be exploited by humans."[73]
But obviously this was PETA self-appointing itself to speak for animals, not
animals speaking for themselves. And this, as in this entire area of nonhuman species' ethics, represents the usual circular anthropogenic reasoning.
What is true for PETA is also true for the Nonhuman Rights Project, a legal
advocacy group working on behalf of animals. In 2017 they filed suit in Con-
necticut Superior Court on behalf of three elephants confined in a zoo. Steven
Wise, speaking for the Nonhuman Rights Project, said they had consulted
"experts" who all agreed that the elephants would rather be free.[74]

Again, this is humans speaking on behalf of animals. No matter how
noble we regard this point of view (personally, I'm opposed to zoos), it is still

Above and following page: **Admittedly, bumper stickers do not lend themselves to
deep philosophy. However, they can be quite indicative of the token environmentalism of the elite. These two messages convey some ironic aspects of speciesism. Are
"beans" not "beings?" Why is it okay to kill one species and not another? "Equal
rights for all species" sounds great, but who will be imposing those rights? At the
risk of sounding absurd, would we accept the rights another species imposed upon
us? So ultimately we are again presented with the unique situation humans find
themselves in, feet in the mud and head in the stars, both animals ourselves but self-
conscious and tasked with environmental responsibility (author's photographs).**

not animals speaking for themselves. Obviously. Furthermore, groups like these claiming to speak on behalf of animals are advocating a philosophical point of view that originates with humans. "Biocentrism" is a human construct and reflects human valuation. Thus Deep Ecology and biocentrism can never escape their anthropogenic origins. Other environmental doomsdayists appeal to human values outright.

Anne and Paul Ehrlich warned that our fate was directly linked with the fate of nonhuman life,[75] regardless of the fact that one species going extinct often creates opportunities for others. A famous example involved dinosaur extinction making room for mammal proliferation. Thomas Lovejoy (inadvertently or not) reflected another anthropocentric view when he wrote, "It is up to science to spread the understanding that the choice is not between wild places or people, it is between a rich or an impoverished existence for

Man."[76] It is no surprise to find nonhuman species' preservationists appealing to our own sense of self-preservation.

And yet ultimately, any given species favors and disfavors other species, usually along the lines of what constitutes food and foe. The human species is no exception. Since the Neolithic we have fostered crops and fought weeds as well as insects and animals hungry for our crops. Since the Paleolithic we have competed with other predators and foragers for food. It is only now, with our luxurious food supply, that we sit back and wax philosophical about things like native and non-native species.

Our species' subjective values are not necessarily mistaken, but we should recognize them and their far-reaching implications for what they are. For example, "cuddly" animals appeal to us emotionally, but also receive more scientific study than do "ugly" animals.[77] Proponents and critics of the Endangered Species Act selectively choose animals that appeal to our emotions or leave us cold.[78] Japanese concepts of "purity" led zoo staff to slaughter dozens of snow monkeys "contaminated" with un-pure genes.[79] Conservation groups openly choose pictures of animals that will appeal to potential donors. We're regularly rescuing birds, sea otters, harbor seals, deer, elk, moose, lions, elephants, tigers, and other animals that elicit our sympathy for one reason or another—but less so entire classifications of fauna like fish, reptiles, and amphibians, much less insects or microorganisms.

There is nothing wrong with this anthrophilia, except in denying we possess it, or that it shapes our perspectives regarding nonhuman life. There are also exceptions, but usually to support advocacy. The California condor (difficult to call majestic) became the poster child in the campaign against DDT. Biologists regularly warn that dying frogs or hermaphrodite frogs are warnings of environmental stress that threatens the wider "ecosystem."

Science fiction writers have explored the obvious possibilities, but the temptation to anthropomorphize is inevitable. There are exceptions, like the Blob, or creatures invented by writers like David Brin or Steven Baxter. More typically, aliens, cyborgs, robots, and androids tend to have faces, eyes, even arms and legs. Even when Mr. Spock mind melds with the creature Horta (which resembles a rug-covered moving boulder), he communicates back to the humans in English.[80] So at the very least nonhuman life forms and their communication must be rendered somehow relatable to humans if the story is to succeed. Maybe the particular strain of primate consciousness is simply too different for us to understand what plants and other nonhuman life forms are "thinking."

Nothing enrages vegetarians more than to point out the secret world of plants. They claim that people talking to plants only stimulates their growth because of added carbon dioxide. But what about plants that apparently thrive in an atmosphere of soothing baroque music but not head banger metal music? What about allelopathy, the chemical warfare flora apparently wages underground (and underwater) out of competition for nutrients and habitat?[81]

Tree scientist Colin Tudge wrote, "How trees remember, I do not know: I have not been able to find out. But they do."[82] He also observed how they seem to anticipate the seasons based upon the length of night. And, like so many others, he concluded that chemical communication explained much of tree behavior.[83] Pines in the New Mexico mountains emit toxins to prevent their cones from sprouting too close to the mother tree, lest competition for water and nutrients kill them both. Some plants emit terpenes when attacked by insects, preventing egg laying and summoning wasps and ladybugs to kill (for example) aphids.[84] Oak trees stagger their acorn production to keep the squirrel population unstable, thus insuring that many acorns will not get eaten during a bounty year.

Lately plant scientists have made remarkable strides that lead us toward a deeper understanding of plant life. Controversy continues, roughly along two sides of the issue first demarcated during the 1970s with the book and following movie *The Secret Life of Plants*.[85] Do plants "know" or "feel" things? Are they "intelligent"? Are we limited to framing such questions anthropocentrically? As Michael Pollan noted, the debate centers around "whether behaviors observed in plants which look very much like learning, memory, decision-making, and intelligence" should be conceived as such, or reserved for organisms with brains.[86] In other words, scientists are grappling with some degree of mammalian subjectivity. But let's suspend that important point for a moment.

Clearly there is an entire world "known" to plants that we are just beginning to grasp. The better botanists appreciate the limits of human perception about many things botanical. Ultimately it is very unlikely that a mammal will ever "know" what it is like to be a plant, any more than humans will "know" what it is like to be a nonhuman mammal. The more dogmatic vegetarians do not want to consider the sentient possibilities of the flora world, for they live off of plants righteously in avoidance of killing "anything with a face," as the inadvertent mammal-centric ideology has it. Mammal-centric ideology is an actual form of speciesism.

Deciding what is allowable and taboo to eat reflects various human values, culturally-constructed and otherwise. For millennia, people all over the world have used all sorts of rules regarding diet. On the other hand, animal experimentation presents us with an entire array of ethical questions that we have yet to answer, at least satisfactorily. The 1966 American Animal Welfare Act specified legal oversight regarding the "humane" treatment of hamsters, dogs, cats, and non-human primates—but did not mention rats or mice, effectively leaving labs more or less free rein regarding these less cuddly rodents.[87] But can there even be "humane" treatment in animal experimentation at all? The fact that we freely use rats and mice for lab experiments (with results dubiously transferrable to humans) illustrates how we value these particular rodents less than the aforementioned animals.

The fact that we have used primates, even for something so important as the polio vaccine, remains very disturbing.[88] Glenn Greenwald and Leighton Akio Woodhouse's recent revelation of experiments on beagles at Wisconsin's Ridglan Farms is so horrific that I will leave it to the more hardy readers to absorb the details themselves.[89] Naming but these two points on a much more complicated spectrum, few would object to experimentation that contributed directly to vaccines against diseases that ravage the human population. But what about testing animals for the adverse effects of frivolous things like cosmetics? This topic is long overdue for entering mainstream debate.

"Speciesism" is central to an environmental dilemma that Green Calvinists are unable to solve. On the one hand, humanity is the evil force harming the environment. Wouldn't it be better if we all died in order to restore the Garden of Eden minus the creature capable of re-causing the fall from grace? So here is where the Green Calvinists hedge their bets. Saving the planet isn't really for the humans (they imply), but rather for the flora and fauna familiar to humanity. Never mind that human fondness for certain flora (like trees) or fauna (especially fellow mammals) represents the subjectivity of homo sapiens. Again, the Green Calvinists have inherited and perpetuated another biblical legacy: the Great Chain of Being.

Persistence of the Great Chain of Being worldview becomes even more clear among variations in the vegetarian world. On one end of the spectrum, vegans forego eggs and dairy products. "The only milk you should have consumed was your mother's," is the sort of phrase you see scrawled in graffiti around Eugene, copied from the vegan sermon. On the other end of the spectrum are vegetarians who avoid only red meat, or some who only eat fish meat. Cows, good. Halibut, who cares? Clearly there are all sorts of sects in the vegetarian religion.

More thoughtful philosophers in this vein of reasoning, such as Mahatma Gandhi or Dick Gregory, practiced and advocated fruitarianism, since harvesting ripe fruit does not harm plants. Too bad that a pure fruitarian diet eventually results in malnutrition, disease, and death for humans. Furthermore, humans eating fruit deprives other entities from this nutrition, whether those entities be birds or bacteria. Who are humans to judge bacteria a lesser life form than homo sapiens? In this case, even fruitarians would likely assert some self-defense on behalf of their own species. So much for complaints about "speciesism."

Hayduke is dead, but the Great Chain of Being lives!

This raises one of the greatest flaws in Jainist and Buddhist philosophy, which advocates no killing. The ancient Jainists and Buddhists can be forgiven for their ignorance of the microscopic world. We know now, of course, that the human body constantly kills millions of microorganisms (such as viruses and bacteria) in order to live. Again, so much of life requires death (or, more metaphysically, transformation). Unless we are embalmed or cremated, natural microorganisms eventually feed off the body that once housed a human life. So at any given moment everyone is killing microorganisms and plants, and many animals are killing other animals. Any thoughtful child faces this common scenario of life requiring death.

I remember watching nature documentaries when I was a kid and how my little sister got upset when a lion killed a gazelle. Dad responded, "But the lion has to eat too." My poor sister (about age seven) did not know how to respond to this. Indeed, how does any thoughtful human come to terms with our own killing?

Again, ancient humanity figured this out. The earliest plant cultivators observed how life (seeds) came from death (that year's crop), and thus prayed, hoped, and worked to facilitate this cycle and thus the perpetuation of humanity. As scholars such as Lotte Motz or Joseph Campbell have amply demonstrated, any number of "primitive" worldviews included a religious gratitude for the sacrifice of animals, through the hunt or a ceremony.[90] Native American traditional religion is replete with genuine reverence for the loss of animal life. This has been trivialized and romanticized and evoked an antidote by Shepard Krech in *The Ecological Indian* (1999). But despite bourgeois white people wishing to create an image obverse to their own culture, there is a deeper aboriginal truth revering sacrifice and regeneration. Salmon ceremonies in the Pacific Northwest and buffalo ceremonies on the Plains demonstrated this, as did James Mooney's 19th-century descriptions of the Cherokee worldview regarding the killing of deer.[91] The Western practice of saying grace before a meal has roots in the ancient Judaic world replete with reverence for sustenance as well as religious dietary rules. Religious gratitude for the dead life sustaining our own is older than recorded history.

This is not to idealize the past. We will never know how many prehistoric Indians were actually or deeply reverent toward the prey they killed or not.

Certainly they utterly depended upon wild food, so it would seem that self-preservation alone would eliminate some if not most of the frivolity and folly associated with luxurious modern life in the developed world. Do any of the environmental misanthropes think about what "developed" world means? i.e., human development of the "raw" environment into farms, productive forests, fisheries, and cities, to start—the basis of said luxury.

Some of the old-fashioned reverence for life and death shows up occasionally. Take, for instance, the observation of James F. McInteer, a wildlife conservationist of the old school, before the modern environmental movement. Back in the 1960s, many hunters and fishers thought of themselves as caretakers of the environment, and certainly they were interested in avoiding the depletion of the species they caught and killed. But McInteer objected to overextending the comparison of agricultural crops with fish and game. He felt taking the life of fish and game should not take place "with the same efficient thoroughness and detachment with which [someone] might dig potatoes or cut corn."[92] McInteer gave wild food "far greater intrinsic value" compared to crops, partly because he saw it as pre-human and part of "a Grand Design which remains forever beyond man's comprehension."[93]

Debatable teleology aside, McInteer's old-fashioned sort of environmental stewardship is something we would do well to appreciate anew. More on this later.

Another example might be David Peterson, who represents a small minority of hunters who seek a spiritual aspect in the endeavor of killing wild animals.[94] Some may object that it hardly approximates the ancient sort of prayer for the departed animal, but maybe that is asking too much. But by contrast, and especially in light of the post-domestication of livestock, the majority of hunters are probably killing animals "for the fun of it" even when they eat the meat.[95] On the other hand, vegetarian and especially vegan ideology reflects a wealthy culture that provides the elaborate nutritional workarounds not available in poorer countries.[96] So today, unfortunately, this sort of self-conscious food consumption has become more a matter of identity politics than the sacred reverence of yore. "Moral contamination" has become a mark of privilege masked as righteousness.[97] For all its fresh local food virtues, Alice Waters' famous Berkeley restaurant (the Chez Panisse) epitomizes this with its $75 to $125 dinners, not exactly the price range of poor folk.

I suppose all we can do is try to remember to have some reverence for the food we kill, whether plant or animal. This is one of the ironies often missed by those who philosophize about hunting. True, some hunters are merely egotistical killers. Many discover some primal thrill in exercising predatory behavior that lies deep in our DNA. Yet others quietly say a prayer of thanks for the beautiful creatures they kill, and part of their reverence is reflected in how they eat all the meat, tan the hide, and certainly try to avoid gratuitous waste. The latter would agree, there's nothing more preposterous than omnivores disparaging hunters while allowing butchers to do their dirty work, out of sight and apparently out of conscience.

Valuations of life require decision. People exercise these decisions all the time, such as the killing of "weeds" that compete with edible vegetables (vegetables that we will kill later). "Weed," of course, is a subjective concept that reflects human value judgment. There goes that mammalian arrogance again. Protect pigs, kill pig weed!

We will likely never supersede our subjective values regarding nonhuman life forms. But we should try to see ourselves now as products of a context, just as earlier people were products of their contexts. This is why the American consensus (for what it was worth) once endorsed the wholesale slaughter of animals (wolves, coyotes, bison) now revered by at least a significant part of the citizenry.[98]

*   *   *

John Copeland Nagle wrote an article that confirmed the practical impossibility of saving all species, but an admonition to do so anyway, as if the Noah flood story were a literal fact.[99] One misinterpretation of the Bible leads to another, for this is actually classic Edenism. Yes, not only is it practically impossible to save every species, but even the desire to do so reflects an untenable fear of inevitable death. When it is not attempting to "restore" species and their habitats to some lost Edenic state, it is seeking to freeze nature in time and place. It ends all human-influenced extinction, which is impossible unless the human species itself goes extinct. And what about evolutionary extinction, in which competition among species results in winners and losers? Isn't that natural, and don't we love nature? What about catastrophic events like asteroid impacts, tsunamis, volcanic eruptions, massive prehistoric global wildfires (any hint of which we attempt to quell now), floods, super storms, and other geological events that have been killing species before humans appeared on the scene? Do we embrace this as part of nature as well?

Misanthropic environmentalists love to focus on the "anthrocene" and exaggerate human-caused extinction. They generally ignore the implications of the five mass extinctions that preceded the arrival of *homo sapiens*. After all, humans cannot be blamed for those extinctions. But these fiver earlier extinctions illustrate the precarious fragility of life on earth through perfectly "natural" forces. That should give us pause and a sense of proportion. It should make us re-think our band-aid approach to species preservation within a false Edenic context.

Of course we should accept the basic fact of life's precariousness on earth—if, for nothing else, because we cannot control natural forces even if we tried. So we circle back to the old familiar: humans are a successful species possessing self-consciousness. We have been gratuitous killers of other life forms, and currently we are in a deep stage of regret for this past behavior … as well we should be. But that does not preclude acknowledging that this does not lead us to Eden, for nothing will. Instead, we're stuck with our stewardship role whether we like it or not, whether we fully understand it or not, and whether or not we fully grasp or even accept the inherent ambiguities that accompany such a role. We can only do our best, and a great many are making heroic efforts. Instead of chastising humanity in the usual hypocritical and misanthropic ways, sometimes we should pause and celebrate human ingenuity and its benefits.

Chapter 7

A Spectrum of Concerns

During the late 1980s, the smog was horrendous in Taipei, Taiwan. The English language newspaper reported that we had four times the vehicle density of Los Angeles (that perennial comparative city when it comes to air pollution). Worse, about three-quarters of those vehicles were two-stroke motor scooters burning a combination of gasoline and oil. We speculated that one motor scooter produced as much smoke as several cars. Then, in a trifecta of misfortune, Taipei lay in a basin of surrounding mountains, and thus high pressure weather systems tended to hold the smog down in the city.

So I undertook an experiment. My Chinese language school was a twenty-minute walk from the international student dormitory where I lived. One day I wore a white polyester shirt and walked to and from school. Upon returning I filled a small plastic tub with warm water—no soap—and soaked the shirt. The water instantly turned gray from the particulates the shirt had absorbed during those forty minutes of walking.

I'm sure Taipei is a cleaner city now, for it was following the familiar trajectory of earlier American and European industrial cities once choked with unfiltered coal smoke. During the 20th century, improved urban air quality tended to accompany a nation's rising standard of living.[1] But I remember the old Taipei as a cautionary tale lost upon the environmentally privileged of my current home in Eugene. There are real environmental problems out there in the developing world. Many cities in China and India still suffer terribly from smog.

I mention this story because the air pollution in Taipei was a real problem—not hysteria, not alarmism, not false science. The human body is nothing if not resilient, but having to breathe in particulates on a daily basis, year after year, is bound to take a toll. In concentrated industrial forms it has often resulted in diseases such as black lung (from coal dust) and brown lung (from textile mill dust), and can contribute to emphysema, mesothelioma, and cardiovascular problems in general. The lungs like oxygen; they will cope with anything else as best they can. Countless residents of Beijing, Shanghai,

New York City, 1953. Smog like this permeated all large American cities during this period, before technologies like smokestack scrubbers and catalytic converters reduced fossil fuel pollutants. In the developing world, such smog persists as a bane upon human health and an assault upon aesthetics. In general, as societies gain wealth they emit less pollution. This has been the pattern regarding air pollution in Japan, western Europe, the United States, and Canada. China and India are among the nations currently struggling to clean their air (photograph by Walter Albertin).

Kolkata, New Delhi, Mumbai, and numerous other cities would readily agree with this.

So I have to laugh when my neighbors express concern over the air quality in western Oregon, which is generally pristine by comparison. Still, environmental quality, including air quality, runs on a spectrum. This is important to remember, especially when we recognize purity does not represent one end of the spectrum. Even in the pre-industrial world people occasionally inhaled wood smoke, coal smoke, and dust or sand during wind storms. Our wondrous bodies have adapted to these realities for millennia. On the other hand, we have not adapted to acute or chronic exposure to any number of substances, especially a variety we have created since the chemical revolution of the mid–20th century.

*   *   *

I used to hike those wonderful trails (especially the La Luz Trail) east of Albuquerque that take you from the high desert (called the "Upper Sonoran Zone") through several more elevation-determined zones, but also including remarkable micro-habitats where a small stream creates marked humidity for about forty paces. Every bend in the trail revealed yet another stunning vista. At the top is or at least used to be a rewarding view of the city below. The last time I hiked up there, around 2000, the main feature was smog. Maybe that was an unlucky windless day.

Various trails in the Jefferson National Forest of western Virginia were also very familiar to me. Many eastern mountain ranges share the summer's humidity haze attributed to the Great Smokies. During the winter you could always separate the natural haze from pollution, for the air would freeze and dry. That is, until the 1980s, when I began to notice the haze year-round. It was no longer merely humidity, but coal smoke blown in from Midwestern power plants. The southern Appalachians in particular have had the misfortune of being downwind from many of these coal-fired plants. Aside from aesthetics, one effect has been the demise of last red spruce and Fraser fir habitats in the highest elevations—leftover species from the Wisconsin glacier retreat thousands of years ago.[2] Ironically, things may improve markedly, now that cheaper and cleaner natural gas seems to be killing off the coal industry.

Aesthetics fit on one part of the air quality spectrum, biological changes (comparatively minor and otherwise) fit on another. It is unlikely and unrealistic that an economic regime is going to change based upon these sorts of considerations alone, even if they preoccupy the Edenists. For example, where I now live, we have LRAPA or the Lane Regional Air Protection Agency, which administers the federal Clean Air Act but relies on local government funding.[3] LRAPA monitors air quality and issues alerts whenever conditions deteriorate. They enforce seasonal bans against outdoor brush burning. When high pressure weather systems dominate during the winter season, they issue warnings against wood fuel burning.

LRAPA means well, but reeks of Edenism, and often impotent Edenism at that. They issue inane public service announcements saying things like people using woodstoves should burn "only short, hot fires," as if wood burners had too much kindling instead of the more typical opposite. Another PSA went, "Even if you have a right to burn yard waste you have a responsibility not to."[4] Are you kidding me? There's an admonition easily ignored. Then they'll say, "Never burn garbage in your woodstove." Everyone burns some paper and/or cardboard to get a fire started, and since the advent of soy inks, these wood-fiber products burn no differently than kindling or logs, and also leave clean ashes. Only an ass burns plastic, which releases dioxin and stinks in that uniquely acrid way that no sane person wants to inhale. What other garbage is left? Metal cans? I don't think so. And with our recent rat outbreak in Eugene people would be better off burning their organic food scraps rather than putting them in composts—er, I mean, rat feeding stations.

An actual culprit LRAPA is powerless to outlaw are fireplaces, which cannot be manipulated with what I call the "blast furnace effect" available in even the most primitive woodstove simply through manipulating air intake and dampened exhaust. Instead of lame public service announcements, LRAPA should advocate common sense, such as keeping an abundant supply of dry kindling available at all times and, if possible, letting all firewood dry for at least two summers. Wood merely "seasoned" for a few months still contains a lot of sap.

I've been heating with wood since the winter of 1970–71, and I have never had a dirty chimney. That's because I burn dry wood, not merely "seasoned" wood, and never ever green wood. But I like gathering wood, splitting and stacking it, and having the "spirit of fire in the house," as my father used to say. I also like having a couple of winter's supply on hand.

In any case, LRAPA reflects a woeful ignorance about wood burning. I remember one winter a few years back, when LRAPA banned visible smoke from residential chimneys. During that ban I rode my bicycle the three miles between my house and the University of Oregon library. It was like being in a closed garage with a car engine running. Tailpipe emissions are obviously the main pollutant in car-culture America, and banning wood smoke when driving cars cannot be banned becomes rather ludicrous. Particulates from wood smoke are irritating; carbon monoxide is deadly. But this, in many ways, epitomizes environmental thinking in America: high wealth, very high energy use, no sacrifice of personal convenience, self-righteous moralizing, no end of hypocrisy from the environmentally privileged, and token environmentalism epitomized by SUVs sporting environmentally-correct bumper stickers.

LRAPA sometimes relies on pseudo-science to justify its existence. In January 2008, during a typical winter high pressure weather system, LRAPA claimed that "exposure to the fine particulates of smoke has been linked to cardiac problems, bronchial and lung trouble and allegories or asthmatic episodes."[5] Notice the passive voice construction: has been linked. By whom? This stinks of the pseudo-science surrounding second-hand smoke[6]; another of countless examples of "agenda-driven science." A little reasoning with the scientific method bears this out. What are scientists doing, cloning people and exposing one to second hand smoke for several decades and the other one not, then measuring the difference? Accounting for all other environmental factors? Genetic predisposition? Of course not. They're guessing, cherry-picking, or even inventing propaganda to support a pre-determined agenda. I dislike cigarette smoke and walk upwind from smoking stations whenever possible. But the false authority becomes a Cry Wolf claim.

But back to the well-intentioned LRAPA. When smoke from a huge wildfire near Coos Bay blew into the Eugene area during the summer of 2017, it broke all previous records for particulates in the atmosphere.[7] It was like literally millions of chimneys producing the sort of smoke you'd expect from burning green wood. After all, no wood gets greener than a living forest. I noticed LRAPA neglected to issue a fine to Mother Nature. And guess what? Wildfire smoke is not nearly so detrimental to health as the Edenists would have you believe, sensationally calling it a "smoke attack."[8] Amid this unprecedented pollution, Dr. Ann Thomas of the Oregon Health Authority observed that the temporary symptoms of breathing in wood smoke, while irritating, are just that—temporary and soon resolved.[9] In other words, it's not detrimental the way carcinogenic materials (like asbestos or coal dust) are, never exiting your lungs and causing health problems and death with prolonged exposure. Obviously the compromised air quality is worse for the frail elderly, but even my mother (whom the doctors claim has COPD) survived quite easily, without complaint, just by staying indoors. Those with preventable handicaps, including the obese and those who have never exercised their cardiovascular system, are asking for trouble in such circumstances.

Don't get me wrong—who is *not* in favor of good air quality? It's just the Edenic premise that renders a potential waste of energy and resources. The small, single-county agency LRAPA costs two million annually, but one could argue that its most regular "benefit" (as featured on local media) is announcing the quality of air in one of six categories: Good, Moderate, Unhealthy for Sensitive Groups, Unhealthy, Very Unhealthy, Hazardous. Do we need an agency telling us what we could surmise by sticking our heads outside and taking a breath? Critics even argue that LRAPA is not necessarily effective when it comes to industrial air pollution,[10] something substantial worth regulation and monitoring. In other parts of Oregon (LRAPA is unique to Lane County) this is done by the state Department of Environmental Quality. I'm not sure what makes Lane County so special, especially when we no more escape high pressure systems and automobile-generated air pollution than does Portland or Salem.

Air pollution in developing countries remains a leading cause of death, more serious than water pollution, and more deadly than diseases like tuberculosis and malaria.[11] That makes common sense as well as scientific sense; the lungs tolerate a great many substances other than the prevalent nitrogen-oxygen mix we call air. Yet, even here, there are the typical medical science difficulties in deriving any precise correlation between varying levels of pollution exposure and its consequences.[12] Generally, everyone wants clean air—but clean air is expensive in the post-industrial world. Dirty air and national poverty coincide. In any case, the smog of a Beijing or a New Delhi is a dire problem far removed from Edenic western Oregon. Still, if there were one last factor to demythologize the illusion of Eden, it is the fact that out here on the West Coast we detect mercury, carbon monoxide, particulates, and ozone that has blown all the way across the Pacific Ocean from China's coal-burning power plants.[13] What, pray tell, is LRAPA going to do about that?

LRAPA is but a subset of a larger phenomenon. The American Lung Association recently released its annual national air quality report.[14] It is, unfortunately, a classic reflection of Edenism and token environmentalism, combined with open fund-seeking and policy advocacy (especially against the perceived threats of the current presidential-congressional regime). The American Lung Association is particularly concerned that the Clean Air Act remain intact and enforced. The usual "scientific" arguments are proffered, with little mention of their problematic nature regarding causation/correlation alone. Climate change makes a convenient bogeyman appearance, as if people in climates warmer or colder or different from that of the current United States were somehow not coping. And finally, the report gives the usual sorts of finger-wagging suggestions about car pooling, using less energy, not burning wood or garbage, and the like[15]—behavior and practices that Americans have been largely ignoring since the 1970s.

More realistically, we're not going to reduce our very high energy use, especially as we continue to use computers, cell phones, televisions, and other electronic devices. Jimmy Carter proved the inefficacy of asking for lower thermostat settings and the donning of sweaters. Most importantly, we're certainly not changing our individual car culture; not only is there little or no personal inclination, but we do not yet have the mass transportation infrastructure that would accommodate group commuters. As for some major sources regarding garbage and wood particulates, municipal incinerators will continue to burn garbage and wildfires will continue to burn. Reducing the massive wildfires would be nice, but so far there has been little political will even to reduce the decades-long accumulation of fuel supply in the western forests.

The genuine air quality problems in the United States remain concentrated in particular places, especially the aforementioned "Cancer Alley" stretch along the Mississippi River between Baton Rouge and New Orleans. Otherwise, and especially compared to parts of south and east Asia, the United States enjoys the relatively healthy air we have come to expect in our wealthy nation. The Clean Air Act and other efforts have been positively effective. Obviously we could eradicate yet more pollution, but that will probably only happen if and when the internal combustion engine becomes obsolete. In the meantime, we should celebrate our improved air and stop measuring the nation's air quality against an impossible Edenic purity.

*   *   *

Numerous laws, if enforced, prevent a reoccurrence of the sort of environmental degradation that took place during the 19th and early 20th centuries. But we have new problems now involving air and water pollution. They are more complex, often more subtle, and just as intertwined (if not more) with industrial profit. I'm not against industry, harbor no conspiracy theories—but someone would have to be naïve to think profit motive is not a serious contender against good environmental stewardship today. The problems, as so often are the case, lie in the details.

It is easy to look back and decry timber stripping or rampant predator killing or highly erosive mining practices. But what about chemicals that invisibly seep into the water table? What about particular neighborhoods that experience a disproportionate amount of downwind air pollution? What about all that lead plumbing (including the solder) in municipal water supplies all over the United States? Many of today's environmental problems are more vexing than those of earlier eras. To offer just one illustration, the point-source pollution problems of the 1960s (pipes dumping waste into waterways directly from factories) lent themselves to straightforward remedies—again, if the law was followed. Non-point source pollution is more insidious, in a way, because it comes from precipitation runoff from nearly every neighborhood, farm, and paved surface. More about that later.

Today there is a middle course between Eden and Pollyanna that must be approximately navigated in many case-by-case situations, depending upon

Agricultural field run-off in Iowa, 1999. Such run-offs carry excess fertilizer and pesticide residue that contribute to "dead zones" in places like the Gulf of Mexico, Chesapeake Bay, and Lake Erie. This "non-point source" pollution persists as a serious problem, decades after Americans vastly mitigated "point source" pollution originating from factories situated next to rivers and lakes (photograph by Lynn Betts).

the problem at hand. These are the real issues of our time; not the poster child favorites of advocates. Ambiguity, mystery, and uncertainty make for poor poster children.

In the United States, Japan, western Europe, and Canada we have made great progress improving air quality. We removed lead from gasoline and began requiring vehicle inspections for emissions. Catalytic converters and more sophisticated automotive technology meant greater gasoline combustion efficiency, and thus less waste, which meant less pollution entering the air. If we ever master non-fossil fuel technologies for large scale use, we may yet see global air quality approximate pre-industrial conditions. This would be an amazing, wondrous, and welcome feat for humanity.

Water quality poses different problems. If anything should cure us of Edenic thinking to ponder real or potential environmental problems, it would be chemical contamination, which shows up in literally thousands of places across the United States. The overall story is complex, sometimes ambiguous, but other times clearly disturbing—particularly when it involves government regulatory and watchdog agencies obfuscating science and thereby compromising public health. This has been engineering professor Marc Edwards's experience since 2003, when he began investigating lead in Washington, D.C., drinking water. He found that the Environmental Protection Agency and the Centers for Disease Control and Prevention and other agencies were uncooperative and even oppositional to his efforts to rectify the situation. Revealing the extent of lead in Flint, Michigan's drinking water propelled Edwards into the international spotlight in 2015—but partly that was from the lessons he had learned in previous years, dealing with the unhelpful regulator agencies.[16] By then he knew how the game was played. We're a long way from the obsolete optimism of "better living through chemistry."[17]

As mentioned, determining precise correlations with illness and varying levels of chemical exposure is problematic, as are so many cause-and-effect scenarios in biological science, and certainly in medical science. This, unfortunately, plays into a common situation in which industry officials and their cohorts use the "doubt factor" to claim (with an element of truth) that the science remains preliminary. In a sense the science will always remain preliminary. We'll never do controlled lab experiments on humans, so there will always be some doubt. This reality unfortunately lends itself to conspiracy theories regarding industry motives.[18]

I myself seem to have a sensitivity to chemicals that probably biases me at least somewhat in favor of the precautionary principle. The abundance of benzene in Pacific Northwest gasoline (from Alaskan crude) makes me feel queasy with just one breath. I once had to stop work on a cabin restoration because (I later learned) a farmer upwind was spraying malathion, a perfectly legal insecticide; all I knew at the time was that I became nauseated, just as I did when planting trees dusted with Thiram, an animal repellant meant to give seedlings a better chance during their first outdoor growing season. In the latter case, my work day only lasted until lunch, at which point I was too nauseated to eat, much less work.

The Hoedads Reforestation Cooperative was the great hippie treeplanting union that negotiated their own terms with landowners. I assume they never tolerated things like Thiram. The treeplanting crew I was on did not benefit from such an arrangement. There were two planters the others semi-derisively referred to as the "Thiram twins" because they would not plant the poison-laced trees. The problem was, you did not know if you were getting Thiram trees or not until after a two-hour (unpaid) commute to the site, invariably located in a remote area far away from the nearest paved road.

The Thiram twins always brought along books to read. This was but a snap-shot of a much wider issue. Chronic workplace exposure to agricultural chem-icals is a serious problem, particularly among migrant laborers.[19]

Sometimes we go too far with the Edenic principle of perfect purity, when it comes to chemical contamination of the soil and water. On the other hand, those dismissing the precautionary principle altogether seem to rep-resent the pendulum swinging too far in reaction. As usual, the policy prob-lems lie in details involving economic and health compromises. Regarding human-made chemicals, a near-pure environment is practically impossible because of costs alone, not to mention toxins like lead, radon, and arsenic—all of which exist in nature. But when it comes to human-made toxins, how much contamination is too much? What levels of toxicity are we willing to accept?

During the early 20th century, and especially during the 1940s and 1950s, we underwent an innovative revolution in the field of chemistry that has given rise to so many daily products that we would have difficulty imagining our world without them now. These products include modern paper pro-duction, wood products (including their glues and preservatives), personal hygiene products, antibiotics and other medicines, and dozens of household goods like carpets, furniture, cooking and cleaning supplies. The upside is the improved material standard of living we practically take for granted. The downside is an enormous array of new chemical wastes, some of which are hazardous to human health and the well being of other life forms.[20]

But that's just the beginning.

Chemical contamination is a vexing topic. On one hand is the leftover hysteria of the overstated Rachel Carson premise of toxic chemicals in the environment. On the other hand, there are toxic chemicals that no one would voluntarily expose themselves to, if they could possibly avoid it. Then there's the strain of aforementioned purity obsession in America that finds its penul-timate expression in germaphobia. No small industry is built around this fear of germs, selling disinfectants, anti-bacterial soaps, disposable counter liners, and all sorts of sprays and cleansers. Ironically, some of those chemicals may do more harm than good, especially given repeated and prolonged exposure. Aside from this voluntary chemical exposure (in the name of purity!), inter-fering with exposure to germs contributes to later immunity problems.

Scholars and observers such as Lomborg, Wildavsky, and Kabat have helped us understand the false scares surrounding disease associated with common food and beverage consumption, living near electrical power lines or using cell phones, and chemicals like DDT, alar, and asbestos. But what about hexavalent chromium? Or mercury? No one would dispute the toxicity of those chemicals. But even here we get into complex issues involving various chemicals and the important difference between acute and chronic exposure.[21] Our Edenic premise must shift in this regard, if we are to deal with this issues rationally.

As Geoffrey Kabat has written, during the 1960s and 1970s, improved detection of human disease causation coincided with the rise of the environmental movement.[22] This fed right into old purity traditions in American culture. Add a sensationalist media, huge payouts for litigation, and we had a perfect storm of overreaction surrounding chemical contamination in places like Times Beach (Missouri) and Love Canal (New York).[23] But yesterday's stories continue today. We are still living, to some degree, in the era of "reaction" against the mid–20th century's chemical revolution—and yet some contaminations are genuinely alarming.

Perfluorooctanoic acid now contaminates drinking water in Hoosick Falls, New York.[24] Long Island residents and those getting drinking water from the Cape Fear River in North Carolina fear contamination through the unregulated chemicals 1,4-dioxane and a fluorochemical called "GenX."[25] As mentioned, the city of Greenville, Illinois, won a $105 million settlement against Syngenta corporation for contaminating drinking water with an herbicide called atrazine.[26] Hexavalent chromium became notorious after Erin Brockovich and Ed Masry investigated and litigated groundwater contamination in and around Hinkley, California.[27] Ironically, lead in drinking water—a purely human-made problem—is a serious environmental hazard in numerous municipalities across the United States.

As you can imagine, politicized and commercialized science gets infused with steroids in such situations. Conspiracy theories abound. But as Allan Freeze illustrated in detail, the actual situation differs from what the popular consciousness (fed by the media) has embraced.[28] What we face now is neither as dire as alarmists claim, but no one educated in chemistry or engineering would claim all is well. Undoubtedly we have become much more sophisticated when it comes to the field of chemistry, and thus prevention of contamination has a fighting chance. In the meantime, remediation of past contamination—and all the controversies, blame, expense, and negative health effects—show no sign of waning.

Contrary to what some believe, there was no corporate conspiracy to dump toxic waste in the environment. Rather, the legacy of environmental contamination we've inherited was more a product of naiveté.[29] It reminds me of those bikini atoll nuclear tests when the top brass (not just enlisted men fodder) were watching, wearing short pants and sunglasses. "Naiveté carried the day," was a caption I remember some author assigning to such a photo. In the field of history, failing to put such events in their historic context is called the "fallacy of presentism." In other words, it is a mistake to read into the past the knowledge and values we hold at present. What *is* important at present, regarding chemical contamination, is dealing with it scientifically. After all, the chemical messes we have made were negative byproducts of our ingeniousness—and only our ingeniousness is going to solve these problems, or at least in the comparatively short timeframe we desire.

Add billions of dollars in profits or losses at stake in the manufacturing of various chemicals, and "commercialized" science becomes difficult to distinguish from detached science. Then stir in media coverage of varying accuracy … and it becomes quite difficult for an average person to distinguish among real problems, false problems, and "acceptable" levels of non-purity. I am very much *not* a conspiracy theorist, but you would have to be naïve not to consider the billions at stake when corporations are involved with controversial substances like BPA and atrazine. Concerned citizens and scientists accuse these corporations of sponsoring bogus "science" to support the safety of their products, while corporations fight back and make similar charges of cherry-picked data.

Then we get to the aforementioned problem of medical consequences. If someone accuses a chemical corporation of their product causing cancer, the corporation is likely to ask, what other factors may have caused or contributed to this cancer? Do the victims smoke, eat processed foods, or regularly expose themselves to other chemicals (for example, common hair sprays, household insecticides, lawn and garden herbicides, carpet off-gassing)? Is the victim obese? After all, around two-thirds of cancer cases supposedly come from self-inflicted sources: smokers and the deadly trifecta of obesity, bad diet, and lack of exercise.[30] You can begin to see "reasonable doubt" leak in at the seams of such a legal case. Of course, often large corporations will settle out of court as a cheaper alternative to a trial and the concurrent bad publicity, but that begs the question regarding science, medicine, chemical exposure, and cause and effect.

Some people have genetic predispositions to certain types of cancer. Expensive cancer "studies" tend to involve over-exposing rodents to various substances—not exactly a replica of daily human lives.[31] And finally, now we're living long enough to get cancer and other diseases when, in all earlier generations, people died much younger from organ failure, accidental injury, blood poisoning, heart attacks and strokes, or what have you. Cancer is, in part, a cruel little gift to our longevity. Lest we forget, during and following the chemistry revolution that has given us so many products (including medicines) as well as new contamination concerns, our longevity has improved.[32]

Most Americans have dozens if not hundreds of artificial foreign chemicals and substances in our blood,[33] yet we are living longer than ever. The body (and the earth) is apparently more resilient than the purity-obsessed would have us imagine. That, of course, does not mean throwing caution to the wind.

On a happy note, veteran environmental engineer Allan Freeze concluded that "litigated science" (my term) tended not to compromise good science in court cases involving toxic waste site remediation.[34] This is remarkable, considering the high stakes involved. Helpful in this regard has been the overwhelming reliance upon judge-only trials rather than jury trials, in Freeze's cases. I had the luck of studying a parallel dynamic myself. I once interviewed Dorman Steelman, an attorney previously involved in a complex property condemnation case who advised his client along these same lines. Steelman was concerned that the case was too esoteric for a jury to understand. His client agreed, and they had a judge-only trial with satisfactory results.[35] Nothing against juries, but Steelman was right; highly technical contentious arguments are probably best put before someone with a graduate degree.

Unfortunately, beyond Freeze's personal experience of judge-only trials involving contaminated sites, there have been cases of "junk science" influencing court decisions.[36] This, of course, merely reflects one of many aspects of an imperfect legal system. Attorneys like Peter Nufeld, Barry Scheck, and Bryon Stevenson have gotten dozens if not hundreds of men off of death row using DNA and other evidence; these were innocent men wrongly convicted because of mistaken eye witnesses and poor original legal representation. Heroic lawyers and science came to the rescue. But there are enormous case loads out there and always a shortage of idealistic people who also possess practical tools.

*   *   *

Aaron Wildavsky compiled an important book just before he died, called *But Is It True?* It is a volume that should serve as an antidote to media hysteria about environmental matters. Yet, perhaps in its eagerness to function as antidote, it functions more to debunk than to offer an entire overview of chemical contamination. There is no mention of unambiguous toxins like lead, mercury, or hexavalent chromium in drinking water or food. In an unfortunate passage Wildavsky wrote, "no human ... has been killed outright by dioxin."[37] But this mis-frames the question. Dioxin is not a matter of life and death as much as it is (overwhelmingly) a matter of problems for the living. These problems include the skin disease chloracne, an apparent increase in still births and miscarriages, higher infant mortality, and an increase in the birth defects spina bifida and anencephaly.[38] Precise effects of dioxin and their extent remain controversial among research scientists, and there is no medical consensus over how dangerous dioxin is. But controversies and missing consensus is practically synonymous with medicine. In fact, the late great philosopher of medicine (and practicing surgeon) Sherwin Nuland embraced uncertainty as central to the entire understanding of medicine.[39] As mentioned, the Times Beach evacuation over dioxin was probably an expensive overkill reaction. The science journalism surrounding the topic at the time, during the 1980s, probably caused more confusion than clarity.[40] On the other hand, the current attempts to mitigate the terrible effects of dioxin in Vietnam (a result of Agent Orange) cannot be undervalued.

Contaminations involving trichloroethylene, perchloroethylene, and other toxic substances do not leave much room for ambiguity. In other situations, dosage of particular chemicals and personal health conditions and susceptibility play enormously important roles. In the workplace, Proctor and Hughes list literally hundreds of chemicals that workers can accidentally inhale or absorb through their skin. We try to categorize exposure based on duration, ranging from hours to years, resulting in acute, subacute, subchronic, or chronic conditions of compromised health.[41] We know from the past that coal miners and textile workers suffered from diseases like black lung, brown lung, and emphysema directly related to their occupations. In other situations cause-and-effect is far more ambiguous.

Wildavsky and others have been critical of the "precautionary principle" when it comes to such environmental matters.[42] But this phrase and concept is used differently by different parties, which adds to the confusion of its meaning and its purported intent. Generally and basically it means having government regulatory bodies prevent environmental problems before they occur.[43] Anne Ingeborg Myhr described argumentative and prescriptive versions. The argumentative version is pragmatic and focuses on economic implications. A prescriptive would focus more on risk and the dangers of scientific uncertainty.[44] All of the above might elicit a grim smile from Professor Marc Edwards in his noble endeavors against lead in drinking water.

The precautionary principle emerged out of the early European environmental movement, particularly in Sweden and Germany beginning in the 1960s. It spread from there, with other nations and organizations (such as the European Union and United Nations) adopting versions of it to address the common list of environmental concerns, such as air and water pollution and chemical contamination.[45] So today the United Nations, for example, recommends that governments should "consider adopting policies based on accepted producer liability principles, where appropriate, as well as precautionary, anticipatory and life-cycle approaches to chemical management, covering manufacturing, trade, transport, use and disposal."[46] Obviously what constitutes risk factors, their anticipated magnitude or likelihood, generates endless debate and disagreement.

"Only a small percentage of the sixty-five thousand or so chemicals known to be in commercial use have been adequately tested for their effects on human health," Allan Freeze wrote.[47] Enough ambiguity remains regarding the human body's reaction to chemicals and combinations of chemicals to merit our ongoing concern and monitoring.[48] Therefore, this is an environmental issue truly worthy of our time and attention, even if regulatory policy remains problematic. Wildavsky largely rejected the precautionary principle as placing an unfair regulatory burden on industry and the public. But many would be leery of rejecting the precautionary principle altogether. True, we are wealthy enough as a nation to be concerned with chemical toxicity, but as long as we overcome our unrealistic Edenic premise—as well as expensive overreactions to perceived rather than real chemical threats—we would certainly do well to be cautious regarding certain chemicals in the environment. The problem lies in the details.

Using legal documents and internal company records, Gerald Markowitz and David Rosner uncovered outright conspiracies in lead and vinyl chloride industries regarding secret scientific studies indicating health problems associated with their products.[49] More controversial is the hypothesis of pesticides, PCBs, xenobiotics, and other chemicals causing endocrine disruption, which possibly leads to infertility, brain damage, and other serious health problems.[50] Central problems of the issue include identifying the diseases involved, establishing valid cause and effect patterns between chemicals and ailments, and the old problem of extrapolating to humans the tests done on rodents involving high doses to small test groups.[51] Because of this situation, Sylvia Tesh concluded that the Environmental Protection Agency's "search for clear risk assessments as an objective guide to policy" regarding regulation of potentially hazardous chemicals was "doomed to failure."[52] Regarding PCBs in particular, Allan Freeze wrote that scientists and regulators had proven "precious little harm," leaving uncertainty to dominate.[53] Naturally, fear is bound to arise from uncertainty.

Some of the typical problems associated with endocrine disrupters, profits, regulations, and science came to light recently. The occasion was the 2012 report issued by the World Health Organization and United Nations Environment Programme (updating the 2002 report) regarding approximately 800 chemicals that many scientists have associated with endocrine disruption in humans and wildlife. James C. Lamb and his team of authors claimed the report was not an update after all, and that it employed biased and outdated scientific views.[54] Åke Bergman and other authors of the 2012 WHO/UNEP report fought back, claiming the Lamb team members were chemical industry lackeys "manufacturing doubt" without any scientific basis, all as a way to generate propaganda and confuse regulators who, of course, are not themselves endocrinology scientists.[55]

The general public is left to think what they may. We've seen in the past how tobacco's profits obscured both science and influenced regulation. Susanne Rust's reporting for the *Milwaukee Sentinel Journal* regarding BPA would almost assuredly indicate a similar pattern. It seems like pure naiveté to think that the corporate profit motive does not generate pseudo-science and propaganda—and yet, it would be a mistake to join the conspiracy theory mentality demonizing all corporations and their behaviors. There are some fairly clear cut cases, but ambiguity probably dominates the overall picture.

As with so many contamination topics, a number of fuzzy corollaries plague any exact science involving chemicals and endocrine disruption. What was a person's or an organism's dosage? Was it in combination with other chemicals? Were there preexisting health conditions? How long was the exposure? It is very tempting to err on the side of medical caution when it comes to such things, but there are almost always other interests, often of an economic nature. There can also be both positive and negative consequences regarding human welfare alone, aside from profit considerations. To some degree, this characterizes the topic of genetically modified organisms (GMOs). There are huge economic factors at stake, but also prospects of reducing pesticide use and feeding people who otherwise would go hungry or malnourished.

Many people raise the precautionary principle regarding GMOs. Not surprisingly, the European Union generally takes a more regulatory approach to GMO foods than does the United States. There are similar contrasts regarding BPA, atrazine, and other environmental concerns. In the case of GMOs, this appears to be because of the dominance of financial interests in the United States, regarding corporations interested in pursuing GMOs. The more socialized EU, by contrast, opts for a predominance of environmental protection, or at least their understanding of such. Compared to European regulators, their American counterparts also appear to have more confidence in science predicting GMO risk.[56]

GMOs are highly controversial in general, and promise to continue being so indefinitely. In a sense, GMOs may seem like an ultimate expression of humanity "playing God." In another sense it may seem like just another extension along an ancient continuum of the human species attempting to manipulate the environment for its own benefit. Definitely there are Edenic elements at play here, as well as the usual perennial question about humanity being a part of or separate from nature. Critics and skeptics often consider GMOs as "unnatural," since they are created by humans, in contrast to "natural" life forms not created or modified by humans. If only it were that simple. One could argue that all agricultural products reflect modified human creations. As Sean Weaver and Michael Morris wrote, "concern about the risks of genetic modification is not merely a debate between scientists on the one hand and well meaning but misinformed lay people on the other."[57]

Aside from philosophical differences and ethical, legal, and cultural concerns, scientists themselves have expressed much disagreement and uncertainty about GMOs based more narrowly upon their experiments and observations. Scientists have worried about genetically modified characteristics spreading from crops into the greater flora habitat, where such characteristics could influence wild plants, especially those plants related to crops. Wind and groundwater could transfer genetic modifications, as well as plant parasites, insects, and through the dispersed dung of herbivores feeding on modified plants.[58]

Ironically, the idea of genetic modification to mimic insecticides (thus aiming to eliminate or reduce the need for chemical spraying) could also develop a sort of resistance seen in chemical spraying, or in antibiotic resistance. Some scientists fear the rise of "super weeds" as a result. Scientists are also concerned that genetic modification for pest control, like its sprayed chemical counterpart, could harm insects we consider beneficial.[59]

We already know that chemical pesticides are not innocuous, even if Rachel Carson may have overstated their toxicity. A pesticide like *Bacillus thuringiensis* remains only on the surface of a crop plant when sprayed, but permeates the crop plant's roots and internal tissues when the plant is modified to carry *Bacillus thuringiensis* genetically. Some scientists are concerned that *Bacillus thuringiensis* will thus persist in the soil in ways it apparently does not when conventionally sprayed.[60]

Again, part of the GMO story reflects human valuation, sometimes obviously so. Many worry about eating GMO crops; fewer would probably argue equally against allowing genetic modification of mosquitos to control their population or a disease like the Zika virus, especially when spraying pesticides is the only other viable option.[61]

Plant geneticist Pamela Ronald has argued that "GMO" is an unscientific term, since all organisms are genetically modified.[62] She has a point. As mentioned, domesticated plants, animals, and ourselves have undergone genetic modification beginning at least as early as the Neolithic,[63] with indications of Paleolithic influences now showing up in the scientific record. Ronald also advocates GMO agriculture for all the usual noble reasons: food security in impoverished countries, reducing or eliminating the use of chemical pesticides, creating new crop varieties (such as flood-tolerant rice), and saving old ones from diseases that have no other cure (such as Hawaii's papayas).[64]

In 2015, popular science media personality Bill Nye stopped opposing GMOs after visiting the Monsanto corporation and actually witnessing gene modification in one of their labs. He was struck by the speed and precision with which the Monsanto scientists did the procedure, as well as how much the procedure had improved since the 1990s. He was also impressed with how careful all the interested players were—Monsanto, the Food and Drug Administration, and U.S. Department of Agriculture—spending years after the initial gene selection before approved modified crops reached the field. Finally, Nye concluded that GMOs were indeed just a sophisticated extension of the agricultural tools humans have employed since farming began.[65] But controversy over GMOs, especially when standard environmental villains like Monsanto are involved, is likely to continue for at least another generation. If the GMO controversy ends, some new development or procedure will likely concern or disturb the producers and consumers of food.

Crime and agriculture have similar dynamics regarding a contest that never ends. Criminals and law enforcement officials vie with each other in a constantly-evolving competition (think of all the new internet crime) that results in a mixture of punished and unpunished crime, use and abuse of authority. In agriculture, "pests" never stop feeding or trying to feed off the food we want for ourselves. We have been fighting them and fending them off for as long as there has been agriculture. Approaches have included the very basic physical human presence in the field or a simulated presence in the way of scarecrows. We have also used natural enemies of pests or predators, such as lady bugs and praying mantises to feed off of aphids and other insects, or llamas among sheep to fend off coyotes, wolves, and cougars. With the chemical age we began employing pesticides against insects and herbicides against weeds. GMOs are among the most recent attempts to combat competition and improve food security.

An old hippie acquaintance of mine used to plant an "extra garden" that she minimally tended, hoping to attract wildlife away from the vegetables she wanted for her family. Spiritually it seemed like a wonderful idea at the time, but it was ineffective in any practical sense. If only the deer knew which gardens we planted for them. If only wolves would prey upon deer and not sheep.

*   *   *

Ironically, instead of the Silent Spring chemical threat from pesticides, or a toxic waste dump contaminating water supplies, probably the most likely and most substantial chemical exposure that most Americans face is from their indoor environments. Worldwide, most people live in cities now and spend far more time indoors than outside. Homes, offices, and schools host an array of chemicals off-gassing from carpets, cleaning solvents, flame retardants, and other sources. Formaldehyde and a group of chemicals generally labeled Volatile Organic Compounds (including phthalates and phenols) appear to be the most common chemicals,[66] but it is the constant exposure that may be more influential, particularly for the usual vulnerable populations of children, the sickly, and the elderly. Connections with health problems remain ever-ambiguous, but some scientists worry that there may be causal links with endocrine disruption, various cancers, and other ailments.[67] Scientists have also found high levels of fluorotelomer alcohols (present in some cleaning liquids, glues, waxes, and paints) in home environments, present in household dust and indoor air. Fluorotelomer alcohols are among the substances that "off-gas," a phenomenon many people experience when smelling new carpet or applying paint (especially some of the primer coats). In 2006 the Environmental Protection Agency decided such chemicals were dangerous enough to require phasing out, and began interactions with industry to achieve this end.[68]

Obviously in the larger general picture, longevity has improved despite the rise of chemicals, indoor or otherwise. Humans have proven to be a resilient lot, despite media's inevitable focus on the exceptions. We should not let the exceptions frighten us too much, and we should not conflate the exceptions with the whole. As we have seen, except for the self-inflicted varieties, cancer is mainly an old age malady. Maybe indoor chemicals contribute to some cancers, but we'll likely never know to what degree. Exposure to potential endocrine-disrupting chemicals and the results are bound to rely upon a number of imprecise or immeasurable factors, such as duration of exposure and dosage, individual sensitivity to chemicals, genetic predisposition toward varying levels of vulnerability, or preexisting ailments or metabolic conditions that may make a person more or less susceptible to disease. In a sense this is but a subset of the eternal mysteries of medical science.

*   *   *

In 1987 a Chinese lady was advising me before I left for Taipei. She was confident I could survive in a then-developing country, for she knew I was not a typical American with a sense of entitlement regarding a high material standard of living. But what became irrelevant to matters of my personal poverty in Taipei was environmental quality. True, I worked all the time when I was there with little time and no money for recreation. I consumed myself with language study and English teaching. But it was the grim urban pollution, not my material standard of living, that really began to wear me down. After about eight months I found myself frequently taking a bus to the eastern edge of the city where I could walk through the forest to and from a beautiful temple situated in the middle of the woods. I can't remember who introduced me to that place, and I cannot remember the name of the park or the temple. But I remember going there with increasing frequency in desperation for a bit of relief from all the traffic and smog. Of course, I was spoiled in this regard, growing up in an American college town that featured a very nice natural environment. The campus environment in general I have written about elsewhere, describing it as a "garden apart." It certainly was and is far removed from the daily lives of the many millions surviving in the world's cities.

Grim environmental quality is a serious problem in the United States as well, and we find it clearly associated with impoverished populations and especially among African American populations. This is a criminally under-told story. Beyond lip service, it is not a concern among the environmentally privileged. It reminds me of white people claiming native identity in academia, which distracts attention from Indian reservations and the dire social problems that persist there. And so the elite pat themselves on their backs for reducing, reusing, recycling and other formulaic rhetoric while poor folk contend with a host of unambiguously grim problems.

1982 belatedly witnessed the rise of the Environmental Justice Movement, which now reflects a well-documented sociopolitical, economic, and demographic reality as well as an established academic field of study.[69] It is a complex topic, but basically it illustrates that non–Caucasian people (especially African Americans) are more likely to live near degraded environmental sites, sometimes specifically labeled TSDFs, or toxic substance disposal facilities.[70] Beyond TSDFs per se, these undesirable locations include close proximity to sewage treatment plants, landfills containing toxic chemicals, abandoned industrial sites (often called brown fields), and smokestacks upwind belching noxious fumes.

Environmental injustice basically involves places where poor people live because they cannot afford to move elsewhere, or because mainstream white society imported hazardous substances to their formerly desirable neighborhood. Regionally there is an "internal colony" aspect involving the South, with a disproportionate burden falling on southern blacks.[71] In terms of millions of pounds of annual toxic release, the EPA's 1995 inventory revealed that, out of the twelve highest averages, seven states were in the South. With the exception of Utah, the other states were in the Rust Belt Midwest.[72] Of the South's hazardous material disposal sites, over 58 percent are in black-majority zip codes, while the South's black population comes in at only 20 percent.[73] The historic pattern of disproportional burden is obvious, as other details illustrate.

For example, according to an EPA report, in 1990 Louisiana ranked first in the nation regarding toxic releases in both air and water. The main source of this was the so-called "industrial corridor"—also called "Cancer Alley"—an eighty-mile stretch of the Mississippi River between Baton Rouge to just below New Orleans. In this corridor, in 1990, there were nearly ninety chemical and petroleum refining plants.[74] The ten parishes of the corridor featured a population that was 38 percent black (with another 3 percent other racial minorities) compared to 31 percent statewide. Nationally the black population was 12 percent. There was a higher rate of exposure to toxic release chemicals in all ten of the parishes, and six of them were in the top ten percentile nationally.[75] Robert Bullard called places in the industrial corridor like Ascension Parish (majority African American) and the town of Alsen (99 percent African American) "toxic sacrifice zones."[76] The fact is, no reasonable person would want to experience the pollution in any of these places.

There are many other locations that exhibit this historic and contemporary pattern of poverty, racism, and environmental degradation: lead contamination in West Dallas, Texas (mostly black and Latino), wood treatment chemical contamination in the segregated black neighborhood of Texarkana, polychlorinated biphenyl (PCB) contamination in all-black Triana, Alabama, and mostly-black Warren County, North Carolina.[77] The latter location was the place that launched the environmental justice movement in 1978,[78] but the overall situation is far from rectified these many decades later.

In a way the problems of environmental racism are like the topic of global over-population: they are tied to much broader and deeper problems involving lack of government representation or responsibility, citizens' poverty, socioeconomic inequality, and consequent access to education and employment. Little wonder that the most serious global chemical contamination problems—and the interrelated problems of population growth, poverty, and environmental degradation in general—occur outside of the United States.[79] Thus environmental justice in its larger sense is an international issue; it is just that aspects of the "developing world" exist quite prominently in parts of the United States. But no matter where these problems exist, population rates go down as standard of living and education levels

goes up. Improved standards of living definitely include improved environmental quality. Reducing poverty is a monumental problem, and thus one
reason the "population bomb" hysteria came and went as an environmental
fad. In typical environmental elitism fashion, it focused on what frightened
the privileged rather than upon the complex problems that continue to plague
complex and multifaceted political economy issues of the poor and oppressed.

Environmental racism in the United States is one of a great many factors
that reveal the legacy of slavery is alive and well. Life expectancy, infant mortality, crime, unemployment, incarceration, broken families, homelessness—
statistics documenting these and other factors remain depressingly conspicuous
among African Americans in all the negative categories. Obviously it is vital
that the environmental justice movement has illustrated the toxic waste issue
as an important part of enslavement's legacy, and generally the legacy of white
supremacy regarding other non–Caucasians who also suffer disproportionately
from environmental racism.

Everyone wants to breathe pure air and drink pure water. Compared to
the tribulations of environmental racism, the environmental preoccupations
of privileged seem trivial. Having said that, the influence of profit at the
expense or risk of public health is disturbing in the United States. It's ironic
that one group sees regulatory agencies as hindering profit, while people like
Marc Edwards have witnessed politicized regulators as corrupting good science. It raises the question about whether or not the objections to regulations
are mere rhetoric, especially in the cases where Edwards found the regulatory
agencies hindering good science at the cost of public health.

Another problem arises with the "revenge of the C student" factor, in
which the lesser science graduate students end up working in regulatory
agencies rather than in more lucrative circles—academia, think tanks, or
industry.[80] I saw elements of this when I worked for the Forest Service, noting
marked contrast in some of the scientists there compared to some of my former professors in those same fields. Private attorneys involved with the Ozark
National Scenic Riverways made similar observations about out-gunning
their federal attorney counterparts. It is also almost a stereotype that the less
ambitious or competent doctors end up working for college infirmaries or
the Veterans Administration. Undoubtedly there are exceptions. But a scientist seeking wealth or fame or even the freedom of original research is
probably not going to work for a regulatory agency. Of course, some of this
becomes a distraction when it comes down to more serious issues involving
politicized science and the entangled world of private and public funding of
academic endeavors.

Like other topics discussed in this book, the future of chemical contamination cannot be predicted. On the negative side of possibilities, we may discover new links between human illness and certain chemicals or chemical combinations. There are bound to be greater biological and ecological impacts and influences we have yet to discern. Geological forces could move contaminated subterranean plumes in ways we cannot anticipate. Most daunting, illegal dumping remains a dire concern.[81] On the other hand, we've discovered new ways of mitigating and even eliminating contamination for all practical purposes. *In situ* destruction or chemical conversion has begun to eclipse earlier approaches at excavation and complete removal. Capping and curtaining plumes is effective in some toxic waste sites; others respond well to thermal treatment. Perhaps most exciting, bioremediation is an effective approach that promises much future potential.[82]

If you have any faith in human ingenuity at all, you have to think that in the future our species will find better ways to deal with hazardous waste before it becomes a problem in the first place. And this is true even though green science and green technology are woefully underappreciated in a popular culture fixated on invented environmental problems, misanthropic lip service regarding the natural place of humanity in the rest of nature, and all-around token environmentalism.

And so we have a spectrum of problems, some more concerning than others, all susceptible to media hyperbole, and all subject to sophisticated solutions or attempted solutions—whether that is remediation of past mistakes or prevention of future contamination. We can be cautiously optimistic as long as scientists and engineers continue to make breakthroughs in green chemistry and green engineering.

Chapter 8

Viable Green

A polite way to describe my high school years was "disinterested." Dropping out of high school after my junior year was a fitting end to five years of marginal participation in studies. Some years later, after college became my ticket out of an old and obsolete street life, I briefly became unreasonably enamored with science. It was clearly not the right fit for me, but for a while I was compensating for having ignored science altogether during my high school years.

The awakening that caused me to abandon geology as a major came during the first week in a chemistry class. I was lucky enough to have a friend who had earned a degree in geochemistry. He gave me some excellent advice that I still remember these thirty-four years later. I told him I had taken no high school science classes and was struggling with the freshman survey chemistry class. "You can pass the class," he predicted, "but you'll likely earn nothing higher than a C. Furthermore, all your other grades are going to suffer. You have to ask yourself if it is worth it."

It did not take long to make up my mind, and not just because I was (by then) unhealthily-preoccupied with earning high grades.

And yet, before I dropped the chemistry class, it had already made a mark on me. On that first day in class, on page one of chapter one, I read the *law of conservation of mass* and suddenly I understood pollution as never before. And that's pretty much the story with mercury released from coal when it is burned and how the rain falling through the smoke carries the mercury to the ocean, to the tuna, to us. It is the persistence of PCBs (polychlorinated biphenyl) on old industrial sites. When we were naughty, greedy, and/or ignorant stewards of our environment, what was out of sight was out of concern. But because of the law of conservation of mass—the first law of chemistry—we now know that many chemicals remain as potent or almost as potent as the day we discarded them.

Chemical contamination of our water supplies is a far more dire problem, generally beyond scientific dispute, than almost all the headline-grabbing environmental issues: speculations about future climate change, hysteria about species extinction or cutting down trees, fantasies about nature in balance, and doomsday predictions here there and everywhere. Not only is chemical contamination beyond scientific doubt, but it is a clear legacy of our past mistakes.

This is the background for green chemistry. Using the first law of chemistry, green chemistry practitioners seek to neutralize chemical toxicity (particularly in solvents) and reduce chemical waste. They also seek more efficient catalysts, which reduce energy requirements in the chemical processes involved with waste water treatment, paper manufacturing, food processing, cooling tower functions, and other procedures. Scientists employing green chemistry pursue the creation of new everyday products, such as detergents, that do not have adverse environmental effects. In the field of energy, green chemists are experimenting with the oft-repeated "alternative energy" forms, attempting to lessen our dependence upon fossil fuels, as well as invent new battery designs.[1] Finally, green chemists seek a new approach to chemical processes that combines minimally-toxic byproducts with economic viability. In a way, green chemistry is merely a more nuanced, more sophisticated sequel to our previous idea of what the chemical industry once naively described as "better living through chemistry."[2]

The "greening" of industry and its chemical processes began with mitigating pollution, then moved on to attempt minimizing or even preventing pollution in the first place. It was naturally reactive, because social consciousness changed in relation to conventional practices.[3] Laws like the Clean Air Act (1963) and the Clean Water Act (1972) reflected this changing social consciousness and new regulatory requirements for industry. By the time Paul T. Anastas coined the term "green chemistry" in 1991,[4] Congress has passed the Pollution Prevention Act (1990). Both reflected the new proactive status quo. Green chemistry actually began in the United States, circa 1990, but afterward became (as with so many environmental topics) a far more robust movement in the European Union. British law professor Joanne Scott noted that European Union green chemistry precedents influenced what followed in California.[5]

In 2008 California passed two laws regarding green chemistry, one establishing a regulatory regime for identifying and assessing hazardous chemicals, the other for educating the public.[6] Governor Arnold Schwarzenegger wrote that the legislation would "create a model for other states and nations to follow."[7] But it is important to remember the European Union precedent. The United States government as a whole has been slow to follow California's example. And except for Greenpeace, American environmental groups have tended to ignore green chemistry because it is too technical, and because they prefer standard agendas like climate change and "renewable energy."[8] Ironically, moving away from petroleum-based manufacturing remains a main goal for those working in green chemistry.

Being an applied science, market competitiveness factors into green chemistry considerations, such as the greater expense of cleaning up a chemical mess rather than preventing it in the first place. Profits also increase if industrialists can find practical uses for waste.[9] The wood products industries where I live reflects the latter; sawdust and wood chips that used to be burned or left to rot (both processes, emitting carbon) now go into laminated beams and other "glue-lam" products that have eliminated vast quantities of former "waste." I remember the first generation of particle board, which fell apart in the rain the same way cardboard did. Now, with improved glues, we can buy chipboard at a fraction of the price of plywood. This requires fewer trees, achieves an acceptable level of structural integrity, and all the while utilizes material that formerly got wasted.

The "notion of eco-efficiency" has become a new philosophy and a new reality. As Fernando J. Diaz Lopez and Carlos Montalvo wrote, "Green chemistry and green engineering concepts, tools, and methods are increasingly being seen as the ultimate stage of evolution supporting sustainable chemicals design and manufacturing."[10] So in a way, all green chemistry represents is our increasingly sophisticated understanding of toxicity. Naturally a toxic environment affects us negatively (along with many other life forms), so avoiding this is merely self-preservation of the common sense variety. That's the general story. The more specific stories involve (like all else in life) an unequal distribution of environmental benefits and hazards.

It is difficult not to see green chemists as among the greater environmental heroes of our time. Their work is also a celebration of human ingenuity and innovation—real solutions to real problems, not hysteria and the emotional satisfaction at being "outraged" or "concerned," which are all too often the fashionable reaction among the comfortable and the sanctimonious.

Another wonderful advancement in chemical understanding has been our improved knowledge of bioremediation. Oil-consuming organisms should not surprise us[11]; after all, crude oil has been bubbling up from the earth of its own accord long before the human species existed. Perhaps counter-intuitively, organisms evolved that consumed it. Another reminder that pre-human "Eden" contains messy and unexpected elements. But even more encouraging is the discovery of microorganisms that appear to consume plastic.[12] Of course, most plastics are made from petrochemicals, so the extension of crude oil consuming microorganisms to a synthesized products is not all that surprising, though most welcome.

Humans, by the way, have also figured out how to turn plastic garbage back into a petrochemical fuel.[13] Carbon-phobic critics downplay this innovation, while those worried about the accumulation of plastics in landfills see potential. Converting plastics to fuel, consuming the fuel and capturing and sequestering the carbon—well, there's a thought that is bound to appeal to those working in green science and technology. And finally, Tipa Sustainable Packaging and others are innovating to manufacture biodegradable substitutes for traditional plastics.[14] Making some plastics obsolete in favor of biodegradable materials could help a great deal.

In any case, no one wants an oil spill, but such disasters inevitably prove to be less dire than reported by the media at the time. Additionally and ironically, the human cleanup in a place like Prince William Sound (the Exxon Valdez oil spill) was destructive in its own right, arguably like the "cure" being worse than the disease.[15] This is an example of extremely expensive (as much as $2 billion) and probably poor stewardship. A less intrusive cleanup with the knowledge that nature would ultimately solve the issue would have been a wiser approach. Instead, admittedly tragic oil-drenched birds invariably make the news.

Oil spills are accidents, but "point source pollution" was common in yesteryear. This was when factories dumped their waste directly into creeks, rivers, lakes, and oceans with no filtering, much less any sort of chemical mitigation. This is how the Cuyahoga River caught on fire in 1969, from discharged or leaking petroleum products. This was why we once thought Lake Erie was going to be devoid of life.[16] I still remember seeing point source pollution as a boy, watching the Mead Pulp Mill drain their effluent directly into Scotts Creek in Sylva, North Carolina. Ironically, the discharge was a few paces away from the municipal swimming pool, so we kids would stand by the creek bank and stare in a sort of fascinated horror, wondering what it would be like to fall in that water that was all foamy and brown. I assume the effluent contained much tannic acid, but also added chemicals (like chlorine, sulfur dioxide, ammonium) depending upon their pulping process.[17] It is difficult to believe anything was alive in that portion of the creek, and who would want to eat the trout anywhere near where Scotts Creek discharged into the Tuckaseegee River?

By the 1960s, the Willamette River near my current home was not unlike the Tuckaseegee or Cuyahoga. Numerous pulp mills dumped their waste directly into the river.[18] Back then we treated rivers like open sewers, until the 1972 Clean Water Act began mandating reforms. I heard the Mead mill in Sylva did not comply with these new mandates for one reason or another, and had ceased operation by the mid–1970s. That was the choice by then: update your technology and comply, or close.

Technically, it is comparatively easy to stop point-source pollution. Doing so was a major accomplishment by the 1990s.[19] We know exactly where it originates. Non-point source pollution is another story. It comes from endless sources and places, like petroleum and anti-freeze run-off from innumerable parking lots and highways, fertilizer and herbicide run-off from farms and forests, as well as lawn chemicals washing into gutters and hence downstream. We have encouraged school children to paint those quaint notices on storm drains, about not dumping toxins, but who could stop anyone from flushing such waste down their toilet?

All of this creates non-point source pollution. The farm and field sources will not change anytime soon, and neither will the lawns owned by the neurotic dandelion chasers who seem to mistake their sod for outdoor carpets. The latter is perhaps the human urge for order gone too far. But at least phytoremediation mitigates some of these pollution impacts. Phytoremediation, like the aforementioned bioremediation, are but two examples of "green science" that is unfolding as we speak.

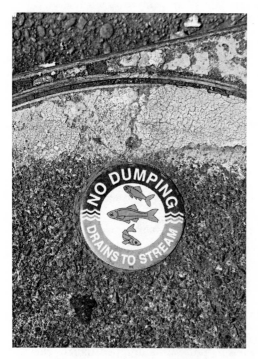

Phytoremediation employs "natural" plants, genetically modified plants, and sometimes a combination of the two to clean soil and water. Where I live these plants include spreading rush (*Juncus patens*), osoberry (*Oemieria cerasiformis*), slough sedge (*Carex obnupta*), and several others. Phytoremediation plants naturally extract chemicals in herbicides and pesticides, and even (astonishingly) heavy metals. Phytoremediation can take time to work, but it ends up being efficient and inexpensive, apparently without negative environmental side effects. The benefits are obvious for water quality alone. The plants interact with toxic substances by storing them or transforming them into inert chemicals. For example, plants can transform

These sorts of notices, commonly found on municipal storm drains throughout the United States, were rudimentary and inadequate ways of addressing non-point source pollution in urban environments (author's photograph).

mercury into mercury oxide. Other plants can store heavy metals that humans can later collect through "phytomining," which sometimes involves burning dried phytoremediation plants and collecting the ash.[20]

Employment of bioremediation and phytoremediation are but modern variations upon a very old theme, using or encouraging natural life forms to combat substances or other life forms we disfavor. Today we call part of this effort "biological pest control."[21] Almost two millennia ago Chinese orange growers placed bamboo poles among and between their mandarin orange trees to encourage predator insects (yellow citrus ants) to move around and feast upon pest insects.[22] There are numerous examples of biological pest control today. You can buy lady bugs and praying mantises to prey upon aphids and arthropods, insects we generally regard as "pests." Forest scientists release wasps to kill the emerald ash-borer and predator beetles (*laricobious*) to hunt

Phytoremediation in action (above, residential; following page, municipal). By planting flora that filters and absorbs chemicals like motor oil, anti-freeze, and lawn-application herbicides, we improve water quality and more effectively address non-point source pollution. While no silver bullet, this is human ingenuity at its best. We created the non-point source pollution problem; it is our responsibility to attempt fixing it (author's photographs).

the wooly adelgids that are devastating hemlock trees in the eastern United States. Agricultural scientists release a predatory mite (*amblyseius cucumeris*) to consume thrips, a common and widespread crop-consuming insect.[23]

Even biological pest control is no magic bullet, and introducing predatory species to attack invasive species should not be undertaken lightly. As in legislative history, environmental history is replete with examples of unintended consequences. Kudzu was wonderful for arresting soil erosion, but a little too aggressive without the Japanese herbivores that coevolved with it.

So we are not Pollyannas here. Environmental problems can be as vexing as their solutions are often ambiguous. But we should pause for a moment and indulge in a little optimism in the face of human ingenuity. Think about it. The coal-fired steam engine was once the wonder of the world; now it is largely obsolete or becoming so. It seems reasonable to imagine the internal combustion engine following the same trajectory. So many scientists and engineers are working on less environmentally-impactful energy sources, that it seems almost inevitable that our great grandchildren's generation will barely recognize the energy technology of our era.

Innovative ideas regarding energy cover a wide spectrum, both "environmentally correct" and not, from new generation nuclear power plants to solar and wind power, to harnessing tides and tapping into natural geothermal temperatures for heating and cooling. Even traditional coal fuel has entirely new potential when combined with carbon capture and sequestration procedures. Both the United Kingdom and Norway use much fossil fuel, but experience growing support for carbon capture and storage.[24] This remains more theoretical than actual for the United States. During the 2016 presidential campaign, Hillary Clinton selling the idea of "clean coal" (zero carbon emissions, when captured) to West Virginia and Pennsylvania miners would have inspired different reactions compared to what she actually said, about coal being yesterday's form of energy. Maybe coal *is* yesterday's fuel. But working people are desperate to stay employed at a living wage and often vote accordingly, whether to the effect they want or not.

"Marry economics to your idealistic cause and you have a chance," I always tell my students. This holds true with technology having the environmental impact (or lack thereof) that we desire. If people are getting jobs in the process, they might go along with the environmental benefits without even appreciating them. A great many would think, "Hey, I've got a good job and I'm helping the environment." Who knows, such a connection could even steer personal behavior toward environmental stewardship and thus help improve the broader culture in that regard.

Some would argue that clean coal—or any of the energy ideas described here—are not economically feasible, to which I often reply, "space shuttle." If we can dedicate billions of subsidies to an unprofitable space program, why not something practical on earth? Annual agricultural subsidies top $20 billion in recent years; why not new allocations or reallocations of public funds? I know, welcome to politics and the eternal fight over a limited pot of money. And I'll leave it to others to debate the complex policy issues at stake, especially when it comes to nuclear energy regulation. For now, let's just consider the technology.

There are many innovations on the forefront of energy, including new tidal technology,[25] a renewed appreciation for geothermal heating and cooling (the cave effect),[26] and innovations in solar and wind technology.[27] The rather old carbon capture technology has also made progress, especially regarding new ways of dealing with the captured carbon.[28] The latter could still yet have enormous implications for "clean coal" and other fossil fuel consumption.

But now to the bogeyman.

I grew up in the era of nuclear energy fear (I was nineteen when the Three Mile Island accident occurred), so upon this topic I must ask my logical mind to intervene. Watching the 2015 documentary *Uranium—Twisting the Dragon's Tail* was helpful. The narrator-physicist actually went to Chernobyl with his Geiger counter to show us that the site may not be what we think it is. Some areas emit radiation negligibly above the planetary average, quite in contrast to genuine hot spots where no one would want to linger. This is the situation with nuclear energy in general; a wide gap between public perception and scientific reality. This is the whipsaw. With all the fear and/or propaganda regarding nuclear holocaust (now passé, but reverberating recently with North Korea and President Trump's "fire and fury" warning), it is difficult to accept the use of a related technology for generation of electricity. And yet, as with so many other topics in our complex world, what do any of us know empirically?

Little appreciated fact: since the mid–1980s France has generated over 70 percent of its electricity through nuclear energy. It even became an exporter of electricity generated from nuclear power.[29] Today the French rely upon nuclear energy for about 80 percent of their electricity and—unlike the United States—recycle their nuclear waste to generate yet more electricity and at least partially avoid the nuclear waste storage issue that plagues America now[30] (another topic that receives only sporadic media coverage).

Recycling radioactive waste is nothing new. Way back in 1951 American nuclear physicists built a "breeder reactor" in Idaho. They called this Experimental Breeder Reactor-I, or EBR-I. This is an expensive type of reactor that offers two enticing features: it is capable of actually consuming nuclear waste as its fuel, and (unlike conventional light water reactors) it has greater failsafe features free of operator actions.[31] Today there are updated nuclear reactors that, like EBR-I, also consume radioactive waste and side-step the design weaknesses of conventional water-cooled reactors.[32] Of course, no reactor is 100 percent safe, and so public fears are bound to remain, especially following highly publicized accidents at Three Mile Island, Chernobyl,[33] and (most recently) Fukushima Daiichi. Yet all three of these accidents featured flawed or outdated designs.

I once heard an old logger make an observation about his dangerous profession. "It's the young bucks and the old veterans who get injured or killed. The young bucks don't know what the hell they're doing, and the old timers have been doing it so long they get careless."

Ironically—and here's the real rub—that old logger himself was fortunate to escape death or at least paralysis in a fluke accident that followed this observation. He was felling his umpteenth thousandth tree, and apparently the vibration of the chainsaw and/or the first slight movement of the falling tree jarred loose a huge dead branch about eighty feet up. The branch came down and clipped his back. A few inches over it would have snapped his neck or caved in his skull, hard hat notwithstanding. It was purely a matter of bad luck that the branch fell, and purely a matter of good luck that he was not injured more seriously (he was out of the hospital within a week).

This is a problem with many dangerous or potentially dangerous human endeavors, I suppose. Regarding a nuclear plant, the team and a fail-safe system can guard against beginners making beginners' mistakes, or old timers growing complacent, as long as enough people follow the rules. So Three Mile Island failed safely (despite the media not emphasizing this at the time). Chernobyl failed unsafely. But what about a fluke accident? What about a tsunami hitting the Fukushima Daiichi plant? And yet the latter became a catastrophe because it relied on water coolant, which in turn relied upon a steady electrical power source. Theoretically, a breeder reactor or one of the other updated designs would not have become a problem in the tsunami's aftermath.

Also, we should remember that oil refineries explode, tankers spill their cargo, and oil tanker train cars derail and catch fire. People heating with woodstoves or space heaters accidentally burn down their houses.

Contrary to some popular fears, environmental engineer Allan Freeze is convinced that nuclear waste is not the most important issue; rather, it is nuclear plant accidents. Nuclear physicists and engineers apparently agree. Freeze believes we can store the high level nuclear waste safely, as long as we choose the proper geology.[34]

And yet I am also intrigued by today's innovations, like Transatomic Power's "molten salt reactor," which (like the earlier breeder reactors) will apparently use less enriched uranium more efficiently, and thus produce less waste. More importantly, and also like the earlier breeder reactors, it is supposed to be a safer design.[35] Conventional reactors only use about 5 percent of the uranium's potential energy. The "pyrometallurgical" process also uses radioactive waste for fuel, reducing the leftover radioactivity contamination window from tens of thousands to hundreds of years, and thus vastly improving long term safety concerns as well as energy efficiency.[36]

Imagine these updated nuclear power plants, with one built near every high level radioactive waste storage site to consume this dangerous fuel while minimizing transportation logistics (and thus potential accidents). Lately, nuclear energy has been uncompetitive economically on the energy market, so a new generation of nuclear plants would likely require government subsidies. But with the Hanford nuclear site consuming billions in annual clean up costs, possibly topping $100 billion before it is completed, perhaps a strong argument for subsidies can be made.[37]

Obviously we would want to continue with our efforts regarding wind, solar, tidal, and geothermal power; but none of these has thus far come close to replacing the grid as we now know it, powered by fossil fuels and hydro-electric dams. Nuclear could replace or more greatly supplement the power source of the grid within a generation, were there the political and social will to do so. As mentioned, in France nuclear energy already supplies 80 percent of their energy; that example would seem to make it plausibly transferrable elsewhere.

But let us remember again the impossibility of predicting. Even if we assume that mitigating or ending our dumping of atmospheric carbon is our goal, massive carbon capture technology could achieve this regarding our current fossil fuel consumption or some future variation upon that consumption. There are so many variables, and much will depend upon which technology becomes the most economically viable, and if that viability can be marketed long enough to bring down costs through the usual process that often evolves from expensive early adoption to much more affordable mass production.

We are working on other things, such as using "thermoelectrics" to capture wasted heat[38] and actually creating fuel *from* carbon dioxide.[39] Scientists have promising ideas and evidence for generating hydrogen fuel from wastewater treatment. They've even made discoveries of using algae to remove pharmaceuticals from wastewater, a problem not solved by traditional wastewater screening, filtering and aeration.[40] Innovators have even come up with the use of titanium dioxide for "consuming" smog,[41] an astonishing development that could improve air quality during the remainder of the traditional fossil fuel consumption era. Speaking of smog, China is unsurprisingly at the forefront of green city concepts and the technology to make it happen.[42] Daan Roosegaarde has used one of his "smog vacuum cleaners" in China.[43] Can you imagine Beijing on a clear day? It could happen sooner or later, depending upon technological and economic viability. In China, the political will to implement such measures seems quite strong, perhaps partly because necessity is mothering and encouraging invention.

Or consider desalination. Obviously you can render potable water from the ocean simply through solar evaporation, but this is not practical on any sizable scale. Contemporary desalination plants use a filtration technique called "reverse osmosis" as well as simply boiling seawater on a massive scale and capturing and condensing the steam. Both require a lot of electricity. Reverse osmosis also requires frequent replacement of membrane materials used to filter salt from water. But now these sorts of desalination plants (like the water-cooled nuclear reactors) are beginning to resemble the Model T. Back in 2013, chemists Richard Crooks (University of Texas) and Ulrich Tallarekat (University of Marburg) developed a technique called "electrochemically mediate seawater desalination," which requires far less energy than traditional ionization desalination.[44] In 2014, MIT engineers enhanced an argument for solar-powered "electrodialysis" for desalinating the sort of mildly saline groundwater found in over half of India's wells.[45] In 2015, Egyptian engineers developed a new type of highly efficient polymeric membrane that makes desalination more efficient, and thus less energy-intensive.[46] Scientists and engineers have also used the new "miracle material" graphene to desalinate water.[47]

It certainly looks like we're on track to develop a low-energy, low-maintenance, cost-effective technique for addressing fresh water availability. Again, it is not a silver bullet (the brackish byproduct must be dealt with), nor do these innovations imply that water conservation efforts should end. But count on humans to keep tinkering with problems and devise better solutions. Fresh water is obviously crucial for direct human consumption, but it also has potential implications for innovative desert food production.[48]

Scientists and engineers will continue to work on many other innovative ideas, from better batteries and new uses for them,[49] to new utilization of solar energy through the metal called *vanadium*,[50] to a nanophotonic fiber that reflects heat and lowers air conditioning energy consumption.[51]

There is really no end to it.

Certainly the energy consumption end of things shows little sign of lessening. In fact, given our fondness for electronic gadgets, it is likely to increase. The United States, with only 5 percent of the world's population, consumes a fourth of the world's energy.[52] Consumption of energy will most likely increase with global population increase, and especially with rise in standards of living, even as population levels off and even drops in some nations, like Japan and Italy. Nevertheless, we can always pursue greater efficiency. Light emitting diode technology will possibly make incandescent bulbs or even those curly fluorescent bulbs look like the computer zip drive that came and went so quickly. LEDs consume a small fraction of either incandescent or fluorescent lighting technology.[53]

This is but a small sampling of science and engineering innovations aimed at addressing true environmental problems. Obviously one could write a very thick book or two about this topic alone and not exhaust all the examples, some of which are bond to become obsolete very quickly. Many more will never become economically viable. Others are or will be technological masterpieces, but whether or not a marketing genius ever discovers them will become another matter. Such is the eternal nature of invention.

And so the point here is to celebrate human ingenuity and offer some guarded confidence that, in spite of all dire predictions to the contrary, we will indeed solve some of our problems and find new tools for helping the environment as we value it. Even if you disagree, what is the alternative? We cannot go back to yesteryear's technology nor even stop contemporary configurations from changing. Forward really is the only direction, even if you feel ambivalent about "progress."

None of this is to advocate unbridled optimism, and obviously there are no silver bullets. For example, MTBE (methyl tertiary butyl ether), once ubiquitous on California gasoline pumps, is now nowhere to be seen. The additive was well-intended, and mitigated air pollution, but proved to be a disastrous ground water pollutant.[54] Even adding chlorine to drinking water, which kills pathogens harmful to humans, also creates potentially carcinogenic "disinfection by-products" like trihalomethanes.[55] We've already seen that wind turbines kill migrating birds, just as old hydro-power dams decimated salmon populations. But even in those areas we engineered salmon ladders, barge transport, and other methods attempting to accommodate migrating fish. And lately there are innovations in bird-friendly wind turbines as well.[56] We tend to do this; always innovating and improving technology, always trying to solve problems and fine-tune procedures when we discover unintended consequences.

This is the sort of work that deserves government grants and private investment, not yet another book based on computer models that repeat (yet again) the climate catastrophe that is supposedly coming and how we should all be "concerned" about it and implement non-solutions through ill-conceived measures like the Kyoto Protocol. Nor do we need yet another antiquarian catalogue, without benefit of a philosophy of species, describing the species we have helped render extinct—not to mention the hundreds of thousands of species that went extinct before humans came on the scene (many of which we will never know about, given the high rarity of conditions leading to fossils).

*   *   *

Philanthropic environmentalism embraces what we are already doing regardless of dogma and ideology: green science and technology. Humans have proven themselves pretty darned ingenious when it comes to engineering our way out of problems. A few doomsdayists romanticize the Paleolithic, as if we could or would want to return to an existence that Hobbes accurately described as "nasty, brutish, and short." But if you have an iota of optimism, you must believe that help is on the way *because* of science and technology, not in spite of it.

All human technologies have impacts upon the environment, because our very presence has an impact. This was true during the Paleolithic and Neolithic eras, when human technology was rudimentary. The differences now are obvious; massive human populations and more influential technologies. But we are also aware of our new problems and capable of attempting solutions. Our species' ingenuity got us into our current ambiguous state; and short of a true apocalypse, it is only our ingenuity that will get us out. Pandora's Box will not recapture the demons it has released, and the Green Calvinists' fantasy of a return to primitivism (easily romanticized when your father is an investment banker) ranks among the most ludicrous of nonsolutions.

Besides, "condemnation of technology is ingratitude," Robert Pirsig wrote.[57] He went on to discuss a great many things about our lives, our perception and attitudes; science, philosophy, and our relationships with technology from both logical and romantic points of view. One of his conclusions was our need to appreciate technology as "a fusion of nature and the human spirit into a new kind of creation that transcends both."[58] Contemporary condemnation of technology tends to come out of the Romantic camp in various flakey forms involving hypocrisy, incoherent selectivity, and deep ironies.[59] The hypocrisy is obvious, since all Romantics use and benefit from technology. The incoherent selectivity involves things like embracing radio or print media while rejecting televised media (the bumper sticker mentality of *Kill your television!* before the internet rendered it quaintly obsolete). Or, supporting a network of dozens of pickup trucks that deliver local food to farmers' markets when a single long distance semi-truck renders a smaller "carbon footprint." Or, the rejecting of mass-produced goods but embracing craft show products, sometimes referred to as "ugly things, all made by hand" (paraphrasing Gertrude Stein).[60] Among the deepest of ironies are the environmental romantics who denounce corporations but unwittingly hold Edenic and doomsday worldviews largely shaped by corporate media.

The ancient and Classical Greeks were skeptical about technology because of the mixed results that could come from its use. Their culture was still familiar with the earlier Neolithic age, in which humanity's connections with nature must have seemed closer (and possibly already romanticized from an advantageous distance). But they also saw how technology could compromise the all-important individual's *arête* (spirit of excellence) or how pride in technology could foster individual hubris. They recognized how technological advantage could exacerbate and intermesh with socioeconomic inequalities,[61] though by now we should realize that *some* level of social inequality is inevitable—or, at least, an egalitarian society has yet to exist.

It was during the Renaissance and Age of Enlightenment that we acquired our optimism regarding technology, and at least for a while that optimism was practically unchecked. The 19th-century Romantics reacted against it, for they saw the dark side of polluted industrial cities, loss of cohesive agrarian villages and families, the abuses of child labor in the cities, and other negative results they associated with technology.[62] This was the era that informed some of Charles Dickens' works. He evocatively described one of those James Watt steam engines (resembled today by the bobbing oil derrick) as "the head of an elephant in a state of melancholy madness."[63]

Overall, we are still living in the Enlightenment's technological trajectory, though by now we are or should be more guarded in our optimism, qualifying our notions of progress. We know technology can cut both ways, and quite commonly produces unintended consequences or otherwise ambiguous results. But no serious person advocates abandoning it. In fact, even a true "primitivist" (if there is such a person) requires technology to survive.

I remember people in early 1980s southeastern Alaska living off of less than a thousand dollars a year—but they bought ammunition for hunting black-tailed deer. They bought skiff gasoline for fishing and kelp gathering. They lived basically and (from my point of view) admirably, but they had no desire to forego technology. It was the technology that fostered the freedom they so craved.

Apparently most philosophers who have pondered the ethics of technology do not support the idea that it is value-neutral, the most obvious reasons being the fact that humans have done terrible things with technology.[64] Any number of military technologies come to mind. But clearly the technology *intended* to solve our environmental problems features positive values, both for ourselves, our environment, and our fellow living creatures—at least the creatures we favor.

Ancient philosophers, who were more apt to blame the user of technology rather than technology itself, realized that our ingeniousness should not cross over into arrogance.[65] In an ironic sense, it could be the height of hubris and the depth of folly to think we can alter our technological uses to influence something massive like the climate, at all. Personally I would not mind watching the experiment of removing carbon from the atmosphere. But thinking we can control something so complex, on a planetary atmospheric scale, as climate? Do we really think we could capture volcanic emissions, which can include methane on a truly apocalyptic scale?

No, it might be better just to do our best in humility.

So, if you wish, call me a fan of the "eco-technocrats" (those who believe in engineering our way toward greenness).[66] With the endless innovators out there looking for better ways to live in our world, avoiding negative environmental impacts as our contemporary values now define them, we should have some hope. Besides, any day I would rather go with the eco-technocrats compared to the doomsdayists and their false premise of emergency that continues, decade in, decade out.

So this chapter and a general message of this book is a celebration of human ingenuity that is too often missing from recent and contemporary environmental dialogue, particularly as it involves the untenable misanthropic Eden mentality. Eco-technocracy is an important foundational philosophy, for there are very real and serious environmental problems out there that don't get half the press compared to climate alarmism and extinction hysteria. There is no sanctuary to return to. Instead, we have to be the best stewards we can be, spending what we can afford and as wisely as possible, informed by pure and applied science, and compassionate for those suffering at the worse end of the spectrum when it comes to environmental conditions. Poor people can already tell you there is no Eden. They would just appreciate a little less purgatory.

So take it from me—a natural born pessimist most of my life—there is far more to be optimistic about than the doomsdayists would lead you to believe. And by the way, rest in peace to the old Jurassic era specialist-turned-doomsdayist. Soon we will be ashes or worm food like him too, but there's not much point in discouraging others before we go.

Chapter 9

Rural Stewardship,
Old and New

Various writers have defined environmental stewardship in different ways, while many others use the term or the concept vaguely without any particular definition at all.[1] I use the term to distinguish from what I consider to be unrealistic philosophies that conceive of nature as static and idyllic as long as humanity agrees not to interfere. Contingent to this Edenic thinking is a separation of humanity from nature, a lip-service pretense toward such separation, or worst of all, the Green Calvinism in which human actions are not only distinct from nonhuman influences, but somehow "sinful." Instead, I see humanity's environmental actions as inevitable. This is because of the unique magnitude of our influence (for good, bad, and ambiguous), our self-consciousness regarding our role and this influence (or at least we *should* be self-conscious about our influence), and our "predicament" of having our "head in the stars and feet in the mud"—i.e., we can dream of the ideal world, like Plato's forms, and yet we're stuck in the mundane world as mammals among other fauna and flora that want to survive, reproduce, fend off competitors for food, fight back against disease, and (of course) eventually succumb to the end of a brief existence.

So, in that sense, stewardship implies humility, gratitude for privilege, compassion, thoughtfulness, and the opposite of misanthropy—philanthropy, in the sense of caring for our fellow humans and, by extension, as many other life forms as practically possible, and not just our favorite megafauna, big trees, or "native species."

Having said all that, it is probably not a specific philosophy coming from me, if it is a philosophy at all. Maybe it is more of an attitude derived from common sense. Certainly every environmental stewardship situation would require particularistic considerations, like applying bioremediation to one chemical spill, complete excavation for another, and allowing another one deemed stable to remain dormant. Or, choosing heavy thinning in one stand of trees compared to light thinning in another, or only firewood harvesting of damaged trees in a third situation. The foregoing are what conscientious people have already been doing or advocating for many years anyway. So in one basic sense stewardship simply means, "try not to break it."

Maybe it's easier to list what *not* to do: avoid greed, avoid wanton killing, and avoid inconsiderate narcissistic behavior. Avoid operating in ignorance. Easier said than done, I know. But just think of how many (but not all) problems would be solved if only people would treat others as they wished to be treated. It's the Golden Rule (or some variety thereof) that has shown up in so many ancient cultures it isn't funny. And yet it remains an idealist's "naïve" pipedream, at least according to the cynics and especially the opportunists.

*   *   *

In 1969, near the apex of the early Environmental Movement, Congress passed the National Environmental Policy Act. In the opening section, Congress recognized the importance of mitigating human impact on the environment, but without neglecting obvious social and economic needs. They wrote that a "productive harmony" between humanity and nature was the goal.[2] In a way this is just common sense. Environmental degradation and short-term greed only make sense for an exploitative few, at the expense of greater society. No society wishes for this, in general. Details are another matter.

Dynamically ambiguous is probably the best term to describe the human role in the environment. It is dynamic because it keeps changing according to our shifting needs, wants, and philosophical values. Also, the environment itself keeps changing, of course. It is ambiguous because the results are rarely entirely evil or good, even in the context of their own times. When we see how long term results sometime play out, the ambiguity deepens. Often by the time we appreciate the consequences of an earlier generation's actions, our values have changed yet again, and it becomes too easy to criticize past actors for their naïve optimism, pessimistic opportunism, ignorance of complexities that later came to light, or what have you.

We can also rest assured that some of our current actions and views will strike some in the future as folly. There are few if any easy and simple scenarios when it comes to the environmental stewardship role we invariably find ourselves fulfilling.

As the foregoing chapter illustrated, innovative technology has the potential to foster better environmental stewardship, even if the results will likely continue to require compromises among environmental, social, and economic values. How we treat animals and plants now reflects our species' ancient high level of influence regarding other life forms; the only odd part is how we often seem to do this semi-blindly, without acknowledging the philosophical values that inform our stewardship choices.

For example, Americans almost wiped out the bison, partly out of gratuitous killing, but also as a way to subdue buffalo-dependent Plains Indians and make way for the white cattle farmer. But then the upper class east coast American Bison Society members brought the buffalo back through pronounced human intervention. Nostalgia for the "lost west" emotionally appealed to them, though more logically they claimed bison preservation would offer others some natural history education. They promoted bison tourism for its economic potential.[3] But as Andrew Isenberg concluded, "while preservationists probably saved the bison from extinction, they saved the species not as a functioning part of the plains environment, but as a curiosity, a tourist attraction, and a target for sport hunters."[4] On the other hand, Canadians have recently been able to bring bison back to Banff National Park,[5] a massive habitat of over 2,500 square miles. One would think that would make the herbivore a "functioning part of the plains environment," at least in that one location.

In recent decades many have advocated for the creation of a "buffalo commons" in the American Great Plains that would bring back tall and short grass prairie, especially now that people are depopulating portions of the mid-continent.[6] After all, the demography of the United States has shifted in recent decades, and people have left the old bison habitat for points east, west, and south. Advanced agricultural technology allows fewer people to harvest more food. So why not create a buffalo commons? Personally I find this very appealing, but I also see it for the stewardship policy that it would constitute, and an interesting idea in light of how a few generations ago we almost hunted the bison to death. We make and have made these sorts of decisions all the time; which species to favor and foster, which species to deter and even eradicate, and a great many we simply ignore. We may see this caretaker role as our privilege or our burden, but it is undeniably a responsibility we cannot escape, owing to our self-consciousness alone.

Shifting demographics, by the way, create all sorts of opportunities along the "buffalo commons" lines. Former neighborhoods in Detroit and other rust belt cities are "returning to nature." The depopulated coalfield regions of the southern Appalachian mountains now have "nature conservancy" potential they did not possess at the height/nadir of strip mining and mountaintop removal. Nature is constantly reclaiming landscapes altered by humans, whether we're actively stewarding the reclamation or not.

And whether we fully appreciate it or not, we are constantly making stewardship choices. Often what makes the news is saving birds or our fellow mammals, particularly when we rescue endearing creatures like baby sea otters or pandas. But there are innumerable other stewardship examples running a wide and complex spectrum of nurturing, killing, and ambiguous "interference." As mentioned, letting "nature take its course" seems to have fallen out of fashion, if we ever thought through the concept in the first place.

For example, the Army Corps of Engineers recently announced a $100 million project to enhance river conditions for salmon and steelhead downstream from western Oregon's Detroit Lake. The project would include a 300-foot tower that would simulate natural waterfall conditions, both accommodating fish migration while pulling up lower level lake water to cool temperatures for downstream habitat.[7] Creation of the lake, an artificial reservoir, compromised the fish habitat in the first place; now we plan to employ environmental engineering to mitigate or reverse our earlier negative effects. This is an example of stewardship in a wealthy nation. Destroying the dam and the reservoir would remove water supplies for both urban human consumption as well as intensive agricultural use, so the $100 million project is a logical response.

Other projects are perhaps more Edenesque. Humans drove the Floreana Island tortoise into extinction during the 19th century, but now scientists are using a captive breeding program for neighboring tortoises to "bring back" the Floreana species. DNA has assured us that this captive breeding and reintroduction will result in a "pure" Floreana species.[8] This seems like a rather weird concept of genetic identity to assuage our ancestral guilt, but (like the bison restoration) that is another response to earlier indiscriminate killing.

Biologists intervene in Montana to bolster the black-footed ferret population, but Midwesterners step in to help the less cuddly Eastern Hellbender Salamander.[9] Heirloom aficionados cultivate rare apple varieties because they fear the hazards of monoculture, decry the homogenized offerings in grocery stores, enjoy variety for variety's sake, have a sense of history—or what have you.[10] By the way, they're preserving apple varieties that already previously co-evolved with human preferences from ancient wild species; now they're just stepping in to revive a flora from that intermediary past, not the primeval past.

In Virginia they have coyote killing tournaments, similar to the Burmese python derbies in Florida.[11] Undoubtedly this is done under the aegis of "invasive species" philosophy, even if coyotes are indigenous (if highly mobile) North American creatures. The same is true in North Carolina and Tennessee, where the National Park Service hunts wild pigs in the Great Smoky Mountains National Park.[12] But let's remember: we introduced the pythons accidentally (or foolishly, by releasing pets), we introduced the pigs deliberately (an old sport hunting idea in places like the Ozarks), then exterminated or greatly reduced large predators like the mountain lion, wolves, and bears. So if we're "preserving Eden" now, it is a highly modified Eden that not only reflects our current and past values, but our current and past (stewardship) practices. There is nothing necessarily "wrong" in any of this, but (again) the Edenic premise is simply wildly inaccurate, thus potentially fostering misguided policy. You cannot return to a place where you've never been before. Most obviously, these examples debunk any notion that humans are separated from nature. We are *hugely* involved with nature, as all these and countless other examples demonstrate.

So, some more examples.

A more nuanced issue arises with wild horses. In eastern Oregon, Indian tribes cope with wild horses who have a tendency to over-populate, over-graze, and damage agricultural crops[13]—all of this description reflecting human values and our stewardship for them. The Bureau of Land Management faces this issue in many parts of the American West. Wild horses are a feral version of a species that went extinct in North America many millennia ago, then in a highly evolved (and much larger form) got reintroduced by the Spanish during the 16th century. This story alone raises one of the obvious themes ignored by the Edenic premise: what even constitutes "invasive," why do we pretend we're not heavily influential when it comes to other life forms, and how are human activities influencing nonhuman life in so many complex ways: obviously and subtly, but also mysteriously and as yet unknown. In a variation upon this theme, human activities may be contributing to whales beaching themselves in New Zealand, to which New Zealanders respond by trying to shepherd the dying animals back into the ocean.[14]

There are endless additional examples, many of which take place in the middle of suburbs and cities. For instance, millions of songbirds in cities adapt to new circumstances in which we accommodate them or discourage them. In fact, more and more of us are living in cities, and we have to trust that we will continue to improve upon urban environmental conditions, both for our sake and the sake of all the flora and fauna existing there—all in reflection of our contemporary and future values (more about this in the following chapter).

The consequences of our stewardship can be bumbling, haphazard, and comic-tragic. We once built hydropower dams here in the Pacific Northwest with little or no thought about how this would wreak havoc on salmon migration and thus future salmon populations. When we learned, we did our best to rectify the situation with fish ladders, but also hatchery-produced fish. The problem with the latter is they learn to surface feed, which makes them ready prey for birds like Caspian Terns and cormorants. They are also vulnerable to sea lions and pike minnows. All of these predator species have experienced population explosions as a result, which causes other problems.[15]

We are constantly making value judgments favoring one species over another, or at least caught in predicaments wondering if we should. The Fish and Wildlife Service was killing cormorants to save fish, until a judge stopped them. We already mentioned the campaign to kill eastern barred owls to favor northern spotted owls. But our accommodations for trumpeter swans in Montana have compromised Arctic grayling trout habitat,[16] giving us a predicament about how to help both, if we can.

It's not easy "playing God." But sometimes it is fun.

Susan Fleming and Sara Marino made a very endearing film about cross-species friendships. A dog and a cheetah were companions, as were a lion and a coyote, a goose and a tortoise. In a truly amazing pairing, a horse that went blind came to depend upon his goat friend to guide the horse to and from pasture.[17] These were wonderful stories to behold, but we should also note that all these cross-species friendships took place within direct human stewardship contexts—not in "wild nature"—and that included the friendship between a wild deer and a domestic dog. Nature is fine and human stewardship is fine—but these cases indicate, yet further, the unique extent and characteristics of human intervention.

In any case, our stewardship role is everywhere, though the media tends to present us with strange examples that rarely include philosophical considerations about why we do what we do. The earlier illustration about ugly speciesism is one obvious example of our subjective behavior. Our preference for megafauna poster species (bison, polar bears, elephants) is another. Urban people often focus on particular species, almost in the abstract, because their city, suburban, or town property tends to be quite limited in size. Rural owners of farms, forests, and rangeland face a very different situation. In a way the rural stewards represent a continuity with old-fashion environmental conservation pre-dating the modern environmental movement.

Aside from fostering particular species or not, a host of rural landowners continues to practice exemplary stewardship of the properties they love. Here in Oregon the childish eco-radicals (overwhelmingly urban folk) have often overshadowed these rural stewards in a microcosm that illustrates overlapping realms of conservation, stewardship, and Edenic environmentalism. The eco-radicals have faded away in recent years, though their contributing legacy helped turn national forests into logging-diminished national parks that now feature annual mega-fires; that has not been helpful. Decades of wildfire suppression have left conditions that only we can now improve, but it will require much intervention in prescribed burning (limited by air quality standards) and mechanical logging (now mostly taboo, especially on federal forest lands).[18]

Allan Freeze rightly gives credit to the early environmental movement for altering our previous exploitative practices. But Freeze is also correct in

A portion of the "Bootheel" region of Southeastern Missouri between the Mississippi River (right), drainage ditches (running southwest on the left), and Highway 412 (bottom), that runs between the towns of Kennett and Hayti. Until the early twentieth century, much of this land was a massive swamp (now called wetlands) surpassed only by the Everglades in magnitude. Then farmers and engineers created an extensive series of drainage ditches to render some of the most productive agricultural land in the United States. Such utilitarian values have changed in the contemporary environmental climate, where such a radical land alteration would likely be legally impossible. And yet, in the broader view, we rendered one habitat from another. If the human species went extinct, undoubtedly the Mississippi River would eventually "reclaim" the Bootheel in its former wetland configuration (enhanced from Google Earth images).

pointing out that those days are past, and continuing obstructionism (often through litigation) and Edenism are no longer tenable.[19] We are late for a new cooperative era that recognizes true environmental problems and tries to solve them in a context of acknowledged philosophical values, whereupon we might try to gauge economic and social costs and benefits.

Another tragedy of contemporary environmentalism has been its obscuring of respect for our conservationist past. True, Americans are notoriously uninterested in history. But in advocating a contemporary and future stewardship we should realize that stewardship itself is not even close to an original idea. Farmers from time immemorial have tried to be good stewards of their land. The Old Testament mentions the necessity of leaving land fallow for—as we now appreciate—regeneration of nutrients, and thus fertility. Farmers have made many mistakes, all the way up to and following the Dust Bowl of the 1930s. But most of those mistakes have been out of ignorance, not maliciousness or greed. Farmers, after all, wish to "sustain" their work throughout their lifetimes and, if possible, continue the tradition into later generations.

Not far from the Ivory Tower—or the righteous downtown protest, or letters to the city newspaper, or testimony to the city council—are an array of country people trying to make a living off the land. Why would they not care about the environment? But, urban dwellers' ignorance of rural stewardship is but one facet of an old urban-rural antagonism that probably goes back to the birth of cities.

*   *   *

James F. McInteer was a wildlife conservationist and the director of Virginia's Commission of Game and Inland Fisheries before the environmental movement of the 1960s and 1970s began to overshadow his sort of caretaking approach to land and creatures. To a some degree, McInteer's old-fashioned sort of environmental stewardship is partly what this current book is about; that is, a cautionary tale in light of acknowledging and celebrating humanity's unique role.

"Plundering this land," McInteer wrote in 1963, "and corrupting this environment, no matter how scientifically done, can be but self-defeating enterprises leading to spiritual as well as material bankruptcy. Stewardship, rather than proprietorship, is the term that best describes each man's relationship to the things of this world over which he claims dominion during his brief stay."[20]

As mentioned before, many writers have debunked Lynn White's simplistic thesis about Judeo-Christianity being responsible for environmental degradation.[21] Here is but another qualification upon that theme. Many environmental stewards of yore and at present recognize an inextricably intertwined combination of a deep care for land and life, some sense of personal spirituality, and an appreciation for the transience of our earthly existence.

Frederick Brown Harris, chaplain to the U.S. Senate, reflected this old ethic in a short essay he wrote in 1958.[22] Besides chastising exploitative industrialists and capitalists, Harris described people as mere "trustees" temporarily caring for the natural environment. He celebrated wilderness sanctuaries as "scenic cathedrals" and warned against the "creeping blight" of civilization.[23] Responding to the question in 2 Samuel 3:12, "Whose is the land?" Harris responded that the land belonged first to God, then to the current land stewards, and lastly to future stewards.[24] The future aspect is important here, and concerns practically every land and forest steward I've ever met. I think this is partly because land and especially trees have a way of evoking our sense of transience and brevity on earth. Planting trees that you know will outlive you has a way of putting you in your longevity place.

It is difficult to know exactly why we get so emotional about trees. Perhaps there is some deeply instinctive remnant of memory from our pre-homo sapiens ancestors who dwelled in trees. That would make trees one of our first homes, and feelings about home are among the most powerful that humans entertain.

Lest we forget, and lest we romanticize too much, we still use a saying that equates the forest with trouble or danger: "We're not out of the woods yet." I heard this saying most of my life without connecting it to a pre–Romantic understanding of wild land, when the forest was a place where large carnivores roamed, people got lost and died from starvation or exposure to harsh weather. No wonder the Grimm stories (set in forested Germany) were replete with children getting lost in the woods, or where wicked witches lived and preyed upon the unsuspecting.

"Environmentalists" hardly invented tree worship. All ancient and following numenistic traditions viewed trees as embodying spirits particular to certain species or entire groves.[25] As such, trees have taken on innumerable religious attributes and associations. Among the more famous are Buddha and the Bodhi tree and the Hebrew Menorah. But the Greco-Roman cultures saw spirits inhabiting every species of tree, and particularly worshiped deities that they associated with, for example, olive tree grove.[26]

And then there were the heavily silvicentric Germanic tribes of northern Europe who interwove trees and forests into their entire worldview. This seems unsurprising, living in a heavily forested geography as they were. No wonder that the Christmas tree came out of this tradition, and not biblical desert regions. The ancient Hebrews had their foundational myth in the Garden of Eden and Tree of Knowledge, but the German tribes had the "world tree" Yggdrasil (alternatively described as an ash or a yew), which gave the tree cosmological preeminence.[27]

Forest and trees were not necessarily benevolent or even benign to these European tribes. Folk tales are replete with descriptions of the forest as a terrifying place. But the forest could also be an enchanting place, particularly associated with sylvan huts and benevolent spells cast. Those who occupied these huts were outside of mainstream society, and harkened back to pre–Christian trickster ideas of maintaining integrity in the prevailing order.[28] No wonder our ancestors developed an ambiguous cultural tradition that regarded the woods with awe, respect, and wonder. Only when our technology safely removed us from the forest did we acquire the luxury to romanticize it, and yet all romanticism aside, we have never lost the religious connection present from time immemorial. As the conservationist Irvin Talton Quinn wrote in 1955, "The majestic tree was the first temple of God and the original tabernacle of man. Beneath its spreading branches and swinging boughs man first held conscious communion with the Divine Spirit of the Universe. In its checkered shade the first off-spring of God's Creation gamboled and frolicked."[29]

For better and worse, today we have relationships with trees and forests that would be unrecognizable to earlier peoples. We have largely dismissed what many would call "superstitious" beliefs associated with the forest. Certainly we have the wherewithal to destroy forests as never before. A great deal has changed. And yet there are strong threads of continuity with past traditions. Kids still find wonderment in climbing trees, and children and adults alike find tree houses fascinating. Twentieth-century cartoons depicting anthropomorphic trees with limbs as arms and roots as feet, sometimes threatening little children, are but a continuation of older traditions.[30]

As the next chapter will demonstrate, remnants of age-old emotionalism regarding trees is alive and well in the city. In this sense, it is mainly urban foresters who have working connections with their rural steward counterparts. In fact, I've met a few arborists who have been rural loggers as well as urban foresters. These people often love trees quite deeply, for that was why they chose to do their dangerous work. They also understand the endless practicalities regarding trees, such as diplomatically trying to explain why a diseased tree needs to come down lest it crush people and property. Disease research also preoccupies certain tree stewards.

For decades there have been massive efforts to bring back the American chestnut tree, widely killed by a blight (*cryphonectria parasitica*) during the early 20th century. This work requires a great deal of patience, for it can take years before discovering whether or not a strain-resistant tree is truly immune to the blight. I wonder if GMO opponents would object to application of such science to revive the chestnut tree? The chestnut species has never completely died. I used to see the sprouts and young trees in the western Virginia forest all the time. But they were never more than a few years old, and succumbed as soon as the wind-borne blight hit them. Researchers have tried many dead-ends, though lately some modified Chestnut strains finally seem to be hardy.[31]

Personally I find these chestnut revival efforts laudable, but that simply reflects my subjective opinion. There is no inherent reason why one tree species is better or worse than another, but humans have all sorts of preferences when it comes to flora and fauna species. For economic reasons we have valued white pines for ship masts, oak for tongue-and-groove flooring, walnut and cherry for furniture, et cetera. We have valued elms for their shade and decried cottonwoods for their brittleness and thus inappropriateness as an urban tree (but helpfulness as an erosion-arresting riverbank tree). We loved sweet gums as fast-growing urban trees until we realized their roots uplifted sidewalks (now we plant other species in berms). All of this simply reflects human valuation, not something in nature that is inherently superior or inferior. So the American chestnut revival attempts are certainly manipulative and revivalist, harkening back to a half-imagined pre-blight era—but they are certainly quite typical of stewardship efforts in general.

Tree and forest stewardship is everywhere.

After decades of effort, China has apparently successfully compensated for an earlier era of intense deforestation,[32] not unlike the timber stripping that once took place in the United States. Japanese and British scientists may have saved the almost-extinct Japanese Birch tree, and sent sprouts to various arboretums in England to encourage their proliferation.[33] Various Oregonians seek to re-establish the once-common (now almost gone) oak savannah landscape that once dominated the Willamette Valley.[34]

The Oregon oak savannah situation illustrates the classic stewardship premise. After the last glaciation, native peoples burned the Willamette Valley regularly, creating the oak savannah in the first place. In the sense that we're using the term, they were effective and good stewards of the land for their purposes. Ironically, what followed mass Indian killing and relegation of survivors to the reservation has been the environmental practices that led to the current trouble: intensive agriculture and forest clearing, industrial logging, fire suppression, and a major drop in logging on federal lands since around 1989.[35] So now we have mega fires. Some argue that these fires are not "nat-

Restoring Oak Groves & Grasslands

Just to your left there is a small oak grove and an adjacent field which are undergoing restoration. Both of these areas, like most of the area around you, have been impacted by human activity. These two areas are being restored to return them to a more natural condition. The goal is to a create a condition that is more supportive of the plants and animals that would normally live in this area.

Historically, fires periodically burned through both the fields and the oak groves. These fires were caused by lightning and were also started by Native American Indians, specifically the Kalapuya Indians that lived in this region. Fire stimulates the growth of new plants and was a key factor in maintaining the health of this environment and the plants, animals and humans that lived here.

Oaks used to be a dominant feature of the Willamette Valley covering 750,000 acres, some living as long as 500 years! More recently, human activities that have been harmful to both the grassland and the oak have included farming, urbanization, fire suppression and the invasion of exotic plants that are not native to this region. Some of these "non-native" plants include Scotch Broom, Himalayan Blackberry and Canadian Thistle.

Part of the Oregon Parks and Recreation Department's (OPRD) mission is to provide and protect natural sites for the enjoyment and education of present and future generations. The restoration work occurring here is part of that effort. Projects have included: removal of fir trees that were shading-out the oaks, re-seeding the field and removal of non-native plants.

Oak groves and grasslands provide a home to a wide variety of native wildflowers, butterflies, birds and mammals. Today, oak groves and grasslands are a rarity within the Willamette Valley. The plants and animals that depend on them are also becoming increasingly threatened and endangered. With the assistance of the Oregon Department of Wildlife, Landwatch and the Oregon Department of Forestry, OPRD is working to restore these sites. The long term goal of both of these projects is to restore them so that they will be more favorable for the Oregon White Oak and to provide habitat for the Gray Squirrel, the Western Bluebird, Oregon's state bird, the Western Meadowlark and other species that would ordinarily live here.

Gray Squirrel

Western Meadowlark

Nature History *Discovery*

This sign reflects an interesting example of environmental stewardship in Elijah Bristow State Park, Oregon. For thousands of years Native Americans used pre-scribed fire that highly influenced the creation of the oak savannah, now almost completely replaced by agricultural lands, Douglas fir forests, and other non-savannah lands. Restoring the oak savannah seeks to recreate an earlier human-influenced environment rather than a pre-human environment (author's photograph).

ural." What they are really saying is that humans caused the current conditions. True. But the oak savannah was caused by humans too. It would be folly to attempt "re-creating" the pre–Wisconsin glaciation landscape, even if we were sure of its details. All of this points toward philosophical values, known or partially-known scientific fact (in this case, regarding silviculture), and stewardship.

Here's another example of stewardship in current circumstances. In southwestern Oregon the U.S. Forest Service proposed using prescribed fire and thinning of Douglas fir trees in order to encourage sugar and Ponderosa pines.[36] This will be a classic stewardship project for several reasons: the Douglas firs are fostering bark beetles that especially attack the pines, but are doing so in a habitat of dense trees already reflecting decades of human fire suppression. Douglas fir is a popular and valuable tree, practically ubiquitous in much of western Oregon, and the source of untold billions of board feet of lumber throughout Oregon's history. So no one is prejudiced against Douglas fir trees—but we humans (and specifically the Forest Service) find this pine habitat unique, so the Forest Service wants to favor them in that particular place. This specific instance of human valuation seems well-reasoned, but valuation and stewardship are invariably intertwined. They also operate in a context of an environment already highly modified by humans.

Eugene resident Tim Hermach, founder and president of the Native Forest Council, is proud of his "no compromise" stance against cutting trees. He claims public forests are in their death throes.[37] Aside from the hysterical exaggeration, the main problem with the public forests arise from the logging moratorium and the accumulation of fuel contributing to mega fires.[38] Furthermore, groups like the Native Forest Council and Cascadia Forest Defenders refuse to accept the fact that the forest already reflects centuries of highly significant human modification. In other words, they are Edenists, but Edenists apparently ignorant of history and blissfully unaware of their own subjective philosophy. In fact, their advocacy is bad policy based upon (green) religion more than reasoned philosophy, uninformed by the scientific facts as we know them.

The aforementioned selectivity regarding which species to revere (or not) reaches new levels in the peculiar religion of tree worship that is central to recent American radical environmentalism. A fanciful interpretation of this religion would trace our ancient lives in trees as primates. But what about the ancient savannah grasses of Africa that sustained our species as we began developing fully-fledged bipedism? The scholar Jan Gonda documented the Hindu worship and appreciation of grasses,[39] but this becomes a bit too esoteric even for adamant environmentalists to bear. Most people can appreciate an emotional attachment to trees; far fewer to grasses. There is also the typically gauche American regard for the spectacular. This means young trees or little trees get no respect, whereas Old Growth forests deserve our highest reverence. Never mind that there is little respect for elder humans in youth-cult America; after all, humans are *bad* and merit no respect, except for the babblers of misanthropy.

By contrast, and in a remarkable reflection of grand environmental stewardship, Shubhendu Sharma and his company Afforestt are undertaking a global reforestation effort.[40] They plant four kinds of forest or tree groves, depending upon a client's specifications. Some simply want an aesthetically-appealing forest, and Sharma chooses the species accordingly. In other cases, using deep-rooted species, watershed protection is the requirement. Humans have a long history of damaging watersheds; it is cheering to watch us reverse such impacts. Afforestt's park trees feature high levels of bird food, a joy to human and avian visitors alike. And finally Sharma will concentrate on groves of fruit and nut trees (among non-food trees) in an agricultural setting.

I find a vicarious joy in imagining these efforts. What a privilege to take care of a small piece of land. There are examples of this all around me in Oregon, and I enjoy the stories of rooted people who have a multi-generational sense of place. In this regard, as a national culture, we may finally be showing signs of settling into more stable people-land modes long established in Europe.

Just a note—none of this is to disparage Old Growth, not in the least. In fact, I pity anyone who does not feel the profound sacredness of being among ancient trees. There is no feeling quite like it. You cannot remain among them for long, for we all have our worldly struggles beckoning us among our fellows. But during our brief visit we should (at the very least) contemplate these life forms that began growing before our parents were born and, with any luck, will endure after our children die. But we should remember that certain contemporary groves of second and third growth could become Old Growth. They will be something future generations can anticipate. In this sense we would also be settling into a long-term environmental configuration already found elsewhere in the world, in places like England, Japan, and Germany.

Early American foresters modeled their silviculture after German practices. This oft-told tale in environmental history goes back to people like Gifford Pinchot, Bernhard Fernow, Teddy Roosevelt, the Biltmore Estate in North Carolina, and early U.S. Forest Service timber policy. The Germans are still legendary for their forestry, and the Black Forest in particular has long ago taken on mythological proportions. Franz Heske, the German scholar of forestry, wrote in 1938 that his nation's woodlands had become "sacred ground, the bedrock of Germany's fate, part of the national organism, the foundation of the lives of those who were, those who are, and those who are to come."[41]

Today the German forest is apparently equal parts romanticized and arranged in scientific order.[42] But it is important to point out that many decades before "sustainability" became an environmental buzzword, German foresters and their American students were using the terms "sustained yield" of timber and "sustained management" of forests.[43] This was the most natural conceivable attitude when people dealt with a limited renewable resource. The overly-exploitative aspect of American logging history was a glaring exception to this norm. And, as mentioned before, we are still in backlash overreaction regarding this earlier rapaciousness. It really is past-due time we moved on.

In the closing minutes of a 2011 lecture at Oregon State University, Paul Owen (president, Vanport International) described the bafflement of a German forester who could not understand the uniquely American objection to harvesting timber from wildfire burn areas or insect-killed timber. European nations, Canada, and other countries generally harvest such timber while it is still salvageable, for products useful to humans. The German forester told Owen, in Germany *he* was the environmentalist, not the enemy of the environment. "What are you talking about? I protect the forest. That's my job."[44] This would be expected from a culture which long ago embraced the idea of the following, written in 1940: "The forest calls out: 'Let us be the monuments of mankind's genius!'"[45] Ironically, the particular Americans who anthropomorphize the forest in their own religious ways would strenuously object to this variant upon the theme. But what a different social context, in which over 80 percent of German citizens support timber production as long as it does not deplete the forest.[46]

This plainly illustrates the differing cultural orientations toward the designed environment. The Germans have been at peace with their highly managed forests for so long they apparently no longer give it a second thought. This is true of Eurasia in general. The Germans made forest management mistakes in the past, freely admit those mistakes, but moved on without abandoning the human role.

So here's a major difference between the United States and Germany or any other part of Europe. In the broad scheme of forestry history, the United States has only recently emerged from a frontier practice of timber stripping, in which timber companies cut every commercially viable tree, put the product on market as fast as they could, then abandoned the land (not worth the expense in property taxes) and left for the next horizon. This is how the northeast was cut, then the upper Midwest. The southern Appalachians were a delayed island of big timber until the late 1800s, when industrial railroads finally penetrated the hills. But it did not end until timber companies finally reached the Pacific Northwest and realized, probably by the early 20th century, that things needed to change now that they had reached the final western horizon.

Germany, on the other hand, has not experienced a frontier's far horizon of forestry or anything else for centuries. We have to go back to the medieval era to find anything approximating a frontier in most parts of Europe. Europeans had no choice but to become forest stewards of their limited acreage, or not have a perpetual forest in the true meaning of "sustainable." So they became stewards, carefully monitoring growth, harvest, and regeneration. The German mentality is not that different from the Japanese, who preserve their limited and precious forest acreage, and thus import wood products from the United States.[47]

Before the word "sustainable" became so hackneyed, it actually evoked a distinctly different approach to forestry compared to the 19th-century era of industrial timber stripping in America, followed by a maximum harvest (and profit) goal in clear-cutting. And yet, upon retrospect, that distinction must break down. After all, clear-cutting is perfectly sustainable in that you can rotate timber sales over a large area, returning for subsequent clear cuts after the earlier ones have grown back. It's just that many people consider clear cuts ugly, and anyone would have to admit their environmental impact is a dramatic shift from acres of forest to acres of seedlings. But they are very profitable economically, especially in Douglas fir forests that put on the most volume when their early decades are spent in full sunlight. Like it or not, economics is a powerful argument.

Only recently has the United States returned to the earlier German silvicultural configuration, and then only partially by twists and turns involving radical environmental objections to cutting any trees at all (at least not in sight or in mind), endangered species habitats as surrogates for trees, and reducing logging on federal forests. But different things have been and are happening on private land, and some of these forest owners have quietly been carrying on old stewardship ideas for many decades.

When I lived in Missouri I had the pleasure and the honor to meet and interview Leo Drey, founder of the 156,000-acre Pioneer Forest, the largest private landholding in the state. Drey bought the acreage just as clear-cutting was taking the timber industry by storm. But Drey stuck to the old German silviculture of individual tree management, once called "selective forestry."[48]

He managed the acreage for modest timber production, allowed no end of graduate students to use plots for their ecological studies, kept a small staff in good employment, and basically behaved as very few wealthy people behave. He cared for the land, and before he died he created a foundation that should perpetuate his stewardship vision indefinitely.[49] As James Guldin wrote, "There is no better example of enlightened and abiding stewardship of NIPF [Non-industrial Private Forest] land, or any timberland, than the stewardship practiced at the Pioneer Forest."[50]

Drey would have loved some of the small forests in Oregon. "Family forestry" accounts for over four million acres of land in Oregon. These families try to make a living, and account for about 11 percent of the state's timber production. But strong emotional bonds to the land tend to override monetary interests.[51] And because of this, it turns out that many small forest owners in Oregon are practicing old-fashioned stewardship. These people often want to leave the forest to their children or for public and ecological benefit at large. They sacrifice potential monetary gain, especially short-term monetary gain, for other values. Here are a couple of specific examples.

Down in southwestern Oregon, the Parsons family recently put their acreage into a conservation easement that allows for selective logging, and thus low impact on water quality or forest habitat for wildlife.[52] This approach puts people and their forest needs in the mix with other life forms and their needs. This is old-fashioned stewardship of the pre-clear-cut era, when German silvicultural practices of individual tree selection still dominated scientific forestry circles, including the U.S. Forest Service (clear-cutting became all the rage during the 1940s).

Steven and Wylda Cafferata manage seventy-nine acres in Lane County, Oregon. Like the Parsons, they have an eye toward wildlife habitat enhancement, watershed protection, and other non-commodity values. They thin their forest against the threat of wildfire, and fight back against Scotch Broom and Himalayan Blackberries, both of which will dominate certain habitats, given the chance. Like the Pioneer Forest, they make their forest available for students to study. But also like the Pioneer Forest, they still want to make a living; they just do so at a lower level of income compared to a forest liquidator. The forest is a very personal place for them; they love working in the woods as well as hosting family gatherings there. The Oregon Tree Farm System named the Cafferatas "Outstanding Tree Farmers of the Year" in 2017.[53]

Many other Oregon family forests are featured in *Forest Family News*, a publication of the Oregon Small Woodlands Association. These are all small operations with various ways of approaching timber and land management.[54]

Specific examples fit into international concepts of sustainable forestry that integrate socioeconomics with ecological health.[55] In stark contrast to timber stripping of the "cut out and get out" era, sustainable forestry at its very basic level involves matching harvest with growth, and in some instances, allowing growth to exceed harvest in order to recover from past excessive exploitation. In contrast to the "boom and bust" economy throughout the history of American mining towns, timber towns, and seafood processing towns (and other volatile and temporary economies), sustainable forestry at least attempts to create a much more stable source of employment, even if severe weather and unpredictable international markets are bound to void all guarantees.[56] But we begin to see how foresters practicing this sort of stewardship interweave the interests of society, economy, and ecology.

The theme of the 2005 documentary film *The Oregon Story: Rethinking the Forests* is basically one of stewardship. The narrators acknowledge a human-influenced forest and an artificial accumulation of fuel from past forest fire suppression policy. Reduced logging has had significant economic impacts on the Oregon economy, and as mentioned, not managing the forest now contributes to mega fires that destroy far more than logging would. Perhaps least excusable of all, because of this reduced logging the "environmental impact" has been shifted elsewhere, for naturally the demand for wood and paper products continues.[57]

For example, circa 2005, following one of the peaks of Amazon forest logging, Brazilians were shipping about 40 percent of rain forest timber abroad. Much of this timber came from illegal logging, and renegades engaged in such crime had zero regard for forest stewardship or "sustainability." Back then Brazil had a notoriously difficult time enforcing its environmental laws, especially over such a vast region. And who was the number one customer for that Brazilian rain forest timber? The United States.[58] So it is easy to become myopically self-righteous at home when part of the consequences for your actions take place out of sight, out of mind. Apparently in more recent years Brazil has had some success mitigating some of this illegal logging,[59] but in 2017 deforestation (legal and illegal) apparently surged in the Amazon again, with illegal logging apparently thriving in Bolivia.[60] Illegal logging continues in many parts of the world. In few places will we find the sort of stewardship forest laws and enforcement as we find in Oregon.

I used to be acquainted with a state forester out here who also worked in Virginia for many years during the early and mid–1990s. He saw the cultural attitude of stewardship in Oregon as remarkable. Here, loggers were generally interested in being informed about the law and complying with it; in Virginia it could become a small ordeal just persuading loggers to do basic things like install a culvert instead of driving trucks through a stream; they were resentful of the law and the state ranger diplomatically asking them to comply.

Ironically, nothing could be more easily sustained than responsible logging. Oregon law has actually required this for a long time. Many decades ago, timber companies trying to practice conscientious stewardship objected to other logging companies that abused the land. Such abuse endangered the health of the forest, the economic health of the industry, and created unfair competition for those trying to be good stewards. Thus some timber companies cooperated with the state to pass and enforce laws like the 1941 Forest Conservation Act. Oregon became the first state to give a state forestry board legal authority over logging practices on private land.[61] The 1941 Forest Conservation Act required leaving stands of seed trees or otherwise re-planting logged acreage. The law also established a research laboratory to find ways to use forest products waste (sawdust, bark, woodchips).[62]

Today stream and river buffers prevent logging too close to water, in the interest of preventing or mitigating erosion or compromising fish habitat (involving water temperature control and turbidity). In addition to the 1972 Forest Practices Act,[63] Oregon was the first state to adopt the 1995 Montreal Process on Criteria and Indicators in sustainable forestry.[64] In other words, Oregon has some of the most progressive and responsible forestry laws in the world, the very opposite end of the spectrum from the old aggressive "cut out and get out" mentality of the 19th and early 20th centuries or, for that matter, the illegal logging that takes place now in other parts of the world.

Lately the Oregon Forest Resource Institute has begun making public service announcements describing the obvious sustainability aspect of Oregon forest practices. This is important. The general cultural shift, beginning in the 1960s and 1970s, turned away from appreciating traditional forest conservation. Many factors caused this, but silviculturalist John J. Garland identified ineffective public relations as one of them,[65] so these public service announcements are vital for addressing that.

Perhaps it is the obviousness of this true sustainability that makes the buzzword utterers grow apoplectic. In a final irony, this land of conscientious stewardship has also been the headquarters of radical environmentalists doing their share for token, environmental elitism—in this case, allowing logging elsewhere in the world, especially in places that lack Oregon's strict logging rules. Meanwhile, some foresters fear that over-bureaucratization has come to cloud the Oregon Forest Practices Act.[66] But then, over-bureaucratization has been a general trend among all government entities, state and national, beginning after World War II at the latest. Yet the forest stewards carry on, and some seem to be surviving fairly well. It helps if profit does not have to be your first priority.

These sorts of stewards—the late Leo Drey, the Parsons, the Cafferatas, and hundreds of small forest owners in many states—reflect a delightful combination of idealism and practicality. It is the same combination that makes me admire a certain select group of attorneys like Bryan Stevenson, Zephaniah Looby, and other idealistic warriors out there fighting the good fight, usually for clients who have little or no money. This is a major reason why I encourage my environmentally-upset students to continue their education. Degrees in forestry, law, engineering, chemistry—these are the tools they will need if they are to effect the changes they seek, or if they want to contribute something substantial in the fields that interest them instead of engaging in ineffective if feel-good protests ... though in the process of their education they are bound to modify their perspective and, hopefully, choose their battles wisely.

We are or should be at a new juncture when it comes to environmental stewardship. We have learned our lessons from previous generations' resource use and abuse. Then we swung back, over-corrected, and created an untenable notion of pure paradise, just when we were discovering the legacy of chemical half-lives underground. But now we have enough knowledge and all the ingredients for a sober philosophical foundation to embrace inevitable stewardship. This stewardship includes, where possible, leaving portions of the landscape with a bare minimum human influence. That includes places formerly altered by humans, even dramatically so. For a while we've been staggering around the new configuration of human presence and impact, territories comparatively free of human presence, and our role in the mix of science, philosophy, and stewardship.

Alston Chase, by the way, was one of the first to describe some of the contortions of stewardship gone awry. As his evocative 1986 book title indicated, *Playing God in Yellowstone* described the inescapable role of humanity: the aforementioned head in the stars, feet in the mud. Yellowstone was one place where the pendulum swung back after earlier rapaciousness. Park Service rangers went from slaughtering wolves, helping render one subspecies extinct, then covertly transplanting a different subspecies and claiming the earlier one was not extinct after all. Amid this was the Edenesque denial of human stewardship, beginning with ignoring the prehistoric Indian presence and how that profoundly shaped the habitats in and around Yellowstone. But as the wolves debacle reflected, the Park Service never quite came to terms with its own stewardship notions or actions. There was precious little true science informing any of their wolf slaughter or reintroduction, partly because we had not yet admitted how little we really knew about ecology in Yellowstone or anywhere else. And, inevitably, there was much political and policy maneuvering behind the public image-consciousness scenes.

In any case, Chase's description of Yellowstone should serve as a cautionary tale. Abandoning Edenic notions and embracing stewardship would be a good first step. Instead of a premise of humanity separated from or distinct from nature, we should accept humanity's relationship with nature as a paradox: we are animals, yet we have a degree of self-consciousness that burdens us with an inescapable stewardship responsibility role. In contrast, humans as distinct from nature causes at least two ironic, yet related problems. The contemporary post-war Edenic view of humans as somehow inherently sullying nature has its counterpart in a worldview that has given some people throughout history the idea that humanity is *superior* to nature. The latter has often resulted in irresponsible resource exploitation, pollution, and other aspects of poor stewardship. But its more recent obverse side, of seeing human-created phenomenon as somehow *inferior* to "natural" phenomenon, or somehow inherently degrading them, is equally misguided. Ancient mythology can actually guide us here.

The idea of humans as environmental stewards, in a way, goes all the way back to the earliest recorded history, as illustrated in the earlier chapter "Cosmos and Chaos." There has always been a strong streak of people who, when enjoying a luxurious moment of not fearing for their future survival, experienced great joy in tending the land. Farmers today know this. The 19th-century Romantics felt it excruciatingly. And ancient people thought they were performing the deepest possible religious act in cultivating the land, tending to orchards, building cities, constructing gardens, fearing and respecting the forest, and rendering their best approximation of Cosmos out of the mundane rendition of cosmic nothingness. It is just that we have lost our way a bit with the contemporary environmental hysteria, elitism, false science, and the sort of environmental lip service and tokenism outlined in this book. It is more than a little ironic, considering most of us live in cities now, where we are obvious caretakers of a highly altered environment immediately surrounding us, but where "nature" thrives nonetheless. Urban ecology is, on one hand, a reflection of nature in the ultimate human-managed environment. And yet, as we shall see, we do not necessarily control nature even in urban settings. Nature has a way of controlling itself, especially in the expression of most life forms struggling to survive, no matter what.

Chapter 10

Modified Habitats

No reasonable person actually advocates dumping plastic in the ocean; rather, it has gathered there from littering, wind blowing over garbage sites, commercial fishers losing their gear, or illegal dumping. The media loves to report the islands of plastic floating in the ocean "twice the size of Texas" or whatever size it actually is.

And yet, fish have made it into a floating habitat. Species like the Trigger fish use the artificial flotsam for sanctuary, similarly to the way they have always used kelp, palm fronds, and other natural materials. Half Moon fish also seek flotsam sanctuary, attracting Sun fish who seek their service in removing parasites. These gathering fish also attract predators, and so the flotsam—whether natural or artificial—become open ocean habitats.[1]

This illustrates at least two things. First, we're not treating our planet the best we can, but when we fail our negative actions are (so far) not the end of the world. Unintended "good" consequences sometimes result, as in the fish finding protection out of unexpected pollution. Second, this illustrates the aforementioned striving of practically all of nature's life forms. We have done much to suppress some species and encourage others, but all species tend to struggle for survival and reproduction whether we want them to or not.

So the "plastic island ecosystem" is just another predictable natural response that we have been witnessing for millennia in cities, whether we noticed or not. Now it is fashionable to study urban ecology, but urban nature has always existed. Just because humans build a concentration of buildings and streets does not mean wildlife stops at the city limits. In fact, nature being nature, certain species have found that the city suits them very well, thank you very much.

If a person were to observe an array of nonhuman homes—say, bird nests, bear dens, squirrel nests, beaver dams, rabbit warrens, or bee hives—they would probably conclude that all of these shelters and constructions were "natural." As mentioned before, back in 1961 Jane Jacobs (the remarkable writer about cities) saw urban settings and their human structures as part of nature.[2] A quarter century later, James Trefil agreed, calling the city a natural ecosystem.[3] Since we've decided to be more picky and reject the entire ecosystem concept as too unscientific, we'll call the city a general habitat (with many a sub-habitat and micro-habitat) that happens to be urban.

So along with these others before me, I am here to argue that human homes, neighborhoods, and cities are no less "natural" than pastures, forests, or wilderness. This premise, probably more than any other in this book, illustrates the further point of people being part of nature. Only Edenists would fail to see cities as the rich and thriving habitats that they have always been. The obvious "niche species" is us, but a plethora of other species thrive. Among the more conspicuous are a great number and variety of birds, insects, rodents, mammals, trees, shrubs, grasses, and weeds.

Aside from habitats intensively or barely influenced by humans, there are intermediary considerations as well. For example, beavers make different dams depending upon what humans are doing in the area (say, cutting down aspen trees or not). Deer, elk, and moose exists in higher populations than at any other time in natural history, owing to our eradication or diminishment of their predator species. The entire salmon fishery of the Pacific Northwest was altered with the advent of hydroelectric dams, then altered again as we created fish ladders, raised fry in hatcheries, and trucked maturing fish downriver. These examples of intermediary human-nonhuman interaction writ large and intensively are, in a sense, what urban ecology is all about: nonhuman life as it has survived or voluntarily adapted to the circumstances we have created, or how we have transplanted flora and fauna, cultivated and nurtured it, but not always controlled it. Other times, just as farmers have done since the Neolithic, we try to remove certain life forms. In the cities and the suburbs it just tends to be entities like weeds and rats rather than crop-feasting crows or lamb-eating eagles.

In fact, one could easily argue that urban ecology and rural ecology are merely points along a continuum of life striving to survive. Human stewardship in any environment is but a variation upon a theme. Thus the concept of rural/wilderness "nature" in contrast to urban artifice breaks down into a false dichotomy parallel with the one separating humans from nature.

If you do not treat your yard with chemicals, and pay attention, every time you mow the grass/weeds you will see ecology at work. In Eugene, we get various low-lying flowers in the spring. I always think about the lowest of those flowers, the ones too close to the ground for the swirling blades, as passing on their genes after escaping decapitation with mowing. Maybe that will increase the likelihood of their survival. I also mow around certain voluntary flowers until they finish blooming, though I'm not sure if I'm helping them propagate or not; still, they show up every year regardless of what I do, so they must like the yard. I also notice hundreds of small spiders that run along the ground, through the grass, ahead of my feet during certain weeks of early spring. My yard is apparently their "ecosystem."

It might have been Henry David Thoreau who once wrote that you could stake out a square yard in the forest and never exhaust the material for study. That is also true of the urban yard, or at least the urban yard left to its own dynamics (save for mowing). And, undoubtedly, in both places one square yard would differ from others side by side. Each would ultimately be unique, and yet we'll never even know the details in most of them, much less all of them. That is an obvious limitation of ecology.

Any close observation of a city reveals a wealth of the urban habitat in nature. Human habitations tend to dominate, of course. But even high-rise apartments feature planter boxes filled with flowers or vegetables. Down on the streets, berms feature grass, shrubs, and trees. Urban parks are the obvious islands of quasi-rural life surrounded by more pronounced city. As long as landlords and homeowners avoid dosing yards with pesticides and herbicides, these grassy places also become rich in flora and insects. And where there are insects there tend to be birds. And finally, with recent trends combating food deserts and favoring the trend of locavorism, urban farms and gardens are multiplying everywhere; often as individual and community food gardens, but also as large-scale commercial concerns utilizing an array of technologies involved with heating, lighting, irrigation, nutrition control, and hydroponics.

As the past issues of *Urban Ecosystems* reveal, there is no end of imagination and urban ecology subjects to study. Scholars have contributed a huge variety of articles dealing with insects, weeds, yards, scavengers, predators, birds, squirrels, urban forests and parks, green roofs, urban aquatic systems (rivers, waterfronts, ponds, wetlands, and storm runoff), and many other topics. The scholarly work is rich and growing richer.

Birds may be the most conspicuous of urban wildlife features. But cities and suburbs also host raccoons, opossums, mice, rats, squirrels, and even larger animals like deer, turkeys, mountain lions, and coyotes. Some towns and cities must be wary of mule deer, elk, and moose, particularly during mating season. And then there are all the animals that accompany humans, mainly house cats and dogs. If you believed in the concept of ecosystem, this would certain constitute one. But let's stick with the more accurate term of habitat and take a look at how life thrives in the city.

The urban habitat differs from the countryside in both obvious and subtle ways, from microclimate, weather patterns, and flora and fauna configurations. The urban habitat (particularly the post-industrial one) is generally warmer and wetter than its country cousin, yet less windy and not as humid.[4] Atmospheric composition is what you might expect; greater than average carbon monoxide, sulfur dioxide, nitrogen oxide, particulates from tire abrasion, and other chemicals related to cars and factories.[5] Even some urban trees (such as oaks, gums, willows, poplars, sycamores, and black locust) emit volatile organic compounds that can negatively effect urban air quality. Conifers, on the other hand, capture more air pollution than broadleaf deciduous trees in general.[6]

The oft-noted "heat island" effect of cities tends to create its own weather of a sort, with all that hot air rising and thus drawing in the surrounding cooler air from the suburbs and countryside. Insects fly higher in the city, making them more conspicuous targets for hungry birds. The heat island also generally creates less frost and thus earlier plant flowering, but in some instances this feature even attracts more southerly plants to migrate and thrive at points to their urban north.[7]

Compared to the countryside, urban settings tend to feature denser populations of birds, but less diversity.[8] This is because certain bird species thrive in the city, while others cannot survive at all. One general distinguishing feature appears to be noise tolerance, and the fluke of having a species' call muted by traffic noise or not.[9] In fact, urban ecologists have organized categories of bird and mammal species depending upon their ability to thrive or not in city and town environments.[10] Cities are famous/notorious for hosting pigeons, but pigeons attract falcons that essentially use skyscrapers as a cliff habitat, where they thrive as long as people allow them to do so. Pigeons have even learned to scurry beneath parked cars when the falcons descend.[11]

And, just as skyscrapers function as cliff habitat for falcons, so does concrete and other masonry surfaces function for plants commonly associated with rural rock outcrops. An examination of "weed" species in Halifax, Nova Scotia reflected such associations.[12] All of this makes common sense. If people abandoned cities, this would be how nature would begin "reclaiming" the habitat. It is exactly how nature has already moved into abandoned industrial sites.[13] The only astonishing part is how so many continue to create false dichotomies of human/non-human environments, human and "natural" environments. Complaints about house cats killing urban birds is the sort of non-issue that arises in this context.[14]

First of all, we tend to foster urban birds by feeding and sheltering them, so if anything, we have increased the population of birds in the city. If we do not want cats to kill them, all we have to do is attach bells to their collars. Of course, that would mean they would not kill anything, including mice. I notice that the songbird aficionados do not seem to mind when house cats kill mice. Ironically, Eyal Shochat and other scholars concluded that urban birds face overall less predation than their rural counterparts, housecats notwithstanding.[15] And thus the housecat-songbird-killing controversy is a tempest in a teapot about an invented, nonexistent problem. But it is a feature of nature we are not familiar with addressing as such, which is true of urban ecology in general.

We and our fellow life forms are participants in any given habitat, including the urban one. Protesting songbird death as if the context were avian paradise is a mistake. Instead, the context is one in which human influence is at its highest and most noticeable. Personally I like both songbirds and house cats, and I've noticed both thrive in my neighborhood and countless others.

Urban ecologists have studied practically everything you can imagine—not just the aforementioned obvious things like air quality and animal presence, but also the chemistry of precipitation runoff and urban soil science.[16] One of my personal favorites has been their study of vacant lots. To no surprise, such places feature unique habitats all their own, with a tendency to host lichens, moss, ferns, and even various trees, shrubs, and flowering plants. Instead of "weeds," urban ecologists like to call many of these plants "pioneers" or more scientifically, *ruderal* plants. Ironically, "native" species often find a place in vacant lots,[17] not competing with herbicides and introduced flora, as they would be in manicured yards. But plenty of "escapees" from yards also show up. Vacant lot plants attract associated insects (milkweed attracts Monarch butterflies, Curly Dock attracts beetles) which, in turn, attract birds and small rodents—which, in turn, attract house cats.[18] Altogether, vacant lots support large varieties of plant, insect, and invertebrate life.[19] It's interesting but unsurprising how an "empty" lot can spawn a food chain.

It's also interesting (and also unsurprising) to discover that the urban habitat has been causing genetic changes in various species.[20] The golden orb-weaving spider apparently grows larger in the city.[21] Grasshoppers change the sound of their mating noise to compete with automobile traffic.[22] Some urban birds have larger brains, and apparently bird body chemistry can change after living in the city.[23] If this sort of evolution is not "natural," then I'm not sure what is. And yet Edenism is so persistent that some urban ecologists transfer their rural and wilderness predecessors' language and mentality to the city. I'm not kidding. It is a little amusing to watch them try to adapt this mindset of buzzwords (holistic, biodiversity, sustainability) to the city habitat.[24] This becomes a ludicrous and untenable separation of humanity from nature, wherein even human-created and abandoned vacant lots somehow become "natural ecosystems" as long as humans do not interfere.[25] What? Not interfere? Beginning when, after abandonment? Before or after building demotion? I'm joking, of course, but this must be the depth of misanthropic environmentalism, wherein even urban life is somehow "corrupted" by humanity.

The realities of urban ecology are much more interesting. For example, in Dunedin, New Zealand, Emily Gray and Yoland van Heezik discovered that urban birds readily interacted with and benefited from both "native" and "exotic" trees.[26] In Mexico City, Monserrat SuárezRodríguez and his team of ecologists observed urban birds using discarded cigarette butts to line their nests, concluding they might have figured out that the residual nicotine fended off a parasitic mite.[27] This should not surprise us. Everything is trying to adapt and survive.

Mark Jordan, a conservation biology professor at Seattle University, got it right. "I would argue that the city is as much a natural area as what we call more wilderness areas," he said. His hidden cameras have captured images of coyotes, raccoons, and opossums in Seattle's parks. He noted that cities have generally become refuges away from large predators.[28] As Simon and Wildavsky wrote, "if humankind is considered to be part of the natural order, then it is not only human beings who must adapt to other species, but those nonhuman forms of life that must also adapt to us."[29] Clearly many species have already done so, and will continue to do so. Some even find these human-intensive habitats most inviting.

How we design cities and what we value will continue to have noticeable impacts upon urban ecology. But as is plain, nonhuman life survives and even thrives in the city no matter what we do. How excellent if we value squirrels and birds and thus give them food and shelter. How excellent if we value cougars and want to create corridors for them to migrate through and around urban areas. But the fact is, we're already interacting a great deal with "nature in the city."

Regarding aforementioned songbirds, around half the American population feeds them.[30] But that's just the beginning. Eight-year-old Gabi Mann of Seattle gained international fame in 2015 when reporters told her story of crows bringing her gifts. This inspired many readers from various countries to relate their own stories of urban crow interactions.[31] Raccoons in one of my former neighborhoods were enormous, undoubtedly feasting on pet food left on porches. Portland, Oregon, hosts an Urban Coyote Project in coordination with the Audubon Society.[32] In Eugene we regularly see flocks of wild turkeys roaming neighborhoods, the community college campus, and even downtown. Many of my neighbors have deer fences to protect their vegetable gardens from the roaming herds, and we're a long way from the city's edge.

In some locations, city dwellers commonly see urban turkeys—along with deer, raccoons, opossums, and many other wildlife species. Viewed from a non–Edenic perspective, cities and suburbs merely represent points on a continuum in a wide spectrum of habitats. One way to describe these habitats is in terms of degrees of minimal and maximum human influences. But whether in a city core or remote wilderness legally set aside, the imprint of human environmental stewardship is practically everywhere on earth (author's photograph).

Some of the most intensive presence of "nature in the city" involves urban forestry. It can change the entire character of a city.[33] For example, the small town of Eureka, California often strikes people as having the "feel" of a city due to its dearth of urban trees. I remember someone I knew coming to visit me in Eugene for the first time, driving up from Eureka. "It's so lush," was the immediate reaction, for in Eugene we have a very rich array of urban trees, making it "feel" much more like a town than a city, despite having five times the population of Eureka (closer to ten times if you count the entire Eugene-Springfield metro area).

Obviously mature trees foster habitat for urban wildlife (particularly birds, squirrels, and raccoons), but urban greenery in general has all sorts of benefits for humans as well, from crime reduction, increase in property values, mitigation of the heat island effect, and muffling of traffic noise.[34] People living near or interacting with these places enjoy the aesthetics, higher levels of social interaction, improved emotional outlook, and an overall better quality of life.[35] The urban forest is a wondrous phenomenon.

As any realtor will tell you, house hunters often distinguish between older, established neighborhoods with mature trees compared to the saplings of a subdivision freshly carved out of a meadow. There is something indescribably pleasing about a tree-lined street that likely lowers one's blood pressure and makes city living more bearable. Trees affect us profoundly, whether we always know it or not. As mentioned in the previous chapter, this is probably because trees evoke some of the most primal emotions people have for flora.

We celebrate innumerable individual dedication or commemoration trees, "champion" or "heritage" trees, and all sorts of emotional activities associated with trees. Barbara Bosworth gathered a collection of "champion" trees around the United States. Thomas Pakenham wrote a series of books about trees all over the world that he found remarkable for one reason or another. College campuses regularly feature plaques dedicating trees to deceased employees, ranging from administrators and professors, to groundskeepers who actually once cared for those same trees. An oak sapling Jesse Owens brought back from his magnificent 1936 Berlin Olympics continues to inspire runners at Rhodes High School in Cleveland.[36] It was world news when scientists discovered a Bosnian pine in northern Greece over a thousand years old.[37] The American Heritage Trees organization focuses on old trees that have survived on farms.[38] Various states and cities feature an official list of outstanding trees.[39]

Shortly after their marriage, Prince William and Duchess Catherine planted an Eastern hemlock in Canada to symbolize their union.[40] The Jeanette Maples Project is a cherry tree planting effort dedicated to a girl who died from severe and prolonged child abuse in Eugene, Oregon.[41] In 2011, after an arsonist targeted a mosque in Corvallis, Oregon, a group of local citizens planted a mountain hemlock tree on its grounds as a symbol of peace and compassion.[42]

Loss or destruction of individual trees also gains notice now. Simon Worrall went in search of the remains of the "world's oldest clove tree" in Ternate, Indonesia.[43] A vandal who attacked a Glastonbury tree with a chainsaw made the BBC News.[44] When age and disease finally claimed it, Philadelphians and tourists alike mourned the Norway maple tree of Philadelphia's Laurel Hill Cemetery, "a witness to history."[45] Similarly, in Virginia, Roanoke College students and staff turned out to say goodbye to an old tulip poplar hit by lightning one too many times.[46] When the city had to take down a diseased, ancient maple tree in the West University neighborhood of Eugene, residents gathered for a farewell ceremony.[47] The Japanese spent around $27 million to salvage the remains of the last pine standing in Rikuzentakata after the 2011 tsunami leveled all others. The salt water killed the 270-year-old tree, but they salvaged it in pieces with plans to reconstruct it as a museum piece.[48]

An old sycamore slated for felling on the Virginia Tech campus elicited all sorts of community grief, including a touching note left on the tree by a woman who once met a man under it for their first date; they later married, then returned to the tree many times over the following years for picnics and music festivals. She sadly wrote that she was watching her children play beneath the tree just before it's demise. "For me and my family it has become more than just an easy landmark," she wrote, "it's a symbol. A symbol of our love, our love for our town, for our family, for our community."[49] I personally remember that tree very well, and spent a great many hours on Henderson Lawn where it once resided during my entire adolescence and young adulthood in Blacksburg. That was a difficult article to read, but I am grateful for the note the woman wrote.

People commonly commemorate dead trees (including the sycamore just mentioned) by making things out of them, like bowls and boxes, furniture and rolling pins.[50] For decades a professional logger named Frank Knight helped protect a 217-year-old elm from Dutch elm's disease in Yarmouth, Maine. When the tree finally succumbed, furniture maker Chris Becksvoort secretly saved some of it for Knight's future casket, and in 2012 Knight was buried in it after a long 103 years of life.[51] Steward and ward were united in a ceremonial rite the ancient forest tribes would have lauded.

Today's tree worship has much more in common with the mid–19th-century Romantic tradition than it does with ancient customs, self-conscious neo-Druidism notwithstanding. For example, in his 1864 book *The Maine Woods*, Henry David Thoreau wrote (in true Romantic fashion) that it was the poet above all others who appreciated the value of trees most; not the utilitarian tradesmen and craftsmen who made lumber, turpentine, and used the tannic acid to cure hides. Plenty of today's woodworkers, including George Nakashima,[52] would disagree with that and probably call Thoreau a bigot in this regard. Thoreau appreciated practical aspects of trees, but wrote of trees as co-equal with humans in their immortality, saying he loved their spirits above all other qualities.[53] Animistic traditions, such as the Maori and Salish canoe makers, would extent the spiritual aspects of trees to the things people ritualistically made *of* them.[54]

Unfortunately, it is Thoreau's sort of romanticism that complicates urban forestry, and nowhere on earth (I assume) than where I live right now, in Eugene, Oregon. Tree worship remains at the heart of the green religion described earlier. And, as so often is the case when it comes to spiritual misunderstandings, the tree religion defies all logic, knowledge, and common sense. It is also deeply ironic, for Eugene and Portland have to rank very high among tree-friendly cities. No wonder; both exist in a state with some of the most progressive forestry laws in the world. But the tree worshippers see it all in their own delusional context.

"The present-day attitude of people to living trees is often sentimental and romantic," Cecil Konijnendijk wrote. "Trees, unlike most other plants, are granted a soul."[55] Konijnendijk also noted the neo–Druid self-conscious association between people and trees.[56] This means arborists in Eugene work in a sociocultural environment that is sometimes irrationally unfriendly to their task. An electrical utility worker told me stories of people in the South Hills (an older, elite section of town) screaming profanities at the tree maintenance crews. These same people would predictably be raising hell after the next ice storm, wondering why it was taking so long to have their electricity restored. The connection between un-maintained trees and limbs and trunks taking out electric lines seemed lost upon them. Such is the power of emotionalism.

Over the years many urban tree worshippers have written into the local capitalistic "alternative" advertising-heavy newspaper, the *Eugene Weekly*, to object to tree cutting (often only if the trees are old and large), to proffer conspiracy theories about why the trees are being cut, and other irrational observations.[57] Sometimes the arborists respond, trying to explain obvious things like the danger of old and diseased trees, how Eugene occupied a treeless prairie before Euroamericans created the urban forest in the first place, or how the Eugene Tree Foundation's team of volunteers plants and waters urban trees on a regular and ongoing basis.[58] I'm sure the educational efforts are worthwhile, even if they will always be wasted among the ideologues.

Yet the emotion is understandable. As just described, even reading about the demise of that old sycamore I once knew, from three thousand miles away, evoked so many sad and wistful emotions for the tree and so many memories I associated with it from a different era that will never come again. But that is life and inevitable death. There is a reasonable middle ground for those who also feel the emotion but understand practical necessities.

Losing an urban tree leaves a special void, particularly since they exist surrounded by yards, houses, streets, and parking lots. When they're gone they trigger primal agoraphobia feelings, at least in me. But any sensitive person knows this or should know it. On the other hand, any sensible person wants to avoid getting houses, cars, people and pets crushed by trees. "Right tree in the right place," is a phrase that urban foresters repeat frequently, while also acknowledging that no tree will survive a severe enough storm.

An urban forest is always a risk, but one worth taking for those of us who enjoy them.

In tree-friendly Eugene, the city's urban foresters always post notices on trees that are planned for removal. The public is invited to inquire or comment. The community college will send a campus-wide email notification for the same reason. When construction of Cascade Manor (a retirement home complex) required the removal of third-growth Douglas fir trees, the feature story made the front page of the local paper.[59] Bob Johnson, a Cascade Manor administrator, expressed his own grief over the trees' removal. "I felt sick when I drove by and saw them gone. My wife was crying," he told the local paper. But Johnson also pointed out that most of the humans living in Cascade Manor were middle-aged when those trees first sprouted.[60] In other words, the trees were young in comparison to the people who ended up living on that same ground. Old people ought to count for something, even in youth-cult America.

In 2008, Whitey Lueck, a horticulturalist of local tree aficionado fame, wrote a touching essay about a huge coast redwood tree he had to take down in his front yard. Obviously he loved the tree, but it had grown large and it's two-trunk split structure made it a looming threat to neighboring people and property. Before the arborists arrived to do their important work, Lueck wrote an explanation for what he was doing and why, and posted it near the tree. He sent flyers to his neighbors informing them of the situation. During the tree's last night, he placed ten luminarios around the base of the tree in a solemn farewell ceremony to his "gentle giant."[61]

From my point of view, that is Eugene at its very best.

During the 2016–17 winter we had an ice storm in Eugene followed by high winds. Times like that remind us of the high price we pay for our luxuriant urban forest. Even before the wind storm exacerbated the millions of dollars in ice storm damage, I asked an arborist when they expected to catch up on their backlog of requests. He half-joked, "Maybe in two years." It wasn't much of an exaggeration. Naturally arborists first focused on fallen trees actually inside houses, leaning against power lines, and other emergencies. Then they moved down the list toward temporarily stable but irreparably damaged trees. Eventually, by late summer, they returned to their normal work of doctoring compromised trees that could be saved through judicious trimming.

A terrible nakedness follows the loss of an urban tree. I lost several in my yard after the storm, and it took weeks to get used to their absence. Every time I walked outside I expected to see them. Instead, I just felt a sense of exposure while standing near where they used to be. But one of the greatest joys in being the steward of a small piece of urban land (i.e., my yard) is planting trees. So soon after I lost two scotch pines and a spruce tree, I nestled in a small Leyland Cypress between a couple of fresh stumps. What a joyous privilege it will be to watch that tree grow. Yet those stumps reminded me to thank all the urban foresters out there literally risking their lives to maintain our wonderful city trees. I especially appreciate their work because in my youth I did a little of it myself, albeit without training or equipment. I hung on with my legs and cut the limbs and the "tops." It is one thing to be afraid of heights; quite another to drop several hundred pounds off a tree top and be clinging up there with your legs, trying to shut off the chainsaw as quickly as possible, feeling that massive trunk swaying from its released stress, and nowhere to run if things go awry. Undoubtedly I was shaking as much as the pine needles.

By the way, it is much more enjoyable planting individual trees with no time constraints, in complete peace, compared to those days up on the mountains with a semi-insane straw boss screaming imprecations at us day labor tree planters. It was my personal privilege to work with the migrants, but a pain to be among the ruffian natives, especially that straw boss, who was "stashing" trees (burying piles of them illegally to collect the per-tree contract money) when the Weyerhauser monitor wasn't looking. I remember that Weyerhauser monitor; some guy named Jim—very professional, very friendly. He was even diplomatic about the obnoxious straw boss, and very respectful and appreciative of those migrant tree planters.

*   *   *

If we love the presence of the forest in the city, more and more we are coming to love the presence of the farm in the city as well. Community gardens are wonderful for all the reasons stated before; they offer practical solutions to the food desert problem in inner cities, they educate school children, and they bring people together in a peaceful activity. Like urban forests, they tend to mitigate crime. They give residents a common vested interest in their neighborhood. But as important as all this is, the commercial urban farm offers a different sort of excitement that could have great benefits for rural areas and the planet at large.

The Dutch are experimenting with indoor, controlled environment farming near the Hague. So far the operation requires more energy costs than conventional farming, but uses no pesticides because there are no insects. No insects removes a major incentive for GMOs, if the latter concerns you. The indoor environment removes the crops from adverse weather, so no food is lost in through sleet, thunderstorms, heat spells, or damaging winds. Indoor

Stadium Woods (center of photo), a little over eleven acres surrounded by the Virginia Tech campus and a Blacksburg residential neighborhood. In recent years this has become a controversial property among those who want to preserve this island of old growth hardwood trees and those who would fell the trees for the expanding university. Urban forests of this size and age have become rare in the United States, especially along the eastern seaboard states. By contrast the Atlantic Rainforest of Brazil (highly diminished and fragmented) remains far larger and more substantial (enhanced from Google Earth images).

conditions also lessen water use through both careful control and limited evaporation. And finally, compared to conventional farming, the operation requires less land to grow the same amount of food.[62] Urban farms in New York and Chicago feature similar dynamics—high demands for electricity and clean water, high per-square yard production, but (in these cases) also apparently regular presence of aphids and thrips, pest insects requiring weekly release of predator insects.[63] Certainly all indoor farms would seem to be immune from large swarms of the usual outdoor predators, whether insects or birds, thus eliminating an age-old problem without resorting to poisoning or killing.

In Singapore—one of the highest urban density populations in the world—the Sky Greens company is growing food in a four-story building, with a gravity-powered water wheel slowly propelling plants up to the sunlight, then down to a hydroponic pool filled with nutrients. Unlike the Dutch operation, Sky Greens uses very little energy, partly by employing a closed-loop hydroponic system.[64]

Green Sense Farms began in Indiana, and is now building a global network of urban warehouses featuring vertical vegetable production.[65] On a much more modest scale, urban farming is popular in my adopted hometown, which features half a dozen community gardens. Other cities, including New York, Atlanta, and Detroit, also feature urban farming operations of varying sizes.[66]

One of the greatest promises of urban commercial agriculture is its potential for alleviating demands upon rural land.[67] If more people in the city grow food more efficiently in warehouses, that raises the possibility of allowing former farmland to return to forest or other habitat for nonhuman life. It will sound like a pipe dream for now, but a hundred years in the future this could be the solution for the megafauna we so adore, now suffering major losses of habitat. The "buffalo commons" idea fits into this pipe dream, as do visions of other large animals we like—wolves, lions, elephants, rhinoceroses, tigers—roaming free on all continents.

Like it or not, most of us live in cities now and the global urbanization trend shows all likelihood of continuing. Given our ongoing environmental concerns, undoubtedly we will continue to think about "green cities" or "biophilic cities" as many have already done in the fields of urban ecology, urban forestry, architecture and urban planning.[68] It appears that we will continue to plan as never before in accommodating nonhuman life in the city. Some obvious (and expensive) projects include cougar corridors in southern California and the fish-friendly seawall in Seattle.[69] But there can be smaller urban design changes that go quite far in accommodating nonhuman species, such as new docks designed to foster aquatic life and adjoining shore life.[70] Urban parks and forests are always a big help, but so is building design that accommodates green roofs or ground-level greenery.

One of the more ambitious projects is the entire "eco city" of Tianjin, a joint project between China and Singapore. Here the plan is to build a city featuring complete non-fossil fuel energy use, a light rail system, and much integration of water and flora features throughout.[71] China, of course, has intensive interest in improving both its urban and rural environments, much as the United States did during the Progressive Era.

Given the high levels of support for "environmentalism" in a generic sense, we are far beyond earlier attitudes of ambiguity toward nature, as well as the "conquering" of it that followed. Now we have the luxury of wanting to blend our lives with nature in cities, the middle of the most intensive human habitats of them all.

* * *

Insects and especially spiders find and make habitat in my firewood stacks. Firewood is my only source of heat, and I try to keep ahead with a two-winter supply. Also, drying the wood for two summers removes all sap. But that's also plenty of time for an entire series of insect habitats to develop among the several cords gathered around my yard at any given time. They are habitats I slowly destroy as I burn the wood. Spiders regularly scramble as I pick up individual pieces of wood. I see their nests of thick gauze, doomed to incineration. Sole wasps hibernating on pieces of wood wake up enough to bite if you don't look for them and snap them off into the yard (where they'll probably become someone else's meal). For a few years I regularly found the remarkable wolf spiders hanging out at the bottom of firewood stacks, probably roaming the upper reaches during earlier months, hunting for insects and other spiders.

If I did not burn the wood it would slowly disintegrate and destroy those habitats differently and more gradually than me removing the logs. But the point is, things obviously change in nature. My firewood stacks foster hundreds if not thousands of insects at any given time, but they are rotating habitats. Some of those insects find new homes as the old ones disappear. These are not "ecosystems"; they are habitats that will remain ultimately mysterious in all their configurations and dynamics. Sometimes I find thousands of sugar ants; other times, barely any at all. The wolf spiders have been scarce lately. Who knows why.

This is the resiliency of nature in general, readily found in habitats ranging from wilderness to field to forest and in any vacant city lot. The undiscerning eye may think the city is dominated by humans without appreciating how immediately nature has moved in. In fact, nature was there in the first place and never left. Nature does not abhor vacuums because there are no vacuums in nature. Nonhuman life adapted to cities immediately, and would quickly take over completely, were we to stop maintaining our fragile expression of civilization in the urban environment.

In the end we cannot escape our self-conscious environmental stewardship role, whether urban, rural, suburban—or in the wilderness areas we've set aside with their own special rules. Even if we deliberately avoid anthropocentric interests, inevitably we are still doing so because *we* (not other species) are making those decisions based upon science and especially upon philosophical value judgments. We cannot escape ourselves. It is pure folly to attempt anything otherwise. Stewardship is our inescapable responsibility, burden, and privilege. The details of this stewardship is where all our energies need to focus, not on a false Edenic premise, a false emergency premise, environmental doomsdayism, nor on the pitfalls of politicized science.

Afterword

One of the strangest aspects of Edenic environmental thinking appears to be lack of appreciation for something very obvious: the transience of our own existence. Edenists seem to think that their paradise is not only perfect, but eternal. After all, non-eternal things grow old, deteriorate, and die. Thus, for them, perhaps Eden occupies some metaphysical exception to what we commonly understand as reality; perhaps by residing in their eternal Eden they can ignore their own mortality. It would be one explanation for why so many doomsdayists preach their creed even during their last days, as if saving Eden will somehow have a bearing upon their own personal future. By contrast, some of the better environmental stewards inherently appreciate that we are but temporary and very brief caretakers inserted into a vast, indifferent phenomenon that has preceded us and (as far as we know) will continue after we are gone. That should humble us. In fact, that should be the cure to practically all pride associated with environmental philosophy and policy.

That great smart aleck Winston Churchill was fond of quoting Hegel, who supposedly wrote, "We learn from history that we do not learn from history." But the study of history should teach us a couple of things: first, the human condition has remained generally constant since recorded time. There have likely always been fairly comparable levels of human greed and generosity, compassion and sociopathic behavior, wisdom and folly, et cetera. No magical force has come along to alter basic human nature. Second, we should appreciate how easy it is to laugh and cringe about past beliefs and worldviews we have come to reject. People once practiced trial by ordeal, burned witches, and thought the ocean would end in a waterfall that fell off the edge of the earth. They believed that strange creatures lived in other lands; people with only one eye, or a human foot coming out of their necks instead of heads. Yet these accounts should alert us to the existence of "quaint beliefs" in our own time, even if we're not always sure of what they might be. Still, we may be confident that they exist.

So, as philosopher of science Anthony O'Hear wrote, "science may be influenced by myths prevalent at a given time and place, and its practitioners respond in their research and theories to the interests and desires of the ruling groups in society."[1] O'Hear added that nature itself would get the last word, for human theories and ideas come and go, while nature never stops inviting us to understand. On the other hand, imposing philosophical values on science tends to render bad science and bad philosophy.[2] The historian Peter J. Bowler observed the obvious subjective philosophical values that color environmental sciences, and how no thoughtful practitioner even attempts denying this anymore.[3] There is nothing inherently wrong about this "death" of objective science—it is just important to try to see ourselves as influenced by the trends, fads, forces, fears, and the values of our times.

Philosopher of science Samir Okasha noted that, in the broad history of science, past empirically-supported scientific theories later turned out to be false,[4] at least according to later generations of scientists. Okasha warned, "we should be cautious about assuming that our current scientific theories are true, however well they fit our data."[5] It's an important point, but some would object to framing the issue in that manner at all, saying the data should determine the theory, not the theory fitting the data. In other words, an inductive (rather than deductive) approach might gradually lead us to a new scientific worldview with fewer mistakes or presumptions along the way. The problem with deducing from a pre-determined worldview—say, anthropogenic climate change, a supposed balance in nature, the existence of ecosystems, or species preservation imperatives—is a temptation to cherry-pick the data (consciously or not), otherwise known as confirmation bias.

We could probably all benefit from an occasional refresher regarding epistemology and empiricism at the common sense level. Much environmental fear in American popular culture is unfounded, and thus unnecessary and counterproductive. Just think about it a moment and ask yourself an honest question: how would you feel about the world and the environment if you did not have the media feeding you doom and gloom? Only those living near toxic waste sites (usually the victims of environmental injustice) would feel imperiled and, indeed, ill. The rest of us would have no indication of impending apocalypse. There are heat waves in summer, and arctic fronts in winter. The ocean shore remains (as it always has been) a foolish place to build a house.

So how much do any of us "know" about the environment? Personal empirical observation of all raw data is humanly impossible, of course. But we can reason from what we do know—such as revisiting the scientific method and appreciating its limitations, and distinguishing philosophical values from scientific facts. Certainly we should learn to be more comfortable

with questions. There is so much about the environment we do *not* know—
so what? We should and will keep exploring. But we're nowhere near finishing
"discovery," as they would say in the legal field, so we're nowhere near deliv-
ering closing arguments.

My niece Emily, pursuing her biology career, talks about a pure day-
dream she knows is unlikely ever to come about: 80 percent of science funding
dedicated to replicating results of earlier studies. Instead, novel "new" science
tends to win the day and the grant. A shift in funding toward replication
would immediately reveal massive problems in many environmental sciences,
just as they have in the aforementioned preliminary checks in the field of
psychology. In the meantime, we also face a great deal of non-science or compromised science relying upon the authority that true science rightly deserves.

Aside from science, as many have noted, there has been a wealth redistribution streak in the environmental movement from the outset.[6] Ironically,
like the overlapping parts of socialist and democratic theories, certain free
market advocates have also seen ending global poverty as a solution to environmental problems, with alleviating human suffering as the first priority.
The end result would be similar. It is the means by which the end is achieved
that differs so starkly, and in this dynamic we get traditional political splits
between confidence in government regulation versus a less regulatory
approach. In the process, the environmental remediation business generates
billions of dollars for lawyers, engineers, technicians, and lobbyists in the
name of environmental cleanup.[7] So, like communist governments everywhere, the aristocracy merely shifted from traditional birth-based families
to the party elite. In America we have watched limousine liberalism develop,
with environmental elites babbling much rhetoric about distributing other
people's money, but only token amounts of their own. There has been no
wealth redistribution of any significance; environmental racism is alive and
well. Outside the United States, disparities regarding poverty, standards of
living, and environmental conditions are often even more stark.

None of this is surprising. As Allan Freeze wrote, "the environmental
movement has historically been a spiritual force rather than a pragmatic
source of practical advice."[8] Freeze felt it was well nigh time for the environmental movement to work past this earlier, useful stage, toward more pragmatic efforts. This is exactly what people like Bjørn Lomborg have been doing
for some years now.

Human population reduction would help any number of ecological matters, such as fossil fuel consumption, carbon emissions, loss of open space,
nonhuman species extinction, et cetera. But because population reduction is
inextricably entangled in much bigger socioeconomic problems associated

with standards of material living, disease and life expectancy, and education levels, it has been and will continue to prove a hard nut to crack in impoverished nations. Addressing these issues is apparently not as rewarding for the crusading mentality, but that is probably the only realistic means toward a more biophilic end. The advocates of an economic approach to environmental problems have an important point in this regard, though the "free market" ideology is always problematic, often merely cloaking an actual non-free market government regulatory regime that favors the proponent's particular interests. But the environmental elite show their true colors by ignoring economics in favor of righteous idealism. It is too easy to "be concerned" about the environment when all your other needs for survival are so sumptuously exceeded.

So what makes an environmentalist? Allan Freeze offered an excellent summary of many important ideas and approaches.[9] He believed environmentalists and all interested parties should attempt to cooperate in a common community of sorts, evolving beyond the villainization that has been so prevalent since environmental litigation became a cottage industry. While past mistakes need rectification, Freeze felt it was more important to focus on careful planning in order to avoid creating future environmental problems. He acknowledged the practical and unavoidable reality of economics and accepted humanity's natural aspirations toward high material standards of living. But he also embraced compassion for multi-generational life, including humanity and our fellow species in general. Finally, he believed that an environmentalist was someone who embraced science as well as the "beauty, awe, reverence, and integrity" inherent in "spiritual knowledge"[10] of the environment. That says a lot, and something worth considering seriously at this mature stage of what began, during the 1960s, as the Environmental Movement.

Aaron Wildavsky wrote, "individuals choose what to fear to support their way of life."[11] That probably holds truth for educated people, but a great deal is feared in ignorance, and that was the case in 1984 when that geologist proffered his environmental doomsdayism to me. In light of what I've learned during the decades since (plus, simply growing old and prospects of a "premature" death long gone) I regret succumbing to that groundless depression. Doomsdayists are often a sort of parasite like that, draining psychic energy from the vulnerable. They take much and contribute little.

So perhaps ironically, a born pessimist like me has come to stand with the optimists when it comes to our species, our planet and its many life forms, and future human generations. I think we have already done a great deal to separate real environmental problems from fictitious ones. More importantly, like any decent humanist, I love to celebrate human ingenuity both ancient and contemporary. Not being a scientist nor an engineer, the joy is almost completely vicarious. When the recent Curiosity/Rover mission to Mars succeeded, I found renewed astonishment that all those engineers had been able to pull off such a complex mission with literally dozens of stages that all had to function perfectly, from entering the orbit of Mars at enormous speed, to slowing down quickly and on time (without even seconds to spare in error), to touching down just so.[12] It is the sort of thing that people suspend their belief for, in order to enjoy science fiction novels. But those Curiosity/Rover people actually did it! And yet I find the same fascination at the ancient Incans' precisely calibrated irrigation ditches that sloped at perfect degrees over long distances. Humanity is fascinating.

We can do it. Whatever we set our minds to, we'll make progress and accomplishments. But even if we failed, it would always be better to go down fighting. If I could go back in time and respond to that doomsday geologist, I would simply repeat what the Brits frequently told each other during World War II: Keep Calm and Carry On.

Chapter Notes

Preface

1. Will Sarvis, *Sacred and Ephemeral: Reflections Upon Land, Place, and Home* (Self-published, 2017).

2. Thucydides, Richard Crawley, trans., *History of the Peloponnesian War*, Book V, https://en.wikisource.org/wiki/History_of_the_Peloponnesian_War/Book_5.

Introduction

1. Alston Chase, *In a Dark Wood: The Fight Over Forests and the Rising Tyranny of Ecology* (New York: Houghton Mifflin, 1995), 165–67.

2. Lauren Sommer, "Planning for the Future of a Park Where the Trees Have One Name," *NPR's Morning Edition* (Aug. 2, 2016).

3. See, for example, Owen Amos, "Where is the Remotest Spot in the United States?" *BBC News* (Dec. 1, 2017). I deal with this subtopic at great length in the chapter, "Misanthropic Eden," in Will Sarvis, *Sacred and Ephemeral: Reflections Upon Land, Place, and Home* (Self-published, 2017).

4. Lior Weissbrod, et al., "Origins of House Mice in Ecological Niches Created by Settled Hunter-Gatherers in the Levant 15,000 Y Ago," *Proceedings of the National Academy of Sciences* 114, no. 16 (Apr. 18, 2017): 4099–4104.

5. Thomas S. Kuhn, *Structure of Scientific Revolutions*, 2nd ed. (1962; Chicago: University of Chicago Press, 1970).

6. Generally shelter is temporary protection from the elements; home is a more established and complex sense of place. See Will Sarvis, "The Homelessness Muddle Revisited," *Urban Lawyer* 49, no. 2 (Spring 2017): 317–354. Also see the chapters "Transitory Home" and "Home in the Breach," in Sarvis, *Sacred and Ephemeral*.

7. Susanne K. Langer, *Philosophy in a New*

Key (Cambridge: Harvard University Press, 1942), 287.

Chapter 1

1. Jamsheed Kairshasp Choksy, *Purity and Pollution in Zoroastrianism: Triumph Over Evil* (Austin: University of Texas Press, 1989), 2, 3.

2. Robert Charles Zaehner, *The Dawn and Twilight of Zoroastrianism* (New York: Putnam, 1961), 20–21, 51–52, 57–58.

3. Robert Ardrey, *The Territorial Imperative: A Personal Inquiry into the Animal Origins of Property and Nations* (New York: Atheneum, 1966).

4. Elaine Pagels, *The Origin of Satan* (New York: Random House, 1995), xxii, 12, 17–18, 47, 85, 87, 107, 110, 111, 119–20, 179, 184.

5. Dwight Jeffrey Bingham, "Irenaeus of Lyons," in *The Routledge Companion to Early Christian Thought*, edited by Dwight Jeffrey Bingham (New York: Routledge, 2010), 144; Denis Minns, *Irenaeus* (Washington, D.C.: Georgetown University Press, 1994), 62, 63; Eric Francis Osborn, *Irenaeus of Lyons* (New York: Cambridge University Press, 2001), 218.

6. Joseph Campbell, *The Hero with a Thousand Faces*, 3rd ed. (Novato, CA: New World Library, 2008), 34; Bruce Chilton, et al., *The Cambridge Companion to the Bible*, 2nd ed. (New York: Cambridge University Press, 2008), 53, 57, 60, 61; Mircea Eliade, *Cosmos and History: The Myth of the Eternal Return*, Willard R. Trask, trans. (New York: Harper, 1959), 5, 6–11, 18; Mircea Eliade, *Myth and Reality* (New York: Harper & Row, 1963), 140–41; Mircea Eliade, *Sacred and the Profane*, Willard R. Trask, trans. (1957; NY: Harper & Row, 1959), 29; N. J. Girardot, *Myth and Meaning in Early Daoism: the Theme of Chaos (Hundun)* (Magdalena, NM: Three Pines Press, 2008), 2, 3, 4.

7. Paul Hamlyn, *Larouse Encyclopedia of*

Mythology (London: Westbook House, 1959), 89–91, 92.

8. Jan De Vries, *The Problem of Loki*, FF Communication no. 110 (Helsinki: Suomalainen Tiedeakatemia Societas Scientiarum Fennica, 1933), 203, 204, 210, 223, 224, 253, 254, 255, 292; John Lindow, *Handbook of Norse Mythology* (Santa Barbara, CA: ABC-CLIO, 2001), 217, 219.

9. William Theodore De Bary, *Sources of Chinese Tradition* (New York: Columbia University Press, 1960), 88. Also see section 3, "The Goodness of Human Nature" in Bryan Van Norden, "Mencius," *Stanford Encyclopedia of Philosophy*: http://plato.stanford.edu/entries/mencius/

10. J. Bronowski and Bruce Mazlish, *The Western Intellectual Tradition: From Leonardo to Hegel* (New York: Harper & Row Pubs., 1962), 62, 74.

11. Shunryu Suzuki, *Zen Mind Beginner's Mind: Informal Talks on Zen Meditation and Practice* (New York: John Weatherhill, 1970), 40, 56, 58, 88, 121.

12. Nassim Nicholas Taleb, *The Black Swan: the Impact of the Highly Improbable* (New York: Random House, 2007); Nassim Nicholas Taleb, *Antifragile: Things That Gain from Disorder* (New York: Random House, 2012).

13. Lao Tzu, *Daodejing*, chapter 5, Chinese Text Project, https://ctext.org/dao-de-jing.

14. Ralph Waldo Emerson, *Nature* (Boston: Thurston, Torry & Co., 1849), 50.

15. Christina Han, "The Aesthetics of Wandering in the Chinese Literati Garden," *Studies in the History of Gardens & Designed Landscapes* 32, no. 4 (2012): 297–98.

16. Kenneth J. Hammond, "Wang Shizhen's Yan Shan Garden Essays: Narrating a Literati Landscape, *Studies in the History of Gardens & Designed Landscapes* 19, no. 3–4 (1999): 277.

17. Paul Avilés, "Seven Ways of Looking at a Mountain: Tetzcotzinco and the Aztec Garden Tradition," *Landscape Journal* 25, no. 2 (2006): 143–157.

18. Achva Benzinberg Stein, "Landscape Elements of the Makam: Sacred Places in Israel," *Landscape Journal* 6, no. 2 (Fall 1987): 123–131.

19. Hamid Shirvani, "The Philosophy of Persian Garden Design: The Sufi Tradition," *Landscape Journal* 4, no. 1 (Spring 1985): 23–30.

20. Jean Cooper, "The Symbolism of the Taoist Garden," *Studies in Comparative Religion* 11, no. 4 (Autumn, 1977): 224, 225; Hui Zou, "The Jing of a Perspective Garden," *Studies in the History of Gardens & Designed Landscapes* 22, no. 4 (2002): 317.

21. Lother Ledderose, "The Earthly Paradise: Religious Elements in Chinese Landscape Art,"

in *Theories of the Arts in China*, edited by Susan Bush and Christian Murck (Princeton: Princeton University Press, 1983), 168–72; Edward H. Schafer, "Cosmos in Miniature: the Tradition of the Chinese Garden," *Landscape* 12, no. 3 (Spring 1963): 24–26; Hui Zou, "The Jing of a Perspective Garden," *Studies in the History of Gardens & Designed Landscapes* 22, no. 4 (2002): 316–17.

22. Patrick Bowe, "The Early Development of Garden Making c. 3000–c. 2000 BCE," *Studies in the History of Gardens & Designed Landscapes* 37, no. 3 (2017): 231–241.

23. Katharine T. Von Stackelberg, "Meaning," in *A Cultural History of Gardens in Antiquity*, edited by Kathryn Gleason (New York: Bloomsburg, 2013), 120–21.

24. *Ibid.*, 125–26.

25. *Ibid.*, 132.

26. Patrick Bowe, "The Sacred Groves of Ancient Greece," *Studies in the History of Gardens & Designed Landscapes* 29, no. 4 (2009): 237.

27. *Ibid.*, 238, 240, 242.

28. *Ibid.*, 240, 242.

29. Gordon Campbell, "Epicurus, the Garden, and the Golden Age," in *Gardening: Philosophy for Everyone*, edited by Dan O'Brien (Malden, MA: Wiley-Blackwell, 2010), 227, 228, 229, 230; Katharine T. Von Stackelberg, "Meaning," in *A Cultural History of Gardens in Antiquity*, edited by Kathryn Gleason (New York: Bloomsburg, 2013), 131, 132.

30. Patrick Bowe, "The Evolution of the Ancient Greek Garden," *Studies in the History of Gardens & Designed Landscapes* 30, no. 3 (2010): 217.

31. *Ibid.*; Clarence J. Glacken, *Traces on the Rhodian Shore: Nature and Culture in Western Thought from Ancient Times to the End of the Eighteenth Century* (1967; Berkeley: University of California Press, 1990), 32–33.

32. Bowe, "The Evolution of the Ancient Greek Garden," 216, 217, 219.

33. Elizabeth Augspach, "Meaning," in *A Cultural History of Gardens in the Medieval Age*, edited by Michael Leslie (New York: Bloomsburg, 2013), 103, 105, 111.

34. Michael Charlesworth, "Sacred Landscape: Signs of Religion in the Eighteenth-Century Garden," *Journal of Garden History* 13, no. 1–2 (Spring-Summer 1993): 56, 57, 66; Patrick Eyres, "Meaning," in *A Cultural History of Gardens in the Age of Enlightenment*, edited by Stephen Bending (New York: Bloomsburg, 2013), 115, 117, 128, 132, 133.

35. See, for example, Young-tsu Wong, *Paradise Lost: the Imperial Garden Yuanming Yuan* (Honolulu: University of Hawaii Press, 2001), 9–10.

36. Patrick Bowe, "The Early Development of Garden Making c. 3000–c. 2000 BCE," *Studies in the History of Gardens & Designed Landscapes* 37, no. 3 (2017): 240.

37. Michel Baridon, "The Scientific Imagination and the Baroque Garden," *Studies in the History of Gardens & Designed Landscapes* 18, no. 1 (1998): 6, 8, 10.

38. Alston Chase, *Playing God In Yellowstone: The Destruction of America's First National Park* (New York: Atlantic Monthly Press, 1986), 176–77.

39. *Genesis*, 1:26, 1:28, 8:17. For one list, see "Bible Versions and Translation," https://www.biblestudytools.com/bible-versions/

40. Rather than repeat all the references here, I refer readers to the numerous citations in Sarvis, *Sacred and Ephemeral*, 253–55.

41. Jane Jacobs, *Death and Life of Great American Cities* (1961; NY: Modern Library, 1993), 579, 580, 584.

42. John Dixon Hunt, "Meaning," in *A Cultural History of Gardens in the Modern Age*, edited by John Dixon Hunt (New York: Bloomsburg, 2013), 119, 124, 129.

43. There are endless examples of this. For a few, see "Annie's Annuals and Urban Tilth," *Growing a Greener World*, season 1, episode 110 (July 18, 2010); Richard A. Fuller and Katherine N. Irvine, "Interactions Between People and Nature in Urban Environments," in *Urban Ecology*, edited by Kevin J. Gaston (New York: Cambridge University Press, 2010), 154; "Growing Power with Will Allen," *Growing a Greener World*, season 1, episode 105 (June 13, 2010); Yvonne Hung, "East New York Farms: Youth Participation in Community Development and Urban Agriculture," *Children, Youth and Environments* 14, no. 1 (2004): 70, 73, 74, 75–76, 77; Elizabeth Royte, "Street Farmer," *New York Times Magazine* (July 1, 2009); Rebecca Severson, "United We Sprout: A Chicago Community Garden Story," in *Meanings of the Garden: Proceedings of a Working Conference to Explore the Social, Psychological and Cultural Dimensions of Gardens*, edited by Mark Francis and Randolph T. Hester, Jr. (University of California, Davis, May 14–17, 1987), 96–104; "New Victory Gardens," *Growing a Greener World*, season 4, episode 420 (Nov. 19, 2013).

44. Catherine Howett, "Gardens are Good Places for Dying," in *Meanings of the Garden*, edited by Mark Francis and Randolph T. Hester, Jr., 181–84; Ian L. McHarg, "Thoughts on the Garden," in *Meanings of the Garden*, edited by Mark Francis and Randolph T. Hester, Jr., 134–35.

45. Catherine Howett, "Gardens Are Good Places for Dying," 184.

46. Jennifer Cousineau, "The Urban Practice of Jewish Space," in *American Sanctuary: Understanding Sacred Spaces*, edited by Louis P. Nelson (Bloomington: Indiana University Press, 2006), 69, 80.

47. This refers to a Zen story I encountered during the late 1970s or early 1980s, but have never been able to re-locate. The basic story as I remember it is that the Zen master orders an aspiring acolyte to carry a pile of stones from one corner of the monastery to another, and from there to another corner, and so forth, potentially endlessly with no "practical" purpose as a feature of self-discipline and meditation.

48. R.C. Lewontin, "Facts and the Factitious in Natural Sciences," in *Questions of Evidence: Proof, Practice, and Persuasion Across the Disciplines*, edited by in James Chandler, et al. (Chicago: University of Chicago Press, 1994), 485.

49. R.C. Lewontin, "A Rejoinder to William Wimsatt," in *Ibid.*, 509.

Chapter 2

1. Alston Chase, *In a Dark Wood: The Fight Over Forests and the Rising Tyranny of Ecology* (New York: Houghton Mifflin, 1995), 347–48; Alston Chase, *Playing God in Yellowstone: The Destruction of America's First National Park* (New York: Atlantic Monthly Press, 1986), 347.

2. Bjørn Lomborg, *Cool It: The Skeptical Environmentalist's Guide to Global Warming* (New York: Knopf, 2007), 5–6.

3. Norwegian Polar Institute, "Polar Bears in Svalbard in Good Condition—So Far," (Dec. 23, 2015), http://www.npolar.no/en/news/2015/12-23-counting-of-polar-bears-in-svalbard.html

4. Matt McGrath, "Arctic Ice 'Grew by a Third' After Cool Summer in 2013," *BBC News* (July 21, 2015); P. Winsor, "Arctic Sea Ice Thickness Remained Constant During the 1990s," *Geophysical Research Letters* 28, no. 6 (March 15, 2001): 1039–1041.

5. Howard Friel, *The Lomborg Deception: Setting the Record Straight About Global Warming* (New Haven: Yale University Press, 2010), 192.

6. Allan Adamson, "More Than 450 Ancient Earthworks Resembling Stonehenge Built In Amazon Rainforest," www.techtimes.com (Feb. 7, 2017); Joanna Klein, "Long Before Making Enigmatic Earthworks, People Reshaped Brazil's Rain Forest," *New York Times* (Feb. 10, 2017).

7. "Sprawling Maya Network Discovered Under Guatemala Jungle," *BBC News* (Feb. 2, 2018).

8. Michael Crichton, *State of Fear* (New York: HarperCollins, 2004), 768.

9. L.L. Jackson, et al., "Ecological Restoration: A Definition and Comments," *Restoration Ecology* 3 (1995): 71.

10. S.T.A. Pickett and V.T. Parker, "Avoiding the Old Pitfalls: Opportunities in a New Discipline," *Restoration Ecology* 2 (1994): 75.

11. S.T.A. Pickett and P.S. White, eds., *The Ecology of Natural Disturbance and Patch Dynamics* (Orlando, FL: Academic Press, 1985).

12. Jacques A. A. Swart, et al., "Valuation of Nature in Conservation and Restoration," *Restoration Ecology* 9, no. 2 (June 2001): 236–37.

13. *Ibid.*, 237.

14. R. van Diggelen, et al., "Ecological Restoration: State of the Art or State of the Science?" *Restoration Ecology* 9, no. 2 (June 2001): 115.

15. *Ibid.*

16. Jörg Pfadenhauer, "Some Remarks on the Socio-Cultural Background of Restoration Ecology," *Restoration Ecology* 9, no. 2 (June 2001): 228.

17. *Ibid.*

18. Keith Winterhalder, et al., "Values and Science in Ecological Restoration—A Response to Davis and Slobodkin," *Restoration Ecology* 12, no. 1 (Mar. 2004), 4.

19. Mark A. Davis and Lawrence B. Slobodkin, "The Science and Values of Restoration Ecology," *Restoration Ecology* 12, no. 1 (Mar. 2004): 1–2.

20. *Ibid.*, 2.

21. Winterhalder, et al., "Values and Science in Ecological Restoration—A Response to Davis and Slobodkin," 5.

22. Society for Ecological Restoration, Mission Statement, Vision Statement, and Guiding Principles, http://www.ser.org/page/Missionand Vision.

23. Bennett Hall, "Floating the Willamette: Initiative Strives to Return the River to a More Natural State," *Eugene Register Guard* (Dec. 18, 2017).

24. Robert C. Walter and Dorothy J. Merritts, "Natural Streams and the Legacy of Water-Powered Mills," *Science* 319, no. 5861 (Jan. 18, 2008): 299–304; John Nielsen, "Study: Are River Restoration Efforts Misguided?" NPR's *All Things Considered* (Jan. 19, 2008); Cornelia Dean, "Follow the Silt," *New York Times* (June 24, 2008).

25. Michael Crichton felt that, in retrospect, Carson was about one-third accurate and two-thirds inaccurate regarding the science of DDT and pesticides. Crichton (who earned a medical degree from Harvard) particularly faulted Carson for over-emphasizing environmental causes for cancer. See the bibliography section in Michael Crichton, *State of Fear* (New York: HarperCollins, 2004), 741.

26. Paul R. Ehrlich and Anne H. Ehrlich, *The Population Bomb* (New York: Ballantine Books, 1968).

27. Lynn Townsend White, Jr., "The Historical Roots of Our Ecologic Crisis," *Science* 155, no. 3767 (Mar. 10, 1967): 1207; Garrett Hardin, "Tragedy of the Commons," *Science* 162 (1968): 1243–48.

28. Will Sarvis, *Sacred and Ephemeral: Reflections Upon Land, Place, and Home* (Self-published, 2017), 136, 254.

29. For a small sampling of typical media stories see, Nithin Coca, "A Growing Crisis: Insects are Disappearing—And Fast," Triplepunditwww (July 13, 2016); Helena Merriman, "How Do We Avoid the Antibiotics Apocalypse?" *BBC News* (Nov. 4, 2016; Jeff Nesbit, "It May Soon Be Too Late to Save the Seas," *U.S. News & World Report* (Apr. 27, 2016); John D. Sutter, "The Era of 'Biological Annihilation,'" *CNN* (July 11, 2017). Even *The Conversation*, which once promised to raise journalism to a higher level, is no different from mainstream media when it comes to sensational environmental doomsdayism. See Andrew Glikson, "We May Survive the Anthropocene, But Need to Avoid a Radioactive 'Plutocene,'" *The Conversation* (Sept. 27, 2017).

30. Sarah Knapton, "Doomsday Clock Set at Two Minutes to Midnight as World Moves Closer to Global Annihilation," *The Telegraph* (Jan. 25, 2018). The wag's quip was in the readers' comment section, which may or may not have survived internet archiving.

31. For examples see Bruce Chilton, et al., *The Cambridge Companion to the Bible*, 2nd ed. (New York: Cambridge University Press, 2008), 58; A.R. Davis, *T'ao Yuan-ming*, vol.1 (Cambridge: Cambridge University Press, 1983), 195–201; Clarence J. Glacken, *Traces on the Rhodian Shore: Nature and Culture in Western Thought from Ancient Times to the End of the Eighteenth Century* (1967; Berkeley: University of California Press, 1990), 133, 705; Frank E. Manuel and Fritzie P. Manuel, *Utopian Thought in the Western World* (Cambridge, MA: Belknap Press, 1979), 433, 586–88; Vernon Louis Parrington, *American Dreams: A Study of American Utopias* (New York: Russell & Russell, 1964), 97.

32. For examples see Thomas R. Dunlap,

Faith in Nature: Environmentalism as Religious Quest (Seattle: University of Washington Press, 2004); Samir Okasha, *Philosophy of Science: A Very Short Introduction*, 2nd ed. (New York: Oxford University Press, 2016), 114; Mark Sagoff, *The Economy of the Earth: Philosophy, Law, and the Environment*, 2nd ed. (Cambridge University Press, 2007), chapter 10, "Environmentalism: Death and Resurrection"; Mark Stoll, "Green versus Green: Religion, Ethics, and the Bookchin-Foreman Dispute," *Environmental History* 6, no. 3 (July 2001): 412–27; Nassim Nicholas Taleb, *Antifragile: Things That Gain from Disorder* (New York: Random House, 2012), 109. Also see Michael Crichton, "Speech to the San Francisco Commonwealth Club," https://www.cs.cmu.edu/~kw/crichton.html.

33. Alston Chase, *In a Dark Wood: The Fight Over Forests and the Rising Tyranny of Ecology* (New York: Houghton Mifflin, 1995), xiii, 105, 112, 118, 130, 132, 148, 151, 159, 249, 250, 251, 294, 413; Alston Chase, *Playing God in Yellowstone: The Destruction of America's First National Park* (New York: Atlantic Monthly Press, 1986), 46, 67, 158 and chapter 17, esp. 315–16, 320, 321; Werner Heisenberg, *Physics and Philosophy: The Revolution in Modern Science* (New York: Harper & Row, 1958), 199; Jay Odenbaugh, "Philosophy of the Environmental Sciences," in *New Waves in Philosophy of Science*, edited by in P.D. Magnus and Jacob Busch (New York: Palgrave Macmillan, 2010), 162, 164, 168; Sagoff, *Economy of the Earth*, 2nd ed., 23, 203.

34. I cover this at length in Sarvis, *Sacred and Ephemeral*, 241–45.

35. George H. Ford, "Felicitous Space: The Cottage Controversy," in *Nature and the Victorian Imagination*, edited by U.C. Knoepflmacher and G.B. Tennyson (Berkeley: University of California Press, 1977), 29–48.

36. There is much literature on this. A good place to begin is Roderick Nash, *Wilderness and the American Mind*, 3rd ed. (New Haven: Yale University Press, 1982), 13–20. Also see John F. Sears, *Sacred Places: American Tourist Attractions in the Nineteenth Century* (New York: Oxford University Press, 1989).

37. John Zerzan, "Drive to Dominate," *Eugene Weekly* (July 23, 2015).

38. John Winthrop, "A Modell of Christian Charity" (1630), Collections of the Massachusetts Historical Society, 3rd series 7:31–48, https://history.hanover.edu/texts/winthmod.html.

39. Aldo Leopold, *A Sand County Almanac and Sketches Here and There* (1949; Oxford University Press, 1968), 199.

40. Quoted in William G. Robbins, *Landscapes of Conflict: the Oregon Story, 1940–2000* (Seattle: University of Washington Press, 2004), 215.

41. *Wilderness Act* of 1964, Public Law 88–577, sec. 2(a).

42. Rumpole to Nick, toward the end of "Rumple and the Honourable Member," found in John Mortimer, *The First Rumpole Omnibus* (Garden City, NY: Doubleday, 1983), 103.

43. Dan Charles, "Hydroponic Veggies Are Taking Over Organic, and a Move to Ban Them Fails," *NPR's Morning Edition* (Nov. 2, 2017).

44. R. Allan Freeze, *The Environmental Pendulum: A Quest for the Truth About Toxic Chemicals, Human Health, and Environmental Protection* (Berkeley: University of California Press, 2000), 100.

45. Melinda A. Zeder, et al., "Documenting Domestication: Bringing Together Plants, Animals, Archaeology, and Genetics," in *Documenting Domestication: New Genetic and Archaeological Paradigms*, edited by Melinda A. Zeder, et al. (University of California Press, 2006), 2.

46. Chase, *In a Dark Wood*, 26–27, 33, 95.

47. Peter J. Bowler, *The Norton History of Environmental Sciences* (New York: W.W. Norton & Co., 1993), 530.

48. Chase, *In a Dark Wood*, 102.

49. John C. Kricher, *The Balance of Nature: Ecology's Enduring Myth* (Princeton: Princeton University Press, 2009).

50. Believe it or not, this sticker is still fairly common around Eugene. I imagine a few other places (maybe Boulder or Bellingham?) also feature some of these Countercultural leftovers.

51. Catherine E. Southward, "A Cap on Waste," *Eugene Weekly* (June 29, 2017).

52. Carrie Gracie, "How Do We Cure Our Plastic Addiction?" BBC World Service's *The Real Story* (Apr. 6, 2018).

53. Lewis Black, "Back in Black: Earth Day," *The Daily Show with Jon Stewart* (Apr. 25, 2007).

54. Ibid.

55. "In Pictures: Transforming a Scarred Landscape," *BBC News* (Nov. 25, 2016).

56. Jonas Geldmann and Juan P. González-Varo, "Conserving Honey Bees Does Not Help Wildlife," *Science* 359, no. 6374 (Jan. 26, 2018): 392–393; Dan Charles, "Honeybees Help Farmers, But They Don't Help the Environment," *NPR's Weekend Edition Saturday* (Jan. 27, 2018).

Chapter 3

1. The speech is widely available online, including the audio transcript at Wikisource:

https://en.wikisource.org/wiki/Eisenhower%27s
_farewell_address_(audio_transcript)

2. For a refreshing approach to this subject, see Steven Shapin, *The Scientific Revolution* (Chicago: University of Chicago Press, 1996).

3. J. Bronowski and Bruce Mazlish, *The Western Intellectual Tradition: From Leonardo to Hegel* (New York: Harper & Row Pubs., 1962), 118; Shapin, *The Scientific Revolution*, 58–59, 60–61, 63, 142.

4. Samir Okasha, *Philosophy of Science: A Very Short Introduction*, 2nd ed. (New York: Oxford University Press, 2016), 114.

5. Shapin, *The Scientific Revolution*, 135–55.

6. See Philip Appleman, ed., *Darwin* (New York: W.W. Norton Co., 2001), 527–33.

7. Sherwin B. Nuland, *The Uncertain Art: Thoughts on a Life in Medicine* (New York: Random House, 2008).

8. Another medical book highly worth considering is Ted J. Kaptchuk, *The Web that Has No Weaver: Understanding Chinese Medicine*, 2nd ed. (Chicago: Contemporary Books, 2000).

9. For examples, see Sharyl Attkisson, "Fake Science," *Full Measure* (May 7, 2017); Richard Harris, *Rigor Mortis: How Sloppy Science Creates Worthless Cures, Crushes Hope, and Wastes Billions* (New York: Basic Books, 2017); Richard Harris, "What Does It Mean When Cancer Findings Can't Be Reproduced?" NPR's *Morning Edition* (Jan. 18, 2017); John P. A. Ioannidis, "Scientific Inbreeding and Same-Team Replication: Type D Personality as an Example," *Journal of Psychosomatic Research* 73 (2012): 408–410; John P. A. Ioannidis, "Why Most Published Research Findings Are False," *PLoS Medicine* 2, no. 8 (Aug. 2005): 696–701; Steve Kolowich, "Meet Retraction Watch, the Blog That Points Out the Human Stains on the Scientific Record," *Chronicle of Higher Education* (Sept. 25, 2015); Debabrata Mukherjee, "Contradicted and Initially Stronger Effects in Highly Cited Clinical Research" *ACC Current Journal Review* (Oct. 2005): 6.

10. Despite endless denials of getting wealthy, and lame excuses such as medical school debt that six-figure salaries are apparently incapable of paying off, American doctors are in one of the more lucrative professions. In 2015 the annual salaries ranged from $189K for pediatricians to $421K for orthopedic doctors. See Lauren F. Friedman, "Here's How Much Money Doctors Actually Make," *Business Insider* (Apr. 21, 2015).

11. For a few examples among many, see Marcia Angell, *The Truth About the Drug Companies: How They Deceive Us and What to Do About It* (Random House, 2004); Paul Basken,

"In Budget Battle, Science Faces New Pressures to Prove It Delivers," *Chronicle of Higher Education* (Nov. 19, 2012); Paul Basken, "Landmark Analysis of an Infamous Medical Study Points Out the Challenges of Research Oversight," *Chronicle of Higher Education* (Sept. 17, 2015); Annie Waldman, "Big Pharma Quietly Enlists Leading Professors to Justify $1,000-Per-Day Drugs," *Propublica* (Feb. 23, 2017).

12. David L. Rosenhan, "On Being Sane in Insane Places," *Science* 179 (1973): 250–58. Also see Lauren Slater, *Opening Skinner's Box: Great Psychological Experiments of the Twentieth Century* (2004), 64–71. For an example of a more recent analysis, see Ferris Jabr, "Self-Fulfilling Fakery: Feigning Mental Illness Is a Form of Self-Deception," *Scientific American* (July 28, 2010).

13. Tom Bartlett, "Power of Suggestion," *Chronicle of Higher Education* (Jan. 20, 2013); Tom Bartlett, "The Results of the Reproducibility Project Are In. They're Not Good," *Chronicle of Higher Education* (Aug. 28, 2015); Benedict Carey, "Many Psychology Findings Not as Strong as Claimed, Study Says," *New York Times* (Aug. 27, 2015); Benedict Carey, "Psychologists Welcome Analysis Casting Doubt on Their Work," *New York Times* (Aug. 28, 2015); Benedict Carey, "New Critique Sees Flaws in Landmark Analysis of Psychology Studies," *New York Times* (Mar. 3, 2016); Mike Drayton, "What's Behind the Rorschach Inkblot Test?" *BBC News Magazine* (July 25, 2012); Christopher D. Green, "The Flaw at the Heart of Psychological Research," *Chronicle of Higher Education* (June 26, 2016); NPR Staff, "Power Poses' Co-Author: 'I Do Not Believe the Effects Are Real'" *NPR's Weekend Edition Saturday* (Oct. 1, 2016).

14. Maarten G., Kleinhans, et al., "Philosophy of Earth Science," in *Philosophies of the Sciences: A Guide*, edited by Fritz Allhoff (Chichester, West Sussex: Wiley-Blackwell, 2010), 213, 227–28, 230–31.

15. Nassim Nicholas Taleb, *Antifragile: Things That Gain From Disorder* (New York: Random House, 2012), 211.

16. Alston Chase, *In a Dark Wood: The Fight Over Forests and the Rising Tyranny of Ecology* (New York: Houghton Mifflin, 1995), 367.

17. *Ibid.*

18. Henri Poincaré, George Bruce Halsted, trans., *The Foundations of Science: Science and Hypothesis (New York*: The Science Press, 1913), 81, 105, 111, 125–26, and chapters three through five.

19. Robert M. Pirsig, *Zen and the Art of Motorcycle Maintenance: An Inquiry into Values*

(1974; New York: Bantam, 1981), 99, 100, 101–02, 236–37.

20. Isaac Newton, letter to Robert Hooke (Feb. 5, 1675), retrieved from the Historical Society of Pennsylvania's digital library, https://digitallibrary.hsp.org/index.php/Detail/objects/9792

21. The article, later retracted, was: Andrew Wakefield, et al., "Ileal-Lymphoid-Nodular Hyperplasia, Non-Specific Colitis, and Pervasive Developmental Disorder in Children," *The Lancet* 351, no. 9103 (1998): 637–41.

22. Silvio O. Funtowicz and Jerome R. Ravetz, "Science for the Post-Normal Age," *Futures* 25, no. 7 (1993): 739, 740, 752–54.

23. Okasha, *Philosophy of Science*, 123–24. The contemporary observation of this general phenomenon basically begins in 1962 with Kuhn, *Structure of Scientific Revolution*, and has generated endless debate ever since. See Thomas S. Kuhn, *Structure of Scientific Revolutions*, 2nd ed. (1962; Chicago: University of Chicago Press, 1970).

24. Chase, *In a Dark Wood*, 99; Paolo Palladino, "Defining Ecology: Ecological Theories, Mathematical Models, and Applied Biology in the 1960s and 1970s," *Journal of the History of Biology* 24, no. 2 (Summer 1991): 225, 226, 238; Peter J. Taylor, "Technocratic Optimism, H.T. Odum, and the Partial Transformation of Ecological Metaphor After World War II," *Journal of the History of Biology* 21, no. 2 (Summer 1988): 227, 229–30, 232, 240.

25. Peter J. Bowler, *The Norton History of Environmental Sciences* (New York: W.W. Norton & Co., 1993), 520; Alston Chase, *Playing God in Yellowstone: The Destruction of America's First National Park* (New York: Atlantic Monthly Press, 1986), 312.

26. Chase, *In a Dark Wood*, xiii, 105; John C. Kricher, *The Balance of Nature: Ecology's Enduring Myth* (Princeton: Princeton University Press, 2009), 86.

27. Paul L. Farber, *Finding Order in Nature: The Naturalist Tradition from Linnaeus to E.O. Wilson* (Baltimore: Johns Hopkins University Press, 2000), 114.

28. Nassim Nicholas Taleb, *The Black Swan: the Impact of the Highly Improbable* (New York: Random House, 2007), 55, 58, 69, 70.

29. Michael G. Barbour, "Ecological Fragmentation in the Fifties," in *Uncommon Ground: Toward Reinventing Nature*, edited by William Cronon (New York: W.W. Norton & Co., 1995), 233–43; Bowler, *Norton History of Environmental Sciences*, 508, 516, 524–25; Malcolm Nicolson, "Henry Allan Gleason and the Individualistic Hypothesis: The Structure of a Botanist's Career," *Botanical Review* 56, no. 2 (Apr. -June, 1990): 107–08, 111–14; Donald Worster, *Nature's Economy: A History of Ecological Ideas*, 2nd ed. (New York: Cambridge University Press, 1994), chapter 11.

30. Chase, *Playing God in Yellowstone*, 313, 315–16, 320, 321; Robert P. McIntosh, *The Background of Ecology* (New York: Cambridge University Press, 1985), 268, 274, 286.

31. Kricher, *Balance of Nature*, 97.

32. K.S. Shrader-Frechette and Earl D. McCoy, "How the Tail Wags the Dog: How Value Judgments Determine Ecological Science," *Environmental Values* 3, no. 2 (Summer 1994): 108–113.

33. Taleb, *Antifragile*, 116.

34. R.C. Lewontin, "A Rejoinder to William Wimsatt," in *Questions of Evidence: Proof, Practice, and Persuasion Across the Disciplines*, edited by James Chandler, et al. (Chicago: University of Chicago Press, 1994), 509.

35. Paul Griffiths, "Philosophy of Biology," *Stanford Encyclopedia of Philosophy* (July 4, 2008), sec. 1, Pre-history of Philosophy of Biology.

36. Shrader-Frechette and McCoy, "How the Tail Wags the Dog," 116.

37. Chase, *In a Dark Wood*, 100–01; Chase, *Playing God in Yellowstone*, 323; McIntosh, *The Background of Ecology*, 310–11; Palladino, "Defining Ecology," 224, 233–34, 238–39; Worster, *Nature's Economy*, 372, 373.

38. Sahotra Sarkar, "Ecology," *Stanford Encyclopedia of Philosophy* (Dec. 23, 2005), sec. 4, "Ecosystem Ecology."

39. Chase, *Playing God in Yellowstone*, 57, 322; Palladino, "Defining Ecology," 230–31, 232–33.

40. Bjørn Lomborg, *The Skeptical Environmentalist: Measuring the Real State of the World* (Cambridge: Cambridge University Press, 2001), 254.

41. Diane Dietz, "University of Oregon's Federal Research Funding in Doubt," *Eugene Register Guard* (Dec. 18, 2016).

42. R. G. Collingwood, *Idea of Nature* (New York: Oxford University Press, 1960), 176.

43. Chase, *Playing God in Yellowstone*, 57, 60–64, and chapter ten in general.

44. *Ibid.*, 315–16.

45. Bowler, *Norton History of Environmental Sciences*, 517, 544–45, 546.

46. Chase, *In a Dark Wood*, 106, 108; Kricher, *Balance of Nature*, 91–92, 109; S.T.A. Pickett and P.S. White, eds. *The Ecology of Natural Disturbance and Patch Dynamics* (Orlando, FL: Academic Press, 1985), xiii, 12, 374, 376, 383.

47. Charles Sutherland Elton, *The Ecology of Invasions by Animals and Plants* (London: Chapman & Hall, 1958; NY: Halsted Press, 1977), 18, 33.

48. *Ibid.*, 110.

49. *Ibid.*, plate 50 (opposite page 145), 158.

50. *Ibid.*, chapter nine, "The Conservation of Variety."

51. Chase, *In a Dark Wood*, 110–111, 117, 118; Kricher, *Balance of Nature*, 90.

52. Kricher, *Balance of Nature*, 91.

53. Shrader-Frechette and McCoy, "How the Tail Wags the Dog," 117.

54. Nancy K. Kubasek and Gary S. Silverman, *Environmental Law* 4th ed. (Upper Saddle River, NJ: Prentice Hall, 2002), 307.

55. Chase, *In a Dark Wood*, 110–111; John Copeland Nagle, "Playing Noah," *Minnesota Law Review* 82 (May 1998): 1173.

56. M. Lynne Corn and Alexandra M. Wyatt, "The Endangered Species Act: A Primer," (Washington, DC: Congressional Information Service, Library of Congress, Sept. 8, 2016), 1.

57. This story is masterfully told in Chase, *In a Dark Wood.* As with Alston Chase's previous book (*Playing God in Yellowstone*), *In a Dark Wood* is really two books: historical and contemporary analysis of the environmental topic at hand, along with a great deal of thoughtful philosophy.

58. Eric Forsman, "A Preliminary Investigation of the Spotted Owl in Oregon" (MS Thesis, Oregon State University, 1976).

59. Chase, *In a Dark Wood*, 132, 148, 247, 248, 249, 250, 251, 314. Also see Chase, *Playing God In Yellowstone*, 67, 251.

60. J. Blakesley, "Habitat Associations," chapter five in Steven P. Courtney, et al., *Scientific Evaluation of the Status of the Northern Spotted Owl* (Portland, OR: Sustainable Ecosystems Institute, 2004); Alan B. Franklin, et al., "Climate, Habitat Quality, and Fitness in Northern Spotted Owl Populations in Northwestern California," *Ecological Monographs* 704 (Nov. 2000): 539–590; Edwin L. McCutchen, "Characteristics of Spotted Owl Nest Trees in the Wenatchee National Forest," *Journal of Raptor Research* 27, no. 1 (Mar. 1993): 1–7; Stan G. Sovern, et al., "Roosting Habitat Use and Selection By Northern Spotted Owls During Natal Dispersal," *Journal of Wildlife Management* 79, no. 2 (2015): 254–262.

61. Associated Press, "Plan to Recommend Killing One Owl to Save Another" (reprinted in Eugene, Oregon's KVAL-13 News, Feb. 7, 2011). A group called Friends of Animals later filed suit against this action. See Associated Press,

"Group Files Suit to Stop Barred Owl Shooting" (reprinted in KVAL-13 News, Oct 2, 2013).

62. Jay Odenbaugh, "Philosophy of the Environmental Sciences," in P.D. Magnus and Jacob Busch, eds. *New Waves in Philosophy of Science* (New York: Palgrave Macmillan, 2010), 155. Other scholars have made similar observations. For example, see Adam Briggle and Carl Mitcham, *Ethics and Science: an Introduction* (Cambridge University Press, 2012), 239; Roman Frigg, "Models in Science," *Stanford Encyclopedia of Philosophy* (Feb. 27, 2006; rev. ed. June 25, 2012), sec. 3, Epistemology: Learning with Models, subsection 3.1, Learning About the Model: Experiments, Thought Experiments and Simulation; Okasha, *Philosophy of Science*, 58; Peter J. Taylor, *Unruly Complexity: Ecology, Interpretation, Engagement* (Chicago: University of Chicago Press, 2005), 1–31; William Wimsatt, "Lewontin's Evidence (That There Isn't Any)," in *Questions of Evidence*, 499; Worster, *Nature's Economy*, 408.

63. Odenbaugh, "Philosophy of the Environmental Sciences," 164, 168.

64. Palladino, "Defining Ecology," 224–25.

65. Alfred Crosby wrote two books that document some of the radical changes wrought by imported flora and fauna. See Alfred W. Crosby, *The Columbian Exchange: Biological and Cultural Consequences of 1492*, new ed. (Westport, CT: Praeger, 2003) and Alfred W. Crosby, *Ecological Imperialism: The Biological Expansion of Europe, 900–1900*, new ed. (New York: Cambridge Univ. Press, 2004).

66. Sherwin B. Nuland, *The Uncertain Art: Thoughts on a Life in Medicine* (New York: Random House, 2008), 51, 52, 54, 58.

67. Pirsig, *Zen and the Art of Motorcycle Maintenance*, 252.

Chapter 4

1. W. Lance. Bennett, *News: The Politics of Illusion.* White Plains (New York: Longman, 1996), x, 37, 120–23; Timothy E. Cook, *Governing with the News: the News Media as a Political Institution* (Chicago: University of Chicago Press, 1998), 164, 175, 191, and generally chapter five.

2. Jason Salzman, *Making the News: A Guide for Activists and Nonprofits* (Boulder, CO: Westview Press, 2003); Lawrence Marshall Wallack, *News for a Change: An Advocate's Guide to Working with the Media* (Thousand Oaks, CA: Sage Publications, 1999).

3. Bennett, *News: The Politics of Illusion*, 197–200.

4. Max Ehrmann, *Desiderata* (1927), https://en.wikipedia.org/wiki/Desiderata.

5. Bennett, *News: The Politics of Illusion*, xv.

6. Monika Djerf-Pierre, "Green Metacycles of Attention: Reassessing the Attention Cycles of Environmental News Reporting 1961–2010," *Public Understanding of Science* 22, no. 4 (2011): 495–512.

7. Jack Stapleton, Jr., interview; Kennett, Missouri, June 6, 1997. Tapes and transcript located in the "Politics in Missouri Oral History Project," Collection #3929, Western Historical Manuscript Collection, Columbia, Missouri.

8. Carol L. Rogers, "The Importance of Understanding Audiences," in *Communicating Uncertainty: Media Coverage of New and Controversial Science*, edited by Sharon M. Friedman, et al. (Mahwah, NJ: L. Erlbaum Associates, 1999), 186–87.

9. R. Allan Freeze, *The Environmental Pendulum: A Quest for the Truth About Toxic Chemicals, Human Health, and Environmental Protection* (Berkeley: University of California Press, 2000), 33.

10. Bennett, *News: The Politics of Illusion*, 19, 20, 73.

11. Rogers, "The Importance of Understanding Audiences," in *Communicating Uncertainty*, 186–87.

12. Sharon M. Friedman, et al., "Introduction," in *Communicating Uncertainty*, xii, xiii; M. Gibbons, "Science's New Social Contract With Society," *Nature* 402, supplement (Dec. 2, 1999): C82, C83-C84; Helga Nowotny and Scott Peter, *Re-Thinking Science: Knowledge and the Public in an Age of Uncertainty* (Cambridge, UK: Polity, 2001), 134, 245, 246, 247.

13. Nowotny and Peter, *Re-Thinking Science*, 258–60.

14. Nowotny and Peter, *Re-Thinking Science*, 213–14.

15. Hans Peter Peters and Sharon Dunwoody, "Scientific Uncertainty in Media Content: Introduction to this Special Issue," *Public Understanding of Science* 25, no. 8 (2016): 894.

16. *Ibid.*, 899. Also see Freeze, *Environmental Pendulum*, 41–42; Nassim Nicholas Taleb, *The Black Swan: the Impact of the Highly Improbable* (New York: Random House, 2007), 75.

17. Geoffrey C. Kabat, *Hyping Health Risks: Environmental Hazards in Daily Life and the Science of Science of Epidemiology* (New York: Columbia University Press, 2008), 5–7, 62–63, 68, 83, 114–15; Gitte Meyer, "Journalism and Science: How to Erode the Idea of Knowledge," *Journal of Agricultural and Environmental Ethics* 19 (2006): 240, 241.

18. Timothy Egan, "Apple Growers Bruised and Bitter After Alar Scare," *New York Times* (July 9, 1991); Freeze, *Environmental Pendulum*, 34–35; Daniel E. Koshland, Jr., "Credibility in Science and the Press," *Science*, New Series, 254, no. 5032 (Nov. 1, 1991): 629.

19. Danielle Haas, "Chemical Fallout: Milwaukee Journal Sentinel and the BPA Story," Columbia University, Journalism School Knight Case Studies Initiative, CSJ-09–0017.0 (Mar. 2009), 18. A conclusion for this paper seems to be missing, but the first twenty-two pages are available at: http://ccnmtl.columbia.edu/projects/caseconsortium/casestudies/12/casestudy/files/global/12/Milwaukee%20Journal%20Sentinel%20and%20the%20BPA%20story_wm.pdf

20. AAAS Mass Media Science & Engineering Fellows Program, https://www.aaas.org/page/about-1

21. "Susanne Rust on Investigating BPA and Other Chemicals," Donald W. Reynolds National Center for Business Journalism (June 24, 2010).

22. Haas, "Chemical Fallout," 20.

23. "The Biologist Who Challenged Agribusiness," *New Yorker* (Dec. 1, 2016); Rachel Aviv, "A Valuable Reputation," *New Yorker* (Feb. 10, 2014); Bruce Chassy, "Turning Science into a Circus: The New Yorker, Rachel Aviv and Tyrone Hayes," *Academics Review* (Mar. 7, 2014); Jon Entine, "Did The New Yorker Botch Puff Piece On Frog Scientist Tyrone Hayes, Turning Rogue into Beleaguered Hero?" *Forbes* (Mar. 10, 2014).

24. *City of Greenville, et al. v. Syngenta Crop Protection*, 904 F.Supp.2d 902 (2012); *City of Greenville, et al. v. Syngenta Crop Protection*, 764 F.3d 695 (2014).

25. Bennett, *News: The Politics of Illusion*, 19, 129–31; Sharon M. Friedman, "The Never-Ending Story of Dioxin," in *Communicating Uncertainty*, 122–23.

26. See, for example, John C. Besley and Matthew Nisbet, "How Scientists View the Public, the Media and the Political Process," *Public Understanding of Science* 22, no. 6 (2011); 644–659; Freeze, *Environmental Pendulum*, 33.

27. Adam Briggle, and Carl Mitcham, *Ethics and Science: An Introduction* (Cambridge University Press, 2012), 260; Alex Jones, "Covering Science and Technology: An Interview with Cornelia Dean. November 22, 2002," *The Harvard International Journal of Press/Politics* 8, no. 2 (2003): 3–4; Kabat, *Hyping Health Risks*, 9–11, 68.

28. Jonathan Schell, "Our Fragile Earth," *Discover Magazine* (Oct. 1989): 47; Stephen H. Schneider, "Don't Bet All Environmental Changes Will Be Beneficial," American Physical Society, *APS News* (Aug./Sept. 1996).

29. Bennett, *News: The Politics of Illusion,* chapter five; Friedman, et al., "Introduction," in *Communicating Uncertainty,* xiii. The uncertainty theme runs throughout the essays in the latter volume.

30. Roy Reed, "Gulf Waters Eating Away a Louisiana Resort Beach," *New York Times* (May 29, 1971), 16.5 square miles annually; "Louisiana Wetlands Are 'Falling Apart,'" *New York Times* (Dec. 15, 1980), 39 square miles annually; William E. Schmidt, "Louisiana's Wetlands Are Steadily Going Out on the Tide," *New York Times* (July 6, 1986), almost 40 square miles annually.

31. Jesse Hardman, "In Louisiana, Rebuilding Mother Nature's Storm Protection: A 'living Coast,'" NPR's *Weekend Edition Saturday* (Aug. 8, 2015).

32. NBC Nightly News, "Christmas Trees Come to the Rescue in Coastal Louisiana" (Jan. 27 2018).

33. Travis Lux, "Louisiana Wants to Use the Muddy Mississippi to Build Up Its Coast," NPR's *Morning Edition* (May 15, 2018).

34. Google Earth Engine, https://earthengine.google.com/timelapse/

35. NBC Nightly News, "Christmas Trees Come to the Rescue in Coastal Louisiana" (Jan. 27 2018).

36. Rita R. Colwell, et al., "Beyond the Basics: a Roundtable Discussion," in *Communicating Uncertainty,* 254, 257–58.

37. Barbara J. Finlayson-Pitts, and James N. Pitts, *Chemistry of the Lower and Upper Atmosphere: Theory, Experiments, and Applications* (San Diego: Academic Press, 2000), chapters 12 and 13.

38. Aaron Wildavsky, *But Is It True? A Citizen's Guide to Environmental Health and Safety Issues* (Cambridge: Harvard University Press, 1995), 310, 315, 317–18, 336–37, 338, 410.

39. Warren Hoge, "In Amazon, Huge Study Aims to Save Jungle Life," *New York Times* (Nov. 23, 1982), page C1; Bayard Webster, "Forest's Role in Weather Documented in Amazon," *New York Times* (July 5, 1983), page C1; John Corry, "TV: Amazon, in 'Nature,'" *New York Times* (Sept. 27, 1987); Malcolm W. Browne, "The Bell Tolls for Rain Forests," *New York Times* (Apr. 19, 1991); Larry Rohter, "Brazil Gambles on Monitoring of Amazon Loggers," *New York Times* (Jan. 14, 2007).

40. Warren Hoge, "Development Is Eating Up the World's Rain Forests," *New York Times* (Aug. 31, 1980), page 16E.

41. This problem is part of a larger phenomenon in the field of science journalism. See

Sharon M. Friedman, et al., eds., *Communicating Uncertainty: Media Coverage of New and Controversial Science* (Mahwah, NJ: L. Erlbaum Associates, 1999), 254; Koshland, "Credibility in Science and the Press," 629; Meyer, "Journalism and Science," 241, 242, 246.

42. The BBC offers some retrospective deforestation statistics from 1988 to 2011, in the article, Justin Rowlatt, "Saving the Amazon: Winning the War on Deforestation," *BBC News* (Jan. 2, 2012).

43. Joseph Novitski, "Prosperity Comes to Urban Brazil, and with It Ecological Woes," *New York Times* (Dec. 3, 1971); Bayard Webster, "In the Rain Forest, a Complex and Threatened World," *New York Times* (Apr. 17, 1979), pages C1-C2; anonymous editorial, "Rain Forest Worth More If Uncut, Study Says," *New York Times* (July 4, 1989); Tony Smith, "Rain Forest Is Losing Ground Faster in Amazon, Photos Show," *New York Times* (June 28, 2003).

44. John Noble Wilford, "Jungle Soil Said to Lack Fertility," *New York Times* (June 17, 1973); Warren Hoge, "Development Is Eating Up the World's Rain Forests," *New York Times* (Aug. 31, 1980), page 16E.

45. Brian Kelly and Mark London, "Bright Spots in the Rain Forest," *New York Times* (Apr. 22, 2004).

46. José Luís Campana Camargo, et al., "Rehabilitation of Degraded Areas of Central Amazonia Using Direct Sowing of Forest Tree Seeds," *Restoration Ecology* 10, no. 4 (Dec. 2002): 636, 642.

47. Elisabeth Rosenthal, "New Jungles Prompt a Debate on Rain Forests," *New York Times* (Jan. 29, 2009). Also see "Amazonian Forest 'More Resilient,'" *BBC News* (Sept. 24, 2007).

48. Thomas K. Rudel, *Tropical Forests: Regional Paths of Destruction and Regeneration in the Late Twentieth Century* (New York: Columbia University Press, 2005), 34.

49. *Ibid.,* 39, 40, 50, 128, 130, 151, 153.

50. Elisabeth Rosenthal, "New Jungles Prompt a Debate on Rain Forests," *New York Times* (Jan. 29, 2009). Also see Brian Kelly and Mark London, "Bright Spots in the Rain Forest," *New York Times* (Apr. 22, 2004) and Justin Gillis, "Restored Forests Breathe Life Into Efforts Against Climate Change," *New York Times* (Dec. 23, 2014).

51. Allan Adamson, "More Than 450 Ancient Earthworks Resembling Stonehenge Built In Amazon Rainforest," techtimes.com (Feb. 7, 2017); Joanna Klein, "Long Before Making Enigmatic Earthworks, People Reshaped Brazil's Rain Forest," *New York Times* (Feb. 10, 2017);

"Sprawling Maya Network Discovered Under Guatemala Jungle," *BBC News* (Feb. 2, 2018).

52. Elisabeth Rosenthal, "New Jungles Prompt a Debate on Rain Forests," *New York Times* (Jan. 29, 2009).

53. Kirsten Barrett, et al., "Ecosystem Services from Converted Land: the Importance of Tree Cover in Amazonian Pastures," *Urban Ecosystems* 16 (2013): 573–591.

54. Estimates inherently vary at any given time and continue to evolve with changing conditions. In 2012, Rowlatt put it at around 80 percent. In 2001, Lomborg had it at 86 percent. See Justin Rowlatt, "Saving the Amazon: Winning the War on Deforestation," *BBC News* (Jan. 2, 2012); Bjørn Lomborg, *The Skeptical Environmentalist: Measuring the Real State of the World* (Cambridge: Cambridge University Press, 2001), 115, 255. No matter how the statistics are gathered and interpreted, from now on we'll need an additional category of re-generated forest.

55. This, relying upon data gathered by the Brazilian National Institute of Space Research (INPE) and the United Nations Food and Agriculture Organization (FAO) data, https://rainforests.mongabay.com/amazon/deforestation_calculations.html

56. Miguel Calmon, et al., "Emerging Threats and Opportunities for Large-Scale Ecological Restoration in the Atlantic Forest of Brazil," *Restoration Ecology* 19, no. 2 (Mar. 2011): 155; Milton Cezar Ribeiro, et al., "The Brazilian Atlantic Forest: How Much Is Left, and How Is the Remaining Forest Distributed? Implications for Conservation," *Biological Conservation* 142 (2009): 1142, 1145, 1149.

57. The small remnants, often in the single percentile or less of original stands are catalogued by Mary Byrd Davis in, "Old Growth in the East: A Survey," http://www.primalnature.org:80/ogeast/contents.html.

58. D.M. Silva Matos, et al., "Fire and Restoration of the Largest Urban Forest of the World in Rio de Janeiro City, Brazil," *Urban Ecosystems* 6 (2002): 151–161.

59. Amber Pariona, "Biggest Old Growth Forests in the United States," *World Atlas* (Apr. 25, 2017), https://www.worldatlas.com/articles/biggest-old-growth-forests-in-the-united-states.html

60. Candace Slater, "Amazonia as Edenic Narrative," in *Uncommon Ground: Toward Reinventing Nature*, edited by William Cronon (New York: W.W. Norton & Co., 1995), 114–31.

61. Bayard Webster, "In the Rain Forest, a Complex and Threatened World," *New York Times* (Apr. 17, 1979), pages C1-C2; Warren Hoge, "In Amazon, Huge Study Aims to Save Jungle Life," *New York Times* (Nov. 23, 1982), page C1; Nancy Beth Jackson, "A Rain-Forest Census Takes Shape, Tree by Tree (Almost Leaf by Leaf)," *New York Times* (June 6, 2006), page F4.

62. Nowotny and Peter, *Re-Thinking Science*, 132, 133.

63. Katherine E. Rowan, "Effective Explanation of Uncertain and Complex Science," in *Communicating Uncertainty*, 207–08.

64. *Ibid.*, 208.

65. Sharon M. Friedman, et al., "Preface," in *Ibid.*, vii.

66. Jones, "Covering Science and Technology," 7.

Chapter 5

1. As described with the U.S. Coast Guard in in Daniel McCabe, dir., prod., writer, *Prediction by the Numbers*, NOVA / PBS (Feb. 28, 2018).

2. Adam Briggle and Carl Mitcham, *Ethics and Science: An Introduction* (Cambridge University Press, 2012), 243.

3. "Futureology" is O'Hear's term, which he used to criticize forecasting of technology innovations. See Anthony O'Hear, *Introduction to the Philosophy of Science* (Oxford: Clarendon Press, 1989), 221.

4. Richard Feynman, *The Character of Physical Law* (1965; NY: Modern Library, 1994), 141.

5. Nassim Nicholas Taleb, *The Black Swan: the Impact of the Highly Improbable* (New York: Random House, 2007), 176. This was also mentioned regarding 1960s weather prediction in McCabe, dir., *Prediction by the Numbers*.

6. Taleb, *Black Swan*, 179.

7. Albert Einstein, *Ideas and Opinions* (New York: Bonanza Books, 1954), 47.

8. Observation of meteorologist Greg Carbin, in McCabe, *Prediction by the Numbers*.

9. Feynman, *The Character of Physical Law*, 151, 152. Also see Robert L. Park, *Voodoo Science: The Road from Foolishness to Fraud* (New York: Oxford University Press, 2000), 9.

10. Bjørn Lomborg, *The Skeptical Environmentalist: Measuring the Real State of the World* (Cambridge: Cambridge University Press, 2001), 268, 272.

11. Peter M. Cox, et al., "Emergent Constraint on Equilibrium Climate Sensitivity from Global Temperature Variability," *Nature* 553 (Jan. 18, 2018): 319–322.

12. Frances Drake, *Global Warming: The Sci-*

ence of Climate Change (New York: Oxford University Press, 2000), 156, 157, 158; Lomborg, The Skeptical Environmentalist, 260–63.

13. Ben Z. Houlton, et al., "Convergent Evidence for Widespread Rock Nitrogen Sources in Earth's Surface Environment," Science 360, no. 6384 (Apr. 6, 2018): 58–62.

14. Nicholas Lewis and Judith Curry, "The Impact of Recent Forcing and Ocean Heat Uptake Data on Estimates of Climate Sensitivity," Journal of Climate 31 (Aug. 2018): 6051–71.

15. For a very small sampling of recent articles, see V. Agilan and N. V. Umamahesh, "Covariate and Parameter Uncertainty in Non-Stationary Rainfall IDF Curve," International Journal of Climatology 38 (2018): 365–383; Louis-Philippe Caron, et al., "On the Variability and Predictability of Eastern Pacific Tropical Cyclone Activity," Journal of Climate 28, no. 24 (Dec. 15, 2015): 9678–9696; Zhiqiang Gong, et al., "Assessment and Correction of BCC_CSM's Performance in Capturing Leading Modes of Summer Precipitation Over North Asia," International Journal of Climatology 38 (2018): 2201–2214; Martin Kohler, et al., "Trends in Temperature and Wind Speed from 40 Years of Observations at a 200-m High Meteorological Tower in Southwest Germany," International Journal of Climatology 38 (2018): 23–34; Xin Li, et al., "Analysis of Variability and Trends of Precipitation Extremes in Singapore during 1980–2013," International Journal of Climatology 38 (2018): 125–141; Xiangwen Liu, et al., "Subseasonal Predictions of Regional Summer Monsoon Rainfall Over Tropical Asian Oceans and Land," Journal of Climate 28, no. 24 (Dec. 15, 2015): 9583–9605; Ruth E. Petrie, "Atmospheric Impact of Arctic Sea Ice Loss in a Coupled Ocean—Atmosphere Simulation," Journal of Climate 28, no. 24 (Dec. 1, 2015): 9606–9622; Rana Samuels, et al., "Evaluation and Projection of Extreme Precipitation Indices in the Eastern Mediterranean Based on CMIP5 Multi-Model Ensemble," International Journal of Climatology 38 (2018): 2280–2297; Shu Wu, et al., "Efficacy of Tendency and Linear Inverse Models to Predict Southern Peru's Rainy Season Precipitation International Journal of Climatology 38 (2018): 2590–2604; Zhen-Qiang Zhou and Shang-Ping Xie, "Effects of Climatological Model Biases on the Projection of Tropical Climate Change," Journal of Climate 28, no. 24 (Dec. 15 2015): 9909–9917.

16. Briggle and Mitcham, Ethics and Science, 237–38, 239.

17. Taleb, Black Swan, xxv.

18. Even the Intergovernmental Panel Cli-mate Change, which fosters so much climate alarmism, has admitted that the role of atmospheric carbon remains mysterious. See IPCC Fourth Assessment Report: Climate Change 2007, Working Group I: The Physical Science Basis, Box 6.2: "What Caused the Low Atmospheric Carbon Dioxide Concentrations During Glacial Times?" https://www.ipcc.ch/publications_and_data/ar4/wg1/en/ch6s6-4.html). Also see Ralph Ellis and Michael Palmer, "Modulation of Ice Ages via Precession and Dust-Albedo Feedbacks," Geoscience Frontiers 7, no. 6 (Nov. 2016): 891–909; Chuck De-Vore, "New Theory: CO2 and Climate Linked—But Not in the Way the 'Consensus' Tells Us," Forbes (June 30, 2016).

19. O'Hear, Introduction to the Philosophy of Science, 221; Taleb, Black Swan, 173. Part Two of Taleb's Black Swan, "We Just Can't Predict," offers numerous examples supporting a strong argument positing prevalent randomness in the world against fake experts offering unscientific predictions. For further examples see Nassim Nicholas Taleb, Antifragile: Things That Gain from Disorder (New York: Random House, 2012), 137, 139, 150.

20. Taleb, Black Swan, xxviii.

21. These four books were: William Kininmonth, Climate Change: a Natural Hazard (Brentwood, Essex: Multi-Science Pub. Co., 2004); Hans H. J. Labohm, et al., Man-Made Global Warming: Unravelling a Dogma (Brentwood, UK: Multi-Science Pub. Co., 2004); Marcel Leroux, Global Warming: Myth or Reality: the Erring Ways of Climatology (Berlin; New York: Springer; 2005); Siegfried Fred Singer and Dennis T. Avery, Unstoppable Global Warming: Every 1,500 Years (Lanham, MD: Rowman & Littlefield Pubs., 2007). Later I encountered the very helpful Frances Drake, Global Warming: The Science of Climate Change (New York: Oxford University Press, 2000), discussed below.

22. How the propagandists created the false notion of consensus (itself a contradiction to how science progresses) is described in Craig D. Idso, et al., Why Scientists Disagree About Global Warming: The NIPC Report on Scientific Consensus, 2nd ed. (Arlington Heights, IL: Heartland Inst., 2016), 10–30.

23. Francis Bacon, First Book of Aphorisms, Aphorism XLVI, available through Fordham University's Modern History SourceBook, http://www.fordham.edu/halsall/mod/bacon-aphor.html

24. Thomas S. Kuhn, Structure of Scientific Revolutions, 2nd ed. (1962; Chicago: University of Chicago Press, 1970), 79. Also see pages 82, 110, 135.

25. *Ibid.*, 5, 23–24, 78, 96.

26. See, for example, Bjørn Lomborg, "Now Even Climate-Change Believers Count as 'Deniers,'" *New York Post* (Oct. 12, 2017).

27. Xiaoquan Zhao, et al., "Partisan Differences in the Relationship Between Newspaper Coverage and Concern Over Global Warming," *Public Understanding of Science* 25, no. 5 (2016): 543–559.

28. Drake, *Global Warming*, 229.

29. *Ibid.*

30. *Ibid.*

31. *Ibid.*, 149.

32. *Ibid.*, 123, 124, 148, 154–55, 171.

33. *Ibid.*, 114, 116–20, 154.

34. *Ibid.*, 156, 157.

35. *Ibid.*, 158. Park (*Voodoo Science*, 33) also notes something that scientists and reporters alike should mention more often: our understanding of past climates is highly incomplete. Thus even if you believed in a "past as prologue" argument (Feynman, et al., would say "No!") the missing data would fatally weaken that argument.

36. Brian M. Fagan, *The Little Ice Age: How Climate Made History, 1300–1850* (New York: Basic Books, 2000).

37. Park, *Voodoo Science*, 33.

38. *Ibid.*, 44.

39. Malthus used "geometric" to mean exponential. See Thomas Malthus, *An Essay on the Principle of Population* (London: J. Johnson, 1798), 17, 21, 23, 88. This book is available for free on one of the best websites ever to come out of the internet, Project Gutenberg, www.gutenberg.org.

40. John Steinbeck, *Grapes of Wrath* (1940; NY: Viking, 1967), 33.

41. Nancy K. Kubasek and Gary S. Silverman, *Environmental Law* 4th ed. (Upper Saddle River, NJ: Prentice Hall, 2002), 319.

42. Paul R. Ehrlich and Anne H. Ehrlich, *The Population Bomb* (New York: Ballantine Books, 1968).

43. Taleb, *Black Swan*, 147.

44. Park, *Voodoo Science*, 87–88.

45. Lomborg asserts that anthropogenic carbon has increased atmospheric carbon by 31 percent (Lomborg, *The Skeptical Environmentalist*, 260). But this is actually problematic, as we do not really know the atmospheric carbon content before the industrial revolution. Furthermore, as detailed below, much more than atmospheric carbon addition or subtraction affects climate change.

46. IPCC Fourth Assessment Report: Climate Change 2007, Working Group I: The Physical Science Basis, Box 6.2: "What Caused the Low Atmospheric Carbon Dioxide Concentrations During Glacial Times?" (available via https://www.ipcc.ch/publications_and_data/ar4/wg1/en/ch6s6–4.html). Also see Ellis and Palmer, "Modulation of Ice Ages via Precession and Dust-Albedo Feedbacks," 891–909; DeVore, "New Theory: CO2 and Climate Linked—But Not in the Way the 'Consensus' Tells Us," *Forbes* (June 30, 2016).

47. Drake, *Global Warming*, 192, 195–97.

48. Barbara J. Finlayson-Pitts and James N. Pitts, *Chemistry of the Lower and Upper Atmosphere: Theory, Experiments, and Applications* (San Diego: Academic Press, 2000), 13, 776, 806, 814–19, 819–20, 821, 822; fig. 1.9, p.12.

49. After analyzing many previous studies, see the conclusion reached by J.R. Houston and R.G. Dean, "Sea-Level Acceleration Based on U.S. Tide Gauges and Extensions of Previous Global-Gauge Analyses," *Journal of Coastal Research* 27, no. 3 (May 2011): 416.

50. Drake, *Global Warming*, 159.

51. See William Ryan and Walter Pitman, *Noah's Flood: The New Scientific Discoveries About the Event That Changed History* (New York: Simon and Schuster, 1998).

52. Craig Welch, "New Island Appears Off U.S. Coast," *National Geographic* (June 27, 2017); Mark Price, "New NC island Was Expected to Eventually Disappear, But Not Like This," *Charlotte Observer* (July 28, 2017).

53. BBC News, "Charcoal Reveals Wildfire History" (July 14, 2006).

54. Quoted in Park, *Voodoo Science*, 31.

55. Phil Jardine, "The Paleocene-Eocene Thermal Maximum," *Paleontology Online* 1, no. 5 (Jan. 10, 2011): 1–7. For some typical speculative climate prognosticating, see Sarah Kaplan, "This Ancient Climate Catastrophe Is Our Best Clue about Earth's Future," *Washington Post* (Mar. 27, 2018).

56. Michael Brüggemann and Sven Engesser, "Between Consensus and Denial: Climate Journalists as Interpretive Community," *Science Communication* 36, no. 4 (2014): 400.

57. Jessica L. Bolin and Lawrence C. Hamilton, "The News You Choose: News Media Preferences Amplify Views on Climate Change," *Environmental Politics* 27, no. 3 (2018): 457–58, 461, 471; Maxwell T. Boykoff, "From Convergence to Contention: United States Mass Media Representations of Anthropogenic Climate Change Science," *Transactions of the Institute of British Geographers* (2007): 482, 483, 486; Jay D. Hmielowski, et al., "An Attack on Science? Media Use, Trust in Scientists, and Perceptions

of Global Warming," *Public Understanding of Science* 23, no. 7 (2014): 868–71, 878, 880; Eric Merkley and Dominik A. Stecula, "Party Elites or Manufactured Doubt? The Informational Context of Climate Change Polarization," *Science Communication* 40, no. 2 (2018): 258–70; Xiaoquan Zhao, et al., "Partisan Differences in the Relationship Between Newspaper Coverage and Concern Over Global Warming," *Public Understanding of Science* 25, no. 5 (2016): 543–559.

58. Lauren Feldman, et al., "Polarizing news? Representations of Threat and Efficacy in Leading U.S. Newspapers' Coverage of Climate Change," *Public Understanding of Science* 26, no. 4 (2017): 481–497; P. Sol Hart and Lauren Feldman, "Threat Without Efficacy? Climate Change on U.S. Network News," *Science Communication* 36, no. 3 (2014): 325–351.

59. Brüggemann and Engesser, "Between Consensus and Denial," 400, 404, 418, 419, 420, 422.

60. Ana Ivanova, et al., "Results from a Survey of German Climate Scientists," *Science Communication* 35, no. 5 (2013): 627, 640, 644.

61. Senja Post, "Communicating Science in Public Controversies: Strategic Considerations of the German Climate Scientists," *Public Understanding of Science* 25, no. 1 (2016): 68.

62. For some recent examples, see Jessica L. Bolin and Lawrence C. Hamilton, "The News You Choose: News Media Preferences Amplify Views on Climate Change," *Environmental Politics* 27, no. 3 (2018): 455–476; Maxwell T. Boykoff, "From Convergence to Contention: United States Mass Media Representations of Anthropogenic Climate Change Science," *Transactions of the Institute of British Geographers* (2007): 477–89; Jay D. Hmielowski, et al., "An Attack on Science? Media Use, Trust in Scientists, and Perceptions of Global Warming," *Public Understanding of Science* 23, no. 7 (2014): 866–883; Eric Merkley and Dominik A. Stecula, "Party Elites or Manufactured Doubt? The Informational Context of Climate Change Polarization," *Science Communication* 40, no. 2 (2018): 258–274.

63. This, according to MIT professor of meteorology, Richard S. Lindzen. See Richard S. Lindzen, "Science and Politics: Global Warming and Eugenics," in *Risks, Costs, and Lives Saved: Getting Better Results from Regulation*, edited by Robert William Hahn (New York: Oxford University Press, 1996), 88.

64. Finlayson-Pitts and Pitts, *Chemistry of the Lower and Upper Atmosphere*, 776, 820; Judith Lean and David Rind, "Climate Forcing by

Changing Solar Radiation," *Journal of Climate* 11 (Dec. 1998): 369–94.

65. Finlayson-Pitts and Pitts, *Chemistry of the Lower and Upper Atmosphere*, 829.

66. Lomborg, *The Skeptical Environmentalist*, 260–63.

67. *Ibid.*, 269–71, 277.

68. *Ibid.*, 269–70, 276–77.

69. Conor Knighton, "On the Trail: Disappearing Glaciers," CBS News (Oct. 23, 2016).

70. Georg Kaser, et al., "Modern Glacier Retreat on Kilimanjaro as Evidence of Climate Change: Observation and Facts," *International Journal of Climatology* 24 (2004): 329, 333, 335–36.

71. Matt McGrath, "Arctic Ice 'Grew by a Third' After Cool Summer in 2013," *BBC News* (July 21, 2015); P. Winsor, "Arctic Sea Ice Thickness Remained Constant During the 1990s," *Geophysical Research Letters* 28, no. 6 (Mar. 15, 2001): 1039–1041.

72. Peter T. Doran, "Antarctic Climate Cooling and Terrestrial Ecosystem Response," *Nature* 415, no. 31 (Jan. 2002): 517–20; Ian Joughin and Slawek Tulaczyk, "Positive Mass Balance of the Ross Ice Streams, West Antarctica," *Science* 295 (Jan. 18, 2002): 476–80.

73. For examples, see Alister Doyle, "Antarctic Seas Defy Global Warming Thanks to Chill from the Deep," *Reuters* (May 30, 2016); Nicole Orttung, "Scientists Reconcile Growth in Antarctic Sea Ice with Global Warming Models," *Christian Science Monitor* (July 6, 2016); Belinda Smith, "Why is Antarctica's Sea Ice Spreading as the Arctic's Shrinks?," *Cosmos News* (May 23, 2016).

74. Jonathan Amos, "Ice Loss Spreads Up Antarctic Glaciers," *BBC News* (Dec. 12, 2016); Chris Mooney, "Antarctic Sea Ice Used to be the Darling of Climate Doubters. Not Anymore," *Washington Post* (Feb. 16, 2017).

75. Andrew Liptak, "Antarctica Is Home to Considerably More Volcanoes Than Previously Thought," *Verge* (Aug. 13, 2017); Hannah Osborne, "NASA Discovers Mantle Plume Almost as Hot as Yellowstone Supervolcano That's Melting Antarctica from Below," *Newsweek* (Nov. 8, 2017); Lewis Page, "Natural Geothermal Heating under Melt-Hit Antarctic Ice Region 'SURPRISINGLY High,'" *The Register* (July 13, 2015); Maximillian Van Wyk De Vries, et al., "A New Volcanic Province: an Inventory of Subglacial Volcanoes in West Antarctica," in M.J. Jamieson, et al., eds., *Exploration of Subsurface Antarctica: Uncovering Past Changes and Modern Processes*, Geological Society, London, Special Publications (2017), https://www.geos.ed.ac.uk/homes/rbingha2/48_2017_Vries.pdf

76. Roger J. Braithwaite, "Glacier Mass Balance: the First 50 Years of International Monitoring," *Progress in Physical Geography* 26, no. 1 (2002): 77, 80, 81, 82.

77. *Ibid.*, 92.

78. Finlayson-Pitts and Pitts, *Chemistry of the Lower and Upper Atmosphere*, 829; Park, *Voodoo Science*, 45. Also, in general, see Bjørn Lomborg, *Cool It: The Skeptical Environmentalist's Guide to Global Warming* (New York: Knopf, 2007).

79. This is what Taleb calls the Black Swan, the topic (and title) of his famous book. Also see Taleb, *Antifragile*, 4.

80. Taleb, *Antifragile*, 93. Also see Taleb, *Black Swan*, xvii, 79, and more generally, Part Two about us not being able to predict.

81. Lomborg, *The Skeptical Environmentalist*, xx. For the mysterious origin of the quote, see Paul F. Velleman, "Truth, Damn Truth, and Statistics," *Journal of Statistics Education* 16:2 (July 2008).

82. Lomborg, *The Skeptical Environmentalist*, 13–19, 31.

83. *Ibid.*, 259, 266. This is also the general thesis in Lomborg's follow-up book, Lomborg, *Cool It*.

84. Lomborg, *The Skeptical Environmentalist*, 26, 30, 249, 259, 266, 275, 278, 287–300, 305–18, 322–24, 329.

85. Park, *Voodoo Science*, 44.

86. John Rennie, et al., "Misleading Math About the Earth," *Scientific American* 286, no. 1 (Jan. 2002): 61.

87. *Ibid.*, 62, 63.

88. Briggle and Mitcham, *Ethics and Science*, 243.

89. Many of these can be found in the opening paragraphs of Gore's 2006 address to the New York University School of Law (Sept. 18, 2006), reproduced in Carolyn Merchant, *Major Problems in American Environmental History*, 3rd ed. (Boston: Wadsworth, Cengage Learning, 2012), 538–43.

90. Rennie, et al., "Misleading Math about the Earth," 65.

91. Warren Hoge, "In Amazon, Huge Study Aims to Save Jungle Life," *New York Times* (Nov. 23, 1982), page C1; Bayard Webster, "Forest's Role in Weather Documented in Amazon," *New York Times* (July 5, 1983), page C1; James Brooke, "Saving Scraps of the Rain Forest May Be Pointless, Naturalists Say," *New York Times* (Nov. 14, 1989).

92. Rennie, et al., "Misleading Math About the Earth," 71.

93. Thomas Lovejoy, "Foreword," in Howard Friel, *The Lomborg Deception: Setting the Record Straight About Global Warming* (New Haven: Yale University Press, 2010), viii.

94. *Ibid.*

95. *Ibid.*, ix.

96. Park, *Voodoo Science*, 44.

97. Friel, *The Lomborg Deception*, 6; Thomas Lovejoy, "Foreword," vii; Rennie, et al., "Misleading Math about the Earth," 65.

98. Rennie, et al., "Misleading Math About the Earth," 62, 65; Friel, *The Lomborg Deception*, 6–18.

99. Alston Chase, *In a Dark Wood: The Fight Over Forests and the Rising Tyranny of Ecology* (New York: Houghton Mifflin, 1995), 313, 415.

100. Rennie, et al., "Misleading Math About the Earth," 63, 65, 66, 67, 68.

101. *Ibid.*, 68, 70.

102. Brent S. Steel, Denise Lach and Vijay A. Satyal, "Ideology and Scientific Credibility: Environmental Policy in the American Pacific Northwest," *Public Understanding of Science* 15 (2006): 484.

103. *Ibid.*

104. Will Sarvis, "The Homelessness Muddle Revisited," *Urban Lawyer*, 49, no. 2 (Spring 2017): 317–354; reproduced in the chapter, "Home in the Breach" in Will Sarvis, *Sacred and Ephemeral: Reflections Upon Land, Place, and Home* (Self-published, 2017).

105. Fred Pearce, "Africans Go Back to the Land as Plants Reclaim the Desert," *New Scientist* 175, no. 2361 (Sept. 21, 2002): 4–5.

106. Zhiliang Zhu and A. David McGuire, eds., "Baseline and Projected Future Carbon Storage and Greenhouse-Gas Fluxes in Ecosystems of Alaska," Professional Paper 1826 (Reston, VA: U.S. Geological Survey, 2016), https://pubs.usgs.gov/pp/1826/pp1826.pdf. Also see Chris Mooney, "Alaska's Huge Climate Mystery—and its Global Consequences," *Washington Post* (June 3, 2016); Chris Mooney, "Thanks to Climate Change, the Arctic Is Turning Green," *Washington Post* (June 27, 2016).

107. Drake, *Global Warming*, 204–05. Also see Lomborg, *Skeptical Environmentalist*, 28–29.

108. Susan Solomon, et al., "Irreversible Climate Change Due to Carbon Dioxide Emissions," *Proceedings of the National Academy of Sciences* 106, no. 6 (Feb. 10, 2009): 1704–09.

109. Harry Collins and Robert Evans, *Rethinking Expertise* (Chicago: University of Chicago Press, 2014), 1, 8, 9.

Chapter 6

1. Julian L. Simon and Aaron Wildavsky, "Species Loss Revisited," *Society* 30 (Nov./Dec. 1992): 45.
2. George Perkins Marsh, *Man and Nature; or, Physical Geography as Modified by Human Action* (New York: Charles Scribner & Co., 1864).
3. The previously-mentioned Crosby volumes catalogue so many details of the modified environment: Alfred W. Crosby, *The Columbian Exchange: Biological and Cultural Consequences of 1492*, new ed. (Westport, CT: Praeger, 2003) and Alfred W. Crosby, *Ecological Imperialism: the Biological Expansion of Europe, 900–1900*, new ed. (New York: Cambridge Univ. Press, 2004).
4. Milton Cezar Ribeiro, et al., "The Brazilian Atlantic Forest: How Much Is Left, and How Is the Remaining Forest Distributed? Implications for Conservation," *Biological Conservation* 142 (2009): 1142.
5. Miguel Calmon, et al., "Emerging Threats and Opportunities for Large-Scale Ecological Restoration in the Atlantic Forest of Brazil," *Restoration Ecology* 19, no. 2 (Mar. 2011): 155; Ribeiro, et al., "The Brazilian Atlantic Forest," 1142, 1145, 1149.
6. Endextinction.org is the San Diego Zoo's program focusing on preserving endangered species.
7. M. Lynne Corn and Alexandra M. Wyatt, "The Endangered Species Act: A Primer," (Washington, DC: Congressional Information Service, Library of Congress, Sept. 8, 2016), 6.
8. *Ibid.*, 6, 13.
9. *Ibid.*, 6.
10. Reed F. Noss, "From Endangered Species to Biodiversity," in *Balancing on the Brink of Extinction: the Endangered Species Act and Lessons for the Future*, edited by Kathryn A. Kohm (Washington, DC: Island Press, 1991), 236–38.
11. Paul L. Farber, *Finding Order in Nature: The Naturalist Tradition from Linnaeus to E.O. Wilson* (Baltimore: Johns Hopkins University Press, 2000), 112.
12. Daniel P. Faith, "Biodiversity," *Stanford Encyclopedia of Philosophy* (June 11, 2003; rev. Dec. 4, 2007), section 1, "Concepts of Biodiversity."
13. Ronnie E. Brenneman, "Controlling Deer Problems in Hardwood Stands," in *Proceedings: Guidelines for Regenerating Appalachian Hardwood Stands*, edited by Arlyn W. Perkey, et al. (USDA Forest Service (Morgantown, WV, May 24–26, 1988), 97–103; Edwin D. Michael,

"Effects of White-Tailed Deer on Appalachian Hardwood Regeneration," in *Proceedings: Guidelines for Regenerating Appalachian Hardwood Stands*, 85–96. Iowans are dealing with their over-population of deer by coordinating increased hunting with food donations. See Josh Buettner, "Deer Hunters Help Combat Food Insecurity in Iowa," *PBS Newshour* (Feb. 12, 2018).
14. W.J. Ripple and R.L. Beschta, "Large Predators Limit Herbivore Densities in Northern Forest Ecosystems," *European Journal of Wildlife Research* (2012), https://ir.library.oregonstate.edu/concern/defaults/1n79h480n.
15. Robert J. Wenke, *Patterns in Prehistory: Humankind's First Three Million Years*, 3rd ed. (New York: Oxford University Press, 1990), 218–219. Also see P.S. Martin and H.E. Wright, Jr., eds., *Pleistocene Extinctions: The Search for a Cause* (New Haven: Yale University Press, 1967).
16. As always, the Stanford Encyclopedia of Philosophy offers a helpful overview of the subject, with many references for further research. See Marc Ereshefsky, "Species," *Stanford Encyclopedia of Philosophy* (July 4, 2002; rev. ed., Aug. 29, 2017).
17. *Ibid.*, sec. 5, "Darwin and Species"; sec. 6, "Summary." Also see Simon and Wildavsky, "Species Loss Revisited," 42–43.
18. Arguments over what constitutes a species have indeed entered the legal arena regarding the ESA. See John Copeland Nagle, "Playing Noah," *Minnesota Law Review* 82 (May 1998): 1180.
19. Corn and Wyatt, "The Endangered Species Act: A Primer," 7.
20. Simon and Wildavsky, "Species Loss Revisited," 44.
21. Bjørn Lomborg, *The Skeptical Environmentalist: Measuring the Real State of the World* (Cambridge: Cambridge University Press, 2001), 256; Simon and Wildavsky, "Species Loss Revisited," 44.
22. Simon and Wildavsky, "Species Loss Revisited," 44.
23. Norman Myers, *The Sinking Ark: A New Look at the Problem of Disappearing Species* (New York: Pergamon Press, 1979), 4–5.
24. Charles C. Mann and Mark L. Plummer, *Noah's Choice: The Future of Endangered Species* (New York: Knopf, 1995), 64.
25. Paul R. Ehrlich and Anne H. Ehrlich, *Extinction: the Causes and Consequences of the Disappearance of Species* (New York: Random House, 1981), 8. Their extinction rates from other studies are cited in Lomborg, *The Skeptical Environmentalist*, 249; Mann and Plummer, *Noah's Choice*, 64; and Nigel E. Stork, "Measur-

ing Global Biodiversity and its Decline," in *Biodiversity II: Understanding and Protecting Our Biological Resources*, edited by Marjorie L. Reaka-Kudla, et al. (Washington, DC: Joseph Henry Press, 1997), table 5–6, pp. 62–63.

26. Edward O. Wilson, *The Diversity of Life* (New York: W.W. Norton, 1992), 280. The same data is repeated on the same page number in the 1999 edition.

27. Lomborg, *The Skeptical Environmentalist*, 254, 256.

28. *Ibid.*, 249.

29. See Lomborg's analysis within a broader natural history context in Lomborg, *The Skeptical Environmentalist*, 249–50, 252, 255.

30. See David Hackett Fischer, *Historians' Fallacies: Toward a Logic of Historical Thought* (New York: Harper, 1970), 109–110.

31. Ehrlich and Ehrlich, *Extinction*, xiii–xiv.

32. Mann and Plummer, *Noah's Choice*, 65. Mann and Plummer offered one glimpse into the slipshod "scientific" methodology that drove early extinction hysteria. See Mann and Plummer, *Noah's Choice*, 66–72.

33. Joel Greenberg, *A Feathered River Across the Sky: The Passenger Pigeon's Flight to Extinction* (New York: Bloomsbury, 2014), xii, 177–78, 186–89, 201, 223–26, 235.

34. *Ibid.*, 199–207.

35. Jerome A. Jackson and Bette J.S. Jackson, "Once Upon a Time in American Ornithology," *Wilson Journal of Ornithology* 119, no. 4 (Dec. 2007): 770.

36. Simon Reeve, "Going Down in History," *Geographical* (Mar. 2001), 64.

37. Robert Whaples, "Book Review: A Feathered River Across the Sky: The Passenger Pigeon's Flight to Extinction, by Joel Greenberg," *Independent Review* 19, no. 3 (Winter 2015): 446.

38. For many examples considering such trade-offs, see R. Allan Freeze, *The Environmental Pendulum: A Quest for the Truth About Toxic Chemicals, Human Health, and Environmental Protection* (Berkeley: University of California Press, 2000), 16, 19, 31, 44–45, 151, 152–53, 158; Lomborg, *Skeptical Environmentalist*, 280–87, 319, 322, 329, 338–39, 341–48.

39. Bernd Brunner, *Birdmania* (Sydney, Australia: Allen & Unwin, 2017); Mark Cocker, *Birders: Tales of a Tribe* (New York: Grove Press, 2001); Jamie Johnson, "Birds: The High Flying Marker of Status," *Vanity Fair* (Apr. 7, 2009); Richard O. Prum, "The Passion and Peril of Birding," *New York Times* (Jan. 23, 2018).

40. Cocker, *Birders: Tales of a Tribe*, 54–55.

41. Sahotra Sarkar, "Ecology," *Stanford Encyclopedia of Philosophy* (Dec. 23, 2005), sec. 4, "Ecosystem Ecology."

42. Donald Worster, *Nature's Economy: A History of Ecological Ideas*, 2nd ed. (New York: Cambridge University Press, 1994), 373, 374, 378, 400, 401, 405, 406, 408, 411, 417, 418–19.

43. *Ibid.*, 419.

44. Daniel P. Faith, "Biodiversity," *Stanford Encyclopedia of Philosophy* (June 11, 2003; rev. Dec. 4, 2007), section 1, "Concepts of Biodiversity."

45. *Ibid.*, section 2, "From Species Values to Biodiversity Values"; subsection 2.2, "Species as Equal Units and SMS." (SMS means "safe minimum standard").

46. Bayard Webster, "In the Rain Forest, a Complex and Threatened World," *New York Times* (Apr. 17, 1979), pages C1–C2; Warren Hoge, "In Amazon, Huge Study Aims to Save Jungle Life," *New York Times* (Nov. 23, 1982), page C1; Nancy Beth Jackson, "A Rain-Forest Census Takes Shape, Tree by Tree (Almost Leaf by Leaf)," *New York Times* (June 6, 2006), page F4.

47. Farber, *Finding Order in Nature*, 112.

48. Faith, "Biodiversity," section 6, "Conclusions."

49. Debbie Elliott, "The Big Stories Behind Small Seeds: This Man Wants to Save Them All," NPR's *Weekend Edition Saturday* (Nov. 4, 2017).

50. John C. Kricher, *The Balance of Nature: Ecology's Enduring Myth* (Princeton: Princeton University Press, 2009), 97.

51. Jason Van Driesche and Roy Van Driesche, *Nature Out of Place: Biological Invasions in the Global Age* (Washington, DC: Island Press, 2000).

52. Peter Alden, et al., *National Audubon Society Field Guide to the Pacific Northwest* (New York: Alfred A. Knopf, 1998), 46–48.

53. *Ibid.*, 47.

54. Dorothy Fadiman, dir., *Butterfly Town, USA* (Concentric Media 2015).

55. The evocatively wonderful phrase is Bjørn Lomborg's, in *The Skeptical Environmentalist*, 330.

56. Will Sarvis, *Sacred and Ephemeral: Reflections Upon Land, Place, and Home* (Self-published, 2017), 1–2.

57. Achva Benzinberg Stein and Jacqueline Claire Moxley, "In Defense of the Nonnative: The Case of the Eucalyptus," *Landscape Journal* 11, no. 1 (Spring 1992): 35–50.

58. *Ibid.*, 42. Also see Jared Farmer, *Trees in Paradise: A California History* (New York: W.W. Norton, 2013), 113, 173–75, 183–84, 198, 202.

59. Stein and Moxley, "In Defense of the Nonnative," 39, 44.

60. *Ibid.*, 36–37, 48.

61. Farmer, *Trees in Paradise*, 190–92.

62. Stein and Moxley, "In Defense of the Nonnative," 48.

63. Farmer, *Trees in Paradise*, 176–79, 188–89.

64. *Save Our Big Trees v. City of Santa Cruz, et al.*, Court of Appeal, Sixth District, California (filed Oct. 23, 2015), 241 Cal.App.4th 694. Also see Emma Marris, "The Great Eucalyptus Debate," *The Atlantic* (Nov. 30, 2016).

65. Brent Walth, *Fire at Eden's Gate: Tom McCall & the Oregon Story* (Portland: Oregon Historical Society, 1994), chapter sixteen, "Visit but Don't Stay."

66. Anna Bramwell, *Ecology in the 20th Century: A History* (New Haven: Yale University Press, 1989), 248. Also see Worster, *Nature's Economy*, 360.

67. Freeze, *Environmental Pendulum*, 45; Aaron Wildavsky, *But Is It True? A Citizen's Guide to Environmental Health and Safety Issues* (Cambridge: Harvard University Press, 1995), 440.

68. The Eugene scene is covered in the "Misanthropic Eden" chapter in Sarvis, *Sacred and Ephemeral.*

69. The article that launched this topic in recent times was Christopher D. Stone, "Should Trees Have Standing?—Towards Legal Rights for Natural Objects," *Southern California Law Review* 45 (1972): 450–501, followed by Roderick Nash, "Do Rocks Have Rights?" *The Center Magazine* 10 (1977): 1–12. Also see Anna Grear, *Should Trees Have Standing?: 40 Years On* (Cheltenham, UK; Northampton, MA: Edward Elgar, 2012); Christopher D. Stone, *Should Trees Have Standing?: Law, Morality, and the Environment* (New York: Oxford University Press, 2010); Brian Smith, "The Rights of Rocks: Towards an Environmental Ethic Without Intrinsicality," Graduate Conference "The Politics of Human Rights," Boston, MA, Mar. 11, 2010.

70. David W. Ehrenfeld, *The Arrogance of Humanism* (New York: Oxford University Press, 1978), 208.

71. *Ibid.*, 209.

72. Bernard Dixon, "Forum: Genes of Yesteryear—What Can We Learn, Bernard Dixon asks, from Disease-Causing Microbes Preserved in the Biosphere?" *New Scientist* (Apr. 9, 1994).

73. Quoted in "Photographer Wins 'Monkey Selfie' Legal Fight," *BBC News* (Sept. 11, 2017).

74. Scott Simon, "The Nonhuman Rights Project Advocates for Zoo Animals," NPR's *Weekend Edition Saturday* (Nov. 18, 2017).

75. Annie H. Ehrlich and Paul R. Ehrlich, "Needed: An Endangered Humanity Act?" in *Balancing on the Brink of Extinction: the Endangered Species Act and Lessons for the Future*, edited by Kathryn A. Kohm (Washington, DC: Island Press, 1991), 302.

76. Kohm, *Balancing on the Brink of Extinction*, Part IV plate quote, page 225.

77. Abigail Beall, "Ugly Animals Overlooked During Scientific Study and Conservation," *Daily Mail* (Mar. 8, 2016); Mark Molloy, "Ugly Animals Are Being 'Shunned' by Scientists—Study," *Telegraph* (Mar. 7, 2016).

78. Dennis D. Murphy, "Invertebrate Conservation," in *Balancing on the Brink of Extinction*, 182, 184; Nagle, "Playing Noah," 1175, 1198–99, 1204, 1208.

79. "Japan Zoo Kills 57 Snow Monkeys Due to 'Alien Genes,'" *BBC News* (Feb. 21, 2017).

80. Star Trek, "Devil in the Dark," season 1, episode 25 (1967).

81. Joel Achenbach, "Who Knew? Plants on the Warpath," *National Geographic Magazine* (Feb. 2004); Jeanna Bryner, "Invasive Plant Conquers with Chemical Warfare," *Live Science* (Oct. 17, 2007); Elroy L. Rice, *Allelopathy*, 2nd ed. (Orlando: Academic Press, 1984); John Timmer, "Chemical Warfare on the Reef," *Ars Technica* (Nov. 9, 2012); Colin Tudge, *The Secret Life of Trees* (London: Allen Lane, 2005), 316.

82. Tudge, *The Secret Life of Trees*, 273.

83. *Ibid.*, 266–68, 273–76. For a wider variety of examples, see Erna Buffie, dir., *What Plants Talk About* (PBS, Nature, 2012).

84. Tudge, *The Secret Life of Trees*, 358.

85. Peter Tompkins and Christopher Bird, *The Secret Life of Plants* (New York: Harper & Row, 1973); Walon Green, dir., *The Secret Life of Plants* (Infinite Enterprises, 1978).

86. Michael Pollan, "The Intelligent Plant," *New Yorker* (Dec. 23 & 30, 2013). This article is a good summation of a great many recent advances in plant science.

87. Animal Welfare Act of 1966, Public Law 89–544, 80 Stat. 350. Also see Anita Guerrini, *Experimenting with Humans and Animals: from Galen to Animal Rights* (Baltimore: Johns Hopkins University Press, 2003), 132.

88. Guerrini, *Experimenting with Humans and Animals*, 115.

89. Glenn Greenwald and Leighton Akio Woodhouse, "Bred to Suffer: Inside the Barbaric U.S. Industry of Dog Experimentation," *The Intercept* (May 17, 2018), https://theintercept.com/2018/05/17/inside-the-barbaric-u-s-industry-of-dog-experimentation/

90. Joseph Campbell, *Transformation of*

Myth Through Time (New York: Harper & Row, 1990), 9–10, 101, 194, 224; Lotte Motz, *The Faces of the Goddess* (New York: Oxford University Press, 1997), 40, 122.

91. James Mooney, *Myths of the Cherokee* (Washington, DC: Bureau of American Ethnology, 1902), 261–64.

92. James F. McInteer, "Where Materialism Falls Short," *Virginia Wildlife* 24, no. 12 (Dec. 1963): 9.

93. *Ibid.*

94. David Peterson, *Heartsblood: Hunting, Spirituality, and Wildness in America* (Washington, DC: Island Press, 2000), 26–27, 78–96, 97, 98.

95. Gene Wunderlich, "Review of Peterson, *Heartsblood*," *Journal of Agricultural and Environmental Ethics* 14, no. 3 (2001): 355–56.

96. Kathryn Paxton George, "The Use and Abuse of Scientific Studies," *Journal of Agricultural and Environmental Ethics* 5, no. 2 (Sept. 1992): 218.

97. Hub Zwart, "A Short History of Food Ethics," *Journal of Agricultural and Environmental Ethics* 12 (2000): 123, 125.

98. The before and after story regarding coyotes can be found in Thomas R. Dunlap, "American Wildlife Policy and Environmental Ideology: Poisoning Coyotes, 1939–1972," *Pacific Historical Review* 55, no. 3 (Aug. 1986): 345–369; Dan L. Flores, *Coyote America: a Natural and Supernatural History* (New York: Basic Books, 2016).

99. Nagle, "Playing Noah," 1193, 1202–03, 1234, 1261.

Chapter 7

1. For two examples, see Cliff I. Davidson, "Air Pollution in Pittsburgh: A Historical Perspective," *Journal of the Air Pollution Control Association* 29, no. 10 (1979) and H. Nishimura, ed. *How to Conquer Air Pollution, A Japanese Experience* (New York: Elsevier Science Pub. Co., 1989), 35–43, 46.

2. Kenneth Edward Diebel, "Isozyme Variation within the Fraser Fir Population on Mt. Rogers, Virginia," (Ph.D. diss., Virginia Polytechnic Institute and State Univ., 1989); Arthur Randolph Shields, "The Isolated Spruce and Spruce-Fir Forests of Southwestern Virginia: A Biotic Study," (Ph.D. diss., Univ. of Tennessee, 1962); Peter S. White, ed., *The Southern Appalachian Spruce-Fir Ecosystem: Its Biology and Threats* (Gatlinburg, TN: Uplands Field Research Laboratory, 1984). Also see Robert H.

Mohlenbrock, "Mount Rogers, Virginia," *Natural History* 99 (Dec. 1990): 72–74, and Joanna Samuels, "The Adelgid Strikes Again," *Audubon* 98 (Mar.–Apr. 1996): 24.

3. Diane Dietz, "The Cost of Clean Air," *Eugene Register Guard* (Apr. 16, 2012).

4. This example is quoted from a local KLCC Radio Public Service Announcement (Nov. 29, 2006).

5. Matt Cooper, "Cold Temps Bring Wood-Burning Restrictions," *Eugene Register Guard* (Jan. 25, 2008).

6. See Geoffrey C. Kabat, *Hyping Health Risks: Environmental Hazards in Daily Life and the Science of Science of Epidemiology* (New York: Columbia University Press, 2008), chapter six, "The Controversy Over Passive Smoking."

7. Elon Glucklich, "Wildfire Smoke Brought Unprecedented Levels of Air Pollution to Eugene Area Last Weekend, New Data Confirm," *Eugene Register-Guard* (Sept. 8, 2017)

8. "We're Really Hoping That Precipitation Helps Clear Some of This Out," *KMTR NBC News* (Sept. 15, l2017).

9. Mary Louise Kelly, "Is All That Wildfire Smoke Damaging My Lungs?" NPR's *Morning Edition* (Sept. 11, 2017).

10. Diane Dietz, "The Cost of Clean Air," *Eugene Register Guard* (Apr. 16, 2012).

11. Niall McCarthy, "Pollution Kills Three Times More Than AIDS, TB and Malaria Combined," *Forbes* (Oct. 23, 2017).

12. Kabat, *Hyping Health Risks*, 35–36.

13. Terence Chea, "China's Pollution Problem Crosses Pacific," *Associated Press* (July 29, 2006).

14. American Lung Association, "State of the Air 2018" (Chicago: American Lung Assoc., 2018), http://www.lung.org/assets/documents/healthy-air/state-of-the-air/sota-2018-full.pdf

15. *Ibid.*, 4–6, 11, 13, 14.

16. Steve Kolowich, "The Water Next Time: Professor Who Helped Expose Crisis in Flint Says Public Science Is Broken," *Chronicle of Higher Education* (Feb. 2, 2016). There is much more testimony to this phenomenon in the disturbing documentaries, Cullen Hoback, dir., *What Lies Upstream* (Hyrax Films, 2017), and Llewellyn M. Smith, dir., *Poisoned Water* (PBS/Nova, 2017).

17. Supposedly a variant from a 1930s advertising slogan from DuPont Corporation that some environmentalists began using ironically during the 1970s.

18. Reiner Grundmann, "Review of Naomi Oreskes and Erik M. Conway, *Merchants of Doubt: How a Handful of Scientists Obscured the*

Truth on Issues from Tobacco Smoke to Global Warming (New York: Bloomsbury Press, 2011)," *BioSocieties* 8, no. 3 (2013): 369–374.

19. This is a focus of the Farmworker Justice organization: https://www.farmworkerjustice. org/content/pesticide-safety

20. R. Allan Freeze, *The Environmental Pendulum: A Quest for the Truth About Toxic Chemicals, Human Health, and Environmental Protection* (Berkeley: University of California Press, 2000), 8–9, 48–51, 57, 61–62.

21. *Ibid.*, 15, 95, 107, 115.

22. Kabat, *Hyping Health Risks*, 3–5.

23. Freeze, *Environmental Pendulum*, 8–9, 10, 32–36, 110–11, 123, 126–27, 128, 140–41; Bjørn Lomborg, *The Skeptical Environmentalist: Measuring the Real State of the World* (Cambridge: Cambridge University Press, 2001), 215; Sylvia Noble Tesh, *Uncertain Hazards: Environmental Activists and Scientific Proof* (Ithaca: Cornell University Press, 2000), 32; Aaron Wildavsky, *But Is It True? A Citizen's Guide to Environmental Health and Safety Issues* (Cambridge: Harvard University Press, 1995), 127.

24. Jesse McKinley, "Lawmakers Skeptical of State's Explanation for Hoosick Falls Water Crisis," *New York Times* (Sept. 7, 2016).

25. Sam Weber and Laura Fong, "Long Island Residents Worry Their Tap Water Is Unsafe," *PBS Newshour* (Dec. 16, 2017); Sam Weber and Laura Fong, "How an Unregulated Chemical Entered a North Carolina Community's Drinking Water," *PBS Newshour* (Dec. 17, 2017).

26. *City of Greenville, et al. v. Syngenta Crop Protection*, 904 F.Supp.2d 902 (2012); *City of Greenville, et al. v. Syngenta Crop Protection*, 764 F.3d 695 (2014).

27. Well publicized in the Hollywood movie: Steven Soderbergh, dir., *Erin Brockovich* (Universal Pictures, 2000).

28. Freeze, *Environmental Pendulum*, 9, 32–36, 110–11, 221–22.

29. *Ibid.*, 148–19, 150.

30. Lomborg, *Skeptical Environmentalist*, 216, 217, 218, 219, 222, 228, 229.

31. *Ibid.*, 231, 235; Freeze, *Environmental Pendulum*, 96, 115, 117, 127; Wildavsky, *But Is It True?*, 8.

32. Freeze, *Environmental Pendulum*, 24.

33. Arianne Cohen, "My Quest to Analyze Every Man-Made Chemical in My Body," *Popular Science* (Nov. 2, 2009). For details, see the massive document: U.S. Department of Health and Human Services, Centers for Disease Control and Prevention, "Fourth National Report on Human Exposure to Environmental Chemicals, Updated Tables," volume one (Mar. 2018),

available at National Report on Human Exposure to Environmental Chemicals, https://www. cdc.gov/exposurereport/index.html

34. Freeze, *Environmental Pendulum*, 272.

35. Dorman L. Steelman Interview (Feb. 9, 1998 in Salem, Missouri), Politics in Missouri Oral History Project, Collection #3929, Western Historical Manuscript Collection, Columbia, Missouri.

36. Although some critics observe that Huber has overstated or mis-stated his case, there are elements of truth in his observation of junk science. Peter W. Huber, *Galileo's Revenge: Junk Science in the Courtroom* (New York: Basic Books, 1991). Also see an interesting essay in its own right: John F. Baughman, "Galileo's Revenge: Junk Science in the Courtroom by Peter W. Huber, Book Review," *Michigan Law Review* 90, no. 6 (May 1992): 1614–1623.

37. Wildavsky, *But Is It True?*, 81.

38. Anh D. Ngo, et al., "Association Between Agent Orange and Birth Defects: Systematic Review and Meta-Analysis," *International Journal of Epidemiology* 35, no. 5 (Oct. 2006): 1220–1230; Jesse King and Cecilia Chou, "Agent Orange Birth Defects: Recording and Contextualizing the Science of Embryos, Development, and Reproduction," *The Embryo Project Encyclopedia* (Arizona State University, School of Life Sciences, Center for Biology and Society, Mar. 7, 2017).

39. Sherwin B. Nuland, *The Uncertain Art: Thoughts on a Life in Medicine* (New York: Random House, 2008), xiii, xiv,–xv, xvi.

40. Sharon M. Friedman, "The Never-Ending Story of Dioxin," in *Communicating Uncertainty: Media Coverage of New and Controversial Science*, edited by Sharon M. Friedman, et al. (Mahwah, NJ: L. Erlbaum Associates, 1999), 119, 122–23.

41. Nick H. Proctor and James P., Hughes, *Proctor and Hughes' Chemical Hazards of the Workplace*, 5th ed. (Hoboken, NJ: Wiley-Interscience, 2004), v–xi, 3–7; Freeze, *Environmental Pendulum*, 15.

42. Wildavsky, *But Is It True?*, conclusion, "Rejecting the Precautionary Principle." Also see Wilfred Beckerman, *Poverty of Reason: Sustainable Development (Oakland, CA: Independent Institute, 2002)*, 43–50.

43. Carolina Moreno, et al., "The Context(s) of Precaution: Ideological and Instrumental Appeals to the Precautionary Principle," *Science Communication* 32, no. 1 (2010): 77, 78.

44. Anne Ingeborg Myhr, "A Precautionary Approach to Genetically Modified Organisms: Challenges and Implications for Policy and Sci-

ence," *Journal of Agricultural and Environmental Ethics* 23 (2010): 504, 505.

45. *Ibid.*, 502.

46. United Nations, Agenda 21, Chapter 19, "Environmentally Sound Management of Toxic Chemicals," section D, "Establishment of Risk Reduction Programmes," subsection 19.49, https://sustainabledevelopment.un.org/content/documents/Agenda21.pdf

47. Freeze, *Environmental Pendulum*, 94.

48. *Ibid.*, 124, 127.

49. Gerald Markowitz and David Rosner, *Deceit and Denial: The Deadly Politics of Industrial Pollution* (Berkeley: University of California Press, 2002), xiii–xv, 7, 108. Generally see chapter six, "Evidence of an Illegal Conspiracy by Industry," and chapter seven, "Damn Liars."

50. Two popular books on this topic were: Theo Colborn, Dianne Dumanoski, and John Peterson Myers, *Our Stolen Future: Are We Threatening Our Fertility, Intelligence and Survival: A Scientific Detective Story* (New York: Dutton, 1996); Sheldon Krimsky, *Hormonal Chaos: The Scientific and Social Origins of the Environmental Endocrine Hypothesis* (Baltimore: Johns Hopkins University Press, 2000).

51. Kabat, *Hyping Health Risks*, 44; Sylvia Noble Tesh, *Uncertain Hazards: Environmental Activists and Scientific Proof* (Ithaca: Cornell University Press, 2000), 27, 28, 30–39; Wildavsky, *But Is It True?*, 38–55.

52. Tesh, *Uncertain Hazards*, 38.

53. Freeze, *Environmental Pendulum*, 113.

54. James C. Lamb IV et al., "Critical Comments on the WHO-UNEP State of the Science of Endocrine Disrupting Chemicals—2012," *Regulatory Toxicology and Pharmacology* 69 (2014), 37.

55. Åke Bergman, et al., "Manufacturing Doubt About Endocrine Disrupter Science—A Rebuttal of Industry-Sponsored Critical Comments on the UNEP/WHO Report "State of the Science of Endocrine Disrupting Chemicals 2012,"" *Regulatory Toxicology and Pharmacology* 73 (2015): 1016.

56. Celina Ramjoué, "The Transatlantic Rift in Genetically Modified Food Policy," *Journal of Agricultural and Environmental Ethics* 20 (2007): 420, 422, 424, 426, 429, 430, 433, 434.

57. Sean A. Weaver and Michael C. Morris, "Risks Associated with Genetic Modification: An Annotated Bibliography of Peer Reviewed Natural Science Publications," *Journal of Agricultural and Environmental Ethics* 18 (2005): 187.

58. *Ibid.*, 158, 159, 170, 171, 173. For earlier examples of some of these arguments, see Simon A. Levin, "An Ecological Perspective," in *The*

Genetic Revolution: Scientific Prospects and Public Perceptions, edited by Bernard D. Davis (Baltimore: Johns Hopkins University Press, 1991), 45–46, 47; Margaret Mellon, "An Environmentalist Perspective," in *The Genetic Revolution*, 61–66; Bernard D. Davis, "Summary and Comments: The Scientific Chapters," in *The Genetic Revolution*, 246.

59. Weaver and Morris, "Risks Associated with Genetic Modification," 159, 165, 171, 173.

60. *Ibid.*, 167.

61. Greg Allen, "Bacteria-Infected Mosquitoes Tested As a Way to Control Population," NPR's *Morning Edition* (Apr. 20, 2017); Nina Fedoroff, "A Secret Weapon Against Zika and Other Mosquito-Borne Diseases," *TED Talks* (Oct. 2016).

62. Pamela Ronald, "The Case for Engineering Our Food," *TED Talks* (Mar. 2015). Also see Pamela Ronald and Raoul Adamchak, *Tomorrow's Table: Organic Farming, Genetics and the Future of Food* (New York: Oxford University Press, 2008).

63. Susan Foster McCarter, *Neolithic* (New York: Routledge, 2007), 17–19; Melinda A. Zeder, et al., eds., *Documenting Domestication: New Genetic and Archaeological Paradigms* (Berkeley: University of California Press, 2006).

64. Ronald, "The Case for Engineering Our Food"; Ronald and Adamchak, *Tomorrow's Table*, 6–10, 58–59, 71, 72, 73, 110.

65. Lydia Ramsey, "Here's the Critical Reason Bill Nye the Science Guy Changed His Mind on GMOs," *Business Insider* (July 13, 2015).

66. Yousef Al Horr, et al., "Occupant Productivity and Office Indoor Environment Quality: A Review of the Literature," *Building and Environment* 105 (2016): 374.

67. Susanna D. Mitro, et al., "Consumer Product Chemicals in Indoor Dust: A Quantitative Meta-Analysis of U.S. Studies," *Environmental Science and Technology* 50 (2016): 10661–672.

68. Xiaoyu Liu, et al., "Determination of Fluorotelomer Alcohols in Selected Consumer Products and Preliminary Investigation of Their Fate in the Indoor Environment," *Chemosphere* 129 (2015): 82; EPA News Release, "EPA's Actions to Restrict PFOA and Similar Chemicals Yield Significant Human Health and Environmental Benefits," (Jan. 15, 2015), available in the EPA web archive, https://archive.epa.gov/epa/newsreleases/epas-actions-restrict-pfoa-and-similar-chemicals-yield-significant-human-health-and.html

69. A good place to begin exploring this topic is through Paul Mohai, et al., "Environmental Justice," *Annual Review of Environment and Re-*

sources 34 (July 2009): 405–30. Also see Freeze, *Environmental Pendulum*, 42–43, 183–84.

70. Mohai, et al., "Environmental Justice," 406, 408–09, 411–12, 413, 415, 422.

71. This theme is elaborated upon in Robert Doyle Bullard, *Dumping in Dixie: Race, Class, and Environmental Quality*, 3rd ed. (Boulder, CO: Westview Press, 2000) and Robert Doyle Bullard and Beverly Wright, *The Wrong Complexion for Protection: How the Government Response to Disaster Endangers African American Communities* (New York: New York University Press, 2012).

72. United States Environmental Protection Agency, "1995 Toxics Release Inventory," (Washington, DC: EPA, Apr. 1997), page 24, table 4–6, "TRI Releases by State, 1995."

73. Bullard, *Dumping in Dixie*, 33–34.

74. U.S. Environmental Protection Agency, "Toxics Release Inventory and Emission Reductions 1987–1990 in the Lower Mississippi River Industrial Corridor," (Washington, DC: EPA, May 1993), 11, 16; Bullard and Wright, *The Wrong Complexion for Protection*, 7.

75. U.S. Environmental Protection Agency, "Toxics Release Inventory and Emission Reductions 1987–1990," 17, 18, 21.

76. Bullard, *Dumping in Dixie*, 55, 106; Bullard and Wright, *The Wrong Complexion for Protection*, 6, 102.

77. Bullard and Wright, *The Wrong Complexion for Protection*, 105–112, 115–18; generally see chapter five, "Response to Toxic Contamination," for these and other examples.

78. Eileen Maura McGurty, "From NIMBY to Civil Rights: The Origins of the Environmental Justice Movement," *Environmental History* 2, no. 3 (July 1997): 302.

79. Freeze, *Environmental Pendulum*, 145. For some grim reminders, see Robert D. Kaplan, *The Ends of the Earth: a Journey at the Dawn of the 21st Century* (New York: Random House, 1996), 4, 12, 46, 55, 57, 63, 75, 248–49, 260, 275–77, 320, 350, 354–55, 381–382, 415–16, 430.

80. Alex Jones, "Covering Science and Technology. An Interview with Cornelia Dean. November 22, 2002," *The Harvard International Journal of Press/Politics* 8, no. 2 (2003): 5. Also see Freeze, *Environmental Pendulum*, 254.

81. Freeze, *Environmental Pendulum*, 277–79.

82. *Ibid.*, 200 (table 15), 205, 210 (table 17), 213, 214–15.

Chapter 8

1. R. Allan Freeze, *The Environmental Pendulum: A Quest for the Truth About Toxic Chem-*
icals, Human Health, and Environmental Protection (Berkeley: University of California Press, 2000), 89; Robert A. Meyers, et al., "Green Chemistry and Chemical Engineering, Introduction," in *Innovations in Green Chemistry and Green Engineering: Selected Entries from the Encyclopedia of Sustainability Science and Technology*, edited by Paul T. Anastas and Julie Beth Zimmerman (New York: Springer, 2013), 1–4; Rashmi Sanghi, et al., "Environment and the Role of Green Chemistry," in *Green Chemistry for Environmental Remediation*, edited by Rashmi Sanghi and Vandana Singh (Hoboken, NJ: John Wiley & Sons, 2012), 4–5, 9, 10.

2. Sanghi, et al., "Environment and the Role of Green Chemistry," 5, 7, 11.

3. Fernando J. Diaz Lopez and Carlos Montalvo, "The Greening of the Chemical Industry: Past, Present and Challenges Ahead," in *Green Chemistry for Environmental Remediation* (Hoboken, NJ: John Wiley & Sons, 2012), 44.

4. Sanghi, et al., "Environment and the Role of Green Chemistry," 9.

5. Joanne Scott, "From Brussels with Love: The Transatlantic Travels of European Law and the Chemistry of Regulatory Attraction," *American Journal of Comparative Law* 57 (Fall 2009): 911–15; p.910, n.74.

6. California Statutes 2008, chapter 559, chapter 560. Also see the Office of Environmental Health Hazard Assessment's summary, https://oehha.ca.gov/risk-assessment/greenchemistry?page=1

7. California Statutes 2008, chapter 560; Definitions, California Health and Safety Code, section 25251.

8. Alastair Iles, "Greening Chemistry: Emerging Epistemic Political Tensions in California and the United States," *Public Understanding of Science* 22, no. 4 (2011): 460, 461, 467, 469, 471–72.

9. Lopez and Montalvo, "The Greening of the Chemical Industry: Past, Present and Challenges Ahead," 44–46, 51.

10. *Ibid.*, 46.

11. "Genetic Potential of Oil-Eating Bacteria from the BP Oil Spill Decoded," *UT News* (May 9, 2016); David Biello, "How Microbes Helped Clean BP's Oil Spill," *Scientific American* (Ap. 28, 2015); Nina Dombrowski, et al., "Reconstructing Metabolic Pathways of Hydrocarbon-Degrading Bacteria from the Deepwater Horizon Oil Spill," *Nature Microbiology* 1 (May 2016).

12. Charles Q. Choi, "Plastic-Eating Bacteria Could Help Make Trash Disappear," www.Livescience.com (Mar. 11, 2016); Ben Lillie, "A Local Bacteria to Solve a Local Problem: Miranda Wang and Jeanny Yao at TED2013," *TED Talks*

Blog (Feb. 27, 2013); Jonathan R. Russell, et al., "Biodegradation of Polyester Polyurethane by Endophytic Fungi," *Applied and Environmental Microbiology* 77, no. 17 (Sept. 2011): 6076–6084.

13. Daniel Robison, "Startup Converts Plastic to Oil, and Finds a Niche," NPR's *Morning Edition* (Mar. 19, 2012).

14. Senay Boztas, "Compostable and Edible Packaging: The Companies Waging War on Plastic," *The Guardian* (Oct. 26, 2016). Tipa Sustainable Packaging's website is: https://tipa-corp.com/

15. Bjørn Lomborg, *The Skeptical Environmentalist: Measuring the Real State of the World* (Cambridge: Cambridge University Press, 2001), 192–94.

16. William McGucken, *Lake Erie Rehabilitated: Controlling Cultural Eutrophication, 1960s–1990s* (Akron, OH: University of Akron Press, 2000); David Stradling and Richard Stradling, *Where the River Burned—Carl Stokes and the Struggle to Save Cleveland* (Ithaca: Cornell University Press, 2015); Donald Worster, *Nature's Economy: A History of Ecological Ideas*, 2nd ed. (New York: Cambridge University Press, 1994), 354–55.

17. María Noel Cabrera, "Pulp Mill Wastewater: Characteristics and Treatment," in *Biological Wastewater Treatment and Resource Recovery*, edited by Robina Farooq and Zaki Ahmad (InTech Open, 2017), 119, 122, 123.

18. Brent Walth, *Fire at Eden's Gate: Tom McCall & the Oregon Story* (Portland: Oregon Historical Society, 1994), 135–36, 139–40, 142, 145, 160, 182, 183, 198–200, 402.

19. Nancy K. Kubasek and Gary S. Silverman, *Environmental Law* 4th ed. (Upper Saddle River, NJ: Prentice Hall, 2002), 107, 134.

20. Elizabeth Pilon-Smits, "Phytoremediation," *Annual Review of Plant Biology* 56 (2005): 17; M.H. Saier, Jr., and J.T. Trevors, "Phytoremediation," *Water, Air, and Soil Pollution*, Supplement 1 (2010): S62.

21. An interesting overview is presented in Shimon Steinberg, "Natural Pest Control... Using Bugs!" *TED Talks* (Apr. 2010).

22. Stephanie Pain, "The Ant and the Mandarin," *New Scientist* (Apr. 14, 2001).

23. "U.S. Releases Parasitic Wasps to Fight Tree-Killing Beetle," *BBC News* (May 25, 2016); Nathan Rott, "National Park Enlists Predator Beetle to Stop Hemlock-Killing Insect," NPR's *Morning Edition* (June 2, 2016); Maina Waruru, "Using Tiny Predators to Tackle Agricultural Pests," *BBC News* (Apr. 7, 2016).

24. Tor Håkon Inderberg and Jørgen Wettestad, "Carbon Capture and Storage in the UK and Germany: Easier Task, Stronger Commitment?" *Environmental Politics* 24, no. 6 (2015): 1015, 1022, 1023–25, 1029–30; Andreas Tjernshaugen, "The Growth of Political Support for CO2 Capture and Storage in Norway," *Environmental Politics* 20, no. 2 (Mar. 2011): 228, 230–36, 242–43.

25. Kirk Johnson, "Project Aims to Harness the Power of Waves," *New York Times* (Sept. 3, 2012).

26. Jeff Barnard, "Geothermal Takes a Technological Step Forward," *Associated Press* (Jan. 12, 2013).

27. Lydia Ramsey, "This Brilliant 13-Year-Old Figured Out How to Make Clean Energy Using a Device that Costs $5," *Business Insider* (Oct. 22, 2016).

28. "Scrubbing the Skies," *Economist* (Mar. 5, 2009); Jonathan Amos, "Experiment 'Turns Waste CO2 to Stone,'" *BBC News* (June 9, 2016); David W. Keith et al., "A Process for Capturing CO2 from the Atmosphere," *Joule* 2 (Aug. 15, 2018): 1–22; Christa Marshall, "In Switzerland, a Giant New Machine Is Sucking Carbon Directly from the Air," *Science Magazine* (Jun. 1, 2017); Chris Mooney, "The Quest to Capture and Store Carbon—and Slow Climate Change—Just Reached a New Milestone," *Washington Post* (Apr. 10, 2017); Dan Zukowski, "Carbon Capture Breakthrough in India Converts CO2 Into Baking Powder," *Ecowatch* (Jan. 3, 2017).

29. David Bodansky, *Nuclear Energy: Principles, Practices, and Prospects* (New York: Springer, 2004), 18, 19 (table 1.4), 47.

30. *Ibid.*, 190, 238.

31. *Ibid.*, 189, 190, 467, 469.

32. William H. Hannum, et al., "Smarter Use of Nuclear Waste," *Scientific American* (Dec. 2005): 84–91. Also see "Technical White Paper," vol. 2.1 (Cambridge, MA: Transatomic Power, Nov. 2016) and "Neutronics Overview," vol. 1.1 (Cambridge, MA: Transatomic Power, Nov. 2016), http://www.transatomicpower.com/

33. Bodansky, *Nuclear Energy*, 371, 372, 417, 419, 421, 422–23 and generally chapter 15.

34. Bodansky, *Nuclear Energy*, 337–38; Freeze, *Environmental Pendulum*, 55, 73–75, 185–94.

35. Explaining the molten salt reactor is Transatomic Energy's Leslie Dewan, who appears toward the end of part two in the PBS documentary *Uranium—Twisting the Dragon's Tail* (Derek Muller, PBS, 2015).

36. William H. Hannum, et al., "Smarter Use of Nuclear Waste," *Scientific American* (Dec. 2005): 85, 86.

37. Nicholas K. Geranios, "Federal Energy Official Warns of More Mishaps at Hanford," *Seattle Times* (June 15, 2017); Fred Pearce,

"Awash in Radioactive Waste," *New York Times* (May 24, 2018).

38. Joe Palca, "A Lot of Heat Is Wasted, So Why Not Convert It Into Power?" NPR's *Morning Edition* (Aug. 20, 2015).

39. Ben Rosen, "Scientists Invent a Way to Create CO2 Fuel from a Solar Leaf," *Christian Science Monitor* (Aug. 1, 2016).

40. Periyasamy Sivagurunathan, et al., "Biohydrogen Production from Wastewaters," in *Biological Wastewater Treatment and Resource Recovery*, edited by Robina Farooq (InTech Open Access, 2017), chapter 11, 197–210; Carla Escapa Santos, et al., "Comparative Assessment of Pharmaceutical Removal from Wastewater by the Microalgae *Chlorella sorokiniana, Chlorella vulgaris and Scenedesmus obliquus*," in *Biological Wastewater Treatment and Resource Recovery*, chapter 6, 99–117, https://mts.intechopen.com/books/biological-wastewater-treatment-and-resource-recovery.

41. Jason Palmer, "'Smog-Eating' Material Breaking into the Big Time," *BBC News* (Nov. 12, 2011).

42. Mark Kinver, "China Tops Global Clean Energy Table," *BBC News* (Mar. 29, 2011).

43. Daan Roosegaarde, "A Smog Vacuum Cleaner and Other Magical City Designs," TED Talks (Apr. 2017).

44. *UT News*, The University of Texas at Austin (Sept. 17, 2013), https://news.utexas.edu/2013/09/17/turning-seawater-into-drinking-water

45. David L. Chandler, "Sun-Powered Desalination for Villages in India," *MIT News* (Sept. 8, 2014).

46. Mona Naim, Mahmoud Elewa, Ahmed El-Shafei and Abeer Moneer, "Desalination of Simulated Seawater by Purge-Air Pervaporation Using an Innovative Fabricated Membrane," *Water Science & Technology* 72, no. 5 (2015): 785–793.

47. Hannah Osborne, "Graphene Sieve Turns Seawater into Clean Drinking Water—and the Technology Can Be Scaled Up," *International Business Times* (Ap. 3, 2017). Also see "Miracle Material Graphene Can Distil Booze, Says Study," *BBC News* (Jan. 27, 2012).

48. Gwen Ifill, "Could Agriculture Bloom in the Desert? Qatar Works to Invent an Innovative Oasis," PBS *Newshour* (June 11, 2013); Alice Klein, "First Farm to Grow Veg in a Desert Using Only Sun and Seawater," *New Scientist* (Oct. 6, 2016).

49. "Tesla Unveils Batteries to Power Homes," *BBC News* (May 1, 2015); Mose Buchelle, "At 94, Lithium-Ion Pioneer Eyes a New Longer-Lasting

Battery," NPR's *All Things Considered* (May 22, 2017); Benjamin Hulac, "Tesla's Elon Musk Unveils Stored Sunlight in Batteries," *Scientific American* (May 1, 2015); Lori Valigra, "MIT Advances Liquid Metal Battery Technology," *Mass High Tech: The Journal of New England Technology* (Feb. 16, 2012).

50. Laurence Knight, "Vanadium: The Metal That May Soon Be Powering Your Neighbourhood," *BBC News* (June 13, 2014).

51. Charles Omedo, "Stanford Scientists Develop Paint Coating Reflects Sunlight and Cools the Planet," *The Westside Story* (Nov. 27, 2014).

52. Kubasek and Silverman, *Environmental Law* 4th ed., 269.

53. "'Most Energy-Efficient' LED Light Revealed by Philips," *BBC News* (Ap. 11, 2013).

54. Kubasek and Silverman, *Environmental Law* 4th ed., 163–64.

55. *Ibid.*, 181–82.

56. Melody Schreiber, "Man-Made 'Wind Trees' Will Finally Make It Possible to Power Homes Using Turbines," *Quartz* (Aug. 23, 2016).

57. Robert M. Pirsig, *Zen and the Art of Motorcycle Maintenance: An Inquiry into Values* (1974; New York: Bantam Books, 1981), 41.

58. *Ibid.*, 262.

59. Carl Mitcham, *Thinking Through Technology: The Path Between Engineering and Philosophy* (Chicago: University of Chicago Press, 1994), 297, 299.

60. "Dirty Things All Made by Hand," in Gertrude Stein, *Three Lives* (New York: Pocket Books, 2003), 45.

61. Mitcham, *Thinking Through Technology*, 277–279, 282–83.

62. *Ibid.*, 283–84, 289, 297, 299.

63. Charles Dickens, *Hard Times and Reprinted Pieces* (London: Chapman & Hall, 1905), 194.

64. Maarten Franssen, et al., "Philosophy of Technology," *Stanford Encyclopedia of Philosophy* (Feb. 20, 2009; rev. Dec. 13, 2013), sec. 3, "Ethical and Social Aspects of Technology," subsection 3.3.1, "Neutrality Versus Moral Agency." Also see Pirsig, *Zen and the Art of Motorcycle Maintenance*, 231.

65. Maarten Franssen, et al., "Philosophy of Technology," *Stanford Encyclopedia of Philosophy* (Feb. 20, 2009; rev. Dec. 13, 2013), sec. 3, "Ethical and Social Aspects of Technology," subsection 3.1, "The Development of the Ethics of Technology."

66. The term appeared in Donald Worster's book, *The Economy of Nature*, 2nd ed., page 370, with attribution to a 1988 Peter J. Taylor article of a different topic altogether (post-war tech-

nocratic optimism, systems ecology, and the work and philosophy of Howard T. Odum). So apparently Worster himself coined the term?

Chapter 9

1. Richard Worrell and Michael C. Appleby, "Stewardship of Natural Resources: Definition, Ethical and Practical Aspects," *Journal of Agricultural and Environmental Ethics* 12 (2000): 265, 266, 268–69.

2. National Environmental Policy Act of 1969, Public law 91–190, 83 Stat. 852, sec. 101(a).

3. Andrew C. Isenberg, "The Returns of the Bison: Nostalgia, Profit, and Preservation," *Environmental History* 2, no. 2 (Apr. 1997): 180, 181, 182.

4. *Ibid.*, 191.

5. Hari Sreenivasan, "How Scientists Brought Bison Back to Banff," *PBS Newshour* (Feb. 28, 2017).

6. Nicholas D. Kristof, "Make Way for Buffalo," *New York Times* (Oct. 29, 2003); Deborah Epstein Popper and Frank J. Popper, "The Great Plains: From Dust to Dust," *Planning Magazine* (Dec. 1987): 12–18.

7. "Fish Recovery Project Could Empty Detroit Lake for 2 Years," *Associated Press* (Jan. 17, 2018).

8. Shivali Best, "Bringing the Galapagos Tortoise Back from the Dead," *Daily Mail* (June 2, 2017).

9. Nate Hegyi, "Biologists with Drones and Peanut Butter Pellets Are on a Mission to Help Ferrets," NPR's *Weekend Edition Sunday* (Dec. 10, 2017); Madeline K. Sofia, "Snot Otters Get a Second Chance in Ohio," NPR's *Morning Edition* (Sept. 14, 2017).

10. Michael Pollan, "Breaking Ground: The Call of the Wild Apple," *New York Times* (Nov. 5, 1998); Mo Rocca, "How's Them Apples?" CBS News This Morning (Nov. 26, 2017).

11. Jacob Demmitt, "Coyote Hunters Converge on Wytheville for Predator Killing Tournament," *Roanoke Times* (Jan. 15, 2017); Lindsey Bever, "Don't Read This Article If You Are Afraid of Giant Snakes Three Times Your Size," *Washington Post* (Dec. 6, 2017); "Snake Catchers from India Hunt Pythons in Florida Everglades," *Associated Press* (Jan. 24, 2017).

12. Nathan Rott, "On the Trail of the Wiley Wild Hog," NPR's *Morning Edition* (May 26, 2016).

13. Natalie Wheeler, "Tribes Tackle Wild Horse Issue," *Eugene Register Guard* (Oct. 27, 2012).

14. "New Zealand Whales: Authorities to Move 300 Carcasses," *BBC News* (Feb. 13, 2017); "What Makes This New Zealand Beach a Whale Graveyard?" *BBC News* (Feb. 13, 2017).

15. This story is told in the documentary, Kate Fulton, et al., prod., *Salmon: Running the Gauntlet* (PBS, 2011).

16. "Wildlife Dilemma: Kill Birds to Save Fish? Cormorants Near the Mouth of the Columbia Are Threatening Fish Runs," *Associated Press* (Aug. 2, 2014); Matthew Daly and Jeff Barnard, "U.S. Moves Ahead with Plan to Shoot Spotted Owl's Rival," *Associated Press* (Feb. 29, 2012); Christopher Joyce, "Saving One Species at the Expense of Another," NPR's *Morning Edition* (July 11, 2013); Peter Payette, "Fish and Wildlife Service May Appeal Judge's Ruling On Cormorants," NPR's *Morning Edition* (June 6, 2016).

17. Susan K. Fleming and Sara Marino, dir., "Animal Odd Couples," *Nature*, season 31, episode 3 (PBS, 2012).

18. Paul Hessburg, "Why Wildfires Have Gotten Worse—And What We Can Do About It," TED Talks (Nov. 7, 2017).

19. R. Allan Freeze, *The Environmental Pendulum: A Quest for the Truth About Toxic Chemicals, Human Health, and Environmental Protection* (Berkeley: University of California Press, 2000), 257, 273, 289.

20. James F. McInteer, "Where Materialism Falls Short," *Virginia Wildlife* 24, no. 12 (Dec. 1963): 3.

21. Will Sarvis, *Sacred and Ephemeral: Reflections Upon Land, Place, and Home* (Self-published, 2017), 253–55.

22. Frederick Brown Harris, "Whose Land Is It?" *Virginia Wildlife* 19, no. 3 (Mar. 1958): 5–7.

23. *Ibid.*, 6, 7.

24. *Ibid.*, 7.

25. James George Frazer, *The Golden Bough* (1890; NY: Oxford Univ. Press, 1994), 84, 87–88; Olof Pettersson, "The Spirit of the Woods: Outlines of a Study of the Ideas About Forest Guardians in African Mythology and Folklore," in *The Supernatural Owners of Nature*, edited by Åke Hultkrantz (Stockholm, Almqvist & Wiksell: 1961), 101–111; J.H. Philpot, *The Sacred Tree, or the Tree in Religion and Myth* (London: Macmillan, 1897), 4–22; Alexander Porteous, *The Forest in Folklore and Mythology* (1928; Mineola, NY: Dover Publications, 2002), 125–43, 160–73.

26. Philpot, *The Sacred Tree*, 40; Porteous, *The Forest in Folklore and Mythology*, 52, 208, 210–11, 221; Leon Yarden, *The Tree of Light: a Study of the Menorah, the Seven-Branched*

Lampstand (Ithaca: Cornell University Press, 1971), 35–40, 42–43.

27. Philpot, *The Sacred Tree*, 109; Porteous, *The Forest in Folklore and Mythology*, 191, 193.

28. For examples, see the following stories in *Complete Grimm's Fairy Tales* (New York: Pantheon Books, 1944). "Snow White," 249–58; "St. Joseph in the Forest," 815–18; "The Hut in the Forest," 698–704; "The Old Woman in the Wood," 558–60; "Hansel and Gretel," 86–94; "The Riddle," 128–31; "Little Red Cap," 139–43. Also see Robert Pogue Harrison, *Forests: The Shadow of Civilization* (Chicago: University of Chicago Press, 1992), 61, 62, 77.

29. I.T. Quinn, "The Tree," *Virginia Wildlife* 16, no. 8 (Aug. 1955): 21.

30. Probably the most famous early example is Burt Gillett, dir., *Flowers and Trees* (Walt Disney, 1932), wherein an old tree stump tries to circumvent romance between two younger trees. For a later example of anthropomorphic trees, see Mario Piluso, dir., *The Halloween Tree* (Hanna-Barbera Productions, 1993).

31. Robbie Harris, "Scientists Work to Bring Back Once-Thriving American Chestnut Tree," NPR's *Weekend Edition Saturday* (Jan. 7, 2017). American Chestnut Cooperators' Foundation offers updates regarding their latest efforts at http://www.accf-online.org/

32. Eva Botkin-Kowacki, "China's Forest Conservation Program Shows Proof of Success," *Christian Science Monitor* (Mar. 19, 2016).

33. Mark Kinver, "UK Team Germinates Critically Endangered Japanese Birch," *BBC News* (Sept. 29, 2015).

34. Mark Freeman, "Oregon Partnership Works to Save Native Oak Savannas," *Eugene Register Guard* (Nov. 5, 2017); John F. Thilenius, "The Quercus Garryana Forests of the Willamette Valley, Oregon," *Ecology* 49, no. 6 (Nov., 1968): 1124–1133.

35. Darius M. Adams, et al., "Estimated Timber Harvest by U.S. Region and Ownership, 1950–2002," (USDA Forest Service, Pacific Northwest Research Station, General Technical Report PNW-GTR-659, Jan. 2006), figure 7, page 14, "Total public harvest, by region, 1957–2002," https://www.fs.fed.us/pnw/pubs/pnw_gtr659.pdf

36. Mark Freeman, "Thinning Project Pitched to Save Forest's Big Pines," *Eugene Register Guard* (Dec. 27, 2016).

37. Bill Bishop, "In His Neck of Our Woods, Compromise Won't Grow on Trees," *Eugene Register Guard* (Jan. 22, 2007). The Native Forest Council's website is: http://www.forestcouncil.org

38. Generally see Alston Chase, *Playing God in Yellowstone: The Destruction of America's First National Park* (New York: Atlantic Monthly Press, 1986), chapter 29.

39. Jan Gonda, *The Ritual Functions and Significance of Grasses in the Religion of the Veda* (New York: North-Holland Pub. Co., 1985).

40. Karen Eng, "The Man Who Plants Trees: Shubhendu Sharma Is Reforesting the World, One Patch at a Time," TED Talks Blog (May 9, 2014), https://blog.ted.com/shubhendusharma/

41. Franz Heske, *German Forestry* (New Haven: Yale University Press, 1938), 231.

42. Michael Imort, "A Sylvan People: Wilhelmine Forestry and the Forest as a Symbol of Germandom," in *Germany's Nature: Cultural Landscapes and Environmental History*, edited by Thomas M. Lekan and Thomas Zeller (New Brunswick: Rutgers University Press, 2005), 56–57. Robert Pogue Harrison traces Germanic self-romanticization in association with the forest all the way back to Roman Empire era, when a partially-assimilated tribal people sought to distinguish themselves from their southern neighbors. See Harrison, *Forests: The Shadow of Civilization*, 177–78.

43. Adalbert Edner, *German Forests: Treasures of a Nation* (New York: German Library of Information, 1940), 25, 26–27, 73, 86; Franz Heske, *German Forestry* (New Haven: Yale University Press, 1938), chapters two and eight; Imort, "A Sylvan People," 71; Will Sarvis, *The Jefferson National Forest: An Appalachian Environmental History* (Knoxville: University of Tennessee Press, 2011), 54, 57, 128.

44. Paul Owen, "World Wood Products Markets: How Do They Impact Oregon?," Starker Lecture Series, Oregon State University, aired on OBP Mar. 26, 2011.

45. Edner, *German Forests*, 124.

46. W. Andreas Hahn and Thomas Knoke, "Sustainable Development and Sustainable Forestry: Analogies, Differences, and the Role of Flexibility," *European Journal of Forest Research* 129 (2010): 792.

47. John Knight, "From Timber to Tourism: Recommoditizing the Japanese Forest," *Development and Change* 31, no. 1 (Jan. 2000): 341–359.

48. Sarvis, *Jefferson National Forest*, chapters 4 and 5.

49. Leo A. Drey Interview (Jan. 1998), Clint Trammel Interview (May 1998), audio recording and transcripts on file with Western Historical Manuscripts Collection, Columbia, Missouri. Missouri Environmental Oral History Collection, coll. # 3966. Trammel was the Pioneer For-

est's chief forester. Also see "Appendix A, Pioneer Forest: A Case Study in Modern Selective Forest Management," in Sarvis, *Jefferson National Forest.*

50. James M. Guldin, "A History of Forest Management in the Ozark Mountains," in James M. Guldin, et al., eds. *Pioneer Forest: A Half Century of Sustainable Uneven-Aged Forest Management in the Missouri Ozarks,* General Technical Report SRS-108 (Asheville, NC: United States Forest Service, Southern Research Station, 2008), 8.

51. Oregon Department of Forestry, "Forest Facts: Oregon's Family-Owned Forests," (Salem: Oregon Department of Forestry, Feb. 2015); Oregon Forest Resource Institute, "Oregon's Family Forestlands: Why They Matter to the State's Quality of Life" (Portland: Oregon Forest Resource Inst., 2008).

52. Mark Freeman, "Oregon Family Ensures Forest Will Stay As Is," *Eugene Register Guard* (Jan. 29, 2018).

53. Mike Barsotti, "Oregon Tree Farm System Announced 2017 Oregon Outstanding Tree Farmers: Steve and Wylda Cafferata," *Oregon Family Forest News* (Oct. 2017), 23; Ed Russo, "A Lane County Couple Is Recognized for Efforts to Help Forests Thrive," *Eugene Register Guard* (Nov. 5, 2017).

54. For examples, see *Oregon Family Forests News* (Oct. 2017), 25–26; *Oregon Family Forests News* (Aug. 2017), 18, 19, 20, 22–23, available via Oregon Small Woodlands Association, https://www.oswa.org/

55. Albert Abee, "Application of Criteria and Indicators of Sustainable Resource Management in the United States," in *Sustainable Forestry: From Monitoring and Modelling to Knowledge Management and Policy Science,* edited by Keith M. Reynolds (Cambridge, MA: CABI, 2007), 76; N. Lowthrop, "Economic Conservation—Hill Holt Wood: the Three Legs of Sustainability in Practice," in *Sustainable Forestry: From Monitoring and Modelling to Knowledge Management and Policy Science,* 189–90. Also see Hahn and Knoke, "Sustainable Development and Sustainable Forestry," 788, 789, 794.

56. Hahn and Knoke, "Sustainable Development and Sustainable Forestry," 791–92.

57. Eric Cain, prod., *The Oregon Story: Rethinking the Forests* (Portland: Oregon Public Broadcasting, 2005).

58. Larry Rohter, "Loggers, Scorning the Law, Ravage the Amazon," *New York Times* (Oct. 16, 2005). Illegal logging continued in following years; see John Collins Rudolf, "Is the Tide Turning on Deforestation?" *New York Times* (July 16, 2010); Tim Boekhout van Solinge,

"Chapter 12.3—Deforestation in the Brazilian Amazon," in *Biological and Environmental Hazards, Risks, and Disasters,* edited by Ramesh Sivanpillai and J.F. Shroder Jr. (Amsterdam: Elsevier Inc., 2016), 374.

59. Justin Rowlatt, "Saving the Amazon: Winning the War on Deforestation," *BBC News* (Jan. 2, 2012).

60. Hiroko Tabuchi, et al., "Amazon Deforestation, Once Tamed, Comes Roaring Back," *New York Times* (Feb. 24, 2017).

61. John J. Garland, "The Oregon Forest Practice Act: 1972 to 1994," section "History and Origins," http://www.fao.org/docrep/W3646E/w3646e07.htm Oregon Board of Forestry, "An Historical Overview of the Establishment of State Forest Lands," section III, "Forest Conservation and Rehabilitation," https://digital.osl.state.or.us/islandora/object/osl%3A20524/datastream/OBJ/view

62. 1941 Oregon Forest Conservation Act, Oregon Laws 1941, chapter 237, section 2; Oregon Laws 1941, chapter 468; Arthur B. Jebens, "State Rural Land Use Legislation in 1941," *The Journal of Land & Public Utility Economics* 18, no. 3 (Aug., 1942): 336, 337.

63. The state legislature has amended and revised the FPA many times since 1972. The contemporary version is found in Oregon Administrative Rules 629–001 through 629–676, available through the Oregon Department of Forestry, http://www.oregon.gov/odf/pages/lawsrules.aspx. John Garland offers an interesting essay from a practitioner and professor's point of view regarding the FPA's first two decades. See John J. Garland, "The Oregon Forest Practice Act: 1972 to 1994," http://www.fao.org/docrep/W3646E/w3646e07.htm

64. Abee, "Application of Criteria and Indicators of Sustainable Resource Management in the United States," in Reynolds, *Sustainable Forestry,* 86.

65. Garland, "The Oregon Forest Practice Act: 1972 to 1994," section "Reasons for increasing forest practices regulations."

66. *Ibid.*

Chapter 10

1. Andy Byatt, prod., David Attenborough, narr., *The Blue Planet: Sea of Life* (BBC Video, 2001), episode one, "Open Ocean," min. 19–25.

2. Jane Jacobs, *Death and Life of Great American Cities* (1961; NY: Modern Library, 1993), 579, 580, 584.

3. James Trefil, *A Scientist in the City* (New York: Anchor Books, 1995), 6–7, 8–14.

4. Trefil, *A Scientist in the City*, 13.

5. Eberhard Parlow, "Urban Climate," in *Urban Ecology: Patterns, Processes, and Applications*, edited by Jari Niemelä (New York: Oxford University Press, 2011), 38–40.

6. Stefan Klotz and Ingolf Kuhn, "Urbanisation and Alien Invasion," in *Urban Ecology*, edited by Kevin J. Gaston (New York: Cambridge University Press, 2010), 122; Rowan A. Rowntree, "Toward Ecosystem Management: Shifts in the Core and the Context of Urban Forest Ecology," in *Urban Forest Landscapes: Integrating Multidisciplinary Perspectives*, edited by Gordon A. Bradley (Seattle: University of Washington Press, 1995), 55; Sri Juari Santosa, "Urban Air Quality," in *Urban Ecosystem Ecology*, edited by Jacqueline Aitkenhead-Peterson and Astrid Volder (Madison, WI: American Society of Agronomy, et al. 2010), 71.

7. Parlow, "Urban Climate," in *Urban Ecology*, Niemelä, ed., 38; Herbert Sukopp, "Urban Ecology—Scientific and Practical Aspects," in *Urban Ecology*, edited by J. Breuste, et al. (New York: Springer, 1998), 4; Trefil, *A Scientist in the City*, 14.

8. Eyal Shochat, et al., "Birds in Urban Ecosystems: Population Dynamics, Community Structure, Biodiversity, and Conservation," in *Urban Ecosystem Ecology*, 75.

9. Stefanie E. LaZerte, et al., "Mountain Chickadees Adjust Songs, Calls and Chorus Composition with Increasing Ambient and Experimental Anthropogenic Noise," *Urban Ecosystems* 20 (2017): 989–1000; Shochat, et al., "Birds in Urban Ecosystems," 78.

10. Karl L. Evans, "Individual Species and Urbanization," in *Urban Ecology*, Gaston, ed., 55; Klotz and Kuhn, "Urbanisation and Alien Invasion," in in *Urban Ecology*, Gaston, ed., 123; Robert McCleery, "Urban Mammals," in *Urban Ecosystem Ecology*, 87–102; Shochat, et al., "Birds in Urban Ecosystems," 75.

11. Trefil, *A Scientist in the City*, 8–10.

12. J.T. Lundholm and A. Marlin, "Habitat Origins and Microhabitat Preferences of Urban Plant Species," *Urban Ecosystems* 9 (2006):139–159.

13. Andrew P. DeWet, et al., "Interactions of Land-Use History and Current Ecology in a Recovering "Urban Wildland,"" *Urban Ecosystems* 2 (1998): 237–262.

14. For a typical example, see Joel Greenberg, *A Feathered River Across the Sky: The Passenger Pigeon's Flight to Extinction* (New York: Bloomsbury, 2014), 206.

15. Richard A. Fuller and Katherine N. Irvine, "Interactions Between People and Nature in Urban Environments," in *Urban Ecology*, Gaston, ed., 136; Shochat, et al., "Birds in Urban Ecosystems," 75, 76, 79.

16. Christopher Joyce, "Soil Doctors Hit Pay Dirt in Manhattan's Central Park," NPR's *Morning Edition* (Oct. 2, 2014); Martin Sauerwein, "Urban Soils—Characterization, Pollution, and Relevance in Urban Ecosystems," in *Urban Ecology*, Niemelä, ed., 45–58; Meredith K. Steele, et al., "Chemistry of Urban, Suburban, and Rural Surface Waters," in *Urban Ecosystem Ecology*, 297–339.

17. Jeremy Lundholm, "Vegetation of Urban Hard Surfaces," in *Urban Ecology*, Niemelä, ed., 99; Matthew F. Vessel and Herbert H. Wong, *Natural History of Vacant Lots* (Berkeley: University of California Press, 1987), 1, 22.

18. Vessel and Wong, *Natural History of Vacant Lots*, 5–6, 23, 24.

19. Sarah L. Robinson and Jeremy T. Lundholm, "Ecosystem Services Provided by Urban Spontaneous Vegetation," *Urban Ecosystems* 15 (2012): 547, 550, 551.

20. Marina Alberti, "Global Urban Signatures of Phenotypic Change in Animal and Plant Populations," *Proceedings of the National Academy of Sciences* (Oct. 31, 2016); Mark Kinver, "Urbanisation Signal Detected in Evolution, Study Shows," *BBC News* (Jan. 7, 2017). Sukopp, "Urban Ecology," in *Urban Ecology*, J. Breuste, et al., eds., 8.

21. Amina Khan, "Spiders Get Bigger When They Live in the City, Study Finds," *Los Angeles Times* (Aug. 20, 2014); Elizabeth C. Lowe, et al., "Urbanisation at Multiple Scales Is Associated with Larger Size and Higher Fecundity of an Orb-Weaving Spider," *PLOS One* (Aug. 20, 2014).

22. "Urban Grasshoppers Change Their Tune for Females," *BBC News* (Nov. 14, 2012); Ulrike Lampe, et al., "Staying Tuned: Grasshoppers from Noisy Roadside Habitats Produce Courtship Signals with Elevated Frequency Components," *Functional Ecology* (Nov. 14, 2012).

23. Ella Davies, "Urban Birds Have Bigger Brains," *BBC News* (Apr. 27, 2011); Alexei A. Maklakov, et al., "Brains and the City: Big-Brained Passerine Birds Succeed in Urban Environments," *Biology Letters* (Apr. 27, 2011); Shochat, et al., "Birds in Urban Ecosystems," 77.

24. For examples see Fuller and Irvine, "Interactions Between People and Nature in Urban Environments," in *Urban Ecology*, Gaston, ed., 134, 136, 156, 161; Klotz and Ingolf Kuhn, "Urbanisation and Alien Invasion," in *Urban Ecol-*

ogy, Gaston, ed., 123–25; Gary W. Luck and Lisa T. Smallbone, "Species Diversity and Urbanisation: Patterns, Drivers and Implications," in *Urban Ecology*, Gaston, ed., 88–199; McCleery, "Urban Mammals," in *Urban Ecosystem Ecology*, 87, 89; Jari Niemelä, "Introduction," in *Urban Ecology*, Niemelä, ed., 1; Martin F. Quigley, "Potemkin Gardens: Biodiversity in Small Designed Landscapes," in *Urban Ecology*, Niemelä, ed., 85–92; Sarah Hayden Reichard, "Insight Out: Invasive Plants and Urban Environments," in *Urban Ecosystem Ecology*, 241–51; Sauerwein, "Urban Soils," in *Urban Ecology*, Niemelä, ed., 45.

25. Vessel and Wong, *Natural History of Vacant Lots*, 51.

26. Emily R. Gray and Yolanda van Heezik, "Exotic Trees Can Sustain Native Birds in Urban Woodlands," *Urban Ecosystems* 19 (2016): 315–329.

27. Matt Kaplan, "City Birds Use Cigarette Butts to Smoke Out Parasites," *Nature* (Dec. 5, 2012).

28. Eric Keto, "How Animal Cameras Are Capturing Seattle's Wild Side," *PBS Newshour* (Jan. 10, 2018).

29. Julian L. Simon and Aaron Wildavsky, "Species Loss Revisited," *Society* 30 (Nov./Dec. 1992): 45.

30. Fuller and Irvine, "Interactions Between People and Nature in Urban Environments," in Gaston, *Urban Ecology*, 155.

31. "Birds That Bring Gifts and Do the Gardening," *BBC News* (Mar. 10, 2015); Katy Sewall, "The Girl Who Gets Gifts from Birds," *BBC News* (Feb. 25, 2015).

32. Eric Mortenson, "Researcher Examining Coyotes That Pick City Life," *Eugene Register Guard* (Dec. 17, 2016).

33. For an interesting historical perspective, see Henry W. Lawrence, "The Neoclassical Origins of Modern Urban Forests," *Forest and Conservation History* 37, no. 1 (Jan. 1993): 26–36.

34. Austin Troy, et al., "The Relationship Between Tree Canopy and Crime Rates across an Urban–Rural Gradient in the Greater Baltimore Region" (*Landscape and Urban Planning*, Apr. 2012), https://www.nrs.fs.fed.us/pubs/jrnl/2012/ nrs_2012_troy_001.pdf Geoffrey H. Donovan and Jeffrey P. Prestemon, "The Effect of Trees on Crime in Portland, Oregon" (*Environment and Behavior*, Sage Journals, Oct. 19, 2010), http://journals.sagepub.com/doi/abs/10.1177/0013916510383238 (abstract only); Austin Troy, et al., "The Relationship Between Tree Canopy and Crime Rates across an Urban–Rural Gradient in the Greater Baltimore

Region" (*Landscape and Urban Planning*, Apr. 2012), https://www.nrs.fs.fed.us/pubs/jrnl/2012/ nrs_2012_troy_001.pdf Also see Astrid Volder and W. Todd Watson, "Urban Forestry," in *Urban Ecosystem Ecology*, 229.

35. Jo Barton and Jules Pretty, "Urban Ecology and Human Health and Well Being," in *Urban Ecology*, Gaston, ed., 202, 203, 205, 206–7, 209–210, 221; Cecil C. Konijnendijk, *The Forest and the City: The Cultural Landscape of Urban Woodland* (New York: Springer, 2008), 135–38; Henry W. Lawrence, "Changing Forms and Persistent Values: Historical Perspectives on the Urban Forest," in *Urban Forest Landscapes*, 29.

36. Mhari Saito, "Jesse Owens' Legacy, And Hitler's Oak Trees," NPR's *Morning Edition* (July 27, 2011).

37. Rachel Feltman, "This Tree Might Be the Oldest Living Thing in Europe," *Washington Post* (Aug. 19, 2016).

38. American Heritage Trees, https://americanheritagetrees.org/

39. For two city examples, see Vancouver, Washington and Seattle, Washington: http://www.cityofvancouver.us/publicworks/page/ heritage-trees and https://www.seattle.gov/ transportation/heritagetree.htm. For two state examples, see Virginia and Oregon: Nancy R. Hugo and Jeff Kirwan, *Remarkable Trees of Virginia* (University of Virginia Press, 2008), and http://ortravelexperience.com/oregon-heritage- trees/about-heritage-trees/

40. Alison Schwartz, "Prince William & Kate Plant a Tree to Symbolize Love," *People Magazine* (July 2, 2011).

41. Karen McCowan, "Friends, Workers, Educators Join to Plant Trees in Memory of Teen," *Eugene Register Guard* (June 5, 2011).

42. Chris McKee, "Corvallis Mosque & Community Plant Peace Tree, Celebrating Differences," *KMTR NBC News* (Feb. 13, 2011).

43. Simon Worrall, "The World's Oldest Clove Tree," *BBC Magazine* (June 23, 2012).

44. "The Mystery Over Who Attacked the Holy Thorn Tree," *BBC Magazine* (Apr. 4, 2012).

45. Edward Colimore, "Laurel Hill Cemetery's Legendary 'Witness Tree' Is Felled," *Philadelphia Inquirer* (May 29, 2016).

46. Matt Chittum, "Roanoke College's Venerable Tree Ready for Its Final Bow," *Roanoke Times* (Apr. 24, 2013).

47. Akiko Hall, "Neighbors Plan Farewell for Old Maple," *Oregon Daily Emerald* (Dec. 1, 2006).

48. Akiko Fujita, "'Miracle Tree' Removed in Ravaged City," *ABC News* (Sept. 12, 2012).

49. David J. Bisset, "Henderson Lawn Sycamore Spreads No More," *ourvalley.org* (July 28, 2010).

50. Mary Hardbarger, "Sycamore's Second Life for Sale at Steppin' Out," *Roanoke Times* (Aug. 4, 2011); "Significant Sycamore Doomed by Storm Damage," *KMTR NBC News* (Jan. 18, 2017).

51. Eric Pfeiffer, "103-Year-Old Man to Be Buried in Coffin Made from Tree He Fought for Decades to Protect," *The Sideshow* (May 15, 2012).

52. George Nakashima, *The Soul of a Tree: A Woodworker's Reflections* (Tokyo, NY: Kodansha International, 1981).

53. Henry David Thoreau, *The Maine Woods / The Writings of Henry David Thoreau* (1864), 209–10.

54. Will Sarvis, "Deeply Embedded: Canoes as an Enduring Manifestation of Spiritualism and Communalism Among the Coast Salish," *Journal of the West* 42, no. 4 (Fall 2003): 74–80.

55. Konijnendijk, *The Forest and the City*, 29.

56. *Ibid.*, 31.

57. Here are but a small sprinkling of examples: Bobbie Cirel, "Pave Paradise," *Eugene Weekly* (Mar. 30, 2006); Shen Steiner, "Silence of the Limbs," *Eugene Weekly* (Feb. 15, 2007); N.L. Bell, "Chainsaw Massacre," *Eugene Weekly* (May 3, 2007); Erin Rokita and Camilla Mortensen, "Timberrrr! Eugene Logs Its Urban Forests," *Eugene Weekly* (Nov. 21, 2007); Shannon Finnell, "Bigleaf Bummer," *Eugene Weekly* (Sept. 23, 2010); Genelle McDaniel, "Don't Cut Any Trees," *Eugene Weekly* (Dec. 16, 2010).

58. Phill Carroll, "Cutting the Old Ones: Our Urban Forest Is Not a Wild Ecosystem," *Eugene Weekly* (Aug. 26, 2004); Alby Thoumsin, "Fate of Our Trees," *Eugene Weekly* (May 17, 2007).

59. Randi Bjornstad, "Cascade Manor's Expansion Project Triggers Distress When Dozens of Trees Are Cut," *Eugene Register Guard* (July 13, 2004).

60. *Ibid.*

61. Whitey Lueck, "A Hole in the Sky—A Hole in My Heart: Reflections on the Removal of a Large Tree," *ETF News*: 11:4 (Fall 2008), 1, 2.

62. Ivette Feliciano, "Could Indoor Farming Help Address Future Food Shortages?" *PBS Newshour* (Nov. 11, 2017).

63. Paul Solman, "Urban Farming," *PBS Newshour* (Oct. 1, 2015).

64. Sam Eaton, "Singapore Looks Skyward to Take Farming in New Directions," *PBS Newshour* (June 12, 2013).

65. Green Sense Farms, https://www.green sensefarms.com/ Also, see Heather Clancy, "Will There Be LEDs in Your Lettuce's Future?" *Forbes* (May 29, 2014); Kevin Gray, "How We'll Grow Food in the Future: Traditional Agriculture Has Bought the Farm," *Popular Science* (Sept. 22, 2015).

66. The Public Television series, "Growing a Greener World," has featured a number of urban farming episodes, such as the following: "Green Roofs & Rooftop Gardens," season one, episode 122 (Oct. 10, 2010); "Hydroponics," season two, episode 206 (Aug. 7, 2011); "NYC Rooftop Farms," season three, episode 322 (Dec. 18, 2012); "Rooftop Farm," season four, episode 409 (Sept. 12, 2013).

67. Michael L. McKinney, "Urban Futures," in *Urban Ecology*, Gaston, ed., 287–308.

68. Much practical advice may be found in Timothy Beatley, *Biophilic Cities: Integrating Nature into Urban Design and Planning* (Washington, DC: Island Press, 2011), and Robbert Snep and Paul Opdam, "Integrating Nature Values in Urban Planning and Design," in *Urban Ecology*, Gaston, ed., 261–86.

69. "World's Largest Wildlife Corridor to Be Built in California," *EcoWatch* (Sept. 27, 2015); Ken Christensen, "Seattle's New Seawall Built to Make Life Easier for Fish," *PBS Newshour* (July 25, 2017).

70. Karen Dyson and Ken Yocom, "Ecological Design for Urban Waterfronts," *Urban Ecosystems* 18 (2015): 189–208.

71. Tianjin Eco City, https://www.tianjineco city.gov.sg/

Afterword

1. O'Hear, Anthony O'Hear, *Introduction to the Philosophy of Science* (Oxford: Clarendon Press, 1989), 210.

2. *Ibid.*, 215, 231–32.

3. Peter J. Bowler, *The Norton History of Environmental Sciences* (New York: W.W. Norton & Co., 1993), 547, 548.

4. Samir Okasha, *Philosophy of Science: A Very Short Introduction*, 2nd ed. (New York: Oxford University Press, 2016), 60.

5. *Ibid.*, 62.

6. Anna Bramwell, *Ecology in the 20th Century: A History* (New Haven: Yale University Press, 1989), 248; R. Allan Freeze, *The Environmental Pendulum: A Quest for the Truth About Toxic Chemicals, Human Health, and Environmental Protection* (Berkeley: University of California Press, 2000), 45; Aaron Wildavsky, *But Is It True? A Citizen's Guide to Environmental*

Health and Safety Issues (Cambridge: Harvard University Press, 1995), 440; Donald Worster, *Nature's Economy: A History of Ecological Ideas,* 2nd ed. (New York: Cambridge University Press, 1994), 360.

7. Freeze, *Environmental Pendulum,* p. 255, table 18, and chapter seven in general.

8. *Ibid.,* 43.
9. *Ibid.,* 46.
10. *Ibid.*
11. Wildavsky, *But Is It True?,* 440.
12. Gail Willumsen, dir., *Ultimate Mars Challenge* (NOVA / WBGH Boston, 2012).

Bibliography

Statutes and Lawsuits

Animal Welfare Act of 1966, Public Law 89–544, 80 Stat. 350.

Bruce Babbit, Secretary of the Interior, et al. v. Sweet Home Chapter of Communities for a Great Oregon 115 S.Ct. 2407 (decided June 29, 1995).

California Statutes 2008, chapter 559, chapter 560.

California Statutes 2008, chapter 560; Definitions, California Health and Safety Code, section 25251.

City of Greenville, et al. v. Syngenta Crop Protection, 764 F.3d 695 (2014).

City of Greenville, et al. v. Syngenta Crop Protection, 904 F.Supp.2d 902 (2012).

Clean Air Act (1963), Public Law 88–206.

Clean Water Act (1972), Public Law 92–500.

Endangered Species Act (1973), Public Law 93–205.

National Environmental Policy Act (1969), Public law 91–190, 83 Stat. 852.

Northern Spotted Owl (Strix Occidentalis Caurina) v. Hodel, 716 F.Supp. 479 (1988).

Northern Spotted Owl v. Lujan, 758 F.Supp. 621 (1991).

Oregon Administrative Rules 629–001 through 629–676. http://www.oregon.gov/odf/pages/lawsrules.aspx

Oregon Forest Conservation Act, Oregon Laws 1941, chapter 237, section 2.

Oregon Forest Practices Act

Pollution Prevention Act (1990), U.S. Code Title 42, "The Public Health and Welfare," chapter 133, "Pollution Prevention," sections 13101–09.

Save Our Big Trees v. City of Santa Cruz, et al., Court of Appeal, Sixth District, California, 241 Cal.App.4th 694 (2015).

Wilderness Act of 1964, Public Law 88–577.

Government Documents

Adams, Darius M., et al. "Estimated Timber Harvest by U.S. Region and Ownership, 1950–2002." USDA Forest Service, Pacific Northwest Research Station, General Technical Report PNW-GTR-659, Jan. 2006. https://www.fs.fed.us/pnw/pubs/pnw_gtr659.pdf

Brenneman, Ronnie E. "Controlling Deer Problems in Hardwood Stands." In *Proceedings: Guidelines for Regenerating Appalachian Hardwood Stands*, edited by Arlyn W. Perkey, et al., 97–103. USDA Forest Service (Morgantown, WV, May 24–26, 1988).

City of Seattle, Washington. "Heritage Tree Program." https://www.seattle.gov/transportation/heritagetree.htm.

City of Vancouver, Washington. "Heritage Trees." http://www.cityofvancouver.us/publicworks/page/heritage-trees.

Corn, M. Lynne, and Alexandra M. Wyatt. "The Endangered Species Act: A Primer." Washington, D.C.: Congressional Information Service, Library of Congress, Sept. 8, 2016.

Guldin, James M. "A History of Forest Management in the Ozark Mountains." In *Pioneer Forest: A Half Century of Sustainable Uneven-Aged Forest Management in the Missouri Ozarks*, General Technical Report SRS-108, edited by in James M. Guldin, et al., 3–8. Asheville, NC: United States Forest Service, Southern Research Station, 2008.

Michael, Edwin D. "Effects of White-Tailed Deer on Appalachian Hardwood Regeneration." In *Proceedings: Guidelines for Regenerating Appalachian Hardwood Stands*, edited by Arlyn W. Perkey, et al., 85–96. USDA Forest Service (Morgantown, WV, May 24–26, 1988).

Oregon Board of Forestry. "An Historical Overview of the Establishment of State Forest Lands." https://digital.osl.state.or.us/islandora/object/osl%3A20524/datastream/OBJ/view

Oregon Department of Forestry. "Forest Facts: Oregon's Family-Owned Forests." Salem: Oregon Department of Forestry, Feb. 2015.

Troy, Austin, et al. "The Relationship Between Tree Canopy and Crime Rates Across an Urban–Rural Gradient in the Greater Baltimore Region." *Landscape and Urban Planning,* April 2012. https://www.nrs.fs.fed.us/pubs/jrnl/2012/nrs_2012_troy_001.pdf

United Nations. Agenda 21, Chapter 19. "Environmentally Sound Management of Toxic Chemicals." https://sustainabledevelopment.un.org/content/documents/Agenda21.pdf

U.S. Department of Health and Human Services, Centers for Disease Control and Prevention. "Fourth National Report on Human Exposure to Environmental Chemicals, Updated Tables." volume one (March 2018). https://www.cdc.gov/exposurereport/index.html

U.S. Environmental Protection Agency. "EPA's Actions to Restrict PFOA and Similar Chemicals Yield Significant Human Health and Environmental Benefits." Jan. 15, 2015. https://archive.epa.gov/epa/newsreleases/epas-actions-restrict-pfoa-and-similar-chemicals-yield-significant-human-health-and.html

U.S. Environmental Protection Agency. "Toxics Release Inventory and Emission Reductions 1987–1990 in the Lower Mississippi River Industrial Corridor." Washington, D.C.: EPA, May 1993.

Zhu, Zhiliang, and A. David McGuire, eds. "Baseline and Projected Future Carbon Storage and Greenhouse-Gas Fluxes in Ecosystems of Alaska." Professional Paper 1826. Reston, VA: U.S. Geological Survey, 2016.

Films

Buffie, Erna, writer and dir. *What Plants Talk About.* PBS/Nature, 2012.

Byatt, Andy, prod., David Attenborough, narr. *The Blue Planet: Sea of Life.* BBC Video, 2001.

Cain, Eric, prod. *The Oregon Story: Rethinking the Forests.* Portland: Oregon Public Broadcasting, 2005.

Campbell, Joseph, narr. *The Power of Myth.* Athena Learning, 1988.

Fadiman, Dorothy dir. *Butterfly Town, USA.* Concentric Media 2015.

Fimeri, Wain, dir., Derek Muller, narr. *Uranium: Twisting the Dragon's Tail.* PBS, 2015.

Fleming, Susan K., and Sara Marino, dirs. *Animal Odd Couples.* PBS/Nature, season 31, episode 3, 2012.

Fulton, Kate, et al., prod. *Salmon: Running the Gauntlet.* PBS, 2011.

Gillett, Burt, dir. *Flowers and Trees.* Walt Disney, 1932.

Green, Walon, dir. *The Secret Life of Plants.* Infinite Enterprises, 1978.

Hoback, Cullen, dir. *What Lies Upstream.* Hyrax Films, 2017.

McCabe, Daniel, dir. *Search for the Super Battery.* PBS/Nova, 2017.

McCabe, Daniel, dir., prod., writer. *Prediction by the Numbers.* PBS/Nova, 2018.

McCabe, Daniel, and Richard Reisz, dirs. *The Great Math Mystery.* WGBH/PBS, 2015.

Ocean Frontiers series (Green Fire Productions/PBS, 2011–2014):
  Great Bear Sea: Reflecting on the Past—Planning for the Future
  Ocean Frontiers: Dawn of a New Era in Ocean Stewardship
  Ocean Frontiers II: A New England Story for Sustaining the Sea
  Ocean Frontiers III: Leaders in Ocean Stewardship and the New Blue Economy

Piluso, Mario, dir. *The Halloween Tree.* Hanna-Barbera Productions, 1993.

Smith, Llewellyn M., dir. *Poisoned Water.* PBS/Nova, 2017.

Soderbergh, Steven, dir. *Erin Brockovich.* Universal Pictures, 2000.

Willumsen, Gail, dir. *Ultimate Mars Challenge.* Nova/WBGH Boston, 2012.

Websites

American Association for the Advancement of Science https://www.aaas.org/

American Chestnut Cooperators' Foundation http://www.accf-online.org/

American Heritage Trees https://americanheritagetrees.org/

Bjørn Lomborg http://www.lomborg.com/

Copenhagen Consensus Center http://www.copenhagenconsensus.com/

Endextinction.org

Eugene Tree Foundation http://eugene2.fatcow.com/

Forest Stewards Guild https://www.forestguild.org

Google Earth Engine https://earthengine.google.com/timelapse/

Green Sense Farms https://www.greensensefarms.com/

Intech: World's Largest Science, Technology and Medicine Open Access book publisher https://www.intechopen.com

Intergovernmental Panel on Climate Change https://www.ipcc

Mongabay Environmental News https://rainforests.mongabay.com

National Report on Human Exposure to Environmental Chemicals https://www.cdc.gov/exposurereport/index.html

The Native Forest Council http://www.forestcouncil.org

Oregon Small Woodlands Association https://www.oswa.org/

Project Gutenberg www.gutenberg.org

San Diego Zoo

Sky Greens https://www.skygreens.com/

Society for Ecological Restoration http://www.ser.org/

Stanford Encyclopedia of Philosophy https://plato.stanford.edu/

Sustainable Forestry Initiative http://www.sfiprogram.org/

Tianjin Eco City https://www.tianjinecocity.gov.sg/

Tipa Sustainable Packaging https://tipa-corp.com/

Transatomic Power http://www.transatomicpower.com

U.S. Environmental Protection Agency http://www.epa.gov/

Oral History Interviews (all by the author)

Drey, Leo A. Interview in St. Louis, Missouri, January 27, 1998. Tapes and transcript located in the "Missouri Environmental Oral History Project," Collection # 3966, Western Historical Manuscript Collection, State Historical Society of Missouri, Columbia, Missouri.

Stapleton, Jack, Jr. Interview in Kennett, Missouri, June 6, 1997. Tapes and transcript located in the "Politics in Missouri Oral History Project," Collection #3929, Western Historical Manuscript Collection, State Historical Society of Missouri, Columbia, Missouri.

Steelman, Dorman L. Interview in Salem Missouri, February 9, 1998. Tapes and transcript located in the "Politics in Missouri Oral History Project," Collection #3929, Western Historical Manuscript Collection, State Historical Society of Missouri, Columbia, Missouri.

Trammel, Clint. Interview in Dent and Shannon Counties, Missouri, May 20, 1998. Tapes and transcript located in the "Missouri Environmental Oral History Project," Collection # 3966, Western Historical Manuscript Collection, State Historical Society of Missouri, Columbia, Missouri.

Books and Articles

Abbey, Edward. *The Brave Cowboy*. New York: Dodd, Mead, & Co., 1956.

Abbott, Derek. "The Reasonable Ineffectiveness of Mathematics." *Proceedings of the IEEE* 101, no. 10 (Oct. 2013): 2147–53.

Abee, Albert. "Application of Criteria and Indicators of Sustainable Resource Management in the United States." In *Sustainable Forestry: From Monitoring and Modelling to Knowledge Management and Policy Science*, edited by Keith M. Reynolds, 75–102. Cambridge, MA: CABI, 2007.

Achenbach, Joel. "Who Knew? Plants on the Warpath." *National Geographic Magazine* (Feb. 2004).

Agilan, V., and N. V. Umamahesh. "Covariate and Parameter Uncertainty in Non-Stationary Rainfall IDF Curve." *International Journal of Climatology* 38 (2018): 365–383.

Aitkenhead-Peterson, Jacqueline, and Astrid Volder, eds. *Urban Ecosystem Ecology*. Madison, WI: American Society of Agronomy, 2010.

Al Horr, Yousef, et al. "Occupant Productivity and Office Indoor Environment Quality: A Review of the Literature." *Building and Environment* 105 (2016): 369–389.

Alberti, Marina. "Global Urban Signatures of Phenotypic Change in Animal and Plant Populations." *Proceedings of the National Academy of Sciences* (Oct. 31, 2016): 1–6.

Alden, Peter, et al. *National Audubon Society Field Guide to the Pacific Northwest*. New York: Alfred A. Knopf, 1998.

Altschull, J. H. *From Milton to McLuhan. The Ideas Behind American Journalism*. New York: Longman, 1990.

American Lung Association. "State of the Air 2018." Chicago: American Lung Assoc., 2018.

Anastas, Paul T., and Julie Beth Zimmerman, eds. *Innovations in Green Chemistry and Green Engineering: Selected Entries from the Encyclopedia of Sustainability Science and Technology*. New York: Springer, 2013.

Angell, Marcia. *The Truth About the Drug Companies: How They Deceive Us and What to Do About It*. New York: Random House, 2004.

Appleman, Philip, ed. *Darwin*. New York: W.W. Norton Co., 2001.

Ardrey, Robert. *The Territorial Imperative: A Personal Inquiry into the Animal Origins of Property and Nations*. New York: Atheneum, 1966.

Augspach, Elizabeth. "Meaning." In *A Cultural History of Gardens in the Medieval Age*, edited by Michael Leslie, 101–115. New York: Blooms-burg, 2013.

Avilés, Paul. "Seven Ways of Looking at a Moun-tain: Tetzcotzingo and the Aztec Garden Tra-dition." *Landscape Journal* 25, no. 2 (2006): 143–157.

Aviv, Rachel. "A Valuable Reputation." *New Yorker* (Feb. 10, 2014).

Bacon, Francis. *First Book of Aphorisms,* Apho-rism XLVI. Fordham University's *Modern History SourceBook* via: http://www.fordham.edu/halsall/mod/bacon-aphor.html.

Barbour, Michael G. "Ecological Fragmentation in the Fifties." In *Uncommon Ground: Toward Reinventing Nature,* edited by William Cronon, 233–55. New York: W.W. Norton & Co., 1995.

Baridon, Michel. "The Scientific Imagination and the Baroque Garden." *Studies in the His-tory of Gardens & Designed Landscapes* 18, no. 1 (1998): 5–19.

Barrett, Kirsten, et al. "Ecosystem Services from Converted Land: the Importance of Tree Cover in Amazonian Pastures." *Urban Ecosys-tems* 16 (2013): 573–591.

Bartlett, Tom. "Power of Suggestion." *Chronicle of Higher Education* (Jan. 20, 2013).

———. "The Results of the Reproducibility Proj-ect Are In. They're Not Good." *Chronicle of Higher Education,* Aug. 28, 2015.

———. "The Results of the Reproducibility Proj-ect Are In. They're Not Good." *Chronicle of Higher Education* (Aug. 28, 2015).

Barton, Jo, and Jules Pretty. "Urban Ecology and Human Health and Well Being." In *Urban Ecology,* edited by Kevin J. Gaston, 202–29. New York: Cambridge University Press, 2010.

Basken, Paul. "In Budget Battle, Science Faces New Pressures to Prove It Delivers." *Chronicle of Higher Education* (Nov. 19, 2012).

———. "Landmark Analysis of an Infamous Medical Study Points Out the Challenges of Research Oversight." *Chronicle of Higher Ed-ucation,* Sept. 17, 2015.

———. "Why Beall's List Died—and What It Left Unresolved About Open Access." *Chronicle of Higher Education* (Sept. 12, 2017).

Baughman, John F. "Galileo's Revenge: Junk Sci-ence in the Courtroom by Peter W. Huber, Book Review." *Michigan Law Review* 90, no. 6 (May 1992): 1614–1623.

Beatley, Timothy. *Biophilic Cities: Integrating Nature into Urban Design and Planning.* Washington, D.C.: Island Press, 2011.

Beckerman, Wilfred. *Poverty of Reason: Sustain-able Development.* Oakland, CA: Independent Institute, 2002.

Bennett, W. Lance. *News: The Politics of Illusion.* White Plains, NY: Longman, 1996.

Bergman, Åke, et al. "Manufacturing Doubt About Endocrine Disrupter Science—A Re-buttal of Industry-Sponsored Critical Com-ments on the UNEP/WHO Report "State of the Science of Endocrine Disrupting Chem-icals 2012."" *Regulatory Toxicology and Phar-macology* 73 (2015): 1007–17.

Besley, John C., and Matthew Nisbet. "How Sci-entists View the Public, the Media and the Political Process." *Public Understanding of Sci-ence* 22:6 (2011): 644–659.

Biello, David. "How Microbes Helped Clean BP's Oil Spill." *Scientific American* (Ap. 28, 2015).

Bingham, Dwight Jeffrey. "Irenaeus of Lyons." In *The Routledge Companion to Early Chris-tian Thought,* edited by Dwight Jeffrey Bing-ham, 137–53. New York: Routledge, 2010.

"The Biologist Who Challenged Agribusiness." *New Yorker* (Dec. 1, 2016).

Black, Lewis. "Back in Black: Earth Day." *The Daily Show with Jon Stewart,* April 25, 2007.

Blakesley, J. "Habitat Associations," chapter five in Steven P. Courtney, et al. *Scientific Evalu-ation of the Status of the Northern Spotted Owl.* Portland, OR: Sustainable Ecosystems Institute, 2004.

Blanke, Olaf, et al. "Neurological and Robot-Controlled Induction of an Apparition." *Cur-rent Biology* 24 (Nov. 17, 2014): 2681–686.

Bodansky, David. *Nuclear Energy: Principles, Practices, and Prospects.* New York: Springer, 2004.

Bolin, Jessica L., and Lawrence C. Hamilton. "The News You Choose: News Media Prefer-ences Amplify Views on Climate Change." *Environmental Politics* 27, no. 3 (2018): 455–476.

Botkin-Kowacki, Eva. "China's Forest Conser-vation Program Shows Proof of Success." *Christian Science Monitor* (March 19, 2016).

Bowe, Patrick. "The Early Development of Gar-den Making c. 3000–c. 2000 BCE." *Studies in the History of Gardens & Designed Landscapes* 37, no.3 (2017): 231–241.

———. "The Evolution of the Ancient Greek Garden." *Studies in the History of Gardens & Designed Landscapes* 30, no.3 (2010): 208–223.

———. "The Sacred Groves of Ancient Greece." *Studies in the History of Gardens & Designed Landscapes* 29, no. 4 (2009): 235–245.

Bowler, Peter J. *The Norton History of Environ-mental Sciences.* New York: W.W. Norton & Co., 1993.

Boykoff, Maxwell T. "From Convergence to Contention: United States Mass Media Representations of Anthropogenic Climate Change Science." *Transactions of the Institute of British Geographers* (2007): 477–89.

Bradley, Gordon A., ed., *Urban Forest Landscapes: Integrating Multidisciplinary Perspectives.* Seattle: University of Washington Press, 1995.

Brainard, Jeffrey. "How a Graduate Student Kindled a Firestorm in Forestry Research." *Chronicle of Higher Education* (April 21, 2006).

Braithwaite, Roger J. "Glacier Mass Balance: The First 50 Years of International Monitoring." *Progress in Physical Geography* 26, no. 1 (2002): 76–95.

Bramwell, Anna. *Ecology in the 20th Century: A History.* New Haven: Yale University Press, 1989.

Breuste, J., et al., eds. *Urban Ecology.* New York: Springer, 1998.

Briggle, Adam, and Carl Mitcham. *Ethics and Science: an Introduction.* Cambridge University Press, 2012.

Bronowski, J., and Bruce Mazlish. *The Western Intellectual Tradition: From Leonardo to Hegel.* New York: Harper & Row Pubs., 1962.

Brüggemann, Michael, and Sven Engesser. "Between Consensus and Denial: Climate Journalists as Interpretive Community." *Science Communication* 36, no. 4 (2014): 399–427.

Brunner, Bernd. *Birdmania.* Sydney, Australia: Allen & Unwin, 2017.

Bryner, Jeanna. "Invasive Plant Conquers with Chemical Warfare." *Live Science* (Oct. 17, 2007).

Bullard, Robert Doyle. *Dumping in Dixie: Race, Class, and Environmental Quality,* 3rd ed. Boulder, CO: Westview Press, 2000.

Bullard, Robert Doyle, and Beverly Wright. *The Wrong Complexion for Protection: How the Government Response to Disaster Endangers African American Communities.* New York: New York University Press, 2012.

Butler, Rhett. "Calculating Deforestation for the Amazon." https://rainforests.mongabay.com/amazon/deforestation_calculations.html.

Cabrera, María Noel. "Pulp Mill Wastewater: Characteristics and Treatment." In *Biological Wastewater Treatment and Resource Recovery,* edited by Robina Farooq and Zaki Ahmad, Chapter 7. InTech Open Access Pub., 2017.

Cahalan, James M. *Edward Abbey: a Life.* Tucson: University of Arizona Press, 2001.

Calmon, Miguel, et al. "Emerging Threats and Opportunities for Large-Scale Ecological

Restoration in the Atlantic Forest of Brazil." *Restoration Ecology* 19, no. 2 (March 2011): 154–58.

Camargo, José Luís Campana, et al. "Rehabilitation of Degraded Areas of Central Amazonia Using Direct Sowing of Forest Tree Seeds." *Restoration Ecology* 10, no. 4 (Dec. 2002): 636–644.

Campbell, Gordon. "Epicurus, the Garden, and the Golden Age." In *Gardening Philosophy for Everyone: Cultivating Wisdom,* edited by Dan O'Brien, 220–31. Malden, MA: Wiley-Blackwell, 2010.

Campbell, Joseph. *The Hero with a Thousand Faces,* 3rd ed. Novato, CA: New World Library, 2008.

———. *Transformation of Myth Through Time.* New York: Harper & Row, 1990.

Carmichael, Jason T., and Robert J. Brulle. "Elite Cues, Media Coverage, and Public Concern: an Integrated Path Analysis of Public Opinion on Climate Change, 2001–2013." *Environmental Politics* 26, no. 2 (2017): 232–252.

Caron, Louis-Philippe, et al. "On the Variability and Predictability of Eastern Pacific Tropical Cyclone Activity." *Journal of Climate* 28, no. 24 (Dec. 15, 2015): 9678–96.

Chandler, James, et al., eds. *Questions of Evidence: Proof, Practice, and Persuasion Across the Disciplines.* Chicago: University of Chicago Press, 1994.

Charlesworth, Michael. "Sacred Landscape: Signs of Religion in the Eighteenth-Century Garden." *Journal of Garden History* 13, no. 1–2 (Spring-Summer 1993): 56–68.

Chase, Alston. *In a Dark Wood: The Fight Over Forests and the Rising Tyranny of Ecology.* New York: Houghton Mifflin, 1995.

———. *Playing God In Yellowstone: The Destruction of America's First National Park.* New York: Atlantic Monthly Press, 1986.

Chassy, Bruce. "Turning Science into a Circus: The New Yorker, Rachel Aviv and Tyrone Hayes." *Academics Review* (March 7, 2014).

Chilton, Bruce, et al. *The Cambridge Companion to the Bible,* 2nd ed. New York: Cambridge University Press, 2008.

Choksy, Jamsheed Kairshasp. *Purity and Pollution in Zoroastrianism: Triumph Over Evil.* Austin: University of Texas Press, 1989.

Clancy, Heather. "Will There Be LEDs In Your Lettuce's Future?" *Forbes* (May 29, 2014).

Cocker, Mark. *Birders: Tales of a Tribe.* New York: Grove Press, 2001.

Cohen, Arianne. "My Quest to Analyze Every Man-Made Chemical in My Body." *Popular Science* (Nov. 2, 2009).

Colborn, Theo, et al. *Our Stolen Future: Are We Threatening Our Fertility, Intelligence and Survival: A Scientific Detective Story.* New York: Dutton, 1996.

Collingwood, Robin George. *Idea of Nature.* New York: Oxford University Press, 1960.

Collins, Harry, and Robert Evans. *Rethinking Expertise.* University of Chicago Press, 2014.

Colwell, Rita R., et al. "Beyond the Basics: a Roundtable Discussion." In *Communicating Uncertainty: Media Coverage of New and Controversial Science,* edited by Sharon M. Friedman, et al., 249–61. Mahwah, NJ: L. Erlbaum Associates, 1999.

Cook, Timothy E. *Governing with the News: the News Media as a Political Institution.* Chicago: University of Chicago Press, 1998.

Cooper, Jean. "The Symbolism of the Taoist Garden." *Studies in Comparative Religion* 11, no. 4 (Autumn, 1977): 224–34.

Cousineau, Jennifer. "The Urban Practice of Jewish Space." In *American Sanctuary: Understanding Sacred Spaces,* edited by in Louis P. Nelson, 65–88. Bloomington: Indiana University Press, 2006.

Cox, Peter M., et al. "Emergent Constraint on Equilibrium Climate Sensitivity from Global Temperature Variability." *Nature* 553 (Jan. 18, 2018): 319–322.

Crichton, Michael. "Speech to the San Francisco Commonwealth Club." San Francisco Commonwealth Club. https://www.cs.cmu.edu/~kw/crichton.html.

———. *State of Fear.* New York: HarperCollins, 2004.

Crockett, Molly. "Beware Neuro-Bunk." TED Talks, Nov. 2012.

Crosby, Alfred W. *The Columbian Exchange: Biological and Cultural Consequences of 1492.* New ed. Westport, CT: Praeger, 2003.

———. *Ecological Imperialism: The Biological Expansion of Europe, 900–1900.* New ed. New York: Cambridge Univ. Press, 2004.

Davidson, Cliff I. "Air Pollution in Pittsburgh: A Historical Perspective." *Journal of the Air Pollution Control Association* 29, no. 10 (1979): 1035–41.

Davis, A.R. *T'ao Yuan-ming,* vol.1. Cambridge: Cambridge University Press, 1983.

Davis, Bernard D. *The Genetic Revolution: Scientific Prospects and Public Perceptions.* Baltimore: Johns Hopkins University Press, 1991.

———. "Summary and Comments: The Scientific Chapters." In *The Genetic Revolution: Scientific Prospects and Public Perceptions,* edited by Bernard D. Davis, 239–65. Baltimore: Johns Hopkins University Press, 1991.

Davis, Mark A., and Lawrence B. Slobodkin. "The Science and Values of Restoration Ecology." *Restoration Ecology* 12, no. 1 (March 2004): 1–3.

Davis, Mary Byrd. "Old Growth in the East: A Survey." http://www.primalnature.org:80/ogeast/contents.html

De Bary, William Theodore. *Sources of Chinese Tradition.* New York: Columbia University Press, 1960.

DeVore, Chuck. "New Theory: CO2 And Climate Linked—But Not In The Way The 'Consensus' Tells Us." *Forbes* (June 30, 2016).

De Vries, Jan. *The Problem of Loki,* FF Communication no. 110. Helsinki: Suomalainen Tiedeakatemia Societas Scientiarum Fennica, 1933.

DeWet, Andrew P., et al. "Interactions of Land-Use History and Current Ecology in a Recovering "Urban Wildland."" *Urban Ecosystems* 2 (1998): 237–262.

Dickens, Charles. *Hard Times and Reprinted Pieces.* London: Chapman & Hall, 1905.

Diebel, Kenneth Edward. "Isozyme Variation within the Fraser Fir Population on Mt. Rogers, Virginia." Ph.D. diss., Virginia Polytechnic Institute and State Univ., 1989.

Dixon. Bernard. "Forum: Genes of Yesteryear—What Can We Learn, Bernard Dixon asks, from Disease-Causing Microbes Preserved in the Biosphere?" *New Scientist* (April 9, 1994).

Djerf-Pierre, Monika. "Green Metacycles of Attention: Reassessing the Attention Cycles of Environmental News Reporting 1961–2010." *Public Understanding of Science* 22, no.4 (2011): 495–512.

Dombrowski, Nina, et al. "Reconstructing Metabolic Pathways of Hydrocarbon-Degrading Bacteria from the Deepwater Horizon Oil Spill." *Nature Microbiology,* 1 (May 2016).

Donovan, Geoffrey H., and Jeffrey P. Prestemon. "The Effect of Trees on Crime in Portland, Oregon." *Environment and Behavior* (Sage Journals, Oct. 19, 2010). http://journals.sagepub.com/doi/abs/10.1177/0013916510383238

Doran, Peter T. "Antarctic Climate Cooling and Terrestrial Ecosystem Response." *Nature* 415, no. 31 (Jan. 2002): 517–20.

Drake, Frances. *Global Warming: The Science of Climate Change.* New York: Oxford University Press, 2000.

Dunlap, Thomas R. "American Wildlife Policy and Environmental Ideology: Poisoning Coyotes, 1939–1972." *Pacific Historical Review* 55, no. 3 (Aug. 1986): 345–369.

———. *Faith in Nature: Environmentalism as Re-*

ligious Quest. Seattle: University of Washington Press, 2004.

Dyson, Karen, and Ken Yocom. "Ecological Design for Urban Waterfronts." *Urban Ecosystems* 18 (2015): 189–208.

Edner, Adalbert. *German Forests: Treasures of a Nation.* New York: German Library of Information, 1940.

Ehrenfeld, David W. *The Arrogance of Humanism.* New York: Oxford University Press, 1978.

Ehrlich, Anne H., and Paul R. Ehrlich. "Needed: An Endangered Humanities Act?" In *Balancing on the Brink of Extinction: the Endangered Species Act and Lessons for the Future,* edited by Kathryn A. Kohm, 298–302. Washington, D.C.: Island Press, 1991.

Ehrlich, Paul R., and Anne H. Ehrlich. *Extinction: The Causes and Consequences of the Disappearance of Species.* New York: Random House, 1981.

———. *The Population Bomb.* New York: Ballantine Books, 1968.

Ehrmann, Max. *Desiderata* (1927). https://en.wikipedia.org/wiki/Desiderata.

Einstein, Albert. *Ideas and Opinions.* New York: Bonanza Books, 1954.

Eisenhower, Dwight David. "Eisenhower's Farewell Address." https://en.wikisource.org/wiki/Eisenhower%27s_farewell_address_(audio_transcript)

Eliade, Mircea. *Cosmos and History: the Myth of the Eternal Return.* Willard R. Trask, trans. New York: Harper, 1959.

———. *Myth and Reality.* New York: Harper & Row, 1963.

———. *The Sacred and the Profane.* Willard R. Trask, trans. 1957; New York: Harper & Row, 1959.

Ellis, Ralph, and Michael Palmer. "Modulation of Ice Ages via Precession and Dust-Albedo Feedbacks." *Geoscience Frontiers* 7, no. 6 (Nov. 2016): 891–909.

Elton, Charles Sutherland. *The Ecology of Invasions by Animals and Plants.* London: Chapman & Hall, 1958; New York: Halsted Press, 1977.

Emerson, Ralph Waldo. *Nature.* Boston: Thurston, Torry & Co., 1849.

Eng, Karen. "The Man Who Plants Trees: Shubhendu Sharma Is Reforesting the World, One Patch at a Time." TED Talks Blog, May 9, 2014.

Entine, Jon. "Did *The New Yorker* Botch Puff Piece on Frog Scientist Tyrone Hayes, Turning Rogue into Beleaguered Hero?" *Forbes* (March 10, 2014).

Ereshefsky, Marc. "Species." *Stanford Encyclopedia of Philosophy* (July 4, 2002; rev. ed., Aug. 29, 2017).

Eubanks, David. "A Guide for the Perplexed." *Intersection.* Association for the Assessment of Learning in Higher Education, Fall 2017.

Evans, Karl L. "Individual Species and Urbanization." In *Urban Ecology,* edited by Kevin J. Gaston, 53–87. New York: Cambridge University Press, 2010.

Eyres, Patrick. "Meaning." In *A Cultural History of Gardens in the Age of Enlightenment,* edited by Stephen Bending, 115–39. New York: Bloomsburg, 2013.

Fagan, Brian M. *The Little Ice Age: How Climate Made History, 1300–1850.* New York: Basic Books, 2000.

Faith, Daniel P. "Biodiversity." *Stanford Encyclopedia of Philosophy* (June 11, 2003; rev. ed. Dec. 4, 2007).

Farber, Paul L. *Finding Order in Nature: The Naturalist Tradition from Linnaeus to E.O. Wilson.* Baltimore: Johns Hopkins University Press, 2000.

Farmer, Jared. *Trees in Paradise: A California History.* New York: W.W. Norton, 2013.

Faulkner, Edward H. *Plowman's Folly.* Norman: University of Oklahoma Press, 1943.

Fedoroff, Nina. "A Secret Weapon Against Zika and Other Mosquito-Borne Diseases." TED Talks, Oct. 2016.

Feldman, Lauren, et al. "Polarizing News? Representations of Threat and Efficacy in Leading U.S. Newspapers' Coverage of Climate Change." *Public Understanding of Science* 26, no. 4 (2017): 481–497.

Feynman, Richard. *The Character of Physical Law* 1965; New York: Modern Library, 1994.

Finlayson-Pitts, Barbara J., and James N. Pitts. *Chemistry of the Lower and Upper Atmosphere: Theory, Experiments, and Applications.* San Diego: Academic Press, 2000.

Fisher, David Hackett. *Historians' Fallacies: Toward a Logic of Historical Thought.* New York: Harper, 1970.

Flores, Dan L. *Coyote America: A Natural and Supernatural History.* New York: Basic Books, 2016.

Ford, George H. "Felicitous Space: The Cottage Controversy." In *Nature and the Victorian Imagination,* edited by U.C. Knoepflmacher and G.B. Tennyson, 29–48. Berkeley: University of California Press, 1977.

Forsman, Eric. "A Preliminary Investigation of the Spotted Owl in Oregon." MS Thesis, Oregon State University, 1976.

Francis, Mark, and Randolph T. Hester, Jr., eds.

Meanings of the Garden: Proceedings of a Working Conference to Explore the Social, Psychological and Cultural Dimensions of Gardens. University of California, Davis, May 14–17, 1987.

Franklin, Alan B., et al. "Climate, Habitat Quality, and Fitness in Northern Spotted Owl Populations in Northwestern California." *Ecological Monographs* 704 (Nov. 2000): 539–590.

Franssen, Maarten, et al. "Philosophy of Technology." *Stanford Encyclopedia of Philosophy* (Feb. 20, 2009; rev. Dec. 13, 2013).

Frazer, James George. *The Golden Bough.* 1890; New York: Oxford University Press, 1994.

Freeze, R. Allan. *The Environmental Pendulum: A Quest for the Truth About Toxic Chemicals, Human Health, and Environmental Protection.* Berkeley: University of California Press, 2000.

Friel, Howard. *The Lomborg Deception: Setting the Record Straight About Global Warming.* New Haven: Yale University Press, 2010.

Frigg, Roman. "Models in Science." *Stanford Encyclopedia of Philosophy* (Feb. 27, 2006; rev. ed. June 25, 2012).

Fuller, Richard A., and Katherine N. Irvine. "Interactions Between People and Nature in Urban Environments." In *Urban Ecology,* edited by Kevin J. Gaston, 134–71. New York: Cambridge University Press, 2010.

Funtowicz, Silvio O., and Jerome R. Ravetz. "Science for the Post-Normal Age." *Futures* 25:7 (1993), 739–55.

Garland, John J. "The Oregon Forest Practice Act: 1972 to 1994." http://www.fao.org/docrep/W3646E/w3646e07.htm

Gaston, Kevin J. *Urban Ecology.* New York: Cambridge University Press, 2010.

Gaston, Kevin J., et al. "Urban Environments and Ecosystem Function." In *Urban Ecology,* edited by Kevin J. Gaston, 35–52. New York: Cambridge University Press, 2010.

Geldmann, Jonas, and Juan P. González-Varo. "Conserving Honey Bees Does Not Help Wildlife." *Science* 359, no. 6374 (Jan. 26, 2018): 392–393.

Genesis. "Bible Versions and Translation." https://www.biblestudytools.com/bible-versions/

George, Kathryn Paxton. "The Use and Abuse of Scientific Studies." *Journal of Agricultural and Environmental Ethics* 5, no. 2 (Sept. 1992): 217–33.

Gibbons, M. "Science's New Social Contract With Society." *Nature* 402, supplement. (Dec. 2, 1999): C81–C84.

Girardot, N. J. *Myth and Meaning in Early Dao-ism: The Theme of Chaos (Hundun).* Magdalena, NM: Three Pines Press, 2008.

Glacken, Clarence J. *Traces on the Rhodian Shore: Nature and Culture in Western Thought from Ancient Times to the End of the Eighteenth Century.* 1967; Berkeley: University of California Press, 1990.

Gonda, Jan. *The Ritual Functions and Significance of Grasses in the Religion of the Veda.* New York: North-Holland Pub. Co., 1985.

Gong, Zhiqiang, et al. "Assessment and Correction of BCC_CSM's Performance in Capturing Leading Modes of Summer Precipitation over North Asia." *International Journal of Climatology* 38 (2018): 2201–2214.

Gore, Al. "Al Gore Explains Why Global Warming Is a Global Crisis, 2006. In *Major Problems in American Environmental History,* 3rd ed., edited by Carolyn Merchant, 538–43. Boston: Wadsworth, Cengage Learning, 2012.

Gray, Emily R., and Yolanda van Heezik. "Exotic Trees Can Sustain Native Birds in Urban Woodlands." *Urban Ecosystems* 19 (2016): 315–329.

Gray, Kevin. "How We'll Grow Food in the Future: Traditional Agriculture Has Bought the Farm." *Popular Science* (Sept. 22, 2015).

Grear, Anna. *Should Trees Have Standing?: 40 Years On.* Cheltenham, UK; Northampton, MA: Edward Elgar, 2012.

Green, Christopher D. "The Flaw at the Heart of Psychological Research." *Chronicle of Higher Education* (June 26, 2016).

Greenberg, Joel. *A Feathered River Across the Sky: The Passenger Pigeon's Flight to Extinction.* New York: Bloomsbury, 2014.

Greenwald, Glenn, and Leighton Akio Woodhouse. "Bred to Suffer: Inside the Barbaric U.S. Industry of Dog Experimentation." *The Intercept* (May 17, 2018). https://theintercept.com/2018/05/17/inside-the-barbaric-u-s-industry-of-dog-experimentation/

Griffiths, Paul. "Philosophy of Biology." *Stanford Encyclopedia of Philosophy* (July 4, 2008).

Grundmann, Reiner. "Review of Naomi Oreskes and Erik M. Conway, *Merchants of Doubt: How a Handful of Scientists Obscured the Truth on Issues from Tobacco Smoke to Global Warming* (New York: Bloomsbury Press, 2011)." *BioSocieties* 8, no. 3 (2013): 370–74.

Guerrini, Anita. *Experimenting with Humans and Animals: from Galen to Animal Rights.* Baltimore: Johns Hopkins University Press, 2003.

Haas, Danielle. "Chemical Fallout: Milwaukee Journal Sentinel and the BPA Story." Columbia University, Journalism School Knight

Case Studies Initiative, CSJ-09-0017.0 (March 2009).

Hahn, Andreas, and Thomas Knoke. "Sustainable Development and Sustainable Forestry: Analogies, Differences, and the Role of Flexibility." *European Journal of Forest Research* 129 (2010): 787–801.

Hamlyn, Paul. *Larouse Encyclopedia of Mythology*. London: Westbook House, 1959.

Hammond, Kenneth J. "Wang Shizhen's Yan Shan Garden Essays: Narrating a Literati Landscape." *Studies in the History of Gardens & Designed Landscapes* 19, no. 3–4 (1999): 276–287.

Han, Christina. "The Aesthetics of Wandering in the Chinese Literati Garden." *Studies in the History of Gardens & Designed Landscapes* 32, no. 4 (2012): 297–301.

Hannum, William H., et al. "Smarter Use of Nuclear Waste." *Scientific American.* (Dec. 2005): 84–91.

Hardin, Garrett. "Tragedy of the Commons." *Science* 162 (1968): 1243–48.

Harris, Frederick Brown. "Whose Land Is It?" *Virginia Wildlife* 19, no. 3 (March 1958): 5–7.

Harris, Richard. *Rigor Mortis: How Sloppy Science Creates Worthless Cures, Crushes Hope, and Wastes Billions.* New York: Basic Books, 2017.

Harrison, Robert Pogue. *Forests: The Shadow of Civilization.* Chicago: University of Chicago Press, 1992.

Hart, P. Sol, and Lauren Feldman. "Threat Without Efficacy? Climate Change on U.S. Network News." *Science Communication* 36, no. 3 (2014): 325–351.

Heisenberg, Werner. *Physics and Philosophy: The Revolution in Modern Science.* New York: Harper & Row, 1958.

Heske, Franz. *German Forestry.* New Haven: Yale University Press, 1938.

Hessburg, Paul. "Why Wildfires Have Gotten Worse—And What We Can Do About It." TED Talks, Nov. 7, 2017.

Hmielowski, Jay D., et al. "An Attack on Science? Media Use, Trust in Scientists, and Perceptions of Global Warming." *Public Understanding of Science* 23, no. 7 (2014): 866–883.

Horton, Richard. "Offline: The Crisis in Scientific Publishing." *Lancet* 388, no. 10042 (July 23, 2016).

Houlton, Ben Z., et al. "Convergent Evidence for Widespread Nitrogen Sources in Earth's Surface Environment." *Science* 360, no. 6384 (April 6, 2018): 58–62.

Houston, J.R., and R.G. Dean. "Sea-Level Acceleration Based on U.S. Tide Gauges and Extensions of Previous Global-Gauge Analyses." *Journal of Coastal Research* 27, no. 3 (May 2011): 409–17.

Howett, Catherine. "Gardens Are Good Places for Dying." In *Meanings of the Garden: Proceedings of a Working Conference to Explore the Social, Psychological and Cultural Dimensions of Gardens,* edited by Mark Francis and Randolph T. Hester, Jr., 180–84. University of California, Davis, May 14–17, 1987.

Huber, Peter W. *Galileo's Revenge: Junk Science in the Courtroom.* New York: Basic Books, 1991.

Hugo, Nancy R., and Jeff Kirwan. *Remarkable Trees of Virginia.* University of Virginia Press, 2008.

Hulac, Benjamin. "Tesla's Elon Musk Unveils Stored Sunlight in Batteries." *Scientific American* (May 1, 2015).

Hung, Yvonne. "East New York Farms: Youth Participation in Community Development and Urban Agriculture." *Children, Youth and Environments* 14, no. 1 (2004): 56–85.

Hunt, John Dixon. "Meaning." In *A Cultural History of Gardens in the Modern Age,* edited by John Dixon Hunt, 117–40. New York: Bloomsburg, 2013.

Idso, Craig D., et al. *Why Scientists Disagree About Global Warming: The NIPC Report on Scientific Consensus,* 2nd ed. Arlington Heights, IL: Heartland Inst., 2016.

Iles, Alastair. "Greening Chemistry: Emerging Epistemic Political Tensions in California and the United States." *Public Understanding of Science* 22, no. 4 (2011): 460–478.

Imort, Michael. "A Sylvan People: Wilhelmine Forestry and the Forest as a Symbol of Germandom." In *Germany's Nature: Cultural Landscapes and Environmental History,* edited by Thomas M. Lekan and Thomas Zeller, 55–80. New Brunswick: Rutgers University Press, 2005.

Inderberg, Tor Håkon, and Jørgen Wettestad. "Carbon Capture and Storage in the UK and Germany: Easier Task, Stronger Commitment?" *Environmental Politics* 24, no. 6 (2015): 1014–1033.

International Panel on Climate Change. Fourth Assessment Report: Climate Change 2007, Working Group I: The Physical Science Basis, Box 6.2: "What Caused the Low Atmospheric Carbon Dioxide Concentrations During Glacial Times?" https://www.ipcc.ch/publications_and_data/ar4/wg1/en/ch6s6-4.html.

Ioannidis, John P. A. "Scientific Inbreeding and Same-Team Replication: Type D Personality as an Example." *Journal of Psychosomatic Research* 73 (2012): 408–410.

_____. "Why Most Published Research Findings Are False." *PLoS Medicine* 2, no. 8 (Aug. 2005): 696–701.

Isenberg, Andrew C. "The Returns of the Bison: Nostalgia, Profit, and Preservation." *Environmental History* 2, no. 2 (April 1997): 179–196.

Ivanova, Ana, et al. "Results From a Survey of German Climate Scientists." *Science Communication* 35, no.5 (2013): 61–70.

Jabr, Ferris. "Self-Fulfilling Fakery: Feigning Mental Illness is a Form of Self-Deception." *Scientific American* (July 28, 2010). https://www.scientificamerican.com/article/faking-mental-illness/.

Jackson, Jerome A., and Bette J.S. Jackson. "Once Upon a Time in American Ornithology." *Wilson Journal of Ornithology* 119, no. 4 (Dec. 2007): 767–772.

Jackson, L. L., et al. "Ecological Restoration: A Definition and Comments." *Restoration Ecology* 3 (1995): 71–75.

Jacobs, Jane. *Death and Life of Great American Cities.* 1961; New York: Modern Library, 1993.

Jardine, Phil. "The Paleocene-Eocene Thermal Maximum." *Paleontology Online* 1, no. 5 (Jan. 10, 2011): 1–7.

Jebens, Arthur B. "State Rural Land Use Legislation in 1941." *The Journal of Land & Public Utility Economics* 18, no. 3 (Aug., 1942): 328–38.

Johnson, Jamie. "Birds: The High Flying Marker of Status." *Vanity Fair* (April 7, 2009).

Jones, Alex. "Covering Science and Technology: An Interview with Cornelia Dean. November 22, 2002." *The Harvard International Journal of Press/Politics,* 8, no. 2 (2003): 3–10.

Joughin, Ian, and Slawek Tulaczyk. "Positive Mass Balance of the Ross Ice Streams, West Antarctica." *Science* 295 (Jan. 18, 2002): 476–80.

Kabat, Geoffrey C. *Hyping Health Risks: Environmental Hazards in Daily Life and the Science of Science of Epidemiology.* New York: Columbia University Press, 2008.

Kaplan, Matt. "City Birds Use Cigarette Butts to Smoke Out Parasites." *Nature* (Dec. 5, 2012).

Kaplan, Robert D. *The Ends of the Earth: a Journey at the Dawn of the 21st Century.* New York: Random House, 1996.

Kaptchuk, Ted J. *The Web That Has No Weaver: Understanding Chinese Medicine,* 2nd ed. Chicago: Contemporary Books, 2000.

Kaser, Georg, et al. "Modern Glacier Retreat on Kilimanjaro as Evidence of Climate Change: Observation and Facts." *International Journal of Climatology* 24 (2004): 329–339.

Keith, David W., et al. "A Process for Capturing CO2 from the Atmosphere." *Joule* 2 (Aug. 15, 2018): 1–22.

King, Jesse, and Cecilia Chou. "Agent Orange Birth Defects: Recording and Contextualizing the Science of Embryos, Development, and Reproduction." *The Embryo Project Encyclopedia.* Arizona State University, School of Life Sciences, Center for Biology and Society (March 7, 2017).

Kininmonth, William. *Climate Change: a Natural Hazard.* Brentwood, Essex: Multi-Science Pub. Co., 2004.

Klein, Alice. "First Farm to Grow Veg in a Desert Using Only Sun and Seawater." *New Scientist* (Oct. 6, 2016).

Kleinhans, Maarten G., et al. "Philosophy of Earth Science." In *Philosophies of the Sciences: A Guide,* edited by Fritz Allhoff, 213–36. Chichester, West Sussex: Wiley-Blackwell, 2010.

Klotz, Stefan, and Ingolf Kühn. "Urbanisation and Alien Invasion." In *Urban Ecology,* edited by Kevin J. Gaston, 120–33. New York: Cambridge University Press, 2010.

Knight, John. "From Timber to Tourism: Recommoditizing the Japanese Forest." *Development and Change* 31, no. 1 (Jan. 2000): 341–359.

Kohler, Martin, et al. "Trends in Temperature and Wind Speed from 40 Years of Observations at a 200-m High Meteorological Tower in Southwest Germany." *International Journal of Climatology* 38 (2018): 23–34.

Kohm, Kathryn A. ed. *Balancing on the Brink of Extinction: The Endangered Species Act and Lessons for the Future.* Washington, D.C.: Island Press, 1991.

Kolowich, Steve. "Meet Retraction Watch, the Blog That Points Out the Human Stains on the Scientific Record." *Chronicle of Higher Education* (Sept. 25, 2015).

_____. "The Water Next Time: Professor Who Helped Expose Crisis in Flint Says Public Science Is Broken." *Chronicle of Higher Education* (Feb. 2, 2016).

Konijnendijk, Cecil C. *The Forest and the City: The Cultural Landscape of Urban Woodland.* New York: Springer, 2008.

Koshland, Daniel E., Jr. "Credibility in Science and the Press." *Science,* New Series 254, no. 5032 (Nov. 1, 1991): 629.

Krech, Shepard. *The Ecological Indian: Myth and History.* New York: Norton, 1999.

Kricher, John C. *The Balance of Nature: Ecology's Enduring Myth.* Princeton: Princeton University Press, 2009.

Krimsky, Sheldon. *Hormonal Chaos: The Scientific and Social Origins of the Environmental*

Endocrine Hypothesis. Baltimore: Johns Hopkins University Press, 2000.

Kubasek, Nancy K., and Gary S. Silverman. *Environmental Law* 4th ed. Upper Saddle River, NJ: Prentice Hall, 2002.

Kuhn, Thomas S. *Structure of Scientific Revolutions,* 2nd ed. 1962; Chicago: University of Chicago Press, 1970.

Labohm, Hans H. J., et al. *Man-Made Global Warming: Unravelling a Dogma.* Brentwood, UK: Multi-Science Pub. Co., 2004.

Lamb, James C. IV, et al. "Critical comments on the WHO-UNEP State of the Science of Endocrine Disrupting Chemicals—2012." *Regulatory Toxicology and Pharmacology* 69 (2014): 22–40.

Lampe, Ulrike, et al. "Staying Tuned: Grasshoppers from Noisy Roadside Habitats Produce Courtship Signals with Elevated Frequency Components." *Functional Ecology* (Nov. 14, 2012).

Langer, Susanne K. *Philosophy in a New Key.* Cambridge: Harvard University Press, 1942.

Lao, Tzu. *Daodejing.* Chinese Text Project. https://ctext.org/dao-de-jing.

Lawrence, Henry W. "Changing Forms and Persistent Values: Historical Perspectives on the Urban Forest." In *Urban Forest Landscapes: Integrating Multidisciplinary Perspectives,* edited by Gordon A. Bradley, 17–40. Seattle: University of Washington Press, 1995.

———. "The Neoclassical Origins of Modern Urban Forests." *Forest and Conservation History* 37, no. 1 (Jan. 1993): 26–36.

LaZerte, Stefanie E., et al. "Mountain Chickadees Adjust Songs, Calls and Chorus Composition with Increasing Ambient and Experimental Anthropogenic Noise." *Urban Ecosystems* 20 (2017): 989–1000.

Lean, Judith, and David Rind. "Climate Forcing by Changing Solar Radiation." *Journal of Climate* 11 (Dec. 1998): 369–94.

Ledderose, Lother. "The Earthly Paradise: Religious Elements in Chinese Landscape Art." In *Theories of the Arts in China,* edited by Susan Bush and Christian Murck, 165–83. Princeton: Princeton University Press, 1983.

Lekan, Thomas M., and Thomas Zeller, eds. *Germany's Nature: Cultural Landscapes and Environmental History.* New Brunswick: Rutgers University Press, 2005.

Leopold, Aldo. *A Sand County Almanac and Sketches Here and There.* 1949; Oxford University Press, 1968.

Leroux, Marcel. *Global Warming: Myth or Reality: the Erring Ways of Climatology.* Berlin; New York: Springer; 2005.

Levin, Simon A. "An Ecological Perspective." In *The Genetic Revolution: Scientific Prospects and Public Perceptions,* edited by Bernard D. Davis, 45–59. Baltimore: Johns Hopkins University Press, 1991.

Lewis, Nicholas, and Judith Curry. "The Impact of Recent Forcing and Ocean Heat Uptake Data on Estimates of Climate Sensitivity." *Journal of Climate* 31 (Aug. 2018): 6051–71.

Lewontin, R.C. "Facts and the Factitious in Natural Sciences." In *Questions of Evidence: Proof, Practice, and Persuasion Across the Disciplines,* edited by James Chandler, et al., 478–91. Chicago: University of Chicago Press, 1994.

———. "A Rejoinder to William Wimsatt." In *Questions of Evidence: Proof, Practice, and Persuasion Across the Disciplines,* edited by James Chandler, et al., 505–09. Chicago: University of Chicago Press, 1994.

Li, Xin, et al. "Analysis of Variability and Trends of Precipitation Extremes in Singapore during 1980–2013." *International Journal of Climatology* 38 (2018): 125–141.

Lillie, Ben. "A Local Bacteria to Solve a Local Problem: Miranda Wang and Jeanny Yao at TED2013." TED Talks Blog, Feb. 27, 2013.

Lindow, John. *Handbook of Norse Mythology.* Santa Barbara, CA: ABC-CLIO, 2001.

Lindzen, Richard S. "Science and Politics: Global Warming and Eugenics." In *Risks, Costs, and Lives Saved: Getting Better Results from Regulation,* edited by Robert William Hahn, 85–103. New York: Oxford University Press, 1996.

Liptak, Andrew. "Antarctica Is Home to Considerably More Volcanoes than Previously Thought." *Verge* (Aug. 13, 2017).

Liu, Xiangwen, et al. "Subseasonal Predictions of Regional Summer Monsoon Rainfall Over Tropical Asian Oceans and Land." *Journal of Climate* 28, no. 24 (Dec. 15, 2015): 9583–9605.

Liu, Xiaoyu, et al. "Determination of Fluorotelomer Alcohols in Selected Consumer Products and Preliminary Investigation of Their Fate in the Indoor Environment." *Chemosphere* 129 (2015): 81–86.

Lomborg, Bjørn. *Cool It: The Skeptical Environmentalist's Guide to Global Warming.* New York: Knopf, 2007.

———. *The Skeptical Environmentalist: Measuring the Real State of the World.* Cambridge: Cambridge University Press, 2001.

Lopez, Fernando J. Diaz, and Carlos Montalvo. "The Greening of the Chemical Industry: Past, Present and Challenges Ahead." In *Green Chemistry for Environmental Remediation,* edited by Rashmi Sanghi and Vandana

Singh, 35–78. Hoboken, NJ: John Wiley & Sons, 2012.

Lowe, Elizabeth C., et al. "Urbanisation at Multiple Scales Is Associated with Larger Size and Higher Fecundity of an Orb-Weaving Spider." *PLOS One* (Aug. 20, 2014).

Lowthrop, N. "Economic Conservation—Hill Holt Wood: the Three Legs of Sustainability in Practice." In *Sustainable Forestry: From Monitoring and Modelling to Knowledge Management and Policy Science,* edited by Keith M. Reynolds, 189–98. Cambridge, MA: CABI, 2007.

Luck, Gary W., and Lisa T. Smallbone. "Species Diversity and Urbanisation: Patterns, Drivers and Implications." In *Urban Ecology,* edited by Kevin J. Gaston, 88–119. New York: Cambridge University Press, 2010.

Lundholm, Jeremy. "Vegetation of Urban Hard Surfaces." In *Urban Ecology: Patterns, Processes, and Applications,* edited Jari Niemelä, 93–102. New York: Oxford University Press, 2011.

Lundholm, J.T., and A. Marlin. "Habitat Origins and Microhabitat Preferences of Urban Plant Species." *Urban Ecosystems* 9 (2006):139–159.

Maklakov, Alexei A., et al. "Brains and the City: Big-Brained Passerine Birds Succeed in Urban Environments." *Biology Letters* (April 27, 2011).

Malthus, Thomas. *An Essay on the Principle of Population.* London: J. Johnson, 1798.

Manes, Christopher. *Green Rage: Radical Environmentalism and the Unmaking of Civilization.* Boston: Little, Brown, 1990.

Mann, Charles C., and Mark L. Plummer. *Noah's Choice: the Future of Endangered Species.* New York: Knopf, 1995.

Manuel, Frank E., and Fritzie P. Manuel. *Utopian Thought in the Western World.* Cambridge, MA: Belknap Press, 1979.

Markowitz, Gerald, and David Rosner. *Deceit and Denial: The Deadly Politics of Industrial Pollution.* Berkeley: University of California Press, 2002.

Marris, Emma. "The Great Eucalyptus Debate." *The Atlantic* (Nov. 30, 2016).

Marsh, George Perkin. *Man and Nature; or, Physical Geography as Modified by Human Action.* New York: Charles Scribner & Co., 1864.

Marshall, Christa. "In Switzerland, a Giant New Machine is Sucking Carbon Directly from the Air." *Science Magazine* (Jun. 1, 2017).

Martin, P.S., and H.E. Wright, Jr., eds. *Pleistocene Extinctions: The Search for a Cause.* New Haven: Yale University Press, 1967.

Matos, D.M. Silva, et al. "Fire and Restoration of the Largest Urban Forest of the World in Rio de Janeiro City, Brazil." *Urban Ecosystems* 6 (2002): 151–161.

McCarter, Susan Foster. *Neolithic.* New York: Routledge, 2007.

McCarthy, Niall. "Pollution Kills Three Times More Than AIDS, TB and Malaria Combined." *Forbes* (Oct. 23, 2017).

McCleery, Robert. "Urban Mammals." In *Urban Ecosystem Ecology,* edited by Jacqueline Aitkenhead-Peterson and Astrid Volder, 87–102. Madison, WI: American Society of Agronomy, 2010.

McCutchen, Edwin L. "Characteristics of Spotted Owl Nest Trees in the Wenatchee National Forest." *Journal of Raptor Research* 27, no. 1 (March 1993): 1–7.

McDonnell, Mark J. "The History of Urban Ecology: A Ecologist's Perspective." In *Urban Ecology: Patterns, Processes, and Applications,* edited Jari Niemelä, 5–13. New York: Oxford University Press, 2011.

McGucken, William. *Lake Erie Rehabilitated: Controlling Cultural Eutrophication, 1960s–1990s.* Akron, OH: University of Akron Press, 2000.

McGurty, Eileen Maura. "From NIMBY to Civil Rights: The Origins of the Environmental Justice Movement." *Environmental History* 2, no. 3 (July 1997): 301–323.

McHarg, Ian L. "Thoughts on the Garden." In *Meanings of the Garden: Proceedings of a Working Conference to Explore the Social, Psychological and Cultural Dimensions of Gardens,* edited by Mark Francis and Randolph T. Hester, Jr., 134–35. University of California, Davis, May 14–17, 1987.

McInteer, James F. "Where Materialism Falls Short." *Virginia Wildlife* 24, no. 12 (Dec. 1963): 3, 9.

McIntosh, Robert P. *The Background of Ecology.* New York: Cambridge University Press, 1985.

McKinney, Michael L. "Urban Futures." In *Urban Ecology,* edited by Kevin J. Gaston, 287–308. New York: Cambridge University Press, 2010.

McWilliams, James E. *Just Food: Where Locavores Get It Wrong and How We Can Truly Eat Responsibly.* New York: Little, Brown and Co., 2009.

Mellon, Margaret. "An Environmentalist Perspective." In *The Genetic Revolution: Scientific Prospects and Public Perceptions,* edited by Bernard D. Davis, 61–66. Baltimore: Johns Hopkins University Press, 1991.

Merkley, Eric, and Dominik A. Stecula. "Party

Elites or Manufactured Doubt? The Informational Context of Climate Change Polarization." *Science Communication* 40, no. 2 (2018): 258–274.

Meyer, Gitte. "Expectations and Beliefs in Science Communication: Learning from Three European Gene Therapy Discussions of the Early 1990s." *Public Understanding of Science* 25, no. 3 (2016): 317–331.

_____. "Journalism and Science: How to Erode the Idea of Knowledge." *Journal of Agricultural and Environmental Ethics* 19 (2006): 239–252.

Meyers, Robert A., et al. "Green Chemistry and Chemical Engineering, Introduction." In *Innovations in Green Chemistry and Green Engineering: Selected Entries from the Encyclopedia of Sustainability Science and Technology,* edited by Paul T. Anastas and Julie Beth Zimmerman, 1–4. New York: Springer, 2013.

Minns, Denis. *Irenaeus.* Washington, D.C.: Georgetown University Press, 1994.

Mitcham, Carl. *Thinking Through Technology: the Path between Engineering and Philosophy.* Chicago: University of Chicago Press, 1994.

Mitro, Susanna D., et al. "Consumer Product Chemicals in Indoor Dust: A Quantitative Meta-Analysis of U.S. Studies." *Environmental Science and Technology* 50 (2016): 10661–672.

Mohai, Paul, et al. "Environmental Justice." *Annual Review of Environment and Resources* 34 (July 2009): 405–30.

Mohlenbrock, Robert H. "Mount Rogers, Virginia." *Natural History* 99 (Dec. 1990): 72–74.

Mooney, James. *Myths of the Cherokee.* Washington, D.C.: Bureau of American Ethnology, 1902.

Moreno, Carolina, et al. "The Context(s) of Precaution: Ideological and Instrumental Appeals to the Precautionary Principle." *Science Communication* 32, no. 1 (2010): 76–92.

Mortimer, John. *The First Rumpole Omnibus.* Garden City, NY: Doubleday, 1983.

Motz, Lotte. *The Faces of the Goddess.* New York: Oxford University Press, 1997.

Mukherjee, Debabrata. "Contradicted and Initially Stronger Effects in Highly Cited Clinical Research." *ACC Current Journal Review* (Oct. 2005).

Murphy, Dennis D. "Invertebrate Conservation. In *Balancing on the Brink of Extinction: the Endangered Species Act and Lessons for the Future,* edited by Kathryn A. Kohm, 181–98. Washington, D.C.: Island Press, 1991.

Myers, Norman. *The Sinking Ark: a New Look at the Problem of Disappearing Species.* New York: Pergamon Press, 1979.

Myhr, Anne Ingeborg. "A Precautionary Approach to Genetically Modified Organisms: Challenges and Implications for Policy and Science." *Journal of Agricultural and Environmental Ethics* 23 (2010): 501–25.

Nagle, John Copeland. "Playing Noah." *Minnesota Law Review* 82 (May 1998): 1171–1261.

Naim, Mona, et al. "Desalination of Simulated Seawater by Purge-Air Pervaporation Using an Innovative Fabricated Membrane." *Water Science & Technology* 72, no. 5 (2015): 785–793.

Nakashima, George. *The Soul of a Tree: A Woodworker's Reflections.* Tokyo, New York: Kodansha International, 1981.

Nash, Roderick. "Do Rocks Have Rights?" *The Center Magazine* 10 (1977): 1–12.

_____. *Wilderness and the American Mind,* 3rd ed. New Haven: Yale University Press, 1982.

Nelson, Louis P., ed. *American Sanctuary: Understanding Sacred Spaces.* Bloomington: Indiana University Press, 2006.

Ngo, Anh D., et al. "Association Between Agent Orange and Birth Defects: Systematic Review and Meta-Analysis." *International Journal of Epidemiology* 35, no. 5 (Oct. 2006): 1220–1230.

Nicolson, Malcolm. "Henry Allan Gleason and the Individualistic Hypothesis: The Structure of a Botanist's Career." *Botanical Review* 56, no. 2 (April-June, 1990): 91–161.

Niemelä, Jari. *Urban Ecology: Patterns, Processes, and Applications.* New York: Oxford University Press, 2011.

Nishimura, H., ed. *How to Conquer Air Pollution, A Japanese Experience.* New York: Elsevier Science Pub. Co., 1989.

Norwegian Polar Institute. "Polar Bears in Svalbard in Good Condition—So Far." (Dec. 23, 2015). http://www.npolar.no/en/news/2015/12-23-counting-of-polar-bears-in-svalbard.html.

Noss, Reed F. "From Endangered Species to Biodiversity." In *Balancing on the Brink of Extinction: the Endangered Species Act and Lessons for the Future,* edited by Kathryn A. Kohm, 227–46. Washington, D.C.: Island Press, 1991.

Nowotny, Helga, and Scott Peter. *Re-Thinking Science: Knowledge and the Public in an Age of Uncertainty.* Cambridge, UK: Polity, 2001.

Odenbaugh, Jay. "Philosophy of the Environmental Sciences." In *New Waves in Philosophy of Science,* edited by in P.D. Magnus and Jacob Busch, 155–171. New York: Palgrave Macmillan, 2010.

O'Hear, Anthony. *Introduction to the Philosophy of Science.* Oxford: Clarendon Press, 1989.

Okasha, Samir. *Philosophy of Science: A Very*

Short Introduction, 2nd ed. New York: Oxford University Press, 2016.

Omedo, Charles. "Stanford Scientists Develop Paint Coating Reflects Sunlight and Cools the Planet." *The Westside Story* (Nov. 27, 2014).

Oregon Forest Resource Institute. "Oregon's Family Forestlands: Why They Matter to the State's Quality of Life." Portland: Oregon Forest Resource Inst., 2008.

Orttung, Nicole. "Scientists Reconcile Growth in Antarctic Sea Ice with Global Warming Models." *Christian Science Monitor* (July 6, 2016).

Osborn, Eric Francis. *Irenaeus of Lyons.* New York: Cambridge University Press, 2001.

Osborne, Hannah. "NASA Discovers Mantle Plume Almost as Hot as Yellowstone Supervolcano That's Melting Antarctica from Below." *Newsweek* (Nov. 8, 2017).

Pagels, Elaine. *The Origin of Satan.* New York: Random House, 1995.

Pain, Stephanie. "The Ant and the Mandarin." *New Scientist* (April 14, 2001).

Palladino, Paolo. "Defining Ecology: Ecological Theories, Mathematical Models, and Applied Biology in the 1960s and 1970s." *Journal of the History of Biology* 24, no. 2 (Summer 1991): 223–243.

Pariona, Amber. "Biggest Old Growth Forests in the United States." *World Atlas,* April 25, 2017. https://www.worldatlas.com/articles/biggest-old-growth-forests-in-the-united-states.html

Park, Robert L. *Voodoo Science: The Road from Foolishness to Fraud.* New York: Oxford University Press, 2000.

Parlow, Eberhard. "Urban Climate." In *Urban Ecology: Patterns, Processes, and Applications,* edited Jari Niemelä, 31–44. New York: Oxford University Press, 2011.

Parrington, Vernon Louis. *American Dreams: A Study of American Utopias.* New York: Russell & Russell, 1964.

Pearce, Fred. "Africans Go Back to the Land as Plants Reclaim the Desert." *New Scientist* 175, no. 2361 (Sept. 21, 2002): 4–5.

Peters, Hans Peter, and Sharon Dunwoody. "Scientific Uncertainty in Media Content: Introduction to this Special Issue." *Public Understanding of Science* 25, no. 8 (2016): 893–908.

Petrie, Ruth E. "Atmospheric Impact of Arctic Sea Ice Loss in a Coupled Ocean–Atmosphere Simulation." *Journal of Climate* 28, no. 24 (Dec. 1, 2015): 9606–9622.

Pettersson, Olof. "The Spirit of the Woods: Outlines of a Study of the Ideas About Forest Guardians in African Mythology and Folk-lore." In *The Supernatural Owners of Nature,* edited by Åke Hultkrantz, 101–111. Stockholm: Almqvist & Wiksell, 1961.

Pfadenhauer, Jörg. "Some Remarks on the Socio-Cultural Background of Restoration Ecology." *Restoration Ecology* 9, no. 2 (June 2001): 220–229.

Philpot, J.H. *The Sacred Tree, or the Tree in Religion and Myth.* London: Macmillan, 1897.

Pickett, S. T., and V.T. Parker. "Avoiding the Old Pitfalls: Opportunities in a New Discipline." *Restoration Ecology* 2 (1994): 75–79.

Pickett, S.T.A., and P.S. White, eds. *The Ecology of Natural Disturbance and Patch Dynamics.* Orlando, FL: Academic Press, 1985.

Pilon-Smits, Elizabeth. "Phytoremediation." *Annual Review of Plant Biology* 56 (2005): 15–39.

Pirsig, Robert M. *Zen and the Art of Motorcycle Maintenance: An Inquiry into Values.* 1974; New York: Bantam, 1981.

Poincaré, Henri. George Bruce Halsted, trans. *The Foundations of Science: Science and Hypothesis.* New York: The Science Press, 1913.

———. George Bruce Halsted, trans. *The Value of Science.* New York: The Science Press, 1913.

———. *Science and Method.* New York: The Science Press, 1913.

Pollan, Michael. "The Intelligent Plant." *New Yorker* (Dec. 23 & 30, 2013).

Popper, Deborah Epstein, and Frank J. Popper. "The Great Plains: From Dust to Dust." *Planning Magazine* (Dec. 1987): 12–18.

Porteous, Alexander. *The Forest in Folklore and Mythology.* 1928; Mineola, NY: Dover Publications, 2002.

Post, Senja. "Communicating Science in Public Controversies: Strategic Considerations of the German Climate Scientists." *Public Understanding of Science* 25, no. 1 (2016): 61–70.

Press, Eyal, and Jennifer Washburn. "The Kept University." *The Atlantic* (March 2000).

Quigley, Martin F. "Potemkin Gardens: Biodiversity in Small Designed Landscapes." In *Urban Ecology: Patterns, Processes, and Applications,* edited Jari Niemelä, 85–92. New York: Oxford University Press, 2011.

Quinn, I.T. "The Tree." *Virginia Wildlife* 16, no. 8 (Aug. 1955): 21.

Ramjoué, Celina. "The Transatlantic Rift in Genetically Modified Food Policy." *Journal of Agricultural and Environmental Ethics* 20 (2007): 419–436.

Reeve, Simon. "Going Down in History." *Geographical* (March 2001): 60–64.

Reich, Lee. *Weedless Gardening.* New York: Workman Pub. Co., 2001.

Reichard, Sarah Hayden. "Inside Out: Invasive Plants and Urban Environments." In *Urban Ecosystem Ecology*, edited by Jacqueline Aitkenhead-Peterson and Astrid Volder, 241–51. Madison, WI: American Society of Agronomy, 2010.

Rennie, John, et al. "Misleading Math about the Earth." *Scientific American* 286, no. 1 (Jan. 2002): 61–71.

Reynolds, Keith M. *Sustainable Forestry: From Monitoring and Modelling to Knowledge Management and Policy Science*. Cambridge, MA: CABI, 2007.

Ribeiro, Milton Cezar, et al. "The Brazilian Atlantic Forest: How Much Is Left, and How Is the Remaining Forest Distributed? Implications for Conservation." *Biological Conservation* 142 (2009): 1141–1153.

Rich, Elroy L. *Allelopathy*, 2nd ed. Orlando: Academic Press, 1984.

Ripple, W. J., and R.L. Beschta. "Large Predators Limit Herbivore Densities in Northern Forest Ecosystems." *European Journal of Wildlife Research* (2012).

Robbins, William G. *Landscapes of Conflict: The Oregon Story, 1940–2000*. Seattle: University of Washington Press, 2004.

Robinson, Sarah L., and Jeremy T. Lundholm. "Ecosystem Services Provided by Urban Spontaneous Vegetation." *Urban Ecosystems* 15 (2012): 545–557.

Rogers, Carol L. "The Importance of Understanding Audiences." In *Communicating Uncertainty: Media Coverage of New and Controversial Science*, edited by Sharon M. Friedman, et al., 179–200. Mahwah, NJ: L. Erlbaum Associates, 1999.

Ronald, Pamela. "The Case for Engineering our Food." TED Talks, March 2015.

Ronald, Pamela, and Raoul Adamchak. *Tomorrow's Table: Organic Farming, Genetics and the Future of Food*. New York: Oxford University Press, 2008.

Roosegaarde, Daan. "A Smog Vacuum Cleaner and Other Magical City Designs." TED Talks, April 2017.

Rosen, Ben. "Scientists Invent a Way to Create CO2 Fuel from a Solar Leaf." *Christian Science Monitor* (Aug. 1, 2016).

Rosenhan, David L. "On Being Sane in Insane Places." *Science* 179 (1973): 250–58.

Rowan, Katherine E. "Effective Explanation of Uncertain and Complex Science." In *Communicating Uncertainty: Media Coverage of New and Controversial Science*, edited by Sharon M. Friedman, et al., 201–23. Mahwah, NJ: L. Erlbaum Associates, 1999.

Rowntree, Rowan A. "Toward Ecosystem Management: Shifts in the Core and the Context of Urban Forest Ecology." In *Urban Forest Landscapes: Integrating Multidisciplinary Perspectives*, edited by Gordon A. Bradley, 43–59. Seattle: University of Washington Press, 1995.

Rudel, Thomas K. *Tropical Forests: Regional Paths of Destruction and Regeneration in the Late Twentieth Century*. New York: Columbia University Press, 2005.

Russell, Jonathan R., et al. "Biodegradation of Polyester Polyurethane by Endophytic Fungi." *Applied and Environmental Microbiology* 77, no. 17 (Sept. 2011): 6076–6084.

Ryan, William, and Walter Pitman. *Noah's Flood: The New Scientific Discoveries About the Event That Changed History*. New York: Simon & Schuster, 1998.

Sagoff, Mark. *The Economy of the Earth: Philosophy, Law, and the Environment*, 2nd ed. Cambridge University Press, 2007.

Saier, M.H., Jr., and J.T. Trevors. "Phytoremediation." *Water, Air, and Soil Pollution*, Supplement 1 (2010): S61-S63.

Salzman, Jason. *Making the News: A Guide for Activists and Nonprofits*. Boulder, CO: Westview Press, 2003.

Samuels, Joanna. "The Adelgid Strikes Again." *Audubon* 98 (Mar.–Apr. 1996): 24.

Samuels, Rana, et al. "Evaluation and Projection of Extreme Precipitation Indices in the Eastern Mediterranean Based on CMIP5 Multi-Model Ensemble." *International Journal of Climatology* 38 (2018): 2280–2297.

Sanghi, Rashmi, and Vandana Singh, eds. *Green Chemistry for Environmental Remediation*. Hoboken, NJ: John Wiley & Sons, 2012.

Sanghi, Rashmi, et al. "Environment and the Role of Green Chemistry." In *Green Chemistry for Environmental Remediation*, edited by Rashmi Sanghi and Vandana Singh, 3–34. Hoboken, NJ: John Wiley & Sons, 2012.

Santos, Carla Escapa, et al. "Comparative Assessment of Pharmaceutical Removal from Wastewater by the Microalgae from Wastewater by the Microalgae *Chlorella sorokiniana, Chlorella vulgaris and Scenedesmus obliquus*," In *Biological Wastewater Treatment and Resource Recovery*, edited by Robina Farooq and Zaki Ahmad, 99–117. InTech Open Access Pub., 2017.

Santosa, Sri Juari. Urban Air Quality." In *Urban Ecosystem Ecology*, edited by Jacqueline Aitkenhead-Peterson and Astrid Volder, 57–74. Madison, WI: American Society of Agronomy, 2010.

Sarkar, Sahotra. "Ecology." *Stanford Encyclopedia of Philosophy* (Dec. 23, 2005).

Sarvis, Will. "The Homelessness Muddle Revisited," *Urban Lawyer* 49, no. 2 (Spring 2017): 317–354.

———. *J.V. Conran and Rural Political Power: Boss Mythology in the Missouri Bootheel.* Lanham, MD: Lexington Books, 2012.

———. *The Jefferson National Forest: An Appalachian Environmental History.* Knoxville: University of Tennessee Press, 2011.

———. *Sacred and Ephemeral: Reflections Upon Land, Place, and Home.* Self-published, 2017.

———. "Save the Planet, Kill Yourself? Unbalanced Nature." *Counterpunch* (Oct. 10, 2012).

Sauerwein, Martin. "Urban Soils—Characterization, Pollution, and Relevance in Urban Ecosystems." In *Urban Ecology: Patterns, Processes, and Applications,* edited Jari Niemelä, 45–58. New York: Oxford University Press, 2011.

Schafer, Edward H. "Cosmos in Miniature: the Tradition of the Chinese Garden." *Landscape* 12, no. 3 (Spring 1963): 24–26

Schell, Jonathan. "Our Fragile Earth." *Discover Magazine.* (Oct. 1989): 45–48.

Schneider, Stephen H. "Don't Bet All Environmental Changes Will be Beneficial." American Physical Society, *APS News* (Aug./Sept. 1996).

Schreiber, Melody. "Man-Made 'Wind Trees' Will Finally Make it Possible to Power Homes Using Turbines." *Quartz* (Aug. 23, 2016).

Schudson, M. *Discovering the News: A Social History of American Newspapers.* New York: Basic Books, 1978.

Schwartz, Alison. "Prince William & Kate Plant a Tree to Symbolize Love." *People Magazine* (July 2, 2011).

Scott, Joanne Scott. "From Brussels with Love: The Transatlantic Travels of European Law and the Chemistry of Regulatory Attraction." *American Journal of Comparative Law* 57 (Fall 2009): 897–943.

"Scrubbing the Skies." *Economist* (March 5, 2009).

Sears, John F. *Sacred Places: American Tourist Attractions in the Nineteenth Century.* New York: Oxford University Press, 1989.

Severson, Rebecca. "United We Sprout: A Chicago Community Garden Story." In *Meanings of the Garden: Proceedings of a Working Conference to Explore the Social, Psychological and Cultural Dimensions of Gardens,* edited by Mark Francis and Randolph T. Hester, Jr., 96–104. University of California, Davis, May 14–17, 1987.

Shapin, Steven. *The Scientific Revolution.* Chicago: University of Chicago Press, 1996.

Shields, Arthur Randolph. "The Isolated Spruce and Spruce-Fir Forests of Southwestern Virginia: A Biotic Study." Ph.D. diss., Univ. of Tennessee, 1962.

Shirvani, Hamid. "The Philosophy of Persian Garden Design: The Sufi Tradition." *Landscape Journal* 4, no. 1 (Spring 1985): 23–30.

Shochat, Eyal, et al. "Birds in Urban Ecosystems: Population Dynamics, Community Structure, Biodiversity, and Conservation." In *Urban Ecosystem Ecology,* edited by Jacqueline Aitkenhead-Peterson and Astrid Volder, 75–86. Madison, WI: American Society of Agronomy, 2010.

Shrader-Frechette, K.S., and Earl D. McCoy. "How the Tail Wags the Dog: How Value Judgments Determine Ecological Science." *Environmental Values* 3, no. 2 (Summer 1994): 107–120.

Simberloff, Daniel. "A Rising Tide of Species and Literature: A Review of Some Recent Books on Biological Invasions." *BioScience* 54, no. 3 (March 2004): 247–254.

Simon Julian L., and Aaron Wildavsky. "Species Loss Revisited." *Society* 30 (Nov./Dec. 1992): 41–46.

Singer, Siegfried Fred, and Dennis T. Avery. *Unstoppable Global Warming: Every 1,500 Years.* Lanham, MD: Rowman & Littlefield Pubs., 2007.

Sivagurunathan, Periyasamy, et al. "Biohydrogen Production from Wastewaters." In *Biological Wastewater Treatment and Resource Recovery,* edited by Robina Farooq and Zaki Ahmad, 197–210. InTech Open Access Pub., 2017.

Sivanpillai, Ramesh, and J.F. Shroder Jr., eds. *Biological and Environmental Hazards, Risks, and Disasters.* Amsterdam: Elsevier Inc., 2016.

Slater, Candace. "Amazonia as Edenic Narrative." In *Uncommon Ground: Toward Reinventing Nature,* edited by William Cronon, 114–31. New York: W.W. Norton & Co., 1995.

Slater, Lauren. *Opening Skinner's Box: Great Psychological Experiments of the Twentieth Century.* New York: W.W. Norton & Co., 2004.

Smith, Brian. "The Rights of Rocks: Towards an Environmental Ethic Without Intrinsicality." Graduate Conference, "The Politics of Human Rights," Boston, MA, March 11, 2010.

Solomon, Susan, et al. "Irreversible Climate Change Due to Carbon Dioxide Emissions." *Proceedings of the National Academy of Sciences* 106, no. 6 (Feb. 10, 2009): 1704–1709.

Sovern, Stan G., et al. "Roosting Habitat Use and Selection By Northern Spotted Owls During Natal Dispersal." *Journal of Wildlife Management* 79, no. 2 (2015): 254–62.

Steel, Brent S., et al. "Ideology and Scientific

Credibility: Environmental Policy in the American Pacific Northwest." *Public Understanding of Science* 15 (2006): 481–495.

Steele, Meredith K., et al. "Chemistry of Urban, Suburban, and rural Surface Waters." In *Urban Ecosystem Ecology,* edited by Jacqueline Aitkenhead-Peterson and Astrid Volder, 297–339. Madison, WI: American Society of Agronomy, 2010.

Stein, Achva Benzinberg. "Landscape Elements of the Makam: Sacred Places in Israel." *Landscape Journal* 6, no. 2 (Fall 1987): 123–131.

Stein, Achva Benzinberg, and Jacqueline Claire Moxley. "In Defense of the Nonnative: The Case of the Eucalyptus." *Landscape Journal* 11, no. 1 (Spring 1992): 35–50.

Stein, Gertrude. *Three Lives.* New York: Pocket Books, 2003.

Steinbeck, John. *Grapes of Wrath.* 1940; New York: Viking, 1967.

Steinberg, Shimon. "Natural Pest Control. .. Using Bugs!" *TED Talk* (April 2010).

Stoll, Mark. "Green versus Green: Religion, Ethics, and the Bookchin-Foreman Dispute." *Environmental History* 6, no. 3 (July 2001): 412–27.

Stone, Christopher D. "Should Trees Have Standing?—Towards Legal Rights for Natural Objects." *Southern California Law Review* 45 (1972): 450–501.

_____. *Should Trees Have Standing?: Law, Morality, and the Environment.* New York: Oxford University Press, 2010.

Stork, Nigel E. "Measuring Global Biodiversity and its Decline." In *Biodiversity II: Understanding and Protecting Our Biological Resources,* edited by Marjorie L. Reaka-Kudla, et al., 41–68. Washington, D.C.: Joseph Henry Press, 1997.

Stradling, David, and Richard Stradling. *Where the River Burned—Carl Stokes and the Struggle to Save Cleveland.* Ithaca: Cornell University Press, 2015.

Sukopp, Herbert. "Urban Ecology—Scientific and Practical Aspects." In *Urban Ecology,* edited by J. Breuste, et al., 3–16. New York: Springer, 1998.

Suzuki, Shunryu. *Zen Mind Beginner's Mind: Informal Talks on Zen Meditation and Practice.* New York: John Weatherhill, 1970.

Swart, Jacques A. A., et al. "Valuation of Nature in Conservation and Restoration." *Restoration Ecology* 9, no. 2 (June 2001): 230–238.

Taleb, Nassim Nicholas. *Antifragile: Things That Gain from Disorder.* New York: Random House, 2012.

_____. *The Black Swan: The Impact of the Highly Improbable.* New York: Random House, 2007.

Taylor, Peter J. "Technocratic Optimism, H.T. Odum, and the Partial Transformation of Ecological Metaphor After World War II." *Journal of the History of Biology* 21, no. 2 (Summer 1988): 213–44.

_____. *Unruly Complexity: Ecology, Interpretation, Engagement.* Chicago: University of Chicago Press, 2005.

Tesh, Sylvia Noble. *Uncertain Hazards: Environmental Activists and Scientific Proof.* Ithaca, New York: Cornell University Press, 2000.

Thilenius, John F. "The *Quercus Garryana* Forests of the Willamette Valley, Oregon." *Ecology* 49, no. 6 (Nov., 1968): 1124–1133.

Thomason, Andy. "Watch John Oliver Blast Exaggerated Scientific Findings." *Chronicle of Higher Education* (May 9, 2016).

Thoreau, Henry David. *The Maine Woods / The Writings of Henry David Thoreau* (1864). https://www.gutenberg.org/files/42500/42500-h/42500-h.htm.

Timmer, John. "Chemical Warfare on the Reef." *Ars Technica* (Nov. 9, 2012).

Tjernshaugen, Andreas. "The Growth of Political Support for CO2 Capture and Storage in Norway." *Environmental Politics* 20, no. 2 (March 2011): 227–45.

Tompkins, Peter, and Christopher Bird. *The Secret Life of Plants.* New York: Harper & Row, 1973.

Trefil, James. *A Scientist in the City.* New York: Anchor Books, 1995.

Troy, Austin, et al. "The Relationship Between Tree Canopy and Crime Rates Across an Urban–Rural Gradient in the Greater Baltimore Region." *Landscape and Urban Planning.* April 2012. https://www.nrs.fs.fed.us/pubs/jrnl/2012/nrs_2012_troy_001.pdf.

Tudge, Colin. *The Secret Life of Trees.* London: Allen Lane, 2005.

Valigra, Lori. "MIT Advances Liquid Metal Battery Technology." *Mass High Tech: The Journal of New England Technology* (Feb. 16, 2012).

van Diggelen, R., et al. "Ecological Restoration: State of the Art or State of the Science?" *Restoration Ecology* 9, no. 2 (June 2001): 115–118.

Van Driesche, Jason, and Roy Van Driesche. *Nature Out of Place: Biological Invasions in the Global Age.* Washington, D.C.: Island Press, 2000.

Van Norden, Bryan. "Mencius." *Stanford Encyclopedia of Philosophy.* Oct 16, 2004; rev., Dec. 3, 2014. http://plato.stanford.edu/entries/mencius/

van Solinge, Tim Boekhout. "Chapter 12.3—Deforestation in the Brazilian Amazon," In *Biological and Environmental Hazards, Risks, and Disasters,* edited by Ramesh Sivanpillai and J.F. Shroder Jr., 373–95. Amsterdam: Elsevier Inc., 2016.

Van Wyk De Vries, Maximillian, et al. "A New Volcanic Province: an Inventory of Subglacial Volcanoes in West Antarctica." In *Exploration of Subsurface Antarctica: Uncovering Past Changes and Modern Processes,* edited by M.J. Jamieson, et al., 461–77. Geological Society, London, Special Publications, 2017.

Velleman, Paul F. "Truth, Damn Truth, and Statistics." *Journal of Statistics Education* 16, no. 2 (July 2008).

Vessel, Matthew F., and Herbert H. Wong. *Natural History of Vacant Lots.* Berkeley: University of California Press, 1987.

Volder, Astrid, and W. Todd Watson. "Urban Forestry." In *Urban Ecosystem Ecology,* edited by Jacqueline Aitkenhead-Peterson and Astrid Volder, 227–40. Madison, WI: American Society of Agronomy, 2010.

Von Stackelberg, Katharine T. "Meaning." In *A Cultural History of Gardens in Antiquity,* edited by Kathryn Gleason, 119–34. New York: Bloomsburg, 2013.

Wakefield, Andrew, et al. "Ileal-Lymphoid-Nodular Hyperplasia, Non-Specific Colitis, and Pervasive Developmental Disorder in Children." *The Lancet* 351, no. 9103 (1998): 637–41.

Wallack, Lawrence Marshal. *News for a Change: an Advocate's Guide to Working with the Media.* Thousand Oaks, CA: Sage Publications, 1999.

Walter, Robert C., and Dorothy J. Merritts. "Natural Streams and the Legacy of Water-Powered Mills." *Science* 319, no. 5861 (Jan. 18, 2008): 299–304.

Walth, Brent. *Fire at Eden's Gate: Tom McCall & the Oregon Story.* Portland: Oregon Historical Society, 1994.

Weaver, Sean A., and Michael C. Morris. "Risks Associated with Genetic Modification: An Annotated Bibliography of Peer Reviewed Natural Science Publications." *Journal of Agricultural and Environmental Ethics* 18 (2005): 157–189.

Weissbrod, Lior, et al. "Origins of House Mice in Ecological Niches Created by Settled Hunter-Gatherers in the Levant 15,000 Y Ago." *Proceedings of the National Academy of Sciences* 114, no. 16 (April 18, 2017): 4099–4104.

Welch, Craig. "New Island Appears Off U.S. Coast." *National Geographic* (June 27, 2017).

Wenke, Robert J. *Patterns in Prehistory: Humankind's First Three Million Years,* 3rd ed. New York: Oxford University Press, 1990.

Whaples, Robert. "Book Review: A Feathered River across the Sky: The Passenger Pigeon's Flight to Extinction, by Joel Greenberg." *Independent Review* 19, no. 3 (Winter 2015): 443–46.

White, Lynn Townsend, Jr. "The Historical Roots of Our Ecologic Crisis." *Science* 155, no. 3767 (Mar. 10, 1967): 1207.

White, Peter S., ed., *The Southern Appalachian Spruce-Fir Ecosystem: Its Biology and Threats.* Gatlinburg, TN: Uplands Field Research Laboratory, 1984.

Wigner, Eugene P. "The Unreasonable Effectiveness of Mathematics in the Nature Sciences." *Communications in Pure and Applied Mathematics* 13, no. 1 (Feb. 1960): 1–14.

Wildavsky, Aaron. *But Is It True? A Citizen's Guide to Environmental Health and Safety Issues.* Cambridge: Harvard University Press, 1995.

Wilson, Edward O. *The Diversity of Life.* New York: W.W. Norton, 1999.

Wimsatt, William. "Lewontin's Evidence (That There Isn't Any)." In *Questions of Evidence: Proof, Practice, and Persuasion Across the Disciplines,* edited by James Chandler, et al., 492–503. Chicago: University of Chicago Press, 1994.

Winsor, P. "Arctic Sea Ice Thickness Remained Constant During the 1990s." *Geophysical Research Letters* 28, no. 6 (March 15, 2001): 1039–1041.

Winterhalder, Keith, et al. "Values and Science in Ecological Restoration—A Response to Davis and Slobodkin." *Restoration Ecology* 12, no. 1 (March 2004): 4–7.

Winthrop, John. "A Modell of Christian Charity" (1630). Collections of the Massachusetts Historical Society, 3rd series 7:31–48. https://history.hanover.edu/texts/winthmod.html.

Wong, Young-tsu. *Paradise Lost: the Imperial Garden Yuanming Yuan.* Honolulu: University of Hawaii Press, 2001.

Worrell, Richard, and Michael C. Appleby. "Stewardship of Natural Resources: Definition, Ethical and Practical Aspects." *Journal of Agricultural and Environmental Ethics* 12 (2000): 263–77.

Worster, Donald. *Nature's Economy: A History of Ecological Ideas,* 2nd ed. New York: Cambridge University Press, 1994.

Wu, Shu, et al. "Efficacy of Tendency and Linear Inverse Models to Predict Southern Peru's Rainy Season Precipitation." *International Journal of Climatology* 38 (2018): 2590–2604.

Wunderlich, Gene. "Review of Peterson, *Hearts-blood.*" *Journal of Agricultural and Environmental Ethics* 14, no. 3 (2001): 355–56.

Yarden, Leon. *The Tree of Light: A Study of the Menorah, the Seven-Branched Lampstand.* Ithaca, New York: Cornell University Press, 1971.

Zaehner, Robert Charles. *The Dawn and Twilight of Zoroastrianism.* New York: Putnam, 1961.

Zeder, Melinda A., et al., eds. *Documenting Domestication: New Genetic and Archaeological Paradigms.* University of California Press, 2006.

Zhou, Zhen-Qiang, and Shang-Ping Xie. "Effects of Climatological Model Biases on the Projection of Tropical Climate Change." *Journal of Climate* 28, no. 24 (Dec. 15 2015): 9909–9917.

Zou, Hui. "The Jing of a Perspective Garden." *Studies in the History of Gardens & Designed Landscapes* 22, no. 4 (2002): 293–326.

Zwart, Hub. "A Short History of Food Ethics." *Journal of Agricultural and Environmental Ethics* 12 (2000): 113–126.

Print, Audio and Visual Media

ABC News
BBC News
Business Insider
CBS News
CNBC News
Conversation
Cosmos News
Ecowatch
Eugene Register Guard
Eugene Tree Foundation News
Eugene Weekly
Full Measure (Sharyl Attkisson)
Growing a Greener World
Guardian
International Business Times
Last Week Tonight (John Oliver)
Los Angeles Times
MIT News
National Public Radio
NBC News
New York Times
Oregon Daily Emerald
Oregon Family Forest News
Oregon Public Broadcasting
Philadelphia Enquirer
ProPublica
Public Broadcasting Service Newshour
Reuters
Roanoke Times
Seattle Times
Sideshow
Techtimes.com
TED Talks
Telegraph
Triplepundit.com
U.S. News & World Report
UT News
Washington Post

Index

Numbers in *bold italics* indicate pages with illustrations

263